# Taking Problem-Solving Courts to Scale

# Taking Problem-Solving Courts to Scale

## Diverse Applications of the Specialty Court Model

Edited by
Eileen M. Ahlin and Anne S. Douds

LEXINGTON BOOKS
*Lanham • Boulder • New York • London*

Published by Lexington Books
An imprint of The Rowman & Littlefield Publishing Group, Inc.
4501 Forbes Boulevard, Suite 200, Lanham, Maryland 20706
www.rowman.com

6 Tinworth Street, London SE11 5AL, United Kingdom

British Library Cataloguing in Publication Information Available

**Library of Congress Cataloging-in-Publication Data**

Names: Ahlin, Eileen M., editor. | Douds, Anne S., editor.
Title: Taking problem-solving courts to scale : diverse applications of the specialty court model / edited by Eileen M. Ahlin and Anne S. Douds.
Description: Lanham, Maryland : Lexington Books, an imprint of The Rowman & Littlefield Publishing Group, Inc., [2021] | Includes bibliographical references and index.
Identifiers: LCCN 2021006387 (print) | LCCN 2021006388 (ebook) | ISBN 9781793608413 (cloth) | ISBN 9781793608420 (ebook) | ISBN 9781793608437 (pbk)
Subjects: LCSH: Criminal justice, Administration of—Social aspects—United States. | Courts of special jurisdiction—United States. | Courts of first instance—United States. | Criminal courts—United States.
Classification: LCC KF9223 .T35 2021 (print) | LCC KF9223 (ebook) | DDC 345.73/0148—dc23
LC record available at https://lccn.loc.gov/2021006387
LC ebook record available at https://lccn.loc.gov/2021006388

# Contents

# List of Figures and Tables

## FIGURES

## TABLES

# Preface

The idea for this book has been percolating for a long time. For many years, we (Eileen and Anne) have discussed producing an edited collection on problem-solving courts because we continue to have questions about community corrections approaches delivered in judicial setting. Our inquiries stem from our various independent and joint projects where we have evaluated and assessed individual and clusters of problem-solving courts. Eileen's evaluative work includes a multi-site national evaluation of adult drug courts focused on expanding and enhancing access to treatment and independent evaluations of drug, community, family treatment, and veterans' treatment courts. Anne and her research team continue to conduct multi-court program evaluations. She recently launched a nationwide assessment of problem-solving courts' policies and practices concerning victims' rights. In addition to our practical work, we have paused to examine the problem-solving court movement in our scholarly writings critically. A recent commentary, *The Problem with Problem-solving Courts*, published in The ASC Division on Corrections & Sentencing Handbook Series, offers suggestions for theoretically informed evaluation. That writing also serves as the intellectual foundation for the present volume. We examine the post hoc application of theoretical explanations to problem-solving courts' building blocks in that piece. We highlight the drug court model's rapid application to myriad criminogenic behaviors or comorbidities, types of crimes, and offenders' characteristics, and discuss how these courts proliferated without well-defined theoretical frameworks. We argued that applying theory and a sound framework, or logic model, came after these courts started operations. Thirty years out, we believe it is time to reflect on the problem-solving court movement to assess their progress, examine how they apply theory to their work, and, with an eye toward the future, highlight opportunities for growth. We also completed a monograph in 2019, *The Veterans Treatment Court Movement: Striving to Serve Those Who Served*, billed as the most comprehensive assessment of veterans courts. We hope that it will motivate other scholars to take a similar, deep-dive approach to other specialized courts. Perhaps this volume will be a step in that direction.

We have invited problem-solving court scholars to delve deeply into the most common applications of the model. These problem-solving court model applications have helped shape the current landscape of alternatives to incarceration and varied treatments in the community. This volume provides detailed descriptions of different problem-solving court manifestations stemming from the first drug court in 1989 Miami. Through a critical lens, this volume contributes to the discourse on the problem-solving court movement by examining the prolific development of these courts so we may better understand their placement within the throes of a call for meaningful criminal justice reform.

## WHY PAUSE TO REFLECT?

It has been thirty years since the first problem-solving court, a drug court in Miami, Florida, was introduced as an alternative to traditional court case processing. Problem-solving courts provide an alternative to traditional court processing by embracing therapeutic jurisprudence. The judge and courtroom workgroup guide clients (rather than defendants) through a series of phases that incrementally reduce reporting requirements as participants work towards graduation and adhere to treatment protocols. These contingency programs use incentives and sanctions to address criminogenic needs that appear to have propelled persons to commit crimes. These courts, also called specialty courts, specialized courts, or therapeutic courts, address criminogenic behavior contributing to an individual's involvement with the criminal justice system. As the first iteration, drug courts sought to provide substance abuse treatment within the confines of close supervision and accountability to various actors in the courtroom workgroup, including the judge, probation, and treatment. These courts were deemed successful anecdotally and through scientific study. Their proliferation and the support they received spurred the advent of spin-off problem-solving courts such as mental health courts, domestic violence courts, and reentry courts.

Initially, many of the treatment courts developed after the Miami court held to the drug court template. Criminal justice practitioners saw that court participants needed more than drug treatment, so they expanded to add mental health treatment, employment assistance, and housing support. Later, problem-solving courts evolved to address demographic similarities (e.g., veterans courts, tribal wellness courts, and community courts) or offense characteristics (e.g., prostitution courts, gambling courts, and sex offender courts).

With an increasing focus on criminal justice reform on both sides of the political aisle, it is essential to reflect on the problem-solving court model's wide-spread expansion. This edited volume takes a comprehensive look into courts that address three aspects: criminogenic needs, offense characteristics, and individual characteristics. The chapters provide brief overviews of the historical development and operations of the courts. Then they describe and assess their implementation and effectiveness, and each concludes with insights and recommendations for how these courts can improve. The volume contains three sections: Section I: Courts Based on Criminogenic Needs; Section II: Courts Based on Individual Characteristics; and Section III: Courts Based on Offense Characteristics. We introduce each curated section and highlight its importance to understanding one of the most prolific advancements in how incarceration alternatives are understood and embraced by criminal justice practitioners. We conclude the volume with a chapter summarizing the findings, contemplating problem-solving courts' future, and proposing policy approaches to respond to some of these courts' perceived weaknesses.

Eileen M. Ahlin and Anne S. Douds

## Section I

# COURTS BASED ON CRIMINOGENIC CHARACTERISTICS

Problem-solving courts originated for a particular purpose. These courts, also called specialty courts, specialized courts, or therapeutic courts, were intended to address criminogenic behavior that contributed to individuals' involvement with the criminal justice system. These courts focus on a criminogenic need. A criminogenic need is one that, in its presence, can contribute to criminal behavior. Conversely, it is assumed that criminal behavior would be tempered or cease to exist in its absence.

Drug courts emerged to center attention on drug use as a criminogenic need. During the late 1980s, courts swelled with cases of defendants presenting with substance use disorders. Drug use is associated with criminal behavior, whether due to reduced capacity due to impairment or as a driving force fueling behaviors to support a drug habit (e.g., stealing to obtain money to buy drugs). Problem-solving courts began because of identifying a criminogenic need and understanding that treatment would change that need. As such, drug courts sought to provide substance abuse treatment within the confines of close supervision and accountability to various actors in the courtroom workgroup, including the judge, probation, and treatment.

Initially, the newer problem-solving courts held to the drug court template and focused on treatment. Like drug courts, these courts' purpose is to address the individuals' criminogenic needs when they become involved with the criminal justice system. Such needs expanded beyond drug use to include mental health treatment and employment and housing. These newer courts also created a separate pathway for persons with alcohol substance use disorders.

In section I, five chapters examine a sampling of courts based on criminogenic needs.

The discussion begins with a superbly researched and thoughtful consideration of the inaugural problem-solving court. In chapter 1, "Drug Courts: The Beginning of the Movement," Cassandra Atkin-Plunk provides a foundational overview describing how these courts emerged as an alternative to traditional court case processing to ease the corrections system's burden. After drawing on the research to provide a comprehensive overview of drug courts, Atkin-Plunk highlights critical issues surrounding operational aspects inherent in court administration and participant recruitment. Readers also learn about drug court evaluations and the evidence surrounding their continued use. The chapter ends with considering what the future of drug courts might entail, given their history.

Chapter 2, "Mental Health Courts: Policy and Practice," by Irina Fanarraga and Deborah Koetzle, explores the expansion of problem-solving courts into another area where treatment could alter the connection between a criminogenic need and criminal behavior. Mental health disorders are not criminogenic; there is no causal link between mental health issues and crime. However, as Fanarraga and Koetzle eloquently describe, the deterioration of mental health treatment in the 1900s, specifically deinstitutionalization and increased police contacts, has contributed to an increased reliance on community-based treatment. Mental health courts emerged as one specific way to provide such treatment to individuals involved with the criminal justice system. The authors cogently illustrate the mental health court model and its similarities to drug courts. The chapter concludes with a discussion of the research evidence and a critical assessment of mental health court strengths and weaknesses.

In chapter 3, "DWI Courts," Carrie Petrucci expertly details the need for alcohol use disorder treatment offered as a balance between courtroom accountability and community-based therapy. Many traffic safety advances have substantially reduced arrests for alcohol-impaired driving (e.g., raising the legal drinking age, ignition interlocks, and lowering the legal limit to 0.08 blood alcohol concentration). However, driving while intoxicated (DWI) remains a common offense. For individuals arrested for one or more DWI, who also present with an alcohol-use disorder, DWI courts offer an alternative to other court processing options. Petrucci describes how DWI courts go beyond license-based sanctions, which restrict driving, to administer needed substance abuse treatment. By outlining how DWI courts are structured and reviewing the extant literature on their effectiveness, she provides a convincing argument that while they are promising, much remains to be studied and considered.

In chapter 4, "Reentry Courts," Lama Hassoun Ayoub and Michael Rempel paint the complex picture of the collateral consequences facing individuals who were formerly incarcerated and how this problem-solving court strives to bolster reentrant success on many outcomes, not just recidivism. The myriad of criminogenic needs resulting from a carceral stay compound existing difficulties far beyond whether someone has a drug use disorder or mental health concern. This chapter expertly outlines such barriers and how reentry courts operate to identify needs across participants. The authors highlight the need for additional research to determine what value may be added by these courts above and beyond community-based supervision.

In chapter 5, "Creating a Home Base for Treatment in Homelessness Courts," Kyle C. Troeger and Anne S. Douds detail the development of a problem-solving court to address what they call the "trifecta [of the] . . . homeless crises." Their astute exploration of economic downturns, waning government housing subsidies, and the deinstitutionalization of mental health services explain how people without homes face increased risk of coming to law enforcement's attention. Homelessness courts do not require any specific treatment and do not adhere to key components, a marked departure from other criminogenic problem-solving courts. Instead, these courts rely on public-private partnerships to address factors associated with homelessness, which drove behaviors leading to their involvement with the criminal justice system (e.g., loitering and panhandling). Their operations embrace standards developed by the American Bar Association. Despite their proliferation, the effectiveness of homelessness courts remains understudied.

We hope that the chapters in Section I provide insights into the problem-solving court movement and how it has flourished beyond the highly touted 1989 Miami-Dade Drug Court to address criminogenic needs among individuals in the criminal justice system. Our reading of these contributions inspires confidence that much progress in advancing criminal justice reform in the past thirty years while also reinforcing the need for rigorous research to maintain momentum. Process and outcome evaluations of these courts will also add credence to their claims and solidify their existence in the continued push to fund and support evidence-based programs.

*Chapter 1*

# Drug Courts

## *The Beginning of the Movement*

### Cassandra Atkin-Plunk

## INTRODUCTION

Widespread criminalization of illicit drug use in the 1980s and 1990s resulted in an exponential increase in the number of individuals with substance use issues cycling in and out of courtrooms across the country (Goldkamp, 1994) and an unprecedented number of drug offenders incarcerated in federal, state, and local correctional facilities (Gillard, 1993). This burden on the criminal justice system, along with the unique needs of these justice-involved individuals and high recidivism rates due to unmet criminogenic substance use disorders, resulted in a distinct confluence of circumstances that set the stage for the development of alternatives to incarceration. As such, states began to devise and create intermediate sanctions (i.e., punishments that fall between traditional probation and incarceration) in an effort to reduce prison crowding, be resource efficient, and provide much needed rehabilitation to offenders that might not otherwise be available in an incarcerative setting (Petersilia, Lurigio, & Byrne, 1992). It is against this backdrop that drug courts were developed. Thus, over the past three decades, substantial and sustained reforms have been made to the way the American criminal justice system responds to and punishes justice-involved individuals with substance use issues (Berman & Feinblatt, 2001; Strong, Rantala, & Kyckelhahn, 2016).

First established in 1989, drug courts draw on various punishment philosophies but have an overarching goal of holding substance-using offenders accountable and providing rehabilitation through effective, intensive treatment. While traditional courts simply seek to adjudicate and sentence, in what has been referred to as "assembly line justice" (Kohler-Hausmann, 2014, p. 615), drug courts strive to change future behavior and increase community safety by addressing the criminogenic needs of substance-using, justice-involved people.

In the past thirty years, drug courts have proliferated across the United States and the percentage of people incarcerated for a drug crime in state correctional facilities has decreased, from 21.9 percent in 2000 to 14.4 percent in 2018 (Carson, 2020; West, Sabol, & Greenman, 2010). Despite this drop, the need for substance use treatment has not decreased over time. Recent data even suggests that the number of illicit drug users is increasing (Substance Abuse and Mental Health Services Administration [SAMHSA], 2019), and the number of people who continue to be entangled in the criminal justice system with unaddressed drug-related issues is pervasive (Bronson, Stroop, Zimmer, & Berzofsky, 2017). Thus, the need for treatment through drug courts is ever-present.

This chapter seeks to provide readers with an overview of drug courts in the United States, their origins, and a look toward their future. The chapter begins by examining the development of drug courts, which began in the War on Drugs era and a court environment with ever-rising caseloads. I then paint a picture of the drug court model and characteristics of typical drug courts, describing how drug courts differ from traditional adversarial courtrooms, and the varying dispositional models used to process people through drug court. The chapter then discusses the ten Key Components of drug courts that provide guidance for the implementation and operation of a model drug court program. This section also examines the difficulty drug courts have in adopting and implementing these components with fidelity. Next, I highlight the proliferation of drug courts across the United States and abroad, and I provide examples of how the adult drug court model has been adapted to serve the needs of other substance-using populations, including juveniles, families, college students, Native Americans, those with alcohol issues, and those suffering from co-occurring disorders. The chapter then goes on to examine the various professional organizations and resources available to drug court personnel, many of which assist with program development, capacity building, and training and technical assistance. This is followed by a comprehensive discussion of the extant research on drug courts, which ultimately supports the effectiveness of drug courts in reducing recidivism. Subsequently, I provide readers with an examination of four critical issues surrounding drug courts, including their coerciveness, due process concerns, net-widening effect, and restrictive eligibility criteria. Finally, this chapter concludes with a discussion on the future of drug courts and the need to implement programs with fidelity, expand eligibility criteria, examine racial disparities, and provide gender-responsive treatment.

## THE BEGINNING OF THE MOVEMENT

The problem-solving court movement began in 1989 when Florida's Eleventh Judicial Circuit established the first drug court in Miami-Dade County

(Goldkamp, 1994). The formation of the Dade County Felony Drug Court came at a time when crime and illicit drug usage, particularly cocaine and crack-cocaine, was on the rise, not just in Miami-Dade but also in other large, urban cities across the United States (Inciardi, 1986; Olson, Lurigio, & Albertson, 2001). During this time, court officials in Miami observed that the vast majority of felony cases coming into the court system were drug-related (Goldkamp, Gottfredson, & Weiland, 1990). The burgeoning number of defendants cycling in and out of the criminal justice system with unaddressed drug-related issues required an innovative response—one that would not only reduce burden on the traditional court system but also provide much-needed treatment to individuals struggling with substance use (Berman & Feinblatt, 2001). As such, the Dade County Felony Drug Court, along with subsequent drug courts, was conceived. These courts, as will be discussed in more detail further, provide an alternative case-processing method that delivers intensive social treatments while holding individuals legally accountable for their actions.

The drug court model was a departure from the deterrent and incapacitative punishment philosophies customarily endorsed in the 1980s and 1990s (Goldkamp, 1994; MacKenzie, 2006). The War on Drugs, which was first promulgated by President Nixon and then expanded by the Reagan administration with the passage of the Anti-Drug Abuse Acts of 1986 and 1988, resulted in incarceration stints for low-level drug users and an exponential increase in the prison population (Carson & Golinelli, 2013; Mauer, 2001). Policymakers and drug court proponents recognized that this crime control approach was not effective at addressing individuals' underlying addiction issues, and that drug treatment was key to long-term behavioral change (Goldkamp, 1994; MacKenzie, 2006). Thus, the new, innovative response represented a paradigm shift that was less punitive and more rehabilitative in nature than previous correctional strategies. As such, drug courts were developed to balance therapeutic interventions with legal sanctions in an effort to reduce drug use and related criminal behavior (Olson et al., 2001).

## THE DRUG COURT MODEL

Although there is no universal, comprehensive drug court model, certain commonalities exist among drug courts throughout the United States. Primarily, these problem-solving courts distinguish themselves from adversarial courtrooms. Instead of two parties vying against each other to quickly adjudicate the case and determine punishment for wrongdoing, drug courts utilize a collaborative approach to handling cases. The drug court team, which typically consists of a judge, prosecutor, defense attorney, supervision officer, and treatment providers, works together with participants (or clients; drug courts shy away from using terms like "offender" or "defendant") in an effort to reduce drug use, the underlying cause of their crime, and thereby curbing criminal behavior. Eligibility criteria, target population, program requirements, and type of treatment vary greatly depending on the program. Drug courts can target adults or juveniles, allow first time or repeat offenders, accept those charged with a felony or misdemeanor, and allow those with or without a documented substance abuse history (MacKenzie, 2006; Olson et al., 2001; U.S. General Accounting Office [GAO], 1997). The Miami-Dade Adult Drug Court, which is still in existence today, generally allows people charged with possessing or purchasing drugs to participate in the drug court. Individuals are ineligible to participate, however, if they have arrests for drug sale or trafficking, a violent history, or more than two non-drug felony convictions (Eleventh Judicial Circuit of Florida, n.d.).

Individuals who meet the drug court's eligibility requirements, agree to the court's conditions of supervision and treatment, and opt in as a client will participate in the court for a set duration of time, which is typically at least one year (Marlowe, Hardin, & Fox, 2016; U.S. GAO, 1997). During this time, participants are required to engage in tailored treatment and be accountable to the drug court judge. Drug courts operate using a phase approach to treatment and programming, where depending on their needs treatment can begin as residential or outpatient and decreases in intensity as participants successfully progress through the program. Throughout their time in the drug court, participants will regularly attend status hearings with a consistent judge and be expected to abide by the conditions of the court. One of the hallmarks of drug courts is that drug court judges take a hands-on approach to managing drug court participants. Judges not only preside over hearings (which can be as often as weekly during the first phase of programming), but they provide encouragement and support, reward progress, and preside over graduation ceremonies. Judges also encourage clients to share with them updates about their progress in treatment (Marlowe et al., 2016).

Drug courts utilize a public health approach and recognize that drug addiction is a disease, and the path to sobriety can, and often does, include setbacks. Thus, not only do judges provide encouragement and support and reward positive behavior but they also use graduated sanctions to hold accountable clients who are unable to comply with court mandates. With graduated sanctions, the severity of sanctions increases with each subsequent rule violation and can begin with a verbal warning and end with dismissal from the program. Other graduated sanctions often used in drug courts include writing an essay, more frequent drug testing, returning to an early phase of the program, increasing treatment intensity, and short terms of incarceration (MacKenzie, 2006). Program dismissal is used in extreme cases when all other options have failed and the participant continues to violate the law and/or use illicit substances.

Drug courts can operate under several dispositional models, including pre-plea diversion, post-plea diversion, post-sentencing, or a hybrid model (GAO, 1997; Marlowe et al., 2016; National Drug Court Resource Center [NDCRC], n.d.). Pre-plea diversion drug courts (also called deferred prosecution) divert individuals from traditional court proceedings and allow them, prior to entering a guilty plea, to participate voluntarily in the drug court as a condition of pretrial supervision. Here, participants are required to waive various due process rights, including their right to a trial, the ability to confront witnesses, and right to an appeal, to name a few. If they successfully complete the drug court, the court will dismiss the arrest charges against them. On the other hand, post-plea diversion drug courts (e.g., deferred sentencing) require individuals to plead guilty or no contest to the charges against them. Their sentence is then deferred while they participate in the drug court. If they successfully complete the drug court, the court can vacate or withdraw the plea and also expunge the arrest or guilty plea from their record (Marlowe et al., 2016). Not all individuals are eligible for diversion, primarily due to the seriousness of their crime or criminal history. Thus, post-sentencing drug courts allow these individuals to participate in the drug court after conviction as a condition of their probation. Within this model, the conviction will remain on the participant's record; however, they avoid incarceration, if successful (Marlowe et al., 2016). Within all dispositional models, if a participant is unsuccessful in completing the requirements of the drug court and is dismissed from the program, the original charges will be brought against them, and they will be processed within the traditional court system (NDCRC, n.d.).

## THE TEN KEY COMPONENTS OF DRUG COURTS

Although the drug court model represented an innovative solution to treating substance-using individuals who were cycling in and out of the criminal justice system, a lack of standardization plagued the drug court movement. In 1997, in an effort to provide guidance to newly established drug courts and define the drug court model, the Bureau of Justice Assistance (BJA) in collaboration with the National Association of Drug Court Professionals (NADCP) published ten Key Components of drug courts (BJA, 2004). These foundational elements were designed to be inspirational and outline the structure and process that drug courts should utilize as the courts are implemented and throughout their operation (Lutze & van Wormer, 2014; Olson et al., 2001). The key components are as follows (BJA, 2004, p. iii):

1. Drug courts integrate alcohol and other drug treatment services with justice system case processing;
2. Using a nonadversarial approach, prosecution and defense counsel promote public safety while protecting participants' due process rights;
3. Eligible participants are identified early and promptly placed in the drug court program;
4. Drug courts provide access to a continuum of alcohol, drug, and other related treatment and rehabilitation services;
5. Abstinence is monitored by frequent alcohol and other drug testing;
6. A coordinated strategy governs drug court responses to participants' compliance;
7. Ongoing judicial interaction with each drug court participant is essential;
8. Monitoring and evaluation measure the achievement of program goals and gauge effectiveness;
9. Continuing interdisciplinary education promotes effective drug court planning, implementation, and operations;
10. Forging partnerships among drug courts, public agencies, and community-based organizations generates local support and enhances drug court program effectiveness.

While the ten Key Components represent a model drug court program, and nearly all espouse these components (Quinn, 2000), drug courts vary in their ability to adopt and implement the various components with fidelity (Lutze & van Wormer, 2014; Olson et al., 2001). Olson and colleagues (2001), for example, found that three drug courts in Chicago, Illinois, were all successfully able to integrate treatment services (Key Component #1), monitor abstinence through urine analysis testing (Key Component #5), and provide ongoing judicial interaction (Key Component #7). The courts, however, varied in their ability to identify and promptly place individuals into the drug court (Key Component #3). One court also had difficulty implementing the courtroom workgroup (Key Components #2 and #6), as the court experienced high rates of staff turnover, which resulted in less stability (Olson et al., 2001).

The variation in adoption of the ten Key Components can also affect the success of drug courts, whereby drug courts that implement and adhere to the ten Key Components are better able to reduce drug use and other criminal behavior (Gottfredson, Najaka, Kearley, & Rocha, 2006; Longshore et al., 2001; Lutze & van Wormer, 2014; Marlowe et al., 2016; Mitchell,

Wilson, Eggers, & MacKenzie, 2012b). Gottfredson and colleagues (2006), for example, found that drug court participants who received more drug treatment, drug testing, judicial monitoring, and probation services were rearrested significantly less during a three-year follow-up than those who received fewer services.

## Proliferation of Drug Courts

In the past thirty years, drug courts (and other problem-solving courts) have proliferated across the United States and abroad (Marlowe et al., 2016). In 1994, Congress passed, and President Clinton signed into law, the Violent Crime Control and Law Enforcement Act. Within this act, the federal government created the Drug Courts Program Office and made available $29 million to support the planning, implementation, and enhancement of state and local drug courts in 1995, while authorizing an additional $971 million to support such courts between 1996 and 2000 (U.S. Department of Justice, n.d.). Currently, BJA's Adult Drug Court Discretionary Grant Program continues to support drug courts financially and provide other assistance in an effort to build drug court capacity and increase participation among clients (BJA, 2020).

As a result of the available funding and support, not just from the federal government, but also from state, local, and private funding mechanisms, the United States has witnessed an exponential increase in the number of operational drug courts, many of which have sustained throughout the years (U.S. GAO, 1997). In 1994, for example, forty-one drug courts existed. By 1997, this number had almost quadrupled to 161 drug courts operating in thirty-eight states, the District of Columbia, and Puerto Rico (U.S. GAO, 1997). Just over a decade later, in 2009, over 2,500 drug courts operated or were in the planning stages in all fifty states, the District of Columbia, Puerto Rico, Guam, the Northern Mariana Islands, and in approximately ninety Tribal locations (Office of National Drug Control Policy [ONDCP], 2011). Furthering its reach, the drug court movement has expanded beyond the United States to include Australia, Belgium, Brazil, Canada, the Caribbean, Ireland, New Zealand, Norway, and Scotland (United Nations Office on Drugs and Crime, 2005; VîlcicĂ, Belenko, Hiller, & Taxman, 2010). Ultimately, over 3,000 drug courts were in operation in 2020, of which half are adult drug courts (BJA, 2020). The rest of the drug courts are the result of policymakers and local leaders adapting the adult drug court model to fit the needs of other substance-using, justice-involved individuals. These variations include juvenile drug, family dependency, campus drug, tribal drug, hybrid driving while intoxicated (DWI)/drug, and co-occurring disorder courts (NDCRC, 2018). While these alternatives utilize standards similar to the adult drug court model described above and adopt a version of the ten Key Components, fundamental differences exist.

Juvenile drug courts, for example, are comparable to adult drug courts in that they seek to provide developmentally appropriate substance abuse treatment to substance-using juveniles who have become involved in the criminal justice system (Belenko & Logan, 2003). Juvenile drug courts differentiate themselves from adult drug courts, however, by delivering comprehensive services to the youth, which take into account the juvenile's family while coordinating with school systems and the community (SAMHSA, n.d.). Family dependency courts also differ from traditional adult drug court. These civil courts (as opposed to criminal courts) target substance-abusing adults who are also custodial parents. Here intervention efforts, including substance abuse treatment and case management, are coordinated with child protective services, with the overarching goal of reuniting the participant with their dependent children (Marlowe & Carey, 2012) (see chapter 6).

Campus drug courts strive to address the complex issue of high-risk drinking and drug use of college students, many of who are facing suspension or expulsion as a result of their substance use, through campus conduct and treatment providers (Asmus, 2002; Dutmers, 2016). While campus drug courts are based on the philosophy of adult drug courts and adopt similar components, these drug courts do not operate within the criminal court system. Instead, campus drug courts typically operate on the university campus, with the drug court team comprising university officials, and the model being adapted for students and available campus resources (Asmus, 2002; Dutmers, 2016).

Tribal drug courts (see chapter 9)—also called tribal healing to wellness courts—focus on the underlying issues associated with pervasive drug and alcohol use within Native American tribes by meeting the individual needs of Indian Nations and tribal justice systems (Tribal Law & Policy Institute, 2003). These courts are designed to take into account the cultural needs and incorporate tribal custom and tradition, which can vary greatly by tribe and reservation. Tribal drug courts also take a holistic approach, stressing the importance of involving family, extended family, and the community in the healing process (Tribal Law & Policy Institute, 1999).

Hybrid DWI/drug courts (see chapter 3) accept justice-involved individuals who are addicted to drugs or alcohol. Operation of these courts tend to mirror those of traditional adult drug courts, with the central difference being the target population (Bouffard, Richardson, & Franklin, 2010). Finally, and similarly, co-occurring disorder courts differ from traditional adult drug courts in their target population. Eligibility requirements for co-occurring disorder courts include having a substance abuse disorder *and* mental illness (see chapter 2). These courts also tend to have fewer participants, provide more intensive services, and be of longer duration than traditional adult drug courts (Peters, Kremling, Bekman, & Caudy, 2012).

## PROFESSIONAL ORGANIZATIONS AND RESOURCES

Professional drug court organizations and supporting resources have developed over the years in an effort to provide guidance to the thousands of operational drug courts and their variations. These organizations, institutes, and associations assist with program development and capacity building, provide technical assistance and training, promote best practices, and disseminate information and research related to drug courts (BJA, 2020). Table 1.1 provides a list of these resources, their purpose, and website.

## THE EFFECTIVENESS OF DRUG COURTS IN REDUCING RECIDIVISM AND DRUG USE

In the three decades since the establishment of the first drug court, these courts have become an extensively researched alternative to incarceration. To date, researchers have conducted over 100 independent evaluations of drug courts all across the country and abroad, from Multnomah County, Oregon, to Brooklyn, New York, to New South Wales, Australia (Mitchell et al., 2012a, 2012b; Rossman, Roman, Zweig, Rempel, & Lindquist, 2011; Sevigny, Fuleihan, & Ferdik, 2013). Generally, examinations of drug courts suggest that this mode of criminal justice is effective at producing positive outcomes for clients and in achieving its overarching goals—reduce recidivism and drug use (Belenko, 2001; Latimer, Morton-Bourgon, & Chrétien, 2006; Lowenkamp, Holsinger, & Latessa, 2005; Mitchell et al., 2012a, 2012b; Rossman et al., 2011; Shaffer, 2011; Wilson, Mitchell, & MacKenzie, 2006).

Despite the breadth of evaluations, the literature base is methodologically weak (Mitchell et al., 2012a; Wilson et al., 2006). Indeed, researchers have conducted only three randomized controlled trials (RCTs) utilizing independent samples to examine the effectiveness of adult drug courts (Deschenes, Turner, & Greenwood, 1995; Gottfredson & Exum, 2002; Shanahan, Lanscar, Hass, Lind, Weatherburn, & Chen, 2004), albeit with numerous publications stemming from these three studies (Sloas, 2020). The following is an overview of three independent RCTs.

**Table 1.1   Drug Court Resources**

| Resource | Purpose | Website |
| --- | --- | --- |
| *General Drug Court Resources* | | |
| Adult Drug Court Research to Practice Initiative | Archive of training resources and webinars related to drug courts | www.ndcrc.org/research2practiceresources/ |
| Center for Court Innovation | Provides training and technical assistance, along with planning and coordination for problem-solving courts | www.courtinnovation.org/areas-of-focus/treatment-courts; https://www.courtinnovation.org/training-ta |
| International Association of Drug Treatment Courts | International clearinghouse for drug courts that provides updates on developments in the United Nations Office of Drug Control Policy | www.iadtc.com |
| National Association of Drug Court Professionals | Provides training and membership for drug court professionals, while advocating for strategies proven to improve the criminal justice response to people with substance use and mental health disorders | www.nadcp.org |
| National Drug Court Institute | Provides standardized, evidence-based training and technical assistance, including customized service, strategic partnerships, coaching, and follow-up | www.ndci.org |
| National Drug Court Resource Center | Provides practical, open, and accessible resources, while encouraging the exchange of research and ideas by connecting treatment court professionals | www.ndcrc.org |
| National Training System for Treatment Court Practitioners | Offers free, national training for treatment court practitioners involved in adult drug, juvenile drug, veterans' treatment, and healing to wellness courts | www.treatmentcourts.org |
| *Specific Drug Court Resources* | | |
| Family Drug Courts Training and Technical Assistance Program | Provides training and technical assistance to state, local, and tribal jurisdictions to develop, enhance, and sustain family drug courts | www.cffutures.org/national-fdc-tta-program |
| Healing to Wellness Training and Technical Assistance Program | Delivers education, research, training, and technical assistance to Native communities to develop and strengthen healing to wellness courts | www.wellnesscourts.org |

*(Continued)*

Table 1.1   **Drug Court Resources** *(Continued)*

| Resource | Purpose | Website |
|---|---|---|
| National Center for DWI Courts | Provides training and technical assistance to jurisdictions seeking to implement, expand, and improve DWI court programs | www.dwicourts .org |
| National Council of Juvenile and Family Court Judges | Judicial membership organization that provides resources, knowledge, and training for professionals in the juvenile and family justice systems | www.ncjfcj.org |
| Office of Juvenile Justice and Delinquency Prevention | Provides guidelines for the development of juvenile drug treatment courts, as well as training and technical assistance | https://ojjdp.ojp.go v/programs/juve nile-drug-treat ment-court-guid elines |
| Tribal Drug Court Training and Technical Assistance Center | Offers training and technical assistance to tribes and tribal organizations using the Strategic Cultural Framework | www.samhsa.gov/ tribal-ttac |

*Sources:* Compiled by the author using information adapted from BJA (2020) and each of the specific web-sites mentioned here.

The earliest RCT of a drug court took place in the Maricopa County First Time Drug Offender (FTDO) program, where 639 probationers were randomly assigned to the FTDO program or standard probation (which used different levels of drug testing) between March 1992 and April 1993 (Deschenes et al., 1995). During the twelve-month follow-up period, there was no significant difference in number of positive urinalysis tests between the treatment and control groups. The FTDO participants, however, were significantly less likely to test positive for cocaine or heroin but more for marijuana compared to those on standard probation. Related to recidivism, there were no significant differences between the FTDO participants and those on standard probation in rearrest, reconviction, or reincarceration rates. FTDO participants, however, were significantly less likely to be sentenced to prison and were less likely to receive a technical violation for a drug violation, alcohol violation, or a nonappearance.

In a series of publications spanning twenty-three years, Gottfredson and colleagues have examined the effects of the Baltimore City's Drug Treatment Court (BCDTC) on a number of different outcomes over time (Banks & Gottfredson, 2003, 2004; Gottfredson & Exum, 2002; Gottfredson, Coblentz, & Harmon, 1997; Gottfredson, Kearely, Najaka, & Rocha, 2005; Gottfredson, Najaka, Kearley, 2003; Gottfredson et al., 2006; Kearley & Gottfredson, 2020). This more than two-decade examination of the BCDTC represents one of the most comprehensive and long-term studies of an adult drug court to date. The BCDTC, which began serving clients in 1994, uses a post-adjudication drug court model, allows for nonviolent adult offenders with misdemeanor or felony charges, and follows the ten Key Components outlined earlier. Between February 1997 and August 1998, researchers randomly assigned 235 eligible BCDTC clients, all of whom had extensive histories of criminal and substance use disorder, to either the BCDTC or treatment as usual (i.e., traditional adjudication) (Gottfredson & Exum, 2002). Ultimately, 139 participants were assigned to the BCDTC, while 96 received traditional adjudication of their case.

Using data from official records, Gottfredson and Exum (2002) presented early findings from the BCDTC study, which suggested that participants of the BCDTC were significantly less likely than the control group to be rearrested, have fewer new arrests, and fewer new charges in the twelve months following randomization. The treatment group, however, was not any less likely than the control group to receive a new charge for a drug crime (Gottfredson & Exum, 2002). Two-year recidivism outcomes, also using official records, provided similar findings (Banks & Gottfredson, 2003; Gottfredson et al., 2003). Particularly, BCDTC participants were significantly less likely to be rearrested compared to the control group, had fewer new arrests, and fewer new charges (Gottfredson et al., 2003). They also had significantly increased time to rearrest (Banks & Gottfredson, 2003). Unlike the one-year follow-up, however, BCDTC participants were significantly less likely than the control group to receive a new drug charge suggesting the program likely had an effect on this outcome (Gottfredson et al., 2003).

Three years post-randomization, drug court participants self-reported significantly less involvement in criminal activity, and when engaged in crime, the crime type was less serious than the control group. The treatment group also reported using fewer illegal substances and had lower scores on an alcohol addiction severity scale than the control group (Gottfredson et al., 2005). Official data support the self-reported behavior of participants, where BCDTC participants were less likely to be rearrested, had fewer new arrests, and were less likely to receive a new drug charge (Gottfredson et al., 2006). Despite these positive findings, there were no significant differences in other outcomes of interest, including employment status, physical and mental health status, and family and social relationships. Thus, while the BCDTC was successful at reducing drug use and criminal behavior, these positive effects did not extend to broader outcomes (Gottfredson et al., 2005).

Results even suggest that the positive effects of drug court participation are sustained long after an individual ceases their involvement in drug court, where BCDTC participants were able to make persistent life changes (Gottfredson et al., 2006; Kearley & Gottfredson, 2002). In a fifteen-year follow-up of the BCDTC, Kearley and Gottfredson (2020) examined the effects of drug court participation on a number of key outcomes, including arrests, convictions, violation of probation, and days incarcerated. Results indicated that BCDTC participants had significantly fewer unique arrests; total charges; total drug, property, and person charges; unique arrest convictions; total charge convictions; and total person and property charge convictions. Participation in the BCDTC, however, did not result in fewer drug charge convictions, total violation of probation charges and convictions, or days of sentenced incarceration (Kearley & Gottfredson, 2020).

Finally, Shanahan and colleagues (2004) conducted an RCT to examine the effectiveness of the New South Wales (Australia) adult drug court in reducing recidivism and costs. Between February 1999 and June 2000, 500 individuals were randomly assigned to the drug court (*n* = 309) or normal judicial processing (*n* = 191). Results of the twenty-three-month evaluation revealed that participants of the drug court committed significantly fewer drug offenses and the time to the first shoplifting or drug offense was significantly longer than that of the control group (Shanahan et al., 2004).

While the aforementioned three RCTs represent the crème-de-la-crème of evaluations, the vast majority of drug court evaluations utilize quasi-experimental designs, with only approximately one in five conducting rigorous quasi-experimental designs (Mitchell et al., 2012a, 2012b). As noted earlier, differences in findings exist between the one-year evaluation of the Maricopa County FTDO program (no recidivism effects), the long-term evaluation of the BCDTC drug court (sustained reductions for multiple measures of recidivism), and the Australian drug court evaluation (reduced recidivism for drug offenses). Notwithstanding the divergences, meta-analytic reviews, systematic reviews, and multi-site evaluations conclude that adult drug courts are effective at reducing recidivism, resulting in an 8–32 percent average reduction in recidivism (Belenko, 2001; Carey et al., 2012; Latimer et al., 2006; Lowenkamp et al., 2005; Mitchell et al., 2012a, 2012b; Rossman et al., 2011; Shaffer, 2011; Wilson et al., 2006). These positive effects remain post-program and extend to at least three years post-drug court entry (Mitchell et al., 2012a, 2012b).

The ability of drug courts to serve as a true alternative to incarceration, however, is less promising. Originally, drug courts were conceived not solely to better allocate court resources, but to conserve correctional resources as well. This was to be done by reducing the number of substance using individuals incarcerated for nonviolent, lesser offenses. Precious correctional resources were to be used, instead, for violent individuals who posed a substantial threat to the community. However, in practice, jail time is commonly used as a punitive graduated sanction for those who are noncompliant with drug court mandates. Participants are also subjected to jail or prison time if they are unsuccessful or drop out of the drug court. In a meta-analysis examining the effects of drug courts on incarceration, Sevigny and colleagues (2013) find that while drug courts reduce the use of incarceration (i.e., drug court participants have lower rates of incarceration than comparison groups), they do not reduce the amount of time incarcerated in jail or prison. This finding is possibly explained by the lengthy sentences drug court participants receive when they fail or drop out of the program. Thus, although drug courts lessen individual-level exposure to incarceration, they do not provide the overall reductions in incarceration and reduced burden on the correctional system that would be expected of a true alternative to incarceration (Sevigny et al., 2013).

## CRITICAL ISSUES SURROUNDING DRUG COURTS

Despite the effectiveness of drug courts in reducing participant recidivism and drug use, a number of substantial concerns surrounding drug courts exist. These concerns not only apply to drug courts but also extend to the broader problem-solving court model. Many scholars contemplate these concerns as they apply to other problem-solving court models. Their carryover perhaps stems from the expediency with which they were implemented. These critical issues should not be overlooked and include the use of coercive, court-mandated treatment, apparent due process violations, net-widening, and restrictive eligibility requirements. Any discussion of drug courts is not complete without an understanding of these issues.

### Drug Court Coerciveness

One of the hallmarks of drug courts is judicial supervision of community-based treatment. As MacKenzie (2006) succinctly states, drug courts use the "coercive power of the court to promote abstinence, treatment attendance, and other prosocial behaviors" (p. 224). This is achieved primarily through the authority and power of the drug court judge who closely monitors participants' progress through treatment and compliance with court mandates (GAO, 1997; Wilson et al., 2006). Although drug courts do not represent the first time the courts have overseen treatment efforts (e.g., see Treatment for Alternatives to Street Crime [TASC]), they substantially diverge from other attempts. Specifically, drug courts are able to hold treatment providers more accountable, do not automatically dismiss a person from the program for relapse (which results in treatment providers being more willing to work with the courts), and they are able to quickly sanction those who violate the conditions of the drug court (MacKenzie, 2006). Questions arise, however, of the appropriateness of drug court judges to pursue rehabilitative interventionism (Miller, 2004).

While the coerciveness of drug courts might undermine the therapeutic philosophy of problem-solving courts (Douds & Ahlin, 2019; Tiger, 2011), research has shown, albeit with mixed results, that mandated treatment can have positive benefits and does not always diminish treatment effectiveness (Farabee, Prendergast, & Anglin, 1998; Parhar, Wormith, Derkzen, & Beauregard, 2008; Rempel & Destefano, 2001). Despite the positive changes of those who enter into drug treatment involuntarily or under the supervision of the court, according to Tiger (2011), drug courts allow for "increased criminal justice oversight of defendants in the name of facilitating recovery" (p. 169).

The coercive extent of problem-solving courts, however, does appear to depend on the target population (e.g., drug, DWI, veteran) and dispositional model of the court (e.g., pre/post-plea diversionary or post-adjudication) (Berman & Feinblatt, 2001; Douds & Ahlin, 2019; Olson et al., 2001). Olson and colleagues (2001), for example, find that misdemeanor drug courts, where participants do not face risk of incarceration for program violations or revocations, had less coercive control over the participants. On the other hand, felony drug courts or those where participants were subject to incarceration if revoked had greater control over participants, as clients faced more punitive sanctions (Olson et al., 2001). The legal status of the participant upon entrance into the problem-solving court also matters (Douds & Ahlin, 2019). For example, veterans' courts that operate using a pre/post-plea diversionary model are able to hold the threat of a criminal conviction and potentially lengthy term of incarceration over the head of the participant as leverage to increase compliance. While post-adjudication veterans' courts are potentially less coercive, as defendants are sentenced to a problem-solving court, judges still have considerable discretion in determining the outcome for those that fail to complete the court program (e.g., revoke probation and impose sentence) and for those that successfully graduate (e.g., dismiss the prosecution and set aside conviction) (Douds & Ahlin, 2019).

## Due Process Considerations

A parallel issue related to drug courts is the inherent due process violations associated with drug court involvement. Recall Key Component #2 that states that "using a nonadversarial approach, prosecution and defense counsel promote public safety while protecting participants' due process rights" (BJA, 2004, p. iii; similar Key Components exist for other problem-solving court models, see Justice for Vets, 2017). Clearly, the courts understand that all defendants, including those interested in participating in a problem-solving court, have inalienable due process rights. Not only are defendants to be treated fairly and with dignity, but they also have a right to effective assistance of counsel, a speedy trial, confront witnesses, and appeal. While the courts consider due process to be flexible and that procedural protections must meet the situational demands (Meyer, 2017), fundamentally, the problem-solving court model calls into question their ability to preserve the substantive and procedural due process rights of participants.

Defense attorneys are essential to preserving clients' legal rights and advocating for fair and equal treatment. The non-adversarial approach to drug courts, however, can hinder their ability to do so. In the name of being a team player, defense counsel, for example, might forego traditional legal defense tactics (e.g., motions to suppress evidence) and encourage their client to disclose a relapse and other potentially damaging information, which can have ramifications for participants (Quinn, 2000). As Quinn (2000) aptly states "in some instances forced non-adversarialism can place defense attorneys in conflict with clients as well as interfere with the provision of competent and zealous representation as required by law" (p. 58). More concerning is that defense attorneys might not even be present during status hearings—allowing for the participant to be questioned and potentially sanctioned by the judge without an attorney present (Quinn, 2000). Even with this, many defense attorneys are ambivalent toward drug courts. This is particularly true, as for decades they have rightfully advocated for their clients to be provided treatment and alternative sanctions (Berman & Feinblatt, 2001).

Additionally, in order to participate in the drug court, individuals are required to enter into a signed plea agreement. These binding agreements typically require participants to waive their right to a trial, to appeal, and to contest warrantless and without cause physical and property searches, among others (Meyer, 2017). The exact outcome a drug court client, whether successful or unsuccessful, can expect for waiving their rights might also be unclear (Quinn, 2000). As a condition of the drug court, many participants are receiving supervision in the community, which may or may not be formal probation depending on their legal status (i.e., in drug court on pre/post-plea diversionary or post-sentence status) (Meyer, 2017). The consequences of being terminated from the drug court, however, are analogous to the consequences of a probation revocation, and at times worse. In the Bronx Treatment Court, for example, participants agree at the outset to a sentence of two to six years imprisonment if they fail to complete treatment—the original charge's statutory minimum of which is only one to three years imprisonment (Quinn, 2000). While this area of law is in flux, some states have ruled that, regardless of participants' legal status, drug court participants who are going to be terminated have the same rights and protections as those on formal probation (Meyer, 2017).

## Net-Widening

During their development and expansion, proponents of drug courts touted them as an alternative to incarceration for substance-addicted individuals.

While drug courts are seen by many as a welcome opportunity to provide treatment to substance-addicted individuals as opposed to the more punitive punishments (e.g., incarceration), some contend that the expansive use of drug courts can result in net-widening (Lilley, 2017; Lilley, Stewart, & Tucker-Gail, 2020; Miller, 2004). Net-widening occurs when new criminal justice reforms target individuals who would have received lesser punishments had the new program not existed (Palumbo, Clifford, & Snyder-Joy, 1992). Essentially, net-widening expands the scope of social control (Petersilia et al., 1992) and results in more people being involved in the criminal justice system.

By year-end 2014, drug courts across the United States were serving over 127,000 participants annually (Marlowe et al., 2016). The extensive use of drug courts opens the door for increased criminal justice involvement for those whose case might have been dismissed or whose punishment might have been less strenuous and burdensome than drug court participation. This is particularly true for those accused of committing relatively minor offenses (Lilley, 2017). Lilley and colleagues, for example, found that jurisdictions with drug courts experienced a 12–17 percent increase in rates of misdemeanor drug use and possession arrests (Lilley, 2017; Lilley et al., 2020). Additionally, while receiving a sanction in drug court is common (Guastaferro & Daigle, 2012; Zettler & Martin, 2020), approximately one in four drug court participants fail to complete drug court due to technical violations or for committing a new offense (Marlowe et al., 2016; Taxman & Bouffard, 2005). This can result in revocation of a plea or sentence, which can then lead to a lengthy prison sentence—a sentence that is possibly unwarranted based on the original charge for which the person was arrested (Quinn, 2000).

Furthermore, studies suggest that over one-thirds of drug court participants do not have chemical dependency, as measured by the Addiction Severity Index, indicating relatively minimal drug use problems (DeMatteo, Marlowe, Festinger, & Arabia, 2009). Because of the intensity of drug court treatment, this type of sanction is not suitable, and can in fact be harmful, for those with minor substance use issues (DeMatteo et al., 2009; Marlow et al., 2016; also see Bonta & Andrews, 2007, for an overview on the risk-needs-responsivity model). Ultimately, it is evident, as Lilley et al. (2020) states that despite the good intentions of drug courts, "the long-term dedication of resources toward relatively minor offenders may have exacerbated the nationwide focus on minor drug offenses, resulting in an unintended net-widening side effect" (p. 301).

## Restrictive Eligibility Requirements

Even with the potential for net-widening, an opposite concern surrounding drug courts is their restrictive eligibility requirements. Since their inception, drug courts have been highly restrictive in their eligibility criteria (Kearley & Gottfredson, 2020; Marlowe et al., 2016). While a plurality (48 percent) of adult drug courts serve individuals charged with a felony, less than 10 percent serve misdemeanants only (Marlowe et al., 2016). This could result in unintended consequences, as individuals whose felony charge is reclassified to a misdemeanor may then be ineligible for drug court participation (Marlowe et al., 2016). Additionally, the majority of drug courts restrict their eligibility to non-violent offenders, which is due, in part, to federal funding constraints (Mitchell et al., 2012a; Strong et al., 2016) and punitive attitudes toward violent offenders (Cullen, Fisher, & Applegate, 2000). Mitchell et al. (2012a), for example, report that of the ninety-two adult drug court studies included in their meta-analysis, only 17 percent allowed violent offenders to participate in the drug court.

These restrictive eligibility criteria can be problematic for a number of reasons. First, drug courts serve only a small percentage of the drug offend-ing population (Marlowe et al., 2016; Sevigny et al., 2013). While lack of resources and capacity are certainly contributing factors in this low inclusion rate, drug courts should consider targeting high-risk, high-need persons, regardless of offense level or client attribute. The extant drug court and cor-rectional rehabilitation literature consistently find that focusing resources on higher-risk offenders (as opposed to lower-risk) results in greater recidivism reductions (Lowenkamp et al., 2005; Marlowe et al., 2006; Marlowe et al., 2016). Second, research demonstrates that drug court participants with a history of violence perform just as well as those with no history of violence (Saum & Hiller, 2008; Saum, Scarpitti, & Robbins, 2001). Additionally, recent research suggests that the public supports a pragmatic approach to sanctioning violent drug offenders, violent offenders with mental health issues, and violent veterans as opposed to a purely punitive response (Atkin-Plunk, 2020; Sloas & Atkin-Plunk, 2019). Specifically, Atkin-Plunk (2020) finds that the majority of the public support a balanced or a rehabilitative-approach to sanctioning violent drug, mental health, and veteran offenders— where a balanced sanctioning approach gives equal emphasis to punishment and rehabilitation. Indeed, drug and other problem-solving courts embrace the ideals of balanced justice, as they not only provide rehabilitation through effective treatment, but also hold participants accountable for their actions. Olson and colleagues (2001, p. 193) best describe the illogical nature of excluding persons with a history of violence from drug court participation:

> It seems almost paradoxical that programs that focus so much effort and energy at "understanding" the extent and nature of an offender's substance abuse prob-lem—the factors that encourage use, the reasons for relapse, and the interrelation-ships among substance abuse, crime, education, and employment—would accept

the position that "anyone with a prior violent conviction is inappropriate for drug treatment court program," particularly when identifying older addicts/criminals, who might have committed a violent crime ten or even twenty years ago.

Although drug-involved individuals have no constitutional right to enter into a drug court, policymakers and drug court stakeholders should closely examine and consider expanding the eligibility criteria of drug courts. They should ensure that drug court are targeting high-risk, high-needs individuals with documented chemical dependency, a criminogenic need. Providing intensive drug treatment to first-time offenders without a documented history of substance abuse could do more harm than good.

## THE FUTURE OF DRUG COURTS

Drug courts have made tremendous strides since their development and have been labeled a promising evidence-based practice (National Institute of Justice, n.d.) that have substantial effects on reducing recidivism (Mitchell et al., 2012a, 2012b). As they continue to evolve, drug courts should look toward improving their operation and increasing effectiveness. Moving forward, drug courts should focus on implementing programs with fidelity, expanding eligibility criteria, reducing racial disparities, and increasing gender-responsiveness.

To begin, drug courts should not only embrace in theory the use of the ten Key Components (BJA, 2004), but they should also work to implement these components with fidelity. Although this will not be done without effort (Olson et al., 2001), research suggests that drug courts that adhere to the 10 Key Components are more successful in reducing drug use and improving community safety (Gottfredson et al., 2006; Longshore et al., 2001; Lutze & van Wormer, 2014; Marlowe et al., 2016; Mitchell et al., 2012b). Additionally, and as previously mentioned, drug court stakeholders should examine the eligibility criteria that individuals must meet to participate in the drug court. Generally, individuals with a history of violence are excluded from participation. It is unwise for drug court officials to assume that substance-using individuals with a violent background are not suitable for and would not benefit from the treatment in a drug court. As research suggests that drug courts should target high-risk, high-needs individuals (Kearley & Gottfredson, 2020; Lowenkamp et al., 2005; Marlowe et al., 2006; Rossman et al., 2011) and the public becomes more pragmatic toward violent offenders (Atkin-Plunk, 2020), there is credence for a reexamination of eligibility criteria.

Relatedly, restricting eligibility to nonviolent individuals can indirectly exclude young, black males from drug court participation (Saum et al., 2001).

Predominately, drug court participants are Caucasian (62 percent), followed by African American (17 percent), then Hispanic (10 percent) (Marlowe et al., 2016). In a unanimous resolution sent out in 2010, the board of directors of the National Association of Drug Court Professionals urged drug courts to examine whether racial and ethnic disparities existed in their courts, and if so, to take corrective measures to eliminate the disparities. While African Americans are slightly overrepresented in drug courts compared to the general population (13 percent), they are substantially underrepresented compared to their involvement in the criminal justice system. Specifically, African Americans represent 30 percent of all drug offense arrestees, 30 percent of probationers, 35 percent of jail inmates, and 37 percent of prisoners (Marlowe et al., 2016). It is not possible, given the lack of information on arrestee's eligibility for drug court, to conclude if drug courts are disproportionately excluding people of color. However, systematic differences in plea-bargaining, charging, and sentencing practices could result in the exclusion of racial and ethnic minorities from drug court.

Further, drug courts should utilize gender-responsive treatment. While females represent 21 percent of those arrested for a drug offense, 25 percent of probationers, 15 percent of jail inmates, and 7 percent of prisoners, they represent 32 percent of the drug court population, ranging from 8 percent to 59 percent representation (Marlowe et al., 2016). Their overrepresentation in drug court compared to their involvement in the criminal justice system is only one reason to provide gender-specific services. Another, and more compelling, reason is that gender-responsive treatment modalities are effective at promoting change. Research has consistently shown that the treatment needs of female drug users are different and more complex than those of male drug users, as justice-involved women have extensive histories of sexual and physical abuse; are more likely to have co-occurring disorders, childcare responsibilities, and parental stress; and have more severe drug use (Binswanger et al., 2010; Messina, Burdon, & Prendergast, 2003; Tuchman, 2010). As such, addressing the specific needs of females, through a trauma-informed approach, can result in positive behavioral change, where women who receive gender-responsive treatment are less likely to recidivate and use drugs, perform better while in treatment, and have improvements in behavioral health (Messina, Calhoun, & Warda, 2012).

## CONCLUSION

The development of drug courts in the late 1980s brought drastic change to how the criminal justice system manages and treats substance-using individuals. Established during an era rife with the criminalization of illicit drug use, drug courts represented a departure from the punitive punishment philosophies of the time by combining community-based treatment and accountability in a therapeutic environment. Thirty years later, these problem-solving courts appear to be a permanent staple in the U.S. criminal justice system. With over 3,000 drug courts serving more than 125,000 participants annually, it is imperative for drug courts to operate utilizing evidence-based practices and target high-risk, high-needs substance-using individuals. Although the extant research supports their effectiveness, it is only through the continued assessment of and reflection on drug courts that their weaknesses will be realized and methods for improvement considered. There is much we do not know about why these courts "work" (see Ahlin & Douds, 2019). Drug courts are not the end-all-be-all to the substance-using justice-involved population or at-capacity corrections system; however, their ability to provide a pragmatic, balanced approach to sanctioning those whose criminogenic substance use contributed to their involvement in the criminal justice system has garnered the support of individuals on both sides of the aisle and ultimately began the problem-solving court movement.

## REFERENCES

Ahlin, E. M., & Douds, A. S. (2019). The problem with problem-solving courts: The black box remains unopened after thirty years. In C. Spohn & P. K. Brennan (Eds.), *Handbook on sentencing policies and practices in the 21st century* (pp. 339–359). Routledge.

Asmus, C. L. (2002). A campus drug court: Colorado State University. *Drug Court Review, 4*(1), 1–38.

Atkin-Plunk, C. A. (2020). Should all violent offenders be treated equally? Perceptions of punishment and rehabilitation for violent offenders with varying attributes. *Victims & Offenders, 15*(2), 218–242.

Baldwin, J. M. (2015). Investigating the programmatic attack: A national survey of veterans treatment courts. *The Journal of Criminal Law & Criminology, 105*(3), 705–751.

Banks, D., & Gottfredson, D. C. (2003). The effects of drug treatment and supervision on time to re-arrest among drug treatment court participants. *Journal of Drug Issues, 33*(2), 385–412.

Banks, D., & Gottfredson, D. C. (2004). Participation in drug treatment court and time to arrest. *Justice Quarterly, 21*(3), 637–658.

Belenko, S. (2001). Research on drug courts: A critical review 2001 update. *National Drug Court Institute Review, 4*, 1–60.

Belenko, S., & Logan, T. K. (2003). Delivering more effective treatment to adolescents: Improving the juvenile drug court model. *Journal of Substance Abuse Treatment, 25*(3), 189–211.

Berman, G., & Feinblatt, J. (2001). Problem-solving courts: A brief primer. *Law & Policy, 23*(2), 125–140.

Binswanger, I. A., Merrill, J. O., Krueger, P. M., White, M. C., Boothe, R. E., & Elmore, J. G. (2010). Gender differences in chronic medical, psychiatric, and substance-dependence disorders among jail inmates. *American Journal of Public Health, 100*(3), 476–482.

Bonta, J., & Andrews, D. A. (2007). *Risk-need-responsivity model for offender assessment and rehabilitation.* Public Safety Canada.

Bouffard, J. A., Richardson, K. A., & Franklin, T. (2010). Drug courts for DWI offenders? The effectiveness of two hybrid drug courts on DWI offenders. *Journal of Criminal Justice, 38*(1), 25–33.

Bronson, J., Stroop, J., Zimmer, S., & Berzofsky, M. (2017). *Drug use, dependence, and abuse among state prisoners and jail inmates, 2007–2009* (NCJ 250546). Bureau of Justice Statistics.

Bureau of Justice Assistance. (2004). *Defining drug courts: The key components* (NCJ 205621). U.S. Department of Justice Office of Justice Programs.

Bureau of Justice Assistance. (2020). *Drug courts* (NCJ 238527). U.S. Department of Justice Office of Justice Programs.

Carson, E. A. (2020). *Prisoners in 2018* (NCJ 253516). Bureau of Justice Statistics.

Carson, E. A., & Golinelli, D. (2013). *Prisoners in 2012: Trends in admissions and releases, 1991–2012* (NCJ 243920). Bureau of Justice Statistics.

Cullen, F. T., Fisher, B. S., & Applegate, B. K. (2000). Public opinion about punishment and corrections. *Crime and Justice, 27*, 1–79.

DeMatteo, D., Marlowe, D. B., Festinger, D. S., & Arabia, P. L. (2009). Outcome trajectories in drug court: Do all participants have serious drug problems? *Criminal Justice and Behavior, 36*(4), 354–368.

Deschenes, E. P., Turner, S., & Greenwood, P. W. (1995). Drug court or probation? An experimental evaluation of Maricopa County's drug court. *Justice System Journal, 18*(1), 55–73.

Douds, A. S., & Ahlin, E. M. (2019). *The veterans treatment court movement: Striving to serve those who served.* Routledge.

Douds, A. S., Ahlin, E. M., Howard, D., & Stigerwalt, S. (2017). Varieties of veterans' courts: A statewide assessment of veterans' treatment court components. *Criminal Justice Policy Review, 28*(8), 740–769.

Dutmers, J. M. (2016). Campus drug courts: How universities may be best equipped to tackle crime and substance abuse in young adults. *Law & Psychology Review, 41*, 191–207.

Eleventh Judicial Circuit of Florida. (n.d.). *Adult drug court.* Retrieved from: https://www.jud11.flcourts.org/Adult-Drug-Court

Farabee, D., Prendergast, M., & Anglin, M. D. (1998). The effectiveness of coerced treatment for drug-abusing offenders. *Federal Probation, 62*(1), 3–10.

Gillard, D. K. (1993). *Prisoners in 1992* (NCJ 141874). Bureau of Justice Statistics.

Goldkamp, J. S. (1994). Miami's treatment drug court for felony defendants: Some implications of assessment findings. *The Prison Journal, 73*(2), 110–166.

Goldkamp, J. S., Gottfredson, M. R., & Weiland, D. (1990). Pretrial drug testing and defendant risk. *Journal of Criminal Law and Criminology, 81*(3), 585–652.

Gottfredson, D. C., Coblentz, K., & Harmon, M. A. (1997). A short-term outcome evaluation of the Baltimore City Drug Treatment Court program. *Perspectives,* Winter, 33–38.

Gottfredson, D. C., & Exum, M. L. (2002). The Baltimore City drug treatment court: One-year results from a randomized study. *Journal of Research in Crime and Delinquency, 39*(3), 337–356.

Gottfredson, D. C., Kearley, B., Najaka, S. S., & Rocha, C. (2005). Baltimore City drug treatment court: Three-year self-report outcome study. *Evaluation Review, 29*(1), 42–64.

Gottfredson, D. C., Najaka, S. S., & Kearley, B. (2003). Effectiveness of drug treatment courts: Evidence from a randomized trial. *Criminology & Public Policy, 2*(2), 171-196.

Gottfredson, D. C., Najaka, S. S., Kearley, B. W., & Rocha, C. M. (2006). Long-term effects of participation in the Baltimore City drug treatment court: Results from an experimental study. *Journal of Experimental Criminology, 2*(1), 67–98.

Guastaferro, W. P., & Daigle, L. E. (2012). Linking noncompliant behaviors and programmatic responses: The use of graduated sanctions in a felony-level drug court. *Journal of Drug Issues, 42*(4), 396–419.

Inciardi, J. A. (1986). *War on drugs: Heroin, cocaine, crime, and public policy.* Mayfield Publishing Co.

Justice for Vets (2017). *Ten key components of veterans treatment courts.* https://justiceforvets.org/resource/ten-key-components-of-veterans-treatment-courts/

Kearley, B., & Gottfredson, D. (2020). Long term effects of drug court participation: Evidence from a 15-year follow-up of a randomized controlled trial. *Journal of Experimental Criminology, 16*(1), 27–47.

Kohler-Hausmann, I. (2014). Managerial justice and mass misdemeanors. *Stanford Law Review, 66,* 611–693.

Latimer, J., Morton-Bourgon, K., & Chrétien, J. (2006). *A meta-analytic examination of drug treatment courts: Do they reduce recidivism?* Research and Statistics Division Department of Justice Canada.

Lilley, D. R. (2017). Did drug courts lead to increased arrest and punishment of minor drug offenses? *Justice Quarterly, 34*(4), 674–698.

Lilley, D. R., Stewart, M. C., & Tucker-Gail, K. (2020). Drug courts and net-widening in U.S. cities: A reanalysis using propensity score matching. *Criminal Justice Policy Review, 31*(2), 287–308.

Longshore, D., Turner, S., Wenzel, S., Morral, A., Harrell, A., McBride, D., . . . Iguchi, M. (2001). Drug courts: A conceptual framework. *Journal of Drug Issues, 31*(1), 7–26.

Lowenkamp, C. T., Holsinger, A. M., & Latessa, E. J. (2005). Are drug courts effective? A meta-analytic review. *Journal of Community Corrections, 15*(1), 5–11.

Lutze, F. E., & van Wormer, J. (2014). The reality of practicing the Ten Key Components in adult drug court. *Journal of Offender Rehabilitation, 53*(5), 351–383.

MacKenzie, D. L. (2006). *What works in corrections: Reducing the criminal activities of offenders and delinquents.* Cambridge University Press.

Marlowe, D. B., & Carey, S. M. (2012). *Research update on family drug courts.* National Association of Drug Court Professionals.

Marlowe, D. B., Festinger, D. S., Lee, P. A., Dugosh, K. L., & Benasutti, K. M. (2006). Matching judicial supervision to clients' risk status in drug court. *Crime & Delinquency, 52*(1), 52–76.

Marlowe, D. B., Hardin, C. D., & Fox, C. L. (2016). *Painting the current picture: A national report on drug courts and other problem-solving courts in the United States.* National Drug Court Institute.

Mauer, M. (2001). The causes and consequences of prison growth in the United States. In D. Garland (Ed.), *Mass imprisonment: Social causes and consequences* (pp. 4–14). Sage.

Messina, N., Burdon, W., & Prendergast, M. (2003). Assessing the needs of women in institutional therapeutic communities. *Journal of Offender Rehabilitation, 37*(2), 89–106.

Messina, N., Calhoun, S., & Warda, U. (2012). Gender-responsive drug court treatment: A randomized controlled trial. *Criminal Justice and Behavior, 39*(12), 1539–1558.

Meyer, W. G. (2017). Constitutional and legal issues in drug courts. In D. B. Marlowe, & W. G. Meyer (Eds.), *The drug court judicial benchbook* (pp. 161–182). National Drug Court Institute.

Miller, E. J. (2004). Embracing addiction: Drug courts and the false promise of judicial interventionism. *Ohio State Law Journal, 65,* 1479–1576.

Mitchell, O., Wilson, D. B., Eggers, A., & MacKenzie, D. L. (2012a). Assessing the effectiveness of drug courts on recidivism: A meta-analytic review of traditional and non-traditional drug courts. *Journal of Criminal Justice, 40*(1), 60–71.

Mitchell, O., Wilson, D. B., Eggers, A., & MacKenzie, D. L. (2012b). Drug courts' effects on criminal offending for juveniles and adults. *Campbell Systematic Reviews, 4.*

National Drug Court Resource Center. (n.d.). *What are drug courts?.* Retrieved from: https://ndcrc.org/what-are-drug-courts-2/

National Drug Court Resource Center. (2018). *Drug treatment court programs in the United States.* Retrieved from: https://ndcrc.org/database/

National Institute of Justice. (n.d.). *Practice profile: Adult drug courts.* Retrieved from: https://www.crimesolutions.gov/PracticeDetails.aspx?ID=7

Office of National Drug Control Policy. (2011). *Drug courts: A smart approach to criminal justice.* Retrieved from: https://obamawhitehouse.archives.gov/ondcp/ondcp-fact-sheets/drug-courts-smart-approach-to-criminal-justice

Olson, D. E., Lurigio, A. J., & Albertson, S. (2001). Implementing the key components of specialized drug treatment courts: Practice and policy considerations. *Law & Policy, 23*(2), 171–196.

Palumbo, D. J., Clifford, M., & Snyder-Joy, Z. K. (1992). From net widening to intermediate sanctions: The transformation of alternatives to incarceration from benevolence to malevolence. In J. M. Byrne, A. J. Lurigio, & J. Petersilia (Eds.), *Smart sentencing: The emergence of intermediate sanctions* (pp. 229–244). Sage.

Parhar, K. K., Wormith, J. S., Derkzen, D. M., & Beauregard, A. M. (2008). Offender coercion in treatment: A meta-analysis of effectiveness. *Criminal Justice and Behavior, 35*(9), 1109–1135.

Peters, R. H., Kremling, J, Bekman, N. M., & Caudy, M. S. (2012). Co-occurring disorders in treatment-based courts: Results of a national survey. *Behavioral Sciences & the Law, 30*(6), 800–820.

Petersilia, J., Lurigio, A. J., & Byrne, J. M. (1992). Introduction: The emergence of intermediate sanctions. In J. M. Byrne, A. J. Lurigio, & J. Petersilia (Eds.), *Smart sentencing: The emergence of intermediate sanctions* (pp. ix–xv). Sage.

Quinn, M. C. (2000). Whose team am I on anyway? Musings of a public defender about drug treatment court practice. *NYU Review of Law and Social Change, 26,* 37–75.

Rempel, M., & Destefano, C. D. (2001). Predictors of engagement in court-mandated treatment: Findings at the Brooklyn Treatment Court, 1996–2000. *Journal of Offender Rehabilitation, 33*(4), 87–124.

Rossman, S. B., Roman, J. K., Zweig, J. M., Rempel, M., & Lindquist, C. H. (Eds.). (2011). *The multi-site adult drug court evaluation: The impact of drug courts.* The Urban Institute.

Saum, C. A., & Hiller, M. L. (2008). Should violent offenders be excluded from drug court participation? An examination of the recidivism of violent and nonviolent drug court participants. *Criminal Justice Review, 33*(3), 291–307.

Saum, C. A., Scarpitti, F. R., & Robbins, C. A. (2001). Violent offenders in drug court. *Journal of Drug Issues, 31*(1), 107–128.

Sevigny, E. L., Fuleihan, B. K., & Ferdik, F. V. (2013). Do drug courts reduce the use of incarceration?: A meta-analysis. *Journal of Criminal Justice, 41*(6), 416–425.

Shaffer, D. K. (2011). Looking inside the black box of drug courts: A meta-analytic review. *Justice Quarterly, 28*(3), 493–521.

Shanahan, M., Lancsar, E., Hass, M., Lind, B., Weatherburn, D., & Chen, S. (2004). Cost-effectiveness analysis of the New South Wales adult drug court program. *Evaluation Review, 28*(1), 3–27.

Sloas, L. B. (2020). Thirty years onward! Citation analysis of randomized experiments on drug and mental health courts. *Journal of Experimental Criminology, 16*(2), 171–181.

Sloas, L. B., & Atkin-Plunk, C. A. (2019). Perceptions of balanced justice and rehabilitation for drug offenders. *Criminal Justice Policy Review, 30*(7), 990–1009.

Strong, S. M., Rantala, R. R., & Kyckelhahn, T. (2016). *Census of problem-solving courts, 2012* (NCJ 249803). Bureau of Justice Statistics.

Substance Abuse and Mental Health Services Administration. (2019). *Key substance use and mental health indicators in the United States: Results from the 2018 National Survey on Drug Use and Health* (HHS Publication No. PEP19-5068). Center for Behavioral Health Statistics and Quality, Substance Abuse and Mental Health Services Administration.

Taxman, F. S., & Bouffard, J. A. (2005). Treatment as part of drug court: The impact on graduation rates. *Journal of Offender Rehabilitation, 42*(1), 23–50.

Tiger, R. (2011). Drug courts and the logic of coerced treatment. *Sociological Forum, 26*(1), 169–182.

Tribal Law & Policy Institute. (1999). *Healing to wellness courts: A preliminary overview of tribal drug courts.* U.S. Department of Justice Office of Justice Programs.

Tribal Law & Policy Institute. (2003). *Tribal healing to wellness courts: The key components (NCJ 188154).* U.S. Department of Justice Office of Justice Programs.

Tuchman, E. (2010). Women and addiction: The importance of gender issues in substance abuse research. *Journal of Addictive Diseases, 29*(2), 127–138.

United Nations Office on Drugs and Crime. (2005). *Drug treatment courts work!* www.unodc.org/documents/drug-treatment/drug_treatment_courts_flyer.pdf

U.S. Department of Justice. (n.d.). *Violent Crime Control and Law Enforcement Act of 1994.* Retrieved from: https://www.ncjrs.gov/txtfiles/billfs.txt

U.S. General Accounting Office. (1997). *Drug courts: Overview of growth, characteristics, and results (GAO/GGD-97-106).* Author.

Vîlcicǎ, E. R., Belenko, S., Hiller, M., & Taxman, F. (2010). Exporting court innovation from the United States to Continental Europe: Compatibility between the drug court model and inquisitorial justice systems. *International Journal of Comparative and Applied Criminal Justice, 34*(1), 139–172.

West, H. C., Sabol, W. J., & Greenman, S. J. (2010). *Prisoners in 2009* (NCJ 231675). Bureau of Justice Statistics.

Wilson, D. B., Mitchell, O., & MacKenzie, D. L. (2006). A systematic review of drug court effects on recidivism. *Journal of Experimental Criminology, 2*(4), 459–487.

Zettler, H. R., & Martin, K. D. (2020). Exploring the impact of technical violations on probation revocations in the context of drug court. *American Journal of Criminal Justice.* DOI: 10.1007/s12103-020-09529-1

*Chapter 2*

# Mental Health Courts

## *Policy and Practice*

### Irina Fanarraga and Deborah Koetzle

## INTRODUCTION

The problem-solving court movement began with the advent of drug treatment courts (see chapter 1) in the late 1980s. Designed to divert nonviolent drug offenders from prison, these early programs quickly gained political support and were soon replicated across the country as they represented a model for providing community-based treatment and supervision. Early drug courts were demonstrated to reduce drug use and recidivism, which led to further expansion of the model. However, these programs are not universally successful, nor are they equally effective across groups. Juvenile drug courts, for example, have often been found to have null or iatrogenic effects and there is ample evidence to suggest that drug treatment courts are more effective under certain conditions, including targeting individuals that are well-matched to the nature and intensity of the services they provide (Shaffer, 2011). Despite these limitations, the success of drug courts spawned the birth of other problem-solving courts, all designed to address specialized populations, including family courts, veteran's courts, and mental health courts. The current chapter provides an overview of mental health treatment courts and their development over time along with an assessment of their effectiveness. In addition, we address criticisms of the problem-solving court model and offer recommendations for improvement.

Mental health courts (MHCs) emerged in the late 1990s, building on the popularity and success of drug treatment courts (DTCs; Burns et al., 2013; Dirks-Linhorst et al., 2011; Tyuse & Linhorst, 2005). The first MHC began operations in 1997 in Broward County, Florida, as a result of a $1.5 million allocation from the state legislature and following recommendations of a multiagency Criminal Justice Mental Health Task Force formed in response to a series of incidents involving individuals with mental illness, including suicides of persons incarcerated in local jails (Castellano & Anderson, 2013; Goldkamp & Irons-Guynn, 2000; Lerner-Wren, 2002). Just as early DTCs focused on nonviolent low-level drug offenders, early MHCs focused on individuals charged with misdemeanors who had mental illness, broadly defined to include psychiatric symptoms, developmental disabilities, and brain injuries (Faraci, 2004).

Like DTCs, MHCs expanded across the United States fairly rapidly. By 2006, MHCs were present in at least thirty-four states (Redlich et al., 2006) and by 2015, in all but a handful of states (Substance Abuse and Mental Health Services Administration, 2019). Today, after DTCs, they are the most common type of problem-solving court. The National Drug Court Institute identified 392 adult MHCs across the United States in 2014 (Marlowe et al., 2016) and the Substance Abuse and Mental Health Services Administration's GAINS center identified 477 adult and 56 juvenile MHCs across the country in 2015 (Substance Abuse and Mental Health Services Administration, 2015). Though more recent numbers are not available, the data suggest that MHCs are prevalent and, like DTCs, have become a core option for jurisdictions seeking to treat persons involved with the criminal justice system, who also have a mental illness, in the community.

## MENTAL HEALTH AND THE
## CRIMINAL JUSTICE SYSTEM

MHCs are intended to reduce recidivism and improve outcomes for justice involved individuals with mental illness, who are often disproportionately involved in the criminal justice system. In part, this overrepresentation can be traced to systematic changes in how mental illness was funded and treated in the mid-1900s (Denckla & Berman, 2001). Throughout much of the 1900s, individuals with serious mental illness were often placed into mental institutions for treatment. As advances in psychiatric medications were being made, there were growing concerns over the civil liberties of individuals who had been institutionalized. Together, these changes led to a decrease in the use of mental health institutions, with a greater reliance on community-based treatment. However, though funding for institutions was decreased, it was not met with increased funding for community-based treatment. As a result, it became more difficult to access treatment services and those in need often faced barriers to receiving meaningful interventions. This ultimately led to more untreated individuals with mental illness in the community coming into increased contact with the police and criminal justice system (Pogrebin & Poole, 1987). Whether deinstitutionalization led to a criminalization of mental illness is a subject of some debate; however, it does appear that the criminal justice system has become arbiters of social control's de facto response for the many individuals they encounter who also struggle with mental illness (Morabito, 2007; Torrey et al., 1992).

Today, individuals with a mental health diagnosis are overrepresented across all levels of the criminal justice system, from arrest to incarceration (Torrey et al., 2010). The 2018 National Survey of Drug Use and Health estimated that 4.6 percent of all adults in the United States met the threshold for serious mental illness in the year prior to the survey being administered (Substance Abuse and Mental Health Services Administration, 2019). And, though estimates vary, the number of individuals in the criminal justice system with mental illness far outweighs that of the general population. Bronson and Bersofsky (2017) estimated that 14 percent of state and federal prisoners and 26 percent of jail inmates reported symptoms consistent with serious psychological distress, and a meta-analysis of sixty-two studies estimates that 14 percent of all incarcerated offenders have some type of serious mental illness, such as schizophrenia and bipolar disorder (Fazel & Danesh, 2002).

One reason for their overrepresentation in prison and jails is simply that people with untreated mental illnesses tend to have a higher rate of police contacts. Theriot and Segal (2005) found that 45 percent of new clients at community mental health centers had at least one police contact, while a recent meta-analysis estimated that 25 percent of people with mental illness have histories of police arrest, and that about 10 percent of individuals with mental illness have at least one police encounter in their pathway to treatment (Livingston, 2016). The reasons for police contact are myriad, but in part reflect the dependency on police to address both public nuisance and criminal events. Individuals with mental illness are more likely to be homeless, have greater health problems, have a substance use disorder, and are more likely to engage in deviant behavior in public settings, which increases the likelihood of police contact and subsequent arrest, as other options are limited to non-existent due to the societal shifts discussed earlier (Castellano & Anderson, 2013; Dickey et al., 2002; Harris & Edlund, 2005).

Upon incarceration, individuals with mental illness tend to remain in prison and jail longer than inmates who do not present with mental illness, which contributes to overcrowding and may increase the criminogenic effect of incarceration (James & Glaze, 2006; Nagin et al., 2009). While incarcerated, they are also more likely to be engaged in major behavioral problems, such as getting involved in fights with other inmates, to be placed in solitary confinement, to be victimized, and to attempt or die by suicide. At the same time, only a third of those in state prisons and less than 20 percent of those in local jails with mental health problems received any type of treatment after admission (James & Glaze, 2006). Perhaps not surprisingly then, individuals with a mental health diagnosis recidivate earlier and at higher rates than individuals without one (Cloyes et al., 2010; Denckla & Berman, 2001; Torrey et al., 2014).

As a result, those with mental illness often cycle back and forth between the communities, courts, and prisons and jails. Thus, as with other problem-solving courts, MHCs are specialized criminal courts created to reduce the cycle of arrest and incarceration of offenders with mental illnesses by diverting them from the criminal justice system into community-based treatment, while at the same time ensuring and maintaining public safety (Almquist & Dodd, 2009; Castellano & Anderson, 2013; Tyuse & Linhorst, 2005). In the next section, we discuss the MHC model and its core elements.

## THE MENTAL HEALTH COURT MODEL

Like many other PSCs, MHCs have evolved in an ad-hoc fashion, but are largely grounded in therapeutic jurisprudence, an approach that regards the law as a potential therapeutic agent. From this perspective, the law should be applied in a manner that emphasizes therapeutic benefits while still maintaining legal safeguards such as due process or other constitutional and related values (Wexler, 2018). In practice, this means that courts can use their authority in ways that encourage positive psychological and emotional outcomes for offenders with mental health diagnoses rather than simply be focused on a sterile application of the law (Burns et al., 2013; Ray et al., 2015; Redlich et al., 2006). A therapeutic approach is consistent with the problem-solving court approach by making participation voluntary, emphasizing collaborative rather than adversarial decision-making, having regular and meaningful interactions between judges and participants, and by placing treatment as a central part of the court (Shaffer, 2011).

Despite the reliance on therapeutic jurisprudence, MHCs developed rather organically and largely drew on elements of DTCs for their design. In 2007, the Bureau of Justice Assistance (BJA) delineated the "essential elements" of MHC design and implementation. As with the original 10 Key Components of drug courts (The National Association of Drug Court Professionals, 1997), the essential elements were based on a variety of sources, including the research literature, interviews with former BJA Mental Health Courts Program grantees, and on-site visits to MHCs. Ten elements were identified: (1) the planning and administration of the court is guided by a range of stakeholders from the criminal justice and mental health systems; (2) eligibility criteria address public safety and consider who can be appropriately served by the court; (3) participants are linked to services as quickly as possible following identification, referral, and enrollment into the court; (4) terms of participation are clear, promote public safety, are individualized, and provide for positive legal outcomes for graduates; (5) potential participants fully understand program requirements before enrollment; (6) participants are connected to treatment and services in the community; (7) safeguards are in place to protect participants' confidentiality; (8) MHC teams receive ongoing training; (9) participants' adherence to court requirements is monitored; and (10) data are collected and analyzed to assess the court's performance (Thompson et al., 2007).

In practice, the ten elements identified by the BJA serve as a guiding framework rather than specific protocols to which must follow and it is not expected that every MHC will have each element, or that these elements will be consistent across courts (Thompson et al., 2007). The lack of specific standards, coupled with the need to reflect local contexts, has led to considerable variation in the characteristics and practices of MHCs across jurisdictions (Almquist & Dodd, 2009; Castellano & Anderson, 2013; Watson et al., 2001).

## Program Model

Individuals can be referred to an MHC from a number of different sources. These include the prosecutor's office, defense attorneys, public defenders, judges, jail staff, treatment providers, law enforcement officers, court liaisons, other problem-solving courts, the individual themselves, family members, or as a result of a competency hearing (Almquist & Dodd, 2009; Goldkamp & Irons-Guynn, 2000; O'Keefe et al., 2013; Snedker et al., 2017; Thompson et al., 2007). Depending on the program, the court may operate as a pre- or post-adjudication program, or as a mix of both, with the post-adjudication model being the most common (Castellano & Anderson, 2013). As with other problem-solving courts, pre-adjudication programs are largely considered diversion programs, and charges are often dropped upon MHC program completion (Goldkamp & Irons-Guynn, 2000; Luskin, 2013). In contrast, post-adjudication programs serve individuals who have entered a guilty plea, often to reduced charges (Bonfine et al., 2016; Herinckx et al., 2005).

## Target Population

Upon referral to the MHC, potential participants are screened for eligibility (Wolff et al., 2011). Eligibility is generally based on current charges and the presence of mental illness, though the severity of charges and mental illness varies across programs. Eligibility is usually determined based on the existence of a psychiatric diagnosis of an Axis I disorder (i.e., schizophrenia, major depression, and bipolar disorder) that is perceived as being associated to the defendant's criminal justice involvement (Burns et al., 2013; Castellano & Anderson, 2013). However, though some MHCs only accept individuals with serious mental illness, other courts accept individuals with less serious diagnoses, and some accept individuals with developmental disabilities (Hiday et al., 2013; Redlich et al., 2006; Thompson et al., 2007). Individuals with co-occurring substance use disorders are usually eligible for admission, though individuals with a substance use disorder and no indication of mental illness would typically be rendered ineligible (Griffin et al., 2002).

In terms of criminal charges, early MHCs only accepted individuals charged with misdemeanors (Griffin et al., 2002). This is still true today for a number of courts, though some now also accept a mix of both misdemeanors and felonies, and a small number of courts only target individuals with felony charges (Fisler, 2005; Frailing, 2010; Hiday et al., 2013; Steadman et al., 2011). This difference is often linked to the way in which MHCs historically developed, given that "first generation" courts tended to focus on nonviolent misdemeanors. As time passed and a "second generation" of MHCs emerged, more and more courts began accepting individuals charged with felonies (Griffin et al., 2002; Redlich et al., 2005). Although the exact reason is unknown, Redlich and colleagues (2005) conjecture that this expansion in eligibility might be linked to a change in goals (to divert people from state prisons rather than from local jails) or as a consequence of policy decisions that resulted in the use of other diversion strategies for misdemeanant offenders.

## Assessment and Screening

In order to determine eligibility, a process of screening, assessment, and negotiation tends to occur, with the nature of formal screening varying across jurisdictions (Almquist & Dodd, 2009; Redlich et al., 2006; Thompson et al., 2007). During this time, participants are also apprised of the terms of the program, including terms of a plea agreement, program duration, level of supervision, and the legal impact of program completion, all of which are negotiated within the program parameters and agreed upon by the relevant stakeholders (Thompson et al., 2007). Following the initial eligibility screening, a more in-depth assessment is conducted to ensure suitability for the program (Wolff et al., 2011). This assessment is typically conducted by the mental health court team, with a focus on behavioral health problems and criminal history. In some courts, a final evaluation screening is conducted by the MHC judge who bases the decision for acceptance into the court on the assessment and, at times, a meeting with the client. Although the mental health assessment of potential participants is a feature shared by most MHCs, less is known about the specific assessment protocols used, whether they are based on clinical judgment or are actuarial in nature, or if the abide by effective rehabilitation practices, such as the risk-needs-responsivity model (Bonfine et al., 2016; Campbell et al., 2015; Wolff et al., 2011). For instance, little is known about whether MHC assesses for risk of recidivism in addition to mental health issues.

## Court Team

As with other PSCs, MHCs utilize a multidisciplinary, non-adversarial team approach that involves consensus decisions between criminal justice (judges, district attorneys, defense attorneys, probation officers) and mental/public health professionals (psychiatrists, psychologists, case managers, social workers) (Almquist & Dodd, 2009; Goldkamp & Irons-Guynn, 2000; Schneider, 2010; Thompson et al., 2007). The MHC team is tasked with conducting screenings and assessments, partnering with community-based treatment service providers, monitoring participants' progress and adherence to program terms, and periodically reviewing and revising court processes to improve its operation (Thompson et al., 2007).

## Treatment Services

Following the problem-solving court perspective, MHC teams develop individually tailored programs that link participants to community-based treatment and services (Boothroyd et al., 2003; Snedker et al., 2017). The most common case management model utilized with MHC participants is Assertive Community Treatment (ACT) (Marlowe et al., 2016). An alternative to inpatient treatment, ACT is a community-based integrative approach meant to serve individuals with severe mental illness whose diagnosis impacts their ability to care for themselves and to function. It involves a multidisciplinary team, which provides clients with support and care 24/7, with a focus on helping clients meet their most basic needs, from access to psychiatric medicine, to aid with housing and other social services (Cosden et al., 2003; Stacy & Atkins, 2012). The use of ACT is well-supported; systematic reviews and meta-analyses have concluded that ACT is an effective approach to treating individuals with severe mental illness in the community. Participation in ACT is associated with reductions in hospital admissions, reductions in homelessness, longer community tenure, and improvements in psychiatric symptoms and quality of life (Bond et al., 2001; Bond & Drake, 2015; Coldwell & Bender, 2007).

Both ACT- and non-ACT-based MHCs refer participants to different types of mental health treatment, including group and individual therapy, medications, counseling, psychotherapy, substance abuse treatment (for participants with co-occurring disorders), outpatient and inpatient services, peer support, and hospital step-down programs (Hendricks et al., 2006; Rubenstein & Yanos, 2019; Snedker et al., 2017). MHCs are also likely to link participants to educational and occupational programs, housing assistance, budgetary counseling, public benefits (i.e., food stamps, Medicaid, health insurance, social security insurance), anger management, parenting classes, and trauma/domestic violence services, though the extent of these types of referrals is unknown (Luskin, 2013; Moore & Hiday, 2006; Rossman et al., 2012; Schneider, 2010).

## Monitoring Program Adherence

In order to determine program compliance, most MHCs rely on regularly scheduled status hearings, although their frequency may vary from court to court (Castellano & Anderson, 2013; Redlich et al., 2006; Thompson et al., 2007). These hearings are presided by one or two dedicated judges who tend to be knowledgeable regarding the particular issues associated with offenders with mental illness (Burns et al., 2013; Frailing, 2010; Rossman et al., 2012). During these hearings, participants receive praise for good behavior, and warnings or sanctions for noncompliance (Redlich et al., 2006; Thompson et al., 2007).

Possible sanctions depend on the individual court but may include verbal warnings or admonishments from the judge, increases in the number and frequency of status hearings and drug tests, stricter treatment conditions, changes in housing, use of electronic monitoring or a global positioning system (GPS), community service, and jail time (Burns et al., 2013; Frailing, 2010; Griffin et al., 2002; Honegger & Honegger, 2019). Because MHCs are grounded in therapeutic jurisprudence, most MHC staff recognize that setbacks are common as participants attempt to change their behavior. However, extreme, ongoing noncompliance can result in a participant's termination from the program, which means that he or she would be sent back to traditional criminal court for disposition (Hiday et al., 2013; Ray et al., 2015; Redlich et al., 2006).

## Phases and Program Length

Some MHCs rely on phases for advancement through the program, modeled off DTCs. Although the number of phases can vary, three to four phases is typical (Desmond & Lenz, 2010; Farley, 2015; Rossman et al., 2012). Progressing from one phase to the next depends on successfully achieving certain milestones, such as compliance with treatment for a set period of time (i.e., attending group and keeping appointments) and consistently testing negative for substance use (Desmond & Lenz, 2010; Rossman et al., 2012). Phase advancement often results in less monitoring and a decrease in the frequency of required status hearings (Bonfine et al., 2016; Burns et al., 2013).

The length of time an individual is under MHC supervision varies across different courts. A review of the literature revealed that program length tends to range between six months to two years. However, these time frames are flexible even within the same court, as offense seriousness and compliance with treatment can have an effect on how long an individual's participation lasts (Bonfine et al., 2016; Desmond & Lenz, 2010; Honegger & Honegger, 2019; Rossman et al., 2012).

## Graduation

As with the advancement through phases, participants "graduate" from an MHC program when they have met program requirements for a determined amount of time. These usually include attending treatment, adhering to their medication, appearing at court for their status hearings, having no new arrests, having no positive drug or alcohol tests for a continued period of time, not owing victim restitution, an ability to live independently, and other more subjective measures that demonstrate "stability" (Castellano & Anderson, 2013; McNiel & Binder, 2007; Redlich et al., 2006; Rossman et al., 2012). MHC graduation rates range from 24 percent to 63 percent of all participants admitted to the program (Burns et al., 2013; Moore & Hiday, 2006; Rubenstein & Yanos, 2019).

## EFFECTIVENESS

Research evaluating the effectiveness of MHC generally focuses on reductions in recidivism, with some studies assessing MHC impact on clinical outcomes. As with other correctional interventions, there is a link between program completion, or graduation, and outcomes. Though relatively few outcome evaluations have been conducted, a number of systematic reviews and meta-analyses have sought to assess whether MHC are effective.

The literature demonstrates that participants who successfully complete an MHC have lower recidivism rates, post-program, than those that fail to complete because of either involuntary termination from the program or opting out of the program (Burns et al., 2013; Hiday et al., 2013; McNiel & Binder, 2007; Steadman et al., 2011). Predictors of graduation include demographics, criminal history, and treatment services utilization. Women, white participants, and those with a higher level of education are more likely to graduate (Hiday et al., 2014; Ray & Dollar, 2013; Rubenstein & Yanos, 2019). Individuals who are unemployed are also more likely to graduate. Though counterintuitive, it may be that the time commitment and responsibilities associated with maintaining a job might act as barriers to treatment compliance, and lead to opting out of participation (Verhaaff & Scott, 2015). Graduation is also more likely for those who do not have a criminal history and for those who had increased exposure to mental health services during program participation (Bonfine et al., 2016; Seto et al., 2018). In contrast, multiple diagnoses or co-occurring disorders, housing instability, charges related to stealing, higher levels of criminogenic risk, and noncompliance in the MHC are associated with program failure (Bonfine et al., 2016; Broner et al., 2009; Dirks-Linhorst et al., 2011; Hiday et al., 2014; Rubenstein & Yanos, 2019; Verhaaff & Scott, 2015). The higher failure rates of individuals with more serious mental health histories and greater risk of recidivism may point to a disconnect between the population being served and the nature of services provided.

The majority of outcome evaluations have found significant reductions in recidivism. Specifically, MHC participation is associated with a decrease in new arrests or charges post-program admission. Herinckx and colleagues (2005) found that the average number of arrests for Clark County MHC participants was significantly reduced from 1.99 one-year pre-enrollment to 0.48 one-year post-enrollment. Studies including treatment-as-usual (TAU) comparison groups have found MHC participation to be associated with lower rearrest rates when compared to control groups (Anestis & Carbonell, 2014; Gallagher et al., 2018; Hiday et al., 2013; Moore & Hiday, 2006; Steadman et al., 2011). Additionally, a study by McNiel and Binder (2007) found that the likelihood of participants enrolled in the San Francisco MHC being charged with a new crime was 26 percent lower than that of a comparable control group.

MHC participation has also been associated with an increase in time to new arrest (Anestis & Carbonell, 2014; McNiel & Binder, 2007). Furthermore, studies have found MHC participation to be associated with statistically significant decreases in incarceration days post-program enrollment (Frailing, 2010; Trupin & Richards, 2003). Steadman and colleagues (2011) found that incarceration days during the eighteen-month post-MHC entry period increased for both the MHC and the TAU groups when compared to the eighteen months prior to enrollment. However, the increase for the MHC group was small (12 percent, from 73 to 82 days), while the increase for the control group was 105 percent (from 74 to 152 days), with the difference between groups being statistically significant.

Finally, studies have found that MHC enrollment is associated with lower severity of new offenses. More specifically, McNiel and Binder (2007) found that, at eighteen months post-program entry, the likelihood of MHC participants being charged with new violent crimes was 55 percent lower than that of individuals in the control group. On the other hand, Moore and Hiday (2006) relied on a summation scale to assess new arrest severity and found that average severity of recidivism for the traditional court control group was significantly higher than that for the MHC group (9.46 vs. 3.90).

Though the majority of studies have found positive effects, some evaluations have failed to find a significant difference in outcomes and, in one program, a negative effect was evidenced (Christy et al., 2005; Cosden et al., 2005). Christy and colleagues' (2005) evaluation of Broward County's MHC did not find any statistically significant differences between the treatment and the control group when it came to the proportion rearrested, mean number of rearrests, and time to new arrest using a one-year follow-up period. In one of the few experiential evaluations, Cosden et al. (2005) found that 12 percent of MHC participants and 10 percent of the TAU group were sent to prison for new crimes during the two-year follow-up period. Although the MHC group had fewer jail days on average than the TAU group (10 versus 15), this difference was not statistically significant.

A small number of studies have evaluated the effectiveness of MHC participation on mental health outcomes. Outcomes were measured in a number of ways, including formal assessments and hospital utilization or psychiatric visits as a proxy for increased symptomatology. Results are mixed. Frailing (2010) found that MHC participants and graduates had significantly fewer psychiatric hospitalization days in the year after graduation than they did in the year before enrollment. Trupin and Richards (2003) found that MHC participation had a positive effect on Global Assessment of Functioning (GAF) ratings when compared to a control group. Cosden and colleagues (2005) found that MHC participation was associated with an increase in independent functioning (GAF scores) and quality of life (QOL scores), and with a reduction in psychological distress (Behavior and Symptom Identification Scale scores) and drug and alcohol problems (Addiction Severity Index drug and alcohol composite scores). However, GAF scores were not significantly higher for MHC participants than for the control group. Similarly, Luskin (2013) found that, although psychiatric hospitalizations declined for MHC participants from pre-court to six months post-enrollment, no significant differences between the treatment and the control group were identified at the six-month follow-up. Remaining studies have found no significant effect on clinical outcomes as measured by formal assessments, contacts with crisis services, emergency room visits, or psychiatric hospital stays (Boothroyd et al., 2003; Ferguson et al., 2008; Keator et al., 2013).

As with drug courts, meta-analytic and systematic reviews have generally been supportive of MHCs but point to the need for additional evaluations, especially those with experimental designs (Arnold, 2019; Cross, 2011; Honegger, 2015; Sarteschi et al., 2011). The most recent meta-analysis, by Arnold (2019), found that mental health courts had a significant impact on rearrest, with MHC participants being 43 percent less likely to be rearrested and 48 percent less likely to be reconvicted, while also spending significantly fewer days in jail than members of the comparison group. These findings, however, should be viewed somewhat cautiously as the majority of evaluations only used a twelve-month follow-up and it is not clear whether differences in recidivism are sustained. This is particularly important to consider, as little is known about whether MHCs systematically address criminogenic needs or influence clinical outcomes.

## CRITICISMS

Despite their success, mental health courts are not immune to criticism. As with other problem-solving courts, there are concerns over net-widening and treatment capacity. Because of the population served, there are additional concerns regarding voluntary consent and the utilization of jail as a sanction.

MHCs, like all problem-solving courts, are theoretically intended to divert individuals from deeper-end involvement in the criminal justice system. Despite this ambition, many of these courts are subject to criticism that they engage in net-widening by incarcerating individuals while awaiting entry into a problem-solving court, and by only admitting cases who are most likely to be successful, such as those who would have been successful with little to no direct supervision (Castellano, 2011). By only admitting cases likely to be successful, problem-solving courts may provide more intensive supervision and monitoring to individuals that would otherwise receive limited intervention (see Koetzle et al., 2015). There is ample research to suggest that increased supervision is associated with increased revocations and rearrests (Petersilia & Turner, 1993), and MHCs, like other problem-solving courts, must be careful to not increase jail and prison time for individuals under the guise of "helping."

Net-widening is of particular concern for MHCs, especially given the model's early focus on limiting eligibility to individuals charged with misdemeanors and restricting individuals with violent offenses. This is particularly problematic, given the evidence to suggest that individuals with mental illness are overrepresented in the criminal justice system. Individuals with mental illness may be arrested for behaviors that others would not be given the changes to how persons with mental illness are handled (discussed earlier); failing to divert these individuals out of the criminal justice system and toward the public health sector could have serious consequences. For example, failing to divert individuals may exacerbate the negative effects associated with arrest, add to an already overburdened court system, and perhaps most importantly, lead to deeper end criminal justice involvement for individuals who are simply in need of treatment (Seltzer, 2005; Stefan & Winick, 2005). For MHCs to operate effectively, they must create specific eligibility and exclusionary criteria that are designed to screen in more serious individuals in need of services and screen out those that do not require intensive supervision or treatment. Using validated risk/need assessments in addition to mental health assessments to determine the likelihood of re-offending and the severity of mental illness is necessary for MHCs hoping to avoid the trap of net-widening (Latessa et al., 2020).

An essential element of MHCs is that participation is voluntary; individuals consent to participate. In other words, individuals agree to participate and to abide by the various program requirements knowingly and willingly. There are three general criticisms of this element. First, although the decision to participate in an MHC is voluntary, compliance with treatment and a myriad of other program requirements is mandatory, and there are sanctions for noncompliance (Redlich et al., 2010; Tyuse & Linhorst, 2005). Though mandated treatment is common across the criminal justice sytem, mandated treatment for mental illness is more controversial, especially as it relates to medical decisions. Individuals have the right to refuse medication, but within a mental health court setting, such a refusal could be paramount to noncompliance, with the associated risks (Crilly, 2008).

Second, choosing to participate in a mental health court often requires entering a guilty plea, which requires adjudicative competence and the ability to make a knowledgable and informed decision (Redlich et al., 2010; Stefan & Winick, 2005; Thompson et al., 2007). Legal standards for consent require voluntariness, knowingness, and competence; there is some question as to whether MHC participants meet these standards at the time of their plea, and whether participation is truly voluntary (Redlich et al., 2006). In a study of 200 MHC clients, Redlich et al. (2010) found that more than half of recent MHC participants indicated they had made the decision to enroll, could identify advantages to participation, and had minimal or no impairment on measures of understanding and reasoning. Yet, more than half also said they did not know the decision to enroll was voluntary, were unaware of the program requirements at the time of enrolling, did not know they could withdraw from participation at any time, and did not identify any disadvantages to participating. Additionally, between 9 and 27 percent of participants had clinically significant impairments in their adjudicative competence.

Third, as with other problem-solving courts, there is a question as to whether program entry is truly voluntary. As noted by Redlich et al. (2010), potential participants are often forced to make a decision between jail or prison and community-based treatment. Given the consequences of declining participation, it is fair to ask whether there is a coercive element to this decision-making process. Moreover, it is not clear that participants view this decision as voluntary. In a review of court transcripts, Boothroyd et al. (2003) found that the voluntary nature of participation of the Broward County (FL) MHC was discussed in only 16 percent of transcripts, and only 53 percent of participants self-reported knowing the decision to participate was voluntary. Given the consequences associated with program failure and noncompliance, it is important that MHCs take additional steps to ensure that program participants are making these decisions free from coercion and with complete understanding of the consequences of their decision.

A core component of drug courts is the use of sanctions and reinforcers, with DTCs using jail as sanction in response to repeated noncompliance or drug use. Because MHCs are based on DTCs, there is some evidence to suggest at least some MHC do the same. In a survey of MHCs, (Redlich et al., 2006) found that 92 percent of programs were willing to use jail in response to noncompliance and that this was more likely when programs accepted individuals charged with felony-level offenses. Though most courts report using sanctions for less than half of their cases, a multi-site exploration into the use of sanctions revealed that over a quarter of MHC participants reported being sent back to jail at least one time for noncompliance (Callahan et al., 2013). While the problem-solving court model generally views brief jail stays as deterrent strategies, Faraci (2004) argues the use of jail time as a sanction is diametrically opposed to the notion of MHCs serving as a therapeutic approach and is inconsistent with the logic of MHCs. That is, if mental illness is the cause of criminal behavior and individuals with mental illness fail to appreciate a deterrent effect of punishment, then jail time is illogical within this framework. Beyond the general inconsistency, the use of jail time as a sanction is potentially problematic when one considers the deleterious effect that incarceration can have on mental health status (Faraci, 2004; Seltzer, 2005).

A final concern regarding MHCs centers around the provision of treatment services. As reviewed in Latessa et al. (2020), there is some debate as to whether mental illness is a singular factor driving criminal behavior or whether mental illness interacts with other risk factors (e.g., criminal thinking, substance use, criminal networks, and poor family support). Many MHCs focus on case management and stabilization of mental illness. Yet, there is ample evidence to suggest there are limits to mental illness as an explanation of criminal behavior and that, for many individuals, a consideration of antisocial beliefs and thoughts and other criminogenic risk factors are equally warranted. This means that MHCs must provide services beyond the scope of mental illness to include treatment needs that are criminogenic in nature.

## CONCLUSIONS AND RECOMMENDATIONS

Jurisdictions have increasingly recognized the need for, and value of, community-based treatment in the past twenty to thirty years. This is likely to continue with ongoing calls for decarceration. As with other problem-solving courts, MHCs enjoy widespread political and public support and it seems likely that the model will continue to grow and serve justice-involved individuals in the community. Though MHCs enjoy modest effects, they only serve a relatively small number of clients when one considers the size and needs of the target population. These programs are already well-poised to provide meaningful treatment while keeping individuals out of prison and jail, but more research is needed on MHCs, both in terms of their effectiveness and how to improve outcomes, especially if capacity increases. And, after more than twenty years of existence, there are still a relatively small number of evaluations and even fewer rigorous evaluations of MHCs (Arnold, 2019).

The current push toward decarceration and a redirection of police funding is consistent with increased calls for a public health approach to mental illness and substance use. Within this context, MHCs are primed to serve as a bridge between the criminal justice and public health sectors. However, to do so successfully will require that MHCs do a number of things. First, they must consider their target population thoroughly and take care not to cherry-pick clients or only serve low-risk individuals. Low-risk individuals should be fully diverted out of the criminal justice system and receive necessary treatment through public health programs without continued court involvement.

Second, they should improve the screening and enrollment process to ensure that all eligible individuals understand the voluntary nature of the MHC, the benefits of participation and consequences of failure, and the advantages and disadvantages of participation. In addition to screening for mental health and risk of recidivism, MHCs should also assess adjudicative competence to ensure participants are capable of making informed decisions. Additionally, MHCs should consider providing court liaisons or social workers to help ensure participants not only meet the legal threshold for competence but also have the capacity to make meaningful treatment decisions (Center for Court Innovation, 2005). Beyond the ethical issues at play, failing to do so may lead to program failures and may actually increase the number of individuals with mental illness in our prisons and jails.

Third, though MHCs are found to reduce recidivism, it is likely that there is room for improvement. Similar to drug courts, MHCs should look to the literature on risk, need, and responsivity to ensure that programmatic and treatment strategies are consistent with the evidence on reducing recidivism (Andrews & Bonta, 2010; Harbinson & Koetzle, 2018; Shaffer, 2011). This will require adopting risk/need assessments, addressing a wider array of treatment needs, and utilizing behavioral strategies both in treatment services and individual interactions. Additional research should explore the impact of MHC on both recidivism and other clinical outcomes.

Finally, consistent with the RNR model, MHCs must take care to treat both mental health and criminogenic needs in order to both stabilize behavior and build skills necessary for coping with high risk situations in the future (see Latessa et al., 2020). As MHCs continue to grow and expand, it will be important that future research consider not only whether these programs are having their intended effects, but also which elements of MHC are effective and which elements are in need of additional improvements.

## REFERENCES

Almquist, L., & Dodd, E. (2009). *Mental health courts: A guide to research-informed policy and practice*. Council of State Governments Justice Center. Retrieved from: https://bja.ojp.gov/sites/g/files/xyckuh186/files/Publications/CSG_MHC_Rese arch.pdf

Andrews, D. A., & Bonta, J. (2010). *The psychology of criminal conduct*. Routledge.

Anestis, J. C., & Carbonell, J. L. (2014). Stopping the revolving door: Effectiveness of mental health court in reducing recidivism by mentally ill offenders. *Psychiatric Services*, *65*(9), 1105–1112.

Arnold, S. (2019). A meta-analysis of mental health courts: State of the research and recommendations [Doctoral dissertation]. In *ProQuest Dissertations and Theses* (2285145859). Drexel University.

Bond, G. R., & Drake, R. E. (2015). The critical ingredients of assertive community treatment. *World Psychiatry*, *14*(2), 240–242.

Bond, G. R., Drake, R. E., Mueser, K. T., & Latimer, E. (2001). Assertive community treatment for people with severe mental illness: Critical ingredients and impact on patients. *Disease Management & Health Outcomes*, *9*(3), 141–159.

Bonfine, N., Ritter, C., & Munetz, M. R. (2016). Exploring the relationship between criminogenic risk assessment and mental health court program completion. *International Journal of Law and Psychiatry*, *45*, 9–16.

Boothroyd, R. A., Poythress, N. G., McGaha, A., & Petrila, J. (2003). The Broward mental health court: Process, outcomes, and service utilization. *International Journal of Law and Psychiatry*, *26*(1), 55–71.

Broner, N., Lang, M., & Behler, S. A. (2009). The effect of homelessness, housing type, functioning, and community reintegration supports on mental health court completion and recidivism. *Journal of Dual Diagnosis*, *5*(3–4), 323–356.

Bronson, J., & Berzofsky, M. (2017). *Indicators of mental health problems reported by prisoners and jail inmates, 2011–12.* Bureau of Justice Statistics. Retrieved from: https://www.bjs.gov/content/pub/pdf/imhprpji1112.pdf

Burns, P. J., Hiday, V. A., & Ray, B. (2013). Effectiveness 2 years postexit of a recently established mental health court. *American Behavioral Scientist, 57*(2), 189–208.

Callahan, L., Steadman, H. J., Tillman, S., & Vesselinov, R. (2013). A multi-site study of the use of sanctions and incentives in mental health courts. *Law and Human Behavior, 37*(1), 1–9.

Campbell, M. A., Canales, D. D., Wei, R., Totten, A. E., Macaulay, W. A. C., & Wershler, J. L. (2015). Multidimensional evaluation of a mental health court: Adherence to the risk-need-responsivity model. *Law and Human Behavior, 39*(5), 489–502.

Castellano, U. (2011). Problem-solving Courts: Theory and practice. *Sociology Compass, 5*(11), 957–967.

Castellano, U., & Anderson, L. (2013). Mental health courts in America: Promise and challenges. *American Behavioral Scientist, 57*(2), 163–173.

Center for Court Innovation. (2005, August 8). *Mental health courts: Challenges, questions and tensions.* Retrieved from: https://www.courtinnovation.org/articles/mental-health-courts-challenges-questions-and-tensions

Christy, A., Poythress, N. G., Boothroyd, R. A., Petrila, J., & Mehra, S. (2005). Evaluating the efficiency and community safety goals of the Broward County mental health court. *Behavioral Sciences & the Law, 23*(2), 227–243.

Cloyes, K. G., Wong, B., Latimer, S., & Abarca, J. (2010). Time to prison return for offenders with serious mental illness released from prison: A survival analysis. *Criminal Justice and Behavior, 37*(2), 175–187.

Coldwell, C. M., & Bender, W. S. (2007). The effectiveness of assertive community treatment for homeless populations with severe mental illness: A meta-analysis. *American Journal of Psychiatry, 164*(3), 393–399.

Cosden, M., Ellens, J. K., Schnell, J. L., Yamini-Diouf, Y., & Wolfe, M. M. (2003). Evaluation of a mental health treatment court with assertive community treatment. *Behavioral Sciences & the Law, 21*(4), 415–427.

Cosden, M., Ellens, J., Schnell, J., & Yamini-Diouf, Y. (2005). Efficacy of a mental health treatment court with assertive community treatment. *Behavioral Sciences & the Law, 23*(2), 199–214.

Crilly, J. F. (2008). An overview of compulsory, noncompulsory, and coercive interventions for treating people with mental disorders in the United States. *International Journal of Mental Health, 37*(3), 57–80.

Cross, B. (2011). *Mental health courts effectiveness in reducing recidivism and improving clinical outcomes: A meta-analysis* (885422878) [Doctoral dissertation]. University of South Florida.

Denckla, D., & Berman, G. (2001). *Rethinking the revolving door: A look at mental illness in the courts.* Center for Court Innovation. Retrieved from: https://www.courtinnovation.org/sites/default/files/rethinkingtherevolvingdoor.pdf

Desmond, B. C., & Lenz, P. J. (2010). Mental health courts: An effective way for treating offenders with serious mental illness. *Mental and Physical Disability Law Reporter, 34*(4), 525–530.

Dickey, B., Normand, S.-L. T., Weiss, R. D., Drake, R. E., & Azeni, H. (2002). Medical morbidity, mental illness, and substance use disorders. *Psychiatric Services*, *53*(7), 861–867.

Dirks-Linhorst, P. A., Kondrat, D., Linhorst, D. M., & Morani, N. (2011). Factors associated with mental health court nonparticipation and negative termination. *Justice Quarterly*, *30*(4), 681–710.

Faraci, S. M. (2004). Slip slidin' away? Will our nation's mental health court experiment diminish the rights of the mentally ill? *Quinnipiac Law Review*, *22*, 811–854.

Farley, E. J. (2015). *A process evaluation of the Manhattan mental health court.* Center for Court Innovation. Retrieved from: https://www.courtinnovation.org/sit es/default/files/documents/MMHC%20Process%20Evaluation%20Final.pdf

Fazel, S., & Danesh, J. (2002). Serious mental disorder in 23 000 prisoners: A systematic review of 62 surveys. *The Lancet*, *359*(9306), 545–550.

Ferguson, A., Hornby, H., & Zeller, D. (2008). *Outcomes from the last frontier: An evaluation of the Anchorage mental health court.* Alaska Mental Health Trust Authority.

Fisler, C. (2005). Building trust and managing risk: A look at a felony mental health court. *Psychology, Public Policy, and Law*, *11*(4), 587–604.

Frailing, K. (2010). How mental health courts function: Outcomes and observations. *International Journal of Law and Psychiatry*, *33*(4), 207–213.

Gallagher, A. E., Anestis, J. C., Gottfried, E. D., & Carbonell, J. L. (2018). The effectiveness of a mental health court in reducing recidivism in individuals with severe mental illness and comorbid substance use disorder. *Psychological Injury and Law*, *11*(2), 184–197.

Goldkamp, J. S., & Irons-Guynn, C. (2000). *Emerging judicial strategies for the mentally ill in the criminal caseload: Mental health courts in Fort Lauderdale, Seattle, San Bernardino, and Anchorage.* Bureau of Justice Assistance.

Griffin, P. A., Steadman, H. J., & Petrila, J. (2002). The use of criminal charges and sanctions in mental health courts. *Psychiatric Services*, *53*(10), 1285–1289.

Harbinson, E., & Koetzle, D. (2018). The effectiveness of the drug court model. In D. Koetzle & S. J. Listwan (Eds.), *Drug courts and the criminal justice system* (pp. 147–164). Lynne Rienner Publishers.

Harris, K. M., & Edlund, M. J. (2005). Use of mental health care and substance abuse treatment among adults with co-occurring disorders. *Psychiatric Services*, *56*(8), 954–959.

Hendricks, B., Werner, T., Shipway, L., & Turinetti, G. J. (2006). Recidivism among spousal abusers: Predictions and program evaluation. *Journal of Interpersonal Violence*, *21*(6), 703–716.

Herinckx, H. A., Swart, S. C., Ama, S. M., Dolezal, C. D., & King, S. (2005). Rearrest and linkage to mental health services among clients of the Clark County mental health court program. *Psychiatric Services*, *56*(7), 853–857.

Hiday, V. A., Ray, B., & Wales, H. W. (2014). Predictors of mental health court graduation. *Psychology, Public Policy, and Law*, *20*(2), 191–199.

Hiday, V. A., Wales, H. W., & Ray, B. (2013). Effectiveness of a short-term mental health court: Criminal recidivism one year postexit. *Law and Human Behavior*, *37*(6), 401–411.

Honegger, L. N. (2015). Does the evidence support the case for mental health courts? A review of the literature. *Law and Human Behavior, 39*(5), 478–488.

Honegger, L. N., & Honegger, K. S. (2019). Criminogenic factors associated with noncompliance and rearrest of mental health court participants. *Criminal Justice and Behavior, 46*(9), 1276–1294.

James, D. J., & Glaze, L. E. (2006). *Mental health problems of prison and jail inmates.* Bureau of Justice Statistics.

Keator, K. J., Callahan, L., Steadman, H. J., & Vesselinov, R. (2013). The impact of treatment on the public safety outcomes of mental health court participants. *American Behavioral Scientist, 57*(2), 231–243.

Koetzle, D., Listwan, S. J., Guastaferro, W. P., & Kobus, K. (2015). Treating high-risk offenders in the community: The potential of drug courts. *International Journal of Offender Therapy and Comparative Criminology, 59*(5), 449–465.

Latessa, E. J., Johnson, S. L., & Koetzle, D. (2020). *What works (and doesn't) in reducing recidivism* (2nd edition). Routledge.

Lerner-Wren, G. (2002). Broward's mental health court: An innovative approach to the mentally disabled in the criminal justice system. In G. Landsberg, M. Rock, L. K. W. Berg, & A. Smiley (Eds.), *Serving mentally ill offenders: Challenges and opportunities for mental health professionals* (pp. 128–132). Springer Publishing Company.

Livingston, J. D. (2016). Contact between police and people with mental disorders: A review of rates. *Psychiatric Services, 67*(8), 850–857.

Luskin, M. L. (2013). More of the same? Treatment in mental health courts. *Law and Human Behavior, 37*(4), 255–266.

Marlowe, D. B., Hardin, C. D., & Fox, C. L. (2016). *Painting the current picture: A national report on drug courts and other problem-solving courts in the United States.* National Drug Court Institute.

McNiel, D. E., & Binder, R. L. (2007). Effectiveness of a mental health court in reducing criminal recidivism and violence. *American Journal of Psychiatry, 164*(9), 1395–1403.

Moore, M. E., & Hiday, V. A. (2006). Mental health court outcomes: A comparison of re-arrest and re-arrest severity between mental health court and traditional court participants. *Law and Human Behavior, 30*(6), 659–674.

Morabito, M. S. (2007). Horizons of context: Understanding the police decision to arrest people with mental illness. *Psychiatric Services, 58*(12), 1582–1587.

Nagin, D. S., Cullen, F. T., & Jonson, C. L. (2009). Imprisonment and reoffending. *Crime and Justice, 38*(1), 115–200.

O'Keefe, M. L., Klebe, K. J., Metzner, J., Dvoskin, J., Fellner, J., & Stucker, A. (2013). A longitudinal study of administrative segregation. *The Journal of the American Academy of Psychiatry and the Law, 41*(1), 49–60.

Petersilia, J., & Turner, S. (1993). *Evaluating intensive supervision probation/parole: Results of a nationwide experiment.* U.S. Department of Justice, Office of Justice Programs, National Institute of Justice.

Pogrebin, M. R., & Poole, E. D. (1987). Deinstitutionalization and increased arrest rates among the mentally disordered. *Journal of Psychiatry and Law, 15*(1), 117–128.

Ray, B., & Dollar, C. B. (2013). Examining mental health court completion: A focal concerns perspective. *Sociological Quarterly*, *54*(4), 647–669.

Ray, B., Kubiak, S. P., Comartin, E. B., & Tillander, E. (2015). Mental health court outcomes by offense type at admission. *Administration and Policy in Mental Health and Mental Health Services Research*, *42*(3), 323–331.

Redlich, A. D., Hoover, S., Summers, A., & Steadman, H. J. (2010). Enrollment in mental health courts: Voluntariness, knowingness, and adjudicative competence. *Law and Human Behavior*, *34*(2), 91–104.

Redlich, A. D., Steadman, H. J., Monahan, J., Petrila, J., & Griffin, P. A. (2005). The second generation of mental health courts. *Psychology, Public Policy, and Law*, *11*(4), 527–538.

Redlich, A. D., Steadman, H. J., Monahan, J., Robbins, P. C., & Petrila, J. (2006). Patterns of practice in mental health courts: A national survey. *Law and Human Behavior*, *30*(3), 347–362.

Rossman, S. B., Buck Willison, J., Mallik-Kane, K., Kim, K., Debus-Sherrill, S., & Downey, P. M. (2012). *Criminal justice interventions for offenders with mental illness: Evaluations of mental health courts in Bronx and Brooklyn, New York*. National Institute of Justice.

Rubenstein, L., & Yanos, P. T. (2019). Predictors of mental health court completion. *The Journal of Forensic Psychiatry & Psychology*, *30*(6), 959–974.

Sarteschi, C. M., Vaughn, M. G., & Kim, K. (2011). Assessing the effectiveness of mental health courts: A quantitative review. *Journal of Criminal Justice*, *39*(1), 12–20.

Schneider, R. D. (2010). Mental health courts and diversion programs: A global survey. *International Journal of Law and Psychiatry*, *33*(4), 201–206.

Seltzer, T. (2005). Mental health courts: A misguided attempt to address the criminal justice system's unfair treatment of people with mental illnesses. *Psychology, Public Policy, and Law*, *11*(4), 570–586.

Seto, M. C., Basarke, S., Healey, L. V., & Sirotich, F. (2018). Correlates of mental health diversion completion in a Canadian consortium. *International Journal of Forensic Mental Health*, *17*(1), 1–12.

Shaffer, D. K. (2011). Looking inside the black box of drug courts: A meta-analytic review. *Justice Quarterly*, *28*(3), 493–521.

Snedker, K. A., Beach, L. R., & Corcoran, K. E. (2017). Beyond the "revolving door?": Incentives and criminal recidivism in a mental health court. *Criminal Justice and Behavior*, *44*(9), 1141–1162.

Stacy, K. M., & Atkins, W. (2012). Assertive community treatment. In K. Key (Ed.), *The gale encyclopedia of mental health* (3rd edition, Vol. 1, pp. 141–144). Gale.

Steadman, H. J., Redlich, A., Callahan, L., Robbins, P. C., & Vesselinov, R. (2011). Effect of mental health courts on arrests and jail days: A multisite study. *Archives of General Psychiatry*, *68*(2), 167–172.

Stefan, S., & Winick, B. J. (2005). A dialogue on mental health courts. *Psychology, Public Policy, and Law*, *11*(4), 507–526.

Substance Abuse and Mental Health Services Administration. (2015, August 19). *Mental health treatment court locators*. Retrieved from: https://www.samhsa.gov/gains-center/mental-health-treatment-court-locators

Substance Abuse and Mental Health Services Administration. (2019). *Key substance use and mental health indicators in the United States: Results from the 2018 National Survey on Drug Use and Health* (HHS Publication No. PEP19-5068; NSDUH Series H-54). Center for Behavioral Health Statistics and Quality, Substance Abuse and Mental Health Services Administration. Retrieved from: https://www.samhsa.gov/data/

The National Association of Drug Court Professionals. (1997). *Defining drug courts: The key components* (Drug Courts Resource Series). Bureau of Justice Assistance.

Theriot, M. T., & Segal, S. P. (2005). Involvement with the criminal justice system among new clients at outpatient mental health agencies. *Psychiatric Services*, 56(2), 179–185.

Thompson, M., Osher, F., & Tomasini-Joshi, D. (2007). *Improving responses to people with mental illnesses: The essential elements of a mental health court.* Bureau of Justice Assistance.

Torrey, E. F., Kennard, S. A. D., Eslinger, S. D., Lamb, R., & Pavle, J. (2010). *More mentally ill persons are in jails and prisons than hospitals: A survey of the states.* Treatment Advocacy Center. Retrieved from: https://www.treatmentadvocacyc enter.org/storage/documents/final_jails_v_hospitals_study.pdf

Torrey, E. F., Stieber, J., Ezekiel, J., Wolfe, S. M., Sharfstein, J., Noble, J. H., & Flynn, L. M. (1992). *Criminalizing the seriously mentally ill: The abuse of jails as mental hospitals.* National Alliance for the Mentally Ill; Public Citizen's Health Research Group.

Torrey, E. F., Zdanowicz, M. T., Kennard, A. D., Lamb, H. R., Eslinger, D. F., Biasotti, M. C., & Fuller, D. A. (2014). *The treatment of persons with mental illness in prisons and jails: A state survey.* Treatment Advocacy Center. Retrieved from: https://www.treatmentadvocacycenter.org/storage/documents/treatment-be hind-bars/treatment-behind-bars.pdf

Trupin, E., & Richards, H. (2003). Seattle's mental health courts: Early indicators of effectiveness. *International Journal of Law and Psychiatry*, 26(1), 33–53.

Tyuse, S. W., & Linhorst, D. M. (2005). Drug courts and mental health courts: Implications for social work. *Health & Social Work*, 30(3), 233–240.

Verhaaff, A., & Scott, H. (2015). Individual factors predicting mental health court diversion outcome. *Research on Social Work Practice*, 25(2), 213–228.

Watson, A., Hanrahan, P., Luchins, D., & Lurigio, A. (2001). Mental health courts and the complex issue of mentally ill offenders. *Psychiatric Services*, 52(4), 477–481.

Wolff, N., Fabrikant, N., & Belenko, S. (2011). Mental health courts and their selection processes: Modeling variation for consistency. *Law and Human Behavior*, 35(5), 402–412.

*Chapter 3*

# DWI Courts

Carrie Petrucci

## INTRODUCTION

One does not have to look far to establish the need for problem-solving courts that focus specifically on drinking and driving. Drunk driving arrests and alcohol-impaired traffic fatalities both present a clear need. Though the number of total arrests for driving under the influence decreased by a third between 2008 and 2018, there were still just over one million drunk driving arrests nationwide in 2018 (Uniform Crime Reports, 2008; 2018). Over the same ten year period, the number of fatalities nationwide for alcohol-impaired driving has virtually held steady (at 10,759 in 2008 and 10,511 in 2018), though this does represent an 8 percent decrease in the overall fatality rate (National Center for Statistics and Analysis, 2019a). If a brighter side can be found, the number of alcohol-impaired fatalities in 2018 represented the lowest percentage of overall fatalities since 1982 at 29 percent (National Center for Statistics and Analysis, 2019b). Still, the estimated tangible economic costs from alcohol-impaired driving remain high ($44 billion), which includes things like lost productivity, medical costs, emergency medical services, and property damage (National Center for Statistics and Analysis, 2019a). Intangible quality-of-life costs add another estimated $201.1 billion nationwide (National Center for Statistics and Analysis, 2019a). Hence, drunk driving arrests and fatalities along with the high tangible and intangible costs support an ongoing focus on the need for interventions that reduce, if not eliminate the problem of drinking and driving.

Driving-while-intoxicated (DWI) courts were the third type of problem-solving court to emerge onto the scene. Some states use the term "driving under the influence" or DUI; DWI and DUI are used interchangeably here. The first DWI court was started in 1995 in New Mexico, following the first drug court in Miami in 1989 and the first community court in Brooklyn in 1993 (Marlowe, Hardin, & Fox, 2016). DWI courts were developed to protect public safety by addressing the underlying causes of repeated driving while intoxicated. The goal of DWI courts is to change the behavior of the alcohol-impaired driver by directly addressing alcohol and substance use through treatment and accountability. This is achieved through a team approach that includes the judge, the prosecutor, the defense attorney, probation officers, law enforcement, and treatment professionals. DWI court participants interact with the judge in regular status hearings to maintain accountability to treatment, alcohol testing, and other supervision requirements (Huddleston, Freeman-Wilson, & Boone, 2004; Marlowe, Hardin, & Fox, 2016). The DWI court approach was patterned after the drug court model outlined in *Defining Drug Courts: Key Components* (National Association of Drug Court Professionals, 1997). The *Ten Guiding Principles of DWI Courts* was published in 2006. Other intervention research emphasizing integrated models that combined a legal approach with treatment also supported DWI courts as an effective means to reduce repeat DWI offenses (DeYoung, 1997; Nochajski & Stasiewicz, 2006; Voas & Fisher, 2001).

The number of DWI courts has steadily increased over the years and includes both DWI courts that deal only with drunk driving and hybrid drug/DWI courts (Huddleston, Freeman-Wilson, & Boone, 2004). In 2004, there were ninety "designated DWI" courts and another eighty-six hybrid DWI/drug courts (Huddleston, Freeman-Wilson, Marlowe, & Roussell, 2005). By 2014, there were 262 designated DWI courts and 407 hybrid DWI/drug courts (Marlowe, Hardin, & Fox, 2016). By 2018, there were a total of 726 DWI courts (National Center for DWI Courts, 2018). There is no doubt that the number of DWI courts is eclipsed by the over 3,400 drug courts nationwide (National Drug Court Month Toolkit, 2019). However, DWI courts remain a mainstay among problem-solving courts, supported by the infrastructure from the National Association of Drug Court Professionals (NADCP), the National Drug Court Institute (NDCI), and the National Center for DWI Courts (NCDC). DWI courts, through NCDC, are also endorsed by multiple key stakeholder organizations that contribute to their sustainability including: Mothers against Drunk Driving (MADD), American Judges Association (AJA), the National District Attorneys Association, the National Sheriffs' Association, the National Association of Prosecutor Coordinators, the International Association of College of Police, the Governors Highway Safety Association, the National Transportation Safety Board, and the National Alcohol Beverage Control Association (see DWIcourts.org).

The purpose of this chapter is to familiarize the reader with DWI courts—their operation and what is known about whether they are successful. This will be accomplished by reviewing the current research on DWI courts, including best practices for implementation and effectiveness in reducing recidivism.

## BEST PRACTICES FOR IMPLEMENTATION

Patterned after drug courts, DWI courts are defined by their focus on addressing underlying substance use as a means to enhance public safety. In the case of DWI courts, this means that alcohol and other substance use is specifically addressed (Huddleston, Freeman-Wilson, & Boone, 2004). A cooperative team approach is taken similar to the drug court model to change defendant behavior related to drinking. Stated simply, the DWI problem-solving approach includes early intervention in the legal process and monitoring of treatment compliance and close community supervision through intensive probation, treatment services, and ongoing interaction with the judge (Huddleston et al., 2005). *The Ten Guiding Principles of DWI Courts* (2006) go into greater detail on what constitutes a well-implemented DWI court. These principles are summarized in table 3.1.

As is evident from table 3.1, the guiding principles are comprehensive, outlining recommended best practices supported by research for everything from establishing which type of DWI-impaired drivers will be included to sustainability (National Center for DWI Courts, 2006). The guidelines begin with clearly defining the target population (principle #1) followed by careful assessment (principle #2), treatment planning (principle #3), and supervision of DWI court participants (principle #4). Establishing partnerships is also essential, given the serious risk to public safety that impaired driving presents. This includes partnering with organizations and agencies that are part of the DWI court team and with community organizations with a vested interest in the DWI court (principle #5). Judicial leadership is an essential component, and arguably, it is considered the most important role of any successful DWI (or problem-solving) court. The judge is the leader and a key motivator for the team, community partners, and court participants to remain engaged and working together toward achieving program goals (principle #6). Case management assures seamless service provision for participants and also carries the responsibility for documentation and sharing of information so that drug court teams are well informed and acting synchronously with one another (principle #7). Unique to DWI courts is the almost universal need by DWI court participants to find an alternative transportation strategy while their license has been revoked so that they can attend all required activities (principle #8). Program evaluation is essential to documenting program successes and proving the worth of the DWI court in reducing future impaired driving among DWI court participants (principle #9).

**Table 3.1  Summary of *Ten Guiding Principles of DWI Courts* (2006)**

| Principle | Key Elements |
|---|---|
| 1. Determine the population | Target the highest-risk offenders with the most need for treatment, based on specific eligibility criteria established through collaboration with community stakeholders. |
| 2. Perform a clinical assessment | Conduct a comprehensive biopsychosocial assessment that includes alcohol use severity, use of substances besides alcohol, level of care, medical and mental health issues, social support, and individual motivation to change. |
| 3. Develop the treatment plan | Individualized treatment approaches from a variety of clinical and medical interventions based on client needs should be developed to support recovery and rehabilitation. Creating an environment in which treatment engagement in the long term is supported is essential. Also important is supporting treatment with participants who are similar in their treatment needs. |
| 4. Supervise the offender | To protect public safety from any further drinking and driving by DWI court participants, collaborative frequent supervision and monitoring of participants' behavior is needed by the court, probation department, and treatment provider. This includes field visits at participants' homes and at work, including urine tests and breathalyzer tests, with the outcome (positive or negative) relayed to the drug court team. Frequent regularly scheduled court contacts through judicial status hearings are also an essential component to assure accountability, praise successes, and to encourage participants toward a clean and sober lifestyle. Clear expectations of consequences of noncompliance as well as incentives for success also need to be communicated and acted on. |
| 5. Forge agency, organization, and community partnerships | The inherent danger to public safety that drunk driving poses makes strong partnerships essential to maintain the credibility, support, and resources needed. Partners should be identified within the court and in the broader community and be continuously informed of the progress of DWI court programs. Accomplishments should also be shared in the media. |
| 6. Take a judicial leadership role | It is essential that the judge take a leadership role of the DWI court team, and exhibit commitment to the role, understand the complex lives of DWI participants, and maintain a belief that treatment and accountability can lead to eliminating driving while impaired. Judges must also be knowledgeable about DWI cases and the nature of addiction and the expected behaviors that go along with it. Judges also need to recognize the important relationship that is built with program participants and how that can affect participant motivation to change. Simply put, judges must be ready to be change agents for program participants, the team, and community stakeholders. |
| 7. Develop case management strategies | A designated case manager assures that all services are seamlessly connected and are accurately documented and shared with the team and with partners. The accurate documentation of data is central to subsequent program evaluations. |

*(Continued)*

**Table 3.1 Summary of *Ten Guiding Principles of DWI Courts* (2006)** *(Continued)*

| Principle | Key Elements |
| --- | --- |
| 8. Address transportation issues | Virtually all DWI court participants will have had their license revoked at least for a period of time and will therefore encounter the need for transportation to attend mandated court hearings, treatment, and other supervision requirements. Programs need to make clear that driving without a license will be monitored by all team members and will be sanctioned. Participants need to be encouraged to solve their transportation problem at the outset of their involvement in DWI court. |
| 9. Evaluate the program | Evaluations are needed to identify what program elements worked best for which types of clients. Evaluations should include a description of participants served, program implementation, and how outcomes were measured. Measured variables not controlled by the program should include: jurisdictional characteristics (environmental context, e.g., suspension of driver's licenses), participant risk factors (e.g., educational achievement and prior DWIs), supervision strategies (alcohol testing, home visits), and treatment characteristics (type and dose of treatment). Program-controlled variables (type of program, eligibility criteria) and non-controlled variables should be included in the evaluation to determine their association with behavioral change among specific types of clients. |
| 10. Ensure a sustainable program | Establishing a sustainable DWI court is reliant upon strategic planning, and ultimately, in proving that DWI court success is an effective strategy to address impaired driving in the community. Strategic planning includes identifying resources, creating partnerships within and outside of the team, establishing protocols, establishing a common goal that everyone works toward, and proactively anticipating obstacles and resolving them together. |

*Sources:* Compiled by the author using Ten Guiding Principles of DUI Courts https://www.dwicourts.org/wp-content/uploads/Guiding_Principles_of_DWI_Court_0.pdf..

Lastly, sustainable programs are achieved through careful strategic planning and collaboration to provide ongoing community support for the DWI court program (principle #10).

Implementation strategies in DWI courts are also supported in the broader alcohol treatment research. Early research emphasized the importance of treatment in combination with abstinence, with self-help groups, and with license revocation. Some of this early work is reviewed here to illustrate the foundation on which DWI courts began. In the case of abstinence and treatment duration, in a randomized clinical trial, abstinence in the first year of treatment predicted better alcohol outcomes in the second year among a sample of 187 men and women diagnosed with either alcohol abuse or alcohol dependence (Maisto, Clifford, Longabaugh, & Betty, 2002). Many DWI courts monitor year-long abstinence of DWI court participants with weekly alcohol testing and intensive supervision. In addition, treatment duration (the number of weeks or months of treatment) may be more important than treatment intensity (the number of sessions per week or month) in reducing subsequent alcohol use (Moos & Moos, 2003; Sloan, Chepke, Davis, Acquah, & Zold-Kilbourn, 2013). DWI courts can require as long as twelve months of individual and group treatment, with intensity varying from weekly to monthly. Participation in Alcoholics Anonymous self-help groups may also have a role in better alcohol related outcomes and reduced need for treatment (Moos & Moos, 2004a; 2004b; 2007) when used in conjunction with formal treatment among those who are alcohol dependent (Dawson, Grant, Stinson, & Chou, 2006). More weeks of treatment was found to predict more weeks of attendance at self-help, which, in turn, predicted a greater likelihood for abstinence (Dennis, Foss, & Scott, 2007). Many DWI courts require eight to twelve months of participation in AA or an equivalent self-help group in combination with treatment (Strong, Rantala, & Kyckelhahn, 2016).

Finally, a combination of license revocation and alcohol treatment/education was more effective in reducing DWI recidivism in comparison to any of these components alone, or to jail alone (DeYoung, 1997; Nochajski & Stasiewicz, 2006; Scott, 2006; Taxman & Piquero, 1998; Voas & Fisher, 2001). License revocation is common among repeat DWI offenders attending DWI courts (National Center for DWI Courts, 2006). Monitoring compliance with not driving is also important. In some DWI courts, illegal driving is closely monitored by probation staff who conduct unannounced home visits. Probation being on board with the sentencing components has been linked to later reductions in recidivism (Nochajski & Stasiewicz, 2006). Taken together, this research suggests that the approach taken by DWI courts, which incorporates longer monitoring and supervision of abstinence and illegal driving, and treatment in conjunction with self-help groups such as Alcoholics Anonymous and license revocation may reduce or eliminate impaired driving due to alcohol and substance use, which, in turn, can greatly enhance public safety.

Another best practice of DWI courts is that the recommended treatment approach as outlined in *The Ten Guiding Principles of DWI Courts* (2006) also incorporates the well-known principles of addiction treatment published by the National Institute of Drug Abuse (NIDA). Table 3.2 matches up four of the *Ten Guiding Principles of DWI Courts* (2006) to the *Principles of Effective Treatment* (NIDA, 1999; 2009) and *Principles of Drug Abuse Treatment for Criminal Justice Populations* (NIDA, 2014). Each of the thirteen principles of addiction treatment (NIDA, 1999; 2009) were conceptually similar to the four DWI court guiding principles relevant to treatment. Eleven of the thirteen principles of drug abuse treatment for criminal justice populations (NIDA, 2014) were conceptually similar to the DWI court guiding principles (two principles more focused on drug court participants were determined to be less relevant to DWI courts).

As is apparent from table 3.2, a clear strength of DWI courts (and treatment courts in general) is their strong emphasis on research-based best practices for treatment. Use of best practices starts at assessment (DWI guiding principle #2 and concomitant NIDA principles) and continues through treatment planning and individualized treatment approaches (DWI guiding principle #3 and concomitant NIDA principles). Another key aspect important in DWI courts is how treatment is incorporated into supervision, starting with an understanding that substance use is a chronic disease, the need for continuous treatment monitoring and testing along with incentives and sanctions (DWI guiding principle #4 and concomitant NIDA principles). Lastly, case management strategies for DWI courts incorporate similar comprehensive approaches espoused by NIDA that address other possible health issues, and also emphasizes coordination between treatment and supervision (DWI guiding principle #7 and concomitant NIDA principles).

In summary, the main focus of DWI courts is public safety. Public safety is achieved by addressing the underlying alcohol and substance use disorders to eliminate the risk of repeated drinking and driving among DWI court participants. An examination of best practices in DWI courts reveals that implementation is firmly embedded in alcohol and treatment research that supports the structure of how DWI courts operate. The strength of DWI court implementation is in its simultaneous focus on supervision and treatment, achieved through a collaborative DWI court team structure.

## HOW EFFECTIVE ARE DWI COURTS IN REDUCING DWI RECIDIVISM?

Establishing effectiveness of DWI courts (or any intervention) in research requires several key considerations. Evaluating programs with a sufficient maturity or number of years of operation (Marlowe et al., 2009; Rempel, 2005), documentation of adherence to best practices (Heck, 2006; National Association of Drug Court Professionals, 2018), and sample sizes of participants of at least 200 per court in order to adequately capture recidivism effects (Rempel, 2005) are just a few considerations. It is debatable as to whether DWI courts have reached these benchmarks, with a clear need for more well-designed studies already noted (Marlowe et al., 2009; Mitchell et al., 2012). Many DWI courts are still relatively new; in a 2012 survey of problem-solving courts, only 28 percent of DWI courts had been in existence for more than six years (Strong et al., 2016). Related to years in operation, multiple years

**Table 3.2** Identification of NIDA *Principles of Effective Treatment* (2009) and *Principles of Drug Abuse Treatment for Criminal Justice Populations* (2014) Most Relevant to *Ten Guiding Principles of DWI Courts* (2006)

| Ten Guiding Principles of DWI Courts (2006) | NIDA Principles of Effective Treatment (1999; 2009) | NIDA Principles of Drug Abuse Treatment for Criminal Justice Populations (2014) |
|---|---|---|
| 2. Perform a clinical assessment | 8. An individual's treatment and service plan must be assessed continually and modified as necessary to ensure that it meets his or her changing needs.<br>9. Many drug-addicted individuals also have other mental disorders. | 4. Assessment is the first step in treatment. |
| 3. Develop the treatment plan | 2. No single treatment is appropriate for everyone. Match treatment services for each individual's treatment needs.<br>3. Treatment needs to be readily available.<br>4. Effective treatment tends to multiple needs of the individual, not just his or her drug abuse.<br>6. Counseling—individual or group—and other behavioral therapies are the most commonly used forms of drug abuse treatment.<br>7. Medications are an important element of treatment for many patients, especially when combined with counseling and other behavioral therapies.<br>10. Medically assisted detoxification is only the first stage of addiction treatment and by itself does little to change long-term drug abuse. | 2. Recovery from drug addiction requires effective treatment, followed by management of the problem over time.<br>5. Tailoring services to fit the needs of the individual is an important part of effective drug abuse treatment for criminal justice populations.<br>7. Treatment should target factors that are associated with criminal behavior.<br>11. Offenders with co-occurring drug abuse and mental health problems often require an integrated treatment approach.<br>12. Medications are an important part of treatment for many drug abusing offenders. |
| 4. Supervise the offender | 1. Addiction is a complex but treatable disease that affects brain function and behavior.<br>5. Remaining in treatment for an adequate period of time is critical.<br>11. Treatment does not need to be voluntary to be effective.<br>12. Drug use during treatment must be monitored continuously, as lapses during treatment do occur. | 1. Drug addiction is a brain disease that affects behavior.<br>3. Treatment must last long enough to produce stable behavior changes.<br>6. Drug use during treatment should be carefully monitored.<br>10. A balance of rewards and sanctions encourages pro-social behavior and treatment participation. |

**Table 3.2** Identification of NIDA *Principles of Effective Treatment* (2009) and *Principles of Drug Abuse Treatment for Criminal Justice Populations* (2014) Most Relevant to *Ten Guiding Principles of DWI Courts* (2006) *(Continued)*

| Ten Guiding Principles of DWI Courts (2006) | NIDA Principles of Effective Treatment (1999; 2009) | NIDA Principles of Drug Abuse Treatment for Criminal Justice Populations (2014) |
|---|---|---|
| 7. Develop case management strategies | 13. Treatment programs should assess patients for the presence of HIV/AIDS, Hepatitis B and C, tuberculosis, and other infectious diseases as well as provide targeted risk-reduction counseling to help patients modify or change behaviors that place them at risk of contracting or spreading infectious diseases. | 8. Criminal justice supervision should incorporate treatment planning for drug abusing offenders, and treatment providers should be aware of correctional supervision requirements. |

*Sources:* Compiled by the author using information from the following resources:
National Center for DWI Courts. The Ten Guiding Principles of DWI Courts. Author. https://www.dwicourt s.org/wp-content/uploads/Guiding_Principles_of_DWI_Court_0.pdf
National Institute on Drug Abuse (NIDA). (2009). Principles of Drug Addiction Treatment. Third Ed. Author. https://www.drugabuse.gov/publications/principles-drug-addiction-treatment-research-based-guide-third -edition/preface
National Institute on Drug Abuse (NIDA). (2009). Principles of Drug Abuse Treatment for Criminal Justice Populations – A Research-Based Guide. Author. https://www.drugabuse.gov/publications/principles-drug-abuse-treatment-criminal-justice-populations-research-based-guide/principles

of DWI court data are needed in research because the number of participants in DWI courts is often relatively low. In the same 2012 survey, two-thirds of surveyed DWI courts had less than fifty participants simultaneously enrolled (Strong et al., 2016). Therefore, it would take approximately four years to achieve the minimum of 200 participants recommended by Rempel (2005). Add to this that the median length of problem-solving courts is one year (Strong et al., 2016), and that a minimum of a two-year post-program follow-up is recommended to track DWI recidivism (as opposed to any type of arrest) (DeYoung, 1997), it becomes clear that most DWI courts cannot be fully evaluated for post-program outcomes until six to seven years of operation.

An additional consideration is there are variations of DWI courts, and this can complicate examination of research results in systematic reviews or meta-analyses. Three important variations deserve our attention. DWI most often refers to alcohol intoxication but may also refer to being intoxicated with any drug, including illegal drugs and prescription and over-the-counter drugs (Berning, Compton, & Wochinger, 2015). This chapter focuses on alcohol because it is the most common type of impairment in DWIs. Potential differences in implementation and the trajectory toward recovery for alcohol-only addiction versus methamphetamine addiction or polydrug use, for example, may need to be considered when combining research results that include various types of addictions (Sloan, Gifford, Eldred, & McCutchan, 2016). Another source of variation in DWI courts are the courts themselves; some are "designated DWI courts," meaning eligibility criteria requires a DWI arrest or conviction, while others are "hybrid" drug-and-DWI courts, which refers to a drug court that also includes DWI arrests or convictions (Huddleston, Freeman-Wilson, Marlowe, & Roussell, 2005). If program implementation was considered to be different across hybrid and designated DWI courts, and initial evidence suggests that it is (Bouffard & Richardson, 2010; Sloan et al., 2016; Strong et al., 2016), this could require doubling sample sizes to be able to separately examine these two types of DWI courts. A third variation is the use of medication-assisted treatment such as naltrex-one, and how this influences program effects (National Association of Drug Court Professionals, 2013).

With the aforementioned issues in mind, if we had to answer the question right now "do DWI courts reduce recidivism," we would echo the conclusion drawn by Mitchell et al. (2012): DWI court research is promising, but more evidence is still needed. This is in contrast to the more definitive conclusion drawn in a 2015 research update that stated there is no question that DWI courts reduce recidivism (Harron & Kavanaugh, 2015). The next section will begin by describing the research basis for Harron and Kavanaugh's (2015) conclusions. This will focus on the available systematic reviews and meta-analyses, including Marlowe et al.'s (2009) systematic review, the Campbell Collaboration meta-analysis (Mitchell, Wilson, Eggers, & MacKenzie, 2012), and the nine studies described by Harron and Kavanaugh (2015).

## Getting to Harron and Kavanaugh's "The Bottom Line"

In Harron and Kavanaugh's (2015) research update titled "The Bottom Line" published by the National Center for DWI Courts, their conclusion states: "That DWI Courts reduce recidivism is no longer a matter of debate or conjecture." The basis of their evidence includes endorsement of DWI courts by the National Transportation Safety Board, results of the Campbell Collaboration meta-analysis of twenty-eight DWI court studies (Mitchell, Wilson, Eggers, & MacKenzie, 2012), and their own analysis of ten high-quality DWI court studies published in 2009 through 2012 (though these studies were also included in the Campbell Collaboration meta-analysis), followed by their critical analysis of positive long-term effects from selected DWI court studies, reductions in car crashes, and cost-effectiveness of DWI courts. The discussion here will focus first on the Campbell Collaboration results and then the ten highlighted DWI court studies, but it is of interest to consider the Campbell Collaboration results in light of an earlier systematic review (Marlowe et al., 2009).

Marlowe et al. (2009) did a systematic review of fourteen published and unpublished DWI court research and evaluation studies. The authors used the Methodological Quality Scale (MQS) adapted from the *Mesa Grande Coding System for Methodological Quality* (Miller & Wilbourne, 2002; Marlowe et al., 2009) to rate the quality of selected studies. This system was developed to rate alcohol treatment evaluations and thus was easily transferable to DWI court settings. The main findings were that favorable outcomes were suggested, but there was still not enough scientific evidence to draw any definitive conclusions about DWI courts due to poor methodological quality (Marlowe et al., 2009).

The Campbell Collaboration meta-analysis was published three years later and included twenty-eight DWI court studies (several of which were also in Marlowe et al., 2009) along with ninety-two adult drug courts and thirty-four juvenile drug courts (Mitchell, Wilson, Eggers, & MacKenzie, 2012). The authors discuss three types of recidivism: general recidivism (defined as any type of arrest), drug recidivism (defined as a drug-related arrest), and drug use (defined as self-reported drug use). While it was not explained in the report, we are left to assume that drug arrests encompass alcohol-related arrests. Results indicated an average of a 12 percent reduction in recidivism for participants in both adult drug courts and DWI courts. Mean significant differences favoring the DWI court participants were also found for general recidivism (for all 28 DWI courts) and for drug-related recidivism (for 14 DWI court studies that included this definition of recidivism). However, when methodological rigor was considered, general recidivism results dropped to non-significance among the four experimental random assignment DWI court studies, but remained significant for methodologically weak, standard, and strong quasi-experimental designs. For drug-related recidivism, only nine standard and strong quasi-experimental designs remained significant, favoring the DWI courts (with no significance found for experimental and weak DWI court studies). In light of these findings, the conclusion drawn for the twenty-eight DWI courts was "DWI drug courts appear to be strong but this evidence is less consistent, especially in experimental evaluations" (Mitchell et al., 2012: 7).

Mitchell et al. (2012) took a closer look at the four randomized DWI court studies by removing the one negative experimental study from the recidivism analysis. When this was done, general recidivism approached significance for the three remaining random studies (meaning the significance value for the difference in mean effect sizes was just over 0.05), while drug-related recidivism remained non-significant. Special note needs to be made regarding this negative study due to its influence in this and subsequent conclusions drawn about DWI court studies. It was published by RAND authors MacDonald, Morral, Raymond, and Ebner (2007) based on a Los Angeles DWI court. This court was initiated for purposes of the RAND study and the program ended at the conclusion of the study (Marlowe et al., 2009) and therefore lacked the program experience or maturity preferred for evaluation (Marlowe et al., 2009; Mitchell et al., 2012). Simply stated, no significant differences in alcohol-related arrests or self-reported DWIs were found in a two-year follow-up in this randomized study (MacDonald et al., 2007). In a separate publication on the same Los Angeles DWI court, three of the same RAND authors acknowledged minimal implementation differences between the treatment and control groups (Eibner, Morral, Pacula, & MacDonald, 2006). Marlowe et al. (2009) also note the lack of difference in recidivism between the randomly assigned treatment and control groups was not unexpected when both received court hearings, considered one of the most important elements of DWI courts.

Perhaps in part as a response to Mitchell et al.'s (2012) somewhat tentative results, Harron and Kavanaugh (2015: 2) include a brief analysis of ten "high-quality evaluations conducted since 2009." By choosing more recent studies, the authors argue there is a greater likelihood that DWI court programs will have reached greater program maturity, making the results more reliable. In seven of these ten studies, statistically significant results favoring the DWI court participants were found in either DWI recidivism or general recidivism (Harron & Kavanaugh, 2015). While the rationale is clear for examining these ten studies more closely, there was not consistency in DWI recidivism results (DWI recidivism on a percentage basis was higher (worse) for DWI courts in two studies, lower (better) in six studies, and not reported in two studies). Percentage differences between DWI court and comparison groups were also small (less than 4 percent in five studies), leading to questionable practical significance. While the evidence presented is promising, it is arguable that it is definitive.

## Variation in DWI Court Programs and Research

In this section, five DWI court studies will be presented that were either not in the previous systematic reviews or meta-analyses or that illustrate a variation of a DWI court that is unusual.

### *Emphasizing Both Process and Outcomes*

Much can be learned from a set of nine DWI court studies in Minnesota published by NPC Research in 2014. Each site was first subjected to a feasibility study, followed by process and quasi-experimental outcome evaluations with one to two year follow-ups for recidivism (NPC Research, 2014). Because process evaluations were conducted at each site, when inconsistent results did occur, the researchers were able to suggest possible reasons why. For example, the general recidivism results (meaning any type of arrest) indicated that five out of nine sites had statistically significant differences in recidivism, favoring the DWI court participants over a matched comparison group. Sites that did not have significant results were noted to have insufficient program implementation, with specific areas identified including poor team cooperation, inadequate testing, and deficits in treatment services. Notably, sites with more high-risk participants tended to have better outcomes compared to sites with more low-risk participants. Recidivism was lower among DWI court participants with an average of 3.5 prior arrests. Several practical recommendations were made by NPC Research on how to accommodate both high- and low-risk participants, most importantly identifying them in the assessment process, developing a less intensive supervision strategy for lower risk participants, and separating low and high-risk participants so that high-risk participants would not negatively influence low risk participants (NPC Research, 2014).

Several encouraging results are notable in the nine Minnesota studies. Perhaps the most encouraging result was the low incidence of DWI recidivism. Another positive result was the high rate of completion among DWI court participants, ranging from 65 to 86 percent. In addition, cost effectiveness studies in six out of seven courts that had sufficient data showed cost savings ranging from $1,694 to $11,386 per participant. These cost savings occurred as a result of positive outcomes, such as fewer rearrests and less time subsequently incarcerated. For every dollar spent, the average rate of return was $2.06 (NPC Research, 2014).

## DUI Monitoring Court with Two Tracks

Carey, Allen, and Einspruch (2012) (also from NPC Research) did a process and outcome evaluation of the San Joaquin, California DUI Monitoring Court. This was not a traditional DWI court in that it had two tracks and served all levels of risk. Track 1 was for low-risk repeat DUI offenders. Track 2 was more intensive and was for Track 1 offenders who failed to comply. The court sample consisted of all participants from its inception in 2008 to 2011 ($n = 1,170$). A historical comparison group was formed using all DWI offenders prior to when the court began ($n = 1,262$). Recidivism follow-ups were eighteen months. Statistically significant results were approached for DWI convictions favoring the DWI court (9 percent versus 12 percent, $p = 0.058$). Statistically significant results favoring the DWI court were found for accidents involving alcohol (1.1 percent versus 3.8 percent, $p < .01$), and fewer license suspensions and revocations (1.7 percent versus 3.8 percent $p < .01$) (Carey et al., 2012). This study was unique due to the unusual structure of the two tracks, with generally positive results, through it might be informative if DWI arrests were also reported.

*Hybrid and DWI Court Evaluation Using Administrative Data*

Sloan et al. (2016) analyzed recidivism data among hybrid drug and DWI courts and DWI-only courts. This study was unique for its use of a very large statewide administrative database for both the specialized court samples and matched comparison groups. The sample included all those with a DWI conviction over a nine-year period (2002 to 2011), with two-year and four-year follow-ups for DWI recidivism. Another unique aspect of this study was that they drew four samples of court participation: those who were *referred and enrolled* in either a hybrid or DWI court or a DWI-only court (two samples), and those who *completed* either a hybrid or DWI court or a DWI-court only (two samples). These samples also allowed comparisons between hybrid drug/DWI courts and DWI-only courts. A total of 1,419 persons were referred to hybrid drug/DWI or DWI-only courts. The comparison group consisted of 131,340 persons with DWI convictions who were never referred to either type of court in the same time frame as the treatment groups. Propensity score matching was used to form the comparison groups.

Given the census nature of Sloan et al.'s (2016) data, the descriptive statistics on their own are of interest. For example, out of the 1,419 persons referred to DWI courts, 58.7 percent went on to enroll ($n = 834$), and 49.8 percent of those who enrolled went on to successfully complete a hybrid or DWI court ($n = 416$). Outcomes were DWI arrest, number of DWI arrests, and DWI convictions in two- and four-year follow-ups. Results were disappointing for the enrolled group. No differences in DWI arrest, convictions, or number of DWI arrests were found in the two- and four-year follow-ups between those who enrolled in either the hybrid or DWI court and the never referred matched comparison group. Results were more positive for those who *completed* the hybrid or DWI courts. Among court completers, significant differences were found at four-year follow-up for all three outcomes favoring the DWI courts, but no differences were found at the two-year follow-up. Another important comparison was between hybrid court outcomes and DWI-only court outcomes. While sample sizes were small for completers of either a hybrid or DWI-only court (sixty-one per group), significant differences were found in DWI arrests favoring DWI-only courts at four-year follow-up. Thus, the authors conclude that while enrolling in a hybrid or DWI-only court did not result in lowered DWI recidivism, participation defined as completing these courts did, and the probability of a subsequent DWI arrest was lower among those who completed a DWI-only court in comparison to a hybrid drug/DWI court. This study illustrates the advantages of utilizing large administrative databases when sufficient data elements are available, and the importance of separate analyses of hybrid and DWI-only courts.

## Incorporating Units-of-Service

Petrucci and Ireland (2008) conducted a process and outcome evaluation of two Orange County DWI courts. One of the two courts was evaluated for four years and included a sample of 374 DWI participants and will be the focus here. Statistically significant results favoring this DWI court were found in up to four-year follow-ups for any type of arrest compared to a historical sample ($n = 114$) (24.9 percent versus 42.1 percent, $p < .01$). Results favoring the DWI court were also found for DWI arrests (9.1 percent versus 16.7 percent, $p < .05$).

What was unique about this evaluation is that it utilized three performance measures described by the National Center for State Courts: units-of-service, retention rate, and graduation rate (Rubio, Cheesman, & Federspiel, 2008). A units-of-service approach was used to describe the treatment and supervision program elements that each participant was expected to receive. The expected *minimum* number of units-of-service for each DWI court participant over the twelve-month program was: 102 alcohol tests, 22 individual counseling sessions, 51 group counseling sessions, 123 self-help meetings, 42 probations meetings (not counting surprise home visits), and 10 judicial status hearings (Petrucci & Ireland, 2008). The retention rate was calculated with the total number of graduates plus the total number of enrollments (both since program inception) and dividing it by the total number of admissions to the program (since program inception). The retention rate was 73.9 percent after four years. The graduation rate was computed with the total number of graduates (since program inception) divided by the total number of graduates plus the total number of terminations (since program inception). The graduation rate was 65.4 percent after four years. Utilizing units-of-service that are defined the same way allows comparisons to be made across courts of expected treatment and dosage and provides insights into participant engagement (Rubio, Cheesman, & Federspiel, 2008).

## Incorporating Treatment Integrity Measurement

Myer and Makarios (2017) analyzed outcomes from six years of a DWI court in a mid-western state. What made their study unique was that they also analyzed treatment integrity. Outcome analyses were somewhat disappointing, particularly given their six-year sample of 485 DWI court participants. Using a matched comparison group, no significant differences were found for any type of arrest or conviction in two-year follow-ups. However, when DWI convictions were grouped against all other types of convictions, statistically significant differences were found, favoring the DWI court (28.7 percent versus 40.4 percent, $p < .05$). While it is not a way to draw conclusions about effectiveness of the DWI court (Rempel, 2005), statistically significant differences were also found between DWI court *completers* and their matched comparisons for any new charge (23.8 percent versus 36.6 percent, $p <$ .001) and any new conviction (20.1 percent versus 34.3 percent, $p < .001$). However, DWI court *non*-completers actually fared worse than their matched comparisons on any new charge (54.0 percent versus 39.8 percent, $p < .01$) and any new conviction (50.2 percent versus 34.5 percent, $p < .001$).

To explain these results, Myer and Makarios (2017) used their data that measured integrity to the drug court model and to treatment. The authors administered the Correctional Program Checklists for Drug Courts and for Referral Agencies (referred to as CPC-DC for drug courts and CPC-RA for treatment referral agencies) developed by researchers at the University of Cincinnati (Blair, Sullivan, Lux, Thielo, & Gormsen, 2016). These two instruments were administered at the DWI court and at the two treatment referral agencies used by the court. The CPC-DC and CPC-RA each rate six complementary areas. The final total scores for the DWI court and the two referral agencies each fell into the "needs improvement" category. The authors state that this could explain the lack of an overall effect of the DWI court. Also relevant was the "ineffective" ratings in two areas—offender assessment and treatment—for the DWI court and both referral agencies. Poor assessment could explain the worse results for DWI court non-completers; perhaps they were low or medium risk and actually ended up doing worse, while the high-risk DWI participants may have done better (Myer & Makarios, 2017).

These more recent studies illustrate several key points about DWI court research. First, documenting and analyzing how DWI courts operate is essential to our understanding of outcomes, including assessment, treatment, and testing. Second, there are relatively easy ways to collect how DWI courts operate through a units-of-service approach or through more labor intensive strategies such as the Correctional Program Checklists or process evaluation. Third, variations in DWI courts need to continue to be contrasted in evaluation research; these include hybrid drug/DWI courts and DWI-only courts, and DWI monitoring courts. Not addressed here but of importance are medication assisted approaches. These variations force us to more carefully consider assessment of risk level and matching to an appropriate constellation of services. Lastly, these studies highlighted the advantages of large sample sizes, often collected over multiple years, but also the importance of accessing available databases for treatment or comparison group analyses.

In closing, these and the other available DWI court research studies suggest promising evidence that DWI courts can make a difference in enhancing public safety, but there is still more work to be done. Continued attention to strong implementation according to best practices and concomitant research that incorporates process and outcomes using both qualitative and quantitative measures is needed to reach more definitive conclusions about the effectiveness of DWI courts.

## REFERENCES

Berning, A., Compton R., & Wochinger, K. (2015). Results of the 2013–2014 National Roadside Survey of alcohol and drug use by drivers. (Traffic Safety Facts Research Note. Report No. DOT HS 812 118). National Highway Traffic Safety Administration.

Blair, L., Sullivan, C. C., Lux, J., Thielo, A. J., & Gormsen, L. (2016). Measuring drug court adherence to the What Works literature: The creation of the Evidence-Based Correctional Program Checklist-Drug Court. *International Journal of Offender Therapy and Comparative Criminology, 60*(2), 165–1688.

Bouffard, J. A., & Richardson, K. A. (2010). Drug courts for DWI offenders? The effectiveness of two hybrid drug courts on DWI offenders. *Journal of Criminal Justice, 38*, 25–33.

Carey, S., Allen, T. H., & Einspruch, E. L. (2012). *San Joaquin DUI Monitoring Court Process and Outcome Evaluation Final Report.* NPC Research.

Dawson, D. A., Grant, B. F., Stinson, F. S., & Chou, P. S. (2006). Estimating the effect of help-seeking on achieving recovery from alcohol dependence. *Addiction, 101*(6), 824–834.

DeYoung, D. J. (1997). An evaluation of the effectiveness of alcohol treatment, driver license actions and jail terms in reducing drunk driving recidivism in California. *Addiction, 92*(8), 989–997.

Dennis, M. L., Foss, M. A., & Scott, C. K. (2007). An eight-year perspective on the relationship between the duration of abstinence and other aspects of recovery. *Evaluation Review, 31*, 585–612.

Eibner, C., Morral, A. R. Pacula, R. L., & MacDonald, J. (2006). Is the drug court model exportable? The cost-effectiveness of a driving-under-the-influence court. *Journal of Substance Abuse Treatment, 31*, 75–85.

Harron, A., & Kavanaugh, M. (2015). *The bottom line. National Center for DWI Courts.* Retrieved from: https://www.dwicourts.org/wp-content/uploads/The%20Bottom%20Line_0.pdf

Heck, C. (2006). *Local drug court research: Navigating performance measures and process evaluations. Monograph series 6.* Alexandria, VA: National Drug Court Institute.

Huddleston III, C. W., Freeman-Wilson, K., & Boone, D. L. (2004). *Painting the current picture: A National report card on drug courts and other problem solving court programs in the United States.* Volume I, Number 1. National Drug Court Institute.

Huddleston III, C. W., Freeman-Wilson, K., Marlowe, D. B., & Roussell, A. (2005). *Painting the current picture: A National report card on drug courts and other problem solving court programs in the United States.* Volume I, Number 2. National Drug Court Institute.

MacDonald, J. M., Morral, A. R., Raymond, B., and Eibner, C. (2007). The efficacy of the Rio Hondo DUI Court: A 2-year field experiment. *Evaluation Review, 31,* 4–23.

Maisto, S. A., Clifford, P. R., Longabaugh, R., & Beattie, M. (2002). The relationship between abstinence for one year following pretreatment assessment and alcohol use and other functioning at two years in individuals presenting for alcohol treatment. *Journal of Studies on Alcohol, 63*(4), 397–403.

Marlowe D. B., Festinger, D. S., Arabia, P. L., Croft, J. R., Patapis, N., & Dugosh, K. L. (2009). A systematic review of DWI court program evaluations. *Drug Court Review, 1*(2), 1–52.

Marlowe, D. B., Hardin, C. D., & Fox, C. L. (2016). *Painting the current picture: A National report on drug courts and other problem-solving courts in the United States.* Drug Court Institute.

Miller, W. R., and Wilbourne, P. L. (2002). Mesa Grande: A Methodological Analysis of Clinical Trials of Treatments for Alcohol Use Disorders. *Addiction, 97,* 265–277.

Mitchell, O., Wilson, D., Eggers, A., & MacKenzie, D. (2012). Drug courts' effects on criminal offending for juveniles and adults. *Campbell Systematic Reviews.* doi: 10.4073/csr.2012.4.

Moos, R. H., & Moos, B. S. (2003). Long-term influence of duration and intensity of treatment on previously untreated individuals with alcohol use disorders. *Addiction, 98,* 325–337.

Moos, R. H., & Moos, B. S. (2004a). Help-seeking careers: Connections between participation in professional treatment and Alcoholics Anonymous. *Journal of Substance Abuse Treatment, 26,* 167–173.

Moos, R. H., & Moos, B. S. (2004b). The interplay between help-seeking and alcohol-related outcomes: Divergent processes for professional treatment and self-help groups. *Drug and Alcohol Dependence, 75,* 155–164.

Moos, R. H., & Moos, B. S. (2007). Treated and untreated alcohol-use disorders: Course and predictors of remission and relapse. *Evaluation Review, 31*(6), 564–584.

Myer, A. J., & Makarios, M. D. (2017). Understanding the impact of a DUI court through treatment integrity: A mixed-methods approach. *Journal of Offender Rehabilitation, 56,* 252–275.

National Association of Drug Court Professionals. (1997). *Defining drug courts: The key components.* Washington, DC: Office of Justice Programs, U.S. Department of Justice. Retrieved from: http://www.ndci.org/sites/default/files/nadcp/Key_Comp onents.pdf

National Association of Drug Court Professionals. (2013). *Drug Court Practitioner Fact Sheet: Extended-Release Naltrexone,* Vol. VIII, No. 2. Alexandria, VA: National Drug Court Institute.

National Association of Drug Court Professionals (2018). *Adult Drug Court Best Practice Standards Volume II Text Revision.* Alexandria, VA. Retrieved from: https://www.nadcp.org/wp-content/uploads/2018/12/Adult-Drug-Court-Best-Prac tice-Standards-Volume-2-Text-Revision-December-2018-1.pdf

National Center for DWI Courts. (2006). *The Ten guiding principles of DWI Courts.* Alexandria, VA: Author. Retrieved from: http://www.dwicourts.org/sites/default/f iles/ncdc/Guiding_Principles_of_DWI_Court_0.pdf

National Center for DWI Courts. (2018). *DWI court fact sheet.* Retrieved from: https ://www.dwicourts.org/wp-content/uploads/2018/04/DWI-Court-Fact-Sheet_2018 .pdf

National Center for Statistics and Analysis. (2019a, December). *Alcohol-impaired driving: 2018 data* (Traffic Safety Facts. Report No. DOT HS 812 864). Washington, DC: National Highway Traffic Safety Administration.

National Center for Statistics and Analysis. (2019b, October). *2018 fatal motor vehicle crashes; Overview* (Traffic Safety Facts Research Note. Report No. DOT HS 812 826). Washington, DC: National Highway Traffic Safety Administration.

*National Drug Court Toolkit. 1989 to 2019: Celebrating 30 years of treatment courts* (2019). Alexandria, VA: National Association of Drug Court Professionals.

National Institute of Drug Abuse (NIDA). (1999). *Principles of drug addiction treatment: A research-based guide.* National Institutes of Health Publication No. 99-4180.

National Institute of Drug Abuse (NIDA). (2009). *Principles of drug addiction treatment: A research-based guide, 2nd edition.* National Institutes of Health Publication No. 09-4180.

National Institute of Drug Abuse (NIDA). (2014). *Principles of drug abuse treatment for criminal justice populations: A Research based guide.* National Institutes of Health Publication No. 11-5316.

Nochajski, T. H., & Stasiewicz, P. R. (2006). Relapse to driving under the influence: A review. *Clinical Psychology Review, 26,* 179–195.

NPC Research. (2014). *Minnesota DWI courts: A summary of evaluation findings in nine DWI court programs.* Retrieved from: https://www.dwicourts.org/wp-conten t/uploads/2016/09/MN_DWI_All_Site_Summary_August_2014_FINAL_FOR_O TS.pdf

Petrucci, C., & Ireland, C. (2008). *Final report: superior court of orange county dui court process and outcome evaluation.* Prepared for Superior Court of Orange County, California.

Rempel, M. (2005). *Recidivism 101: Evaluating the impact of your drug court.* New York: Center for Court Innovation.

Rubio, D. M., Cheesman, F., & Federspiel, W. (2008). *Performance measurement of drug courts: The state of the art.* Statewide Technical Assistance Bulletin, Volume 6. Williamsburg, VA: national Center for State Courts. Retrieved from: http://cdm 16501.contentdm.oclc.org/cdm/ref/collection/spcts/id/

Sloan, F. A., Chepke, L. M., Davis, D. V., Acquah, K., & Zold-Kilbourn, P. (2013). Effects of admission and treatment strategies of DWI courts on offender outcomes. *Accident Analysis and Prevention 53,* 12–120.

Sloan, F. A., Gifford, E. J., Eldred, L. M., & McCutchan, S. A. (2016). Does the prob- ability of DWI arrest fall following participation in DWI and hybrid drug treatment court programs? *Accident Analysis and Prevention, 97,* 197–205.

Strong, S. M., Rantala, R. R., & Kyckelhahn, T. (2016). *Census of Problem-Solving Courts, 2012.* U.S. Department of Justice, Office of Justice Programs, Bureau of Justice Statistics. NCJ 249803.

Taxman, F. S., & Piquero, A. (1998). On preventing drunk driving recidivism: An Examination of rehabilitation and punishment approaches. *Journal of Criminal Justice, 26*(2), 129–143.

Uniform Crime Reports. (2008). Table 29: Estimated Number of Arrests, United States 2008. Retrieved from: https://www2.fbi.gov/ucr/cius2008/data/table_29.html

Uniform Crime Reports. (2018). Table 29: Estimated Number of Arrests, United States 2018. Retrieved from: https://ucr.fbi.gov/crime-in-the-u.s/2018/crime-in-the-u.s.-2018/tables/table-29

Voas, R. B., & Fisher, D. A. (2001). Court procedures for handling intoxicated drivers. *Alcohol Research and Health, 25*(1), 32–42.

*Chapter 4*

# Reentry Courts

## Lama Hassoun Ayoub and Michael Rempel

### INTRODUCTION AND DEFINITION OF THE MODEL

Reentry courts are a type of problem-solving court, taking primary inspiration and guidance from drug courts (see chapter 1). Reentry courts share many of the core elements that define problem-solving courts generally, such as court-ordered treatment, judicial monitoring, stakeholder collaboration, and nontraditional roles (Berman & Feinblatt, 2001; Casey & Rottman, 2003). While there were only an estimated 30 reentry courts nationwide in 2014, compared to more than 3,000 drug courts (Marlowe, Hardin, & Fox 2016), these programs present a promising model for helping people transition from jails and prisons to the community. This chapter describes the reentry court model, research on its effectiveness, and major issues and challenges that distinguish this model from other problem-solving courts.

### Goals and Origins

Unlike most problem-solving courts, which specialize in one or a few discrete needs (e.g., drug addiction, mental illness, truancy, or trauma resulting from military combat), reentry courts seek to provide a coordinated and comprehensive response to the *multiple needs and collateral consequences* that formerly incarcerated individuals may face upon their release.

The then-director of the National Institute of Justice, Jeremy Travis, first proposed the idea of reentry courts in 1999, and they began to appear soon thereafter. Interest in reentry courts originated from two converging movements in the late 1990s and early 2000s: (1) a growing recognition that formerly incarcerated persons have extremely high recidivism rates brought about by an array of unmet needs; and (2) the spread of other problem-solving courts, drug courts especially, throughout the 1990s coupled with research pointing to their effectiveness in reducing both recidivism and drug use.

## Addressing the Multiple Barriers of Reentry

Ninety-five percent of people held in prison are released at some point (Hughes & Wilson, 2018). The vast majority go on to re-offend. A Bureau of Justice Statistics study found that 77 percent of those released in 2005 were rearrested within five years; and more than half of this recidivist subgroup was rearrested in the very first year (Durose, Cooper, & Snyder, 2014).

In turn, rearrest often triggers a revolving door of re-incarceration on parole violations. When those who are re-incarcerated due to a new charge are combined with those who are re-incarcerated on *technical* parole violations (e.g., for positive drug tests, missing parole officer check-ins, or other noncompliance with specific terms of parole), imprisonment for parole violations accounts for a sizable proportion of America's state prison population—as many as half of those held in prison around 2000, when reentry courts began to emerge (Petersilia, 2000; Travis & Lawrence, 2002).

Moreover, both the disturbingly high recidivism rates found among people released from prison, and their related exposure to re-incarceration, were well known by the turn of the millennium. Indeed, Jeremy Travis, Joan Petersilia, and many others spent the early 2000s drawing repeated attention to the multiple needs and lack of employable skills among released individuals—directly precipitating their recidivism (e.g., Petersilia, 2000, 2003, 2005; Travis, Solomon, & Waul, 2001; Travis, 2005). Substance abuse, mental illness, and barriers to stable housing, in particular, proved all too common in the released population, highlighting structural inequities in reentry (e.g., Belenko & Peugh, 2005; Clear & Cadora, 2003). In part reflecting these problems, but also reflecting collateral legal consequences of incarceration—that is, the refusal of many employers to hire formerly incarcerated individuals—unemployment was also widespread (e.g. Petersilia, 2000; Raphael & Weiman, 2007). With mass incarceration concentrated in communities of color, both back in 2000 (e.g., Beck & Harrison, 2001) and currently (Carson, 2018), the effects of labor market discrimination and systemic racism in employment are compounded for those with a criminal record (Holzer et al., 2003).

In this context, the Second Chance Act (SCA) passed in 2008, leading the Department of Justice to administer an array of multi-million-dollar grants intended to strengthen reentry services and programs nationwide. The National Reentry Resource Center estimates that since 2009, more than 800 federal grants were distributed as a direct result of SCA legislation. While the SCA was not driven by a specific interest in expanding specialized reentry courts per se, and most of the funding went to other reentry programs. However, SCA funds provided early support to the Harlem Parole Reentry

Court (Hassoun Ayoub & Pooler, 2015) and, later, to reentry courts across the country, eight of which were evaluated as part of *NIJ's Evaluation of Second Chance Act Adult Reentry Courts* (Carey et al., 2018). Thus, reentry courts clearly reflected a growing interest in the manifold problems posed by reentry in general, apart from any specific interest in a new type of problem-solving court. Nonetheless, without the larger problem-solving court movement, reentry courts per se may never have surfaced, in lieu of other ways of responding to the growing demand for reentry programming.

## The Role of the Antecedent Problem-Solving Court Movement

The nation's first drug court opened in Miami-Dade County in 1989. More than 1,000 drug courts had opened by 2002, and after five years the number reached to 2,000 by 2007 (Huddleston & Marlowe, 2011). Mirroring this surge in reentry courts specifically, the early 2000s saw a general expansion of the "problem-solving court" model to underlying issues besides the problem of substance abuse that gave rise to drug courts. In fact, the National Drug Court Institute estimates that in a mere three-year period from 2004 to 2007, the number of problem-solving courts *other than drug courts* doubled, from just over 500 to just over 1,000 (Huddleston & Marlowe, 2011). Put simply, problem-solving courts quickly became a full-on fad. Federal and state funders found them appealing, inducing local jurisdictions to establish specialized dockets for increasing numbers of problems to bring in federal dollars to their court systems.

However, it is noteworthy that by 2009, the National Drug Court Institute cited a total of twenty-six reentry courts, only four fewer than it estimated five years later in 2014. Unlike drug courts, whose expansion continued at varying curves over three decades, reentry courts arrived, and then stabilized, almost exclusively within the first key decade of the 2000s.

Beyond the lure of funding, models such as reentry courts may have also seemed attractive, given the largely positive drug court research literature converging in the early 2000s, including favorable multi-site evaluations of drug courts in Las Vegas and Portland (Goldkamp, White, & Robinson, 2002) and Kansas City and Escambia County, Florida (Truitt et al., 2000); statewide evaluations in New York (Rempel et al., 2003) and Ohio (Latessa, Shaffer, & Lowenkamp, 2002); a well-publicized randomized trial in Baltimore (Gottfredson, Najaka, & Kearley, 2003); and, finally, a positive meta-analysis of all drug court evaluations to date (Wilson, Mitchell, & MacKenzie, 2006).

A thorough problem-solving court literature review would point to a continuing stream of problem-solving court evaluations over the ensuing decade (many reviewed in chapters presented in this volume). Yet, given a lack of subsequent growth in reentry court numbers, they are best understood in terms of a dramatic and fast-moving confluence of policy and research trends—both reentry-specific and general to other problem-solving courts—concentrated in the first five years of the millennium.

## Common Components

In 1999, drawing from the established drug court model, the Department of Justice (DOJ) outlined the key components that they deemed essential to reentry courts. Specifically, they stated that reentry courts should involve risk and needs assessment; monitoring through judicial oversight and community supervision (probation or parole); service provision through community-based providers; case management through dedicated case managers; the use of graduated and parsimonious sanctions; and positive incentives for success (Office of Justice Programs, 1999). One of the key assumptions of the model was that recently released individuals could benefit from the interest and involvement of a judge, who was fully invested in successful reentry. Since then, pre-release contact, through pre-release assessment or services, has also emerged as an important component of reentry programs (LaVigne et al., 2008). The next few sections briefly review these key components.

### Risk-Need Assessment

Validated risk-need assessment tools are designed both to classify an individual's likelihood of re-offense (e.g., as low, moderate, or high) and to aid treatment planning by estimating the severity of different types of needs and problems. To be validated, a risk-need assessment must be based on empirical research that supports the resulting classifications. Preferably, a tool's accuracy is supported by multiple large-scale validation studies with diverse populations and subgroups. Moreover, the use of risk-needs assessment tools has become a common, often required, practice in problem-solving courts; and reentry courts are no exception.

Following the widely researched risk-need-responsivity model, the intensity of supervision (i.e., its frequency, duration, and scope) should be based on the risk score, with higher risk participants assigned to more intensive supervision. While case management planning should be based on needs, specific interventions should be "responsive," in that they should be tailored to the characteristics and learning styles of the individual (Andrews & Bonta, 2010; Bonta & Andrews, 2007).

In multi-site studies of reentry courts, risk-need assessments were one of the most consistently utilized evidence-based practice. One way of under-standing this finding is as a perfectly logical outgrowth of the multiple, varying needs that different formerly incarcerated persons possess—making a quality assessment perhaps even more imperative than in a drug court, where, by definition, treatment can at least target a drug addiction in all cases. Carey and colleagues (2017) found that reentry court participants received more effective use of risk-need assessment than their counterparts in regular community supervision.

A full review of risk-need assessment tools is beyond the scope of this chapter (see Serin & Lowenkamp, 2015). However, we highlight some important considerations to the ongoing use of risk-need assessment tools in reentry programs. First, these tools are not similarly validated with all populations, even when some studies or tool developers claim they are. For example, tools validated with a reentering Native American population in a non-tribal urban setting may not be appropriate for use in a tribal court or reentry program.

Second, there is ongoing debate in the field about the potential contribution of risk-assessment tools to racial disparities. Research to date has found that risk assessments tend to misclassify higher percentages of black than white individuals as "high risk" (Angwin et al., 2016; Picard et al., 2019). Misclassifying people means, in effect, that the tool classified people as high risk, who did not, in fact, re-offend. On the other hand, sizable racial disparities in incarceration and other criminal sanctions existed well prior to the advent of risk assessments, resulting from judicial or supervision officer discretion. Thus, scholars differ over whether risk assessments should be used at all, with some positing that, if they continue to be used, there should be standardized safeguards, such as curtailing their role in incarceration decisions (Picard et al., 2019). In this regard, the adverse ramifications of risk assessments might be viewed as less consequential in a reentry court context; here, risk assessments would mainly impact the intensity of supervision, not an incarceration decision. But even then, if more frequent supervision exposes people to more opportunities to be caught engaging in noncompliance, leading to a greater likelihood of revocation, incarceration could ultimately be at stake. Thus, risk assessment should also be conducted with care and intentionality, with a specific focus and review of how a tool may be contributing to further justice-related racial/ethnic disparities.

On the other hand, there is less debate over the essential role of *needs assessments* in aiding supervision officers, case managers, or other staff who may work in correctional programs to place people in services they truly need. Especially in a reentry context, there is little argument not to thoroughly assess the needs and strengths of each participant.

## Individualized Case Management

Building upon information gathered during intake and, especially, the administration of a risk-need assessment, reentry court staff develop individualized case management plans, tailored to the needs and situation of each participant. Notably, the literature to date suggests that it is often both common and productive to implement reentry service delivery in stages: Reentry court participants often have immediate stabilization needs that, once met, then facilitate the introduction of additional longer-term services. Initial stabilization services can include help obtaining proper identification, housing stability, and registration for public assistance programs (Carey et al., 2017; Boar & Watler, 2012), whereas subsequent services might expand into long-term drug or mental health treatment, employment assistance, or cognitive-behavioral therapy.

To orchestrate services effectively, strength-based pre-release intake forms or questionnaires can guide discharge planning. As in the case of the Harlem parole reentry court (Boar & Watler, 2012), reentry courts should seek to identify participants' strengths and challenges in addition to their risks and needs, which will allow for case management aimed at leveraging strengths and efficiently tackling obstacles.

Depending on the resources of each reentry court, some offer in-house employment services or cognitive behavioral therapy (Hassoun Ayoub, 2020), while others refer participants to local community-based agencies (Boar & Walter, 2012). Reentry court staff have drawn attention to substance use and mental health treatment as especially common needs, leading staff to believe that strong partnerships with community-based local service providers can contribute to positive participant outcomes (Carey et al., 2017). Some reentry courts also link participants to services from faith-based institutions, which offer a wide variety of reentry related services, including post-release care packages (Hassoun Ayoub, 2020), temporary housing, housing assistance (Carey et al., 2017), and drug treatment (Martinez & Graf, 2020).

Boar and Walter (2012), in their reentry court toolkit, emphasize the nurturing of strong partnerships with local service organizations as a key implementation step. They also state that external community-based programs, including substance abuse or mental health treatment, should be fully vetted to ensure that the program is a good match. Vetting may include determining if the program fills the needs of the reentry court participants, determining the volume of participants that can be accommodated, identifying specialized programming (e.g., parenting or gender-based programs), or reviewing the use of evidence-based practices.

*Judicial Oversight & Community Supervision*

Participation in most reentry courts is voluntary, with a focus on high-risk, high-need individuals. Programs vary in length, with reports of programs as short as six months to eighteen months post-release (Lindquist et al., 2013). Supervision is usually intense, given the higher risk levels of participants, including frequent drug testing, close monitoring of treatment and service provision and engagement, and regular (biweekly or monthly) non-adversarial hearings (Aiken, 2019; Hassoun Ayoub, 2020). These status hearings usually involve the participants, the judge, a supervision officer, case manager, and other reentry court staff; they may also include supporters or family members of the participant (Maruna & LeBel, 2003).

Reentry courts combine judicial oversight with parole or probation supervision to seek recidivism reductions and address client needs. Process studies have found that judicial involvement can have many potential benefits. An effective judge can help to increase accountability of both the reentry court team (for providing necessary services) and of the participant (for compliance) (Salvatore et al., 2020). In addition, the judge can provide supports to the participant (e.g., emotional); assist in improving services or coordination with other parts of the criminal justice system; and positively impact perceptions of procedural justice, which may be linked to reduced recidivism or increased compliance (Atkin-Plunk & Armstrong, 2016).[1] Finally, in some cases, the judge is responsible for the final decision on violations, revocations, and returns to incarceration, even when a supervision officer issues them. In those situations, the judge's in-depth knowledge of the participant can guide decision-making (Farole, 2003; Hassoun Ayoub, 2020). Ideally, the judge may be able to restrain what is sometimes a traditional community supervision culture of resorting to quickly to re-incarceration—though research cited further in the text suggests that it has not always worked out this way in reentry courts. Notably, as compared to reentry courts' ongoing use of judicial supervision, individuals on standard community supervision typically see a judge only after a violation has been filed (Lindquist et al., 2018).

## Sanctions and Incentives

Graduated sanctions and incentives have long been considered an effective mechanism for improving compliance with community supervision (Taxman & Soule, 1999). While many different models of graduated sanctions and incentives have been proposed, most scholars agree that they must be *swift* and *certain*. Certainty refers to the knowledge of the participant; that is, participants must know what the responses to their behavior are likely to be from the beginning of their program participation; and those responses must, in fact, be imposed each time. Swiftness refers to the timeliness of the response; responses to participants' actions, whether sanctions or incentives, should occur soon after the behavior, an outcome facilitated by the scheduling of regular hearings before the judge, when responses may be swiftly applied.

Swift and certain sanctions have been increasingly implemented in numerous criminal justice contexts (Hawken et al., 2016; O'Connell et al., 2011). In 2016, Hamilton and colleagues published a study on the first statewide implementation of swift and certain sanctions in community supervision. In this quasi-experimental study, they found that participants who received such sanctions showed reduced recidivism, received a higher dosage of treatment, were incarcerated for fewer days after a violation, and there were lower correctional costs. The authors noted that effective implementation of sanctions required significant staff training, support from staff and leadership, and prioritization and investment by correctional agencies.

In addition to certainty and swiftness, the National Reentry Resource Center has identified several other features of effective sanctions and incentives in reentry contexts. Specifically, the Resource Center proposes that sanctions and incentives should be proportional and appropriate, given the participants' behavior. They must also be fair and perceived as fair and just by the participant. Last, sanctions and incentives must be individualized in that they must consider the participant's needs and risks when they are implemented (Lowe et al., 2013).

Positive incentives (aka "rewards") are equally important, if not more important, than graduated sanctions. But evidence indicates that they are less consistently applied in reentry courts (Lindquist et al., 2014; Taxman & Soule, 1999). Incentives may include praise by the supervision officer or judge, fewer required hearings or less treatment, more travel or curfew flexibility, small gifts, certificates, a reduced supervision period, and other incentives depending on the court context (Aiken, 2019; Gottschall & Armour, 2016; Hamilton, 2010; Hassoun Ayoub & Pooler, 2015; Lindquist et al., 2018). In a randomized trial of the Harlem parole reentry court, reentry court participants were significantly more likely to report receiving positive incentives (96 percent) than people on traditional parole (77 percent). Participants also were significantly less likely to receive sanctions (30 percent) than the control group (63 percent). This greater reliance on incentives over sanctions may have contributed to better outcomes: the self-reported positive incentives were a *stronger* predictor of reduced rearrest than negative sanctions, though both had statistically significant effects (Hassoun Ayoub & Pooler, 2015).

A recent longitudinal study revealed further evidence of the importance of incentives. Investigators found that positive incentives, such as supervision officer praise, were associated with significantly less recidivism and substance use, while sanctions were associated with greater recidivism and substance use (Mowen et al., 2018).

## Pre-Release Services

Experts consider pre-release engagement an essential component of reentry courts, potentially contributing to an improved likelihood of participant success. Pre-release engagement allows the case manager or supervision officer to begin building a relationship at a time when participants are most receptive to assistance (Boar & Watler, 2012). Most such engagement occurs thirty to sixty days before release when a risk-needs assessment can be conducted.

For programs operating with limited pre-release service capabilities, handbooks and resource guides have become a popular approach to providing access to information for soon-to-be-released individuals (LaVigne et al., 2008). Specifically, reentry programs may use standardized handbooks or resource manuals to deliver information without a designated case manager or a complex relationship with the correctional system.

## Evidence on Reentry Courts

Unlike the literature on drug courts, which has a long history, the evidence on reentry courts is limited and mixed. Recent studies have utilized rigorous methodologies (e.g., strong quasi-experimental designs, multi-method), but have shown inconsistent findings, which scholars have linked to variations in implementation quality (e.g., use of evidence-based practices or not), as well as the wide and varying scope of different reentry courts.

A recent quasi-experimental outcome evaluation of one federal reentry court provided evidence that the program did not reduce rearrests but did reduce revocations while increasing access to social services and future employment (Taylor, 2020).

Similar results were found in a randomized controlled trial (RCT) published in 2020 for the reentry court in Harlem. This study yielded no evidence of significant differences in rearrest or reconviction, but a significant 45 percent reduction in revocations for reentry court participants (Hassoun Ayoub, 2020). The same RCT also involved interviews with individuals in both the reentry court and the control group, which showed significant positive intermediate outcomes (Hassoun Ayoub & Pooler, 2015). Specifically, reentry court participants were significantly more likely than the control group to report current school enrollment or employment (75 percent versus 45 percent). Participants also reported working for more months since their release, with an average of nearly eight months of employment (over a twelve- to eighteen-month timeframe), compared to only four months for the control group. Reentry court participants worked more hours per week and had higher quality employment (e.g., paid sick leave) than the control group. Positive outcomes were also reported for substance use, family support and relationships, supervision experience, and procedural justice. The authors suggested that perceptions of procedural fairness, attitudes toward the judge, number of case manager and probation officer meetings, sanctions, and housing status may have played a role in reducing revocations.

The same Harlem reentry court had also been evaluated in the past through a quasi-experimental design. That study yielded mixed results as well, with reductions in rearrest and reconviction but increased revocations compared to a matched comparison group (Hamilton, 2010). The program made significant changes in response, including focusing on implementing RNR principles to reduce any supervision effect (Hassoun Ayoub & Pooler, 2015).

In 2017, Carey and colleagues published a multi-site study of reentry courts, involving process, outcome, and cost evaluations. This comprehensive study primarily showed mixed results; the process study provided significant insight on the differences among the reentry courts. Only one site consistently demonstrated positive outcomes in comparison to business-as-usual by successfully reducing recidivism (rearrest and reconviction), reducing incarceration (revocation and period of incarceration), delivering more substance use treatment and other services, and showing significant costs savings. The remaining reentry courts in the study were divided evenly: two showed neutral results (trending positive, but not significant), two with mixed results (e.g., fewer rearrests but increased re-incarceration), and two with consistently negative results (e.g., more rearrests and incarceration than comparison group).

Based on the process evaluation, the most successful reentry court in this study differed from the other courts in several key areas: (a) reliance on a validated risk-need assessment tool for supervision and case management decisions; (b) intense and consistent service provision, including substance abuse treatment and services for other key criminogenic needs; (c) highly involved supervision officers; and (d) heavy use of praise, incentives, and sanctions by the judge. The authors argued that reentry courts with less positive results may not have had the appropriate levels of supervision or types of services consistently available to best serve the risk levels of their participants, essentially violating the principles of risk-need-responsivity when assigning participants to supervision or services (Carey et al., 2017; Lindquist et al., 2014). While other sites may have implemented some of these elements, high-quality implementation appears to have made the difference between consistent positive recidivism results and mixed or negative results.

Considering the high costs of incarceration, reducing recidivism in reentry courts may be associated with substantial cost savings to the public. Cost studies or cost-benefit analyses of reentry courts, however, have been limited with mixed results, usually highly dependent on implementation strategies and program effectiveness. A study of a reentry court in Indiana found a cost savings of about $9,000 per participant per year, but this was only in comparison to incarceration (Pearson-Nelson, 2009). A multi-court study in California showed that reduced revocation-related incarceration among reentry court participants saved the state approximately $6 million (Carey & Zil, 2014); however, this may have been offset by higher rearrest for the reentry court, although a comprehensive cost-benefit analysis that incorporated further expenses was not conducted.

The multi-site study by Carey and colleagues involved a rigorous cost evaluation of multiple reentry courts nationwide, with mixed results. Only two reentry courts showed cost savings, primarily due to reduced recidivism and lower victimization costs for reentry court participants ($2,500–$6,700 saved per participant); other reentry courts incurred financial losses (ranging from −$1,000 to −$17,000 loss per participant)[2] (Carey et al., 2017).

Another study of six reentry courts in California examined parole revocations and rearrests, finding that reentry court programs were successful in reducing revocations: reentry court participants were revoked less often than members of the comparison group in the year following program entry. Consequently, they spent significantly less time incarcerated than comparison group members. Rearrest results were mixed. Reentry court participants were more likely to be arrested in the first year following program entry and had a higher number of arrests on average in the year following program entry (Zil & Carey, 2014).

## RECOMMENDATIONS

The number of reentry courts around the country grew quickly for several years, despite a lack of research to drive expansion. In recent years, there appears to have been a plateau in growth,[3] although the reasons are unclear. While reentry programs more generally have yielded consistent, rigorous research about their effectiveness, documented in a national "what works" in reentry clearinghouse,[4] reentry courts have a much weaker track record. While new studies will continue to emerge in the coming years, a few key lessons should be considered by practitioners, researchers, and justice agencies.

1. *Implementation matters.* Results from the few completed studies suggest that when reentry courts engaged in careful, evidence-based implementation, they *may* be effective in achieving their goals, but those with low-quality implementation may contribute to worse outcomes for their participants. Thus, reentry court planners and managers should seek to implement evidence-based strategies, as described

earlier, with fidelity and high quality. Related, reentry courts should ensure that the use of both sanctions and positive incentives is swift, certain, proportional, consistent, and fair. As shown in the study by Hamilton (2010), when programs do not apply RNR principles properly (lower risk participants receiving fewer services; higher risk participants in more intense supervision), this can lead to a "supervision effect" where lower-risk participants may be recidivating due to unnecessarily intense supervision. By contrast, research on drug courts has reached a stage where it is possible to conclude that they reduce recidivism on average and, even when they don't, the result is typically no effect, with worse outcomes in but a tiny fraction of programs (Mitchell et al., 2012).

2. *Reentry courts may not outperform evidence-based community supervision.* The real possibility that reentry courts can do harm absent strong implementation is not a low-stakes problem; if people can benefit more from "business-as-usual" community supervision, jurisdictions might consider integrating well-implemented evidence-based practices (e.g., RNR and risk assessment; revised supervision caseloads; service provision) into existing supervision practices, instead of initiating or investing in a brand new court-based model. The option of improving community supervision becomes especially attractive when there is no clear evidence that a reentry court model would outperform a well-implemented community- or corrections-based reentry program. Since the reentry court model takes so many elements from the same evidence-based practices encouraged in reentry programs, generally, research to date is insufficient to conclude that the primary additional component—judicial oversight—yields clear added value. If the mere fact of establishing a reentry court and adhering in broad terms to its key components cannot produce positive average impacts, as drug courts have been able to achieve, overlaying judicial oversight onto community supervision may not be sufficiently justified, over and above efforts to invest in more robust services and better practices in a community supervision framework.

   In fact, the comparison between the reentry court model and community- or corrections-based reentry programs has never been done. Those two types of reentry programs are most programs around the country and among those funded by the federal government (National Reentry Resource Center, 2017). However, given the wealth of research on effective reentry practices in both community programs and correctional initiatives, a comparison of a similar investments in a reentry court versus community or corrections-based programs is warranted.

3. *The use of formal risk-needs assessment tools and other elements of the risk-need-responsibility (RNR) model may improve outcomes.* The multisite study by Carey et al (2018), as well as the randomized trial of a reentry court in Harlem, suggested that reentry courts can produce more positive outcomes when they integrate risk-needs assessment tools—and then use assessment findings to link people to substance abuse treatment or services like cognitive-behavioral therapy for their other key criminogenic needs. It is unclear whether *risk* assessments were specifically responsible for these promising findings or whether they had more to do with systematically assessing and classifying the severity of a wide range of *needs*—an uncertainty worth underscoring given the more controversial status of risk than need assessment. But without rigorously disentangling the effects of risk versus needs assessment, or for that matter of any other highly specific program component, the limited reentry court literature to date would seem to provide, at most, modest support for RNR-informed practice.

4. *Reentry court judges should have enough authority to make the overlay of judicial oversight worthwhile in the first place.* This observation would not merit attention in the context of any other problem-solving court model, including drug, mental health, and veterans courts. In these other models, the initial criminal case has yet to be adjudicated, a reality that virtually assures a central role for the judge. But in reentry courts, the individual has already been adjudicated, convicted, and sentenced. Accordingly, judges in reentry courts may share legal authority to a far greater extent with the parole and probation agencies that are traditionally in the driver's seat post-release. And, in fact, some reentry courts have supervision officers that wield more power than a judge in final decisions on arrests or revocations (Lindquist et al., 2013). But reentry court planners can, by contrast, reach an understanding that investing in this model means increasing the judge's authority to be more akin to its level in other problem-solving courts. For example, in the most regularly evaluated reentry court, the Harlem Parole Reentry Court, different evaluators have highlighted the importance of the judge in that particular reentry court; in this case, the administrative law judge who oversees Harlem's reentry court also handles violations and revocation hearings for the participants and other formerly incarcerated persons, thereby building on their in-depth knowledge of the individual before them (Farole, 2003; Hamilton, 2010; Hassoun Ayoub, 2020; Hassoun Ayoub & Pooler, 2015). Thus, the lesson is not necessarily that judges cannot ever play a central role in a reentry context as that it is more important to negotiate the judge's authority and role at the planning stages in reentry courts than, for example, in drug or mental health courts, where the judicial role will be inherently central.

5. *Beyond Recidivism: Reentry Courts, funders, and researchers should focus on outcomes other than recidivism.* While many reentry practitioners working day-to-day with formerly incarcerated individuals recognize the importance of every "win," small or big, researchers, senior officials, and funders are usually uninterested in outcomes other than recidivism. This issue plagues most of criminal justice reform and research (Sharlein, 2016; Heidemann et al., 2016; Pelletier & Evans, 2019; Maruna, 2020), and it is particularly important in reentry contexts for two reasons. First, participants are working on succeeding in several areas (e.g., employment/education and treatment). Many of these areas are connected to recidivism through past research, but they also warrant consideration as separate important outcomes. Other outcomes that have been shown to be important to recently released individuals or service providers include family reunification and support, parenting successes, cultural and community connections, entrepreneurship, and much more (Hassoun Ayoub & Pooler, 2015; Fox, 2019; Maruna, 2020). Second, the numerous well-documented pervasive biases in criminal justice arrest and incarceration rates also infiltrate criminal justice data. That is, recidivism data is less a reflection of current crime and more a reflection of disparate police and court practices. Hassoun Ayoub (2020) hinted at this issue in explaining poor outcomes in a randomized controlled trial of a reentry court, highlighting that similar arrest rates (between treatment and control) are likely a result of over-policing in Harlem.

## CONCLUSION

In sum, reentry courts present an interesting approach to creating a collaborative and supportive reentry experience for individuals recently released from incarceration or on community supervision. However, the results from multiple rigorous studies have shown that reentry court impacts have been mixed, at best, with significant challenges to high-quality implementation involving the effective use (or lack thereof) of evidence-based practices. Although reentry courts have not proliferated as much as drug courts, some common problems have also emerged, including an inability to scale to larger contexts (i.e., low court volume), thereby greatly limiting any potential impact that they might have. In the case of reentry courts, the current pause in the expansion is likely a positive development, as the field takes the time to consider the research results and the best use of limited resources dedicated to the improvement of reentry programming—a clear need that exists with or without a court-based model.

## NOTES

1. More recent research shows that the connection between recidivism and procedural justice is mixed. A recent study indicated that the relationship did not exist and that it may vary by race/ethnicity. Specifically, black problem-solving court clients' showed significantly lower perceptions of procedural justice, while also having a lower likelihood of recidivism. Perceptions of procedural justice did not influence recidivism outcomes (Atkin-Plunk et al., 2017).

2. Reentry court program investment costs were examined, but the comparison of cost estimates is limited to outcomes and does not include net benefits based on investment in traditional case processing comparison groups.

3. As of the writing of this chapter, the most recent reentry court estimate is at least a decade old. There is no evidence that their numbers continue to grow.

4. What works in reentry clearinghouse is available at: https://whatworks .csgjusticecenter.org/

## REFERENCES

Andrews, D. A., & Bonta, J. (2010). *The psychology of criminal conduct 5th ed.* LexisNexis.

Angwin, J., Kirchner, L., Larson, J., & Surya, M. (2016). Machine bias. *ProPublica.*

Beck, A. J., & Harrison, P. M. (2001). *Prisoners in 2000.* Bureau of Justice Statistics.

Belenko, S., & Peugh, J. (2005). Estimating drug treatment needs among state prison inmates. *Drug and Alcohol Dependence, 77*(3), 269–281.

Bonta, J., & Andrews, D. A. (2007). *Risk-need-responsivity model for offender assessment and rehabilitation.* Public Safety Canada.

Carey, S. M., Rempel, M., Lindquist, C., Cissner, A. B., Ayoub, L. H., Kralstein, D., & Malsch, A. (2017). *Reentry Court Research: Overview of Findings from the National Institute of Justice's Evaluation of Second Chance Act Adult Reentry Courts.* NPC Research.

Carson, A. (2020). *Prisoners in 2018.* Bureau of Justice Statistics.

Casey, P., & Rottman, D. (2003). *Problem-solving courts: Models and trends.* National Center for State Courts.

Clear, T. R., & Cadora, E. (2003). *Community justice.* Wadsworth Press, Series on Contemporary Issues in Crime and Justice.

Durose, M. R., Cooper, A. D., & Snyder, H. N. (2014). *Recidivism of prisoners released in 30 States in 2005: Patterns from 2005 to 2010 – Update.* Bureau of Justice Statistics.

Fox, D. L. (2019). *Measuring recidivism risk outcomes: A pilot project in collaboration with the Flathead Reservation Reentry Program* (Doctoral dissertation, University of Montana).

Goldkamp, J. S., White, M. D., & Robinson, J. B. (2001). *From whether to how drug courts work: retrospective evaluation of drug courts in Clark County (Las Vegas) and Multnomah County (Portland)*. Final Project Report, August 2001. Criminal Justice Research Institute.

Gottfredson, D., Najaka, S. S., & Kearley. B. (2003). Effectiveness of drug treatment courts: Evidence from a randomized trial. *Criminology and Public Policy, 2*(2), 171–196.

Hassoun Ayoub, L., & Pooler, T. (2015). *Coming home to harlem: A randomized controlled trial of the Harlem Parole reentry court*. Center for Court Innovation.

Hassoun Ayoub, L. (2020). The impact of reentry court on recidivism: A randomized controlled trial in Harlem, New York. *Journal of Experimental Criminology,16*, 101–117.

Heidemann, G., Cederbaum, J. A., & Martinez, S. (2016). Beyond recidivism: How formerly incarcerated women define success. *Affilia, 31*(1), 24–40.

Holzer, H., Raphael, S., & Stoll, M. (2003). Employment dimensions of reentry: understanding the nexus between prisoner reentry and work. Urban Institute Reentry Roundtable. Retrieved from: ResearchGate website: https://goo.gl/2ZuCWW

Huddleston, W., & Marlowe, D. B. (2011). *Painting the current picture: A national report on drug courts and other problem-solving court programs in the United States*. National Drug Court Institute.

Hughes, T., & Wilson, D. J. (2016). *Reentry trends in the U.S.* Bureau of Justice Statistics.

Latessa, E. J., Shaffer, D. K., & Lowenkamp, C. (2002). *Outcome evaluation of Ohio's drug court efforts*. Report submitted to the Ohio Office of Criminal Justice, July 2002.

Lindquist, C., Walters, J. H., Rempel, M., & Carey, S. M. (2013). *The National Institute of Justice's evaluation of second chance act adult reentry courts: program characteristics and preliminary themes from year 1*. US Department of Justice.

Lindquist, C., Hassoun Ayoub, L. H., Dawes, D., Harrison, P. M., Malsch, A. M., Walters, J. H., & Carey, S. M. (2014). *The national institute of justice's evaluation of second chance act adult reentry courts: Staff and client perspectives on reentry courts from year 2*. US Department of Justice.

Lindquist, C., Hassoun Ayoub, L., & Carey, S. M. (2018). *The National Institute of Justice's evaluation of second chance act adult reentry courts: Lessons learned about reentry court program implementation and sustainability*. NPC Research.

Marlowe, D. B., Hardin, C. D., & Fox, C. L. (2016). *Painting the current picture: A national report on drug courts and other problem-solving courts in the United States*. National Drug Court Institute.

Maruna, S. (2020). *Beyond recidivism: New approaches to research on prisoner reentry and reintegration*. NYU Press.

Mitchell O., Wilson D. B., Eggers E., & MacKenzie, D. L. (2012). Assessing the effectiveness of drug courts on recidivism: A meta-analytic review of traditional and non-traditional drug courts. *Journal of Criminal Justice, 40*, 60–71.

Pelletier, E., & Evans, D. (2019). Beyond recidivism. *Journal of Correctional Education, 70*(2), 49–68.

Petersilia, J. (2000). "When Prisoners Return to the Community: Political, Economic, and Social Consequences." In *Sentencing & Corrections, Issues for the 21st*

*Century,* 9 (Bureau Justice Statistics Publication No. NCJ 184253). National Institute of Justice.

Petersilia, J. (2003). *When prisoners come home: Parole and prisoner reentry.* Oxford University Press.

Petersilia, J. (2005). Hard time: Ex-convicts returning home after prison. *Corrections Today,* American Correctional Association.

Picard, S., Watkins, M., Rempel, M., & Kerodal, A. (2019). *Beyond the algorithm: Pretrial reform, risk assessment, and racial fairness.* Center for Court Innovation.

Rafael, S., & Weiman, D. (2007). The Impact of local labor market conditions on the likelihood that parolees return to custody. In *Barriers to Reentry? The Labor Market for Released Prisoners in Post-Industrial America.* Russell Sage Foundation.

Rempel, M., Fox-Kralstein, D., Cissner, A., Cohen, R., Labriola, M., Farole, D., Bader, A., & Magnani, M. (2003). *The New York State adult drug court evaluation: Policies, participants, and impacts.* Center for Court Innovation.

Salvatore, C., Michalsen, V., & Taylor, C. (2020). Reentry court judges: The key to the court. *Journal of Offender Rehabilitation, 59*(4), 198–222.

Serin, R. C., & Lowenkamp, C. (2015). *Selecting and using risk and need assessments.* National Drug Court Institute. National Drug Court Institute.

Sharlein, J. (2018). Beyond recidivism: Investigating comparative educational and employment outcomes for adolescents in the juvenile and criminal justice systems. *Crime & Delinquency, 64*(1), 26–52.

Travis, J. (2005). *But they all come back: Facing the challenges of prisoner reentry.* Urban Institute Press.

Travis J., & Lawrence, S. (2002). *Beyond the prison gates: The state of parole in America.* Urban Institute.

Travis, J., Solomon, A. L., & Waul, M. (2001). *From prison to home: The dimensions and consequences of prisoner reentry.* Urban Institute.

Truitt, L., Rhodes, W. M., Seeherman, A. M., Carrigan, K., & Finn, P. (2000). *Phase I: Case studies and impact evaluations of Escambia County, Florida and Jackson County, Missouri Drug Courts.* Abt Associates.

Vance, S. E. (2011). Federal reentry court programs: A summary of recent evaluations. *Federal Probation, 75*(2), 108–120

Wilson, D., Mitchell, O., & MacKenzie, D. (2006). A systematic review of drug court effects on recidivism. *Journal of Experimental Criminology, 2,* 459–487.

Zil, C., & Carey, S. (2014). *Judicial Council Report to the Legislature: California Parolee Reentry Court Evaluation Report.* Judicial Council of California.

*Chapter 5*

# Creating a Home Base for Treatment in Homeless Courts

Kyle C. Troeger and Anne S. Douds

## INTRODUCTION

Homeless persons' issues dominated public discourse in late 2019 when the U.S. Supreme Court, in *City of Boise v. Martin*, confirmed that the Constitution "prohibits the imposition of criminal penalties for sitting, sleeping, or lying on public property for homeless individuals who cannot obtain shelter" (*City of Boise v. Martin*, 2019, p. 31). Contemporaneously, national dialogue became inflamed when President Trump made remarks disparaging cities such as Los Angeles and San Francisco, for their failure to clear homeless persons from their sidewalks (Stein & Rucker, 2019). Some view homelessness as a social ill or a by-product of untreated mental illness (Torrey, 1998). Others sidestep the origin of the problem and point out that, regardless of why persons are homeless, their presence outside of restaurants and shops discourages patronage and diminishes cities' aesthetics (Iovino, 2020). Still others take a different approach, criticizing laws that outlaw vagrancy, loitering, and sleeping in public as unfair criminalization of conditions beyond the offenders' control that have disproportionate minority impacts (NLCHP, 2019). Pundits continue to offer familiar, conflicting arguments on social and traditional media, with all sides remaining entrenched in their perspectives (Cava, Fritze, & Chandler, 2019; Pollak, 2019).

In response to these arguments and others, many jurisdictions have created specialized courts to deal with the underlying causes of homelessness (Worrall & Nugent-Borakove, 2008). Proponents of these courts claim that they "expand access to justice, reduce court costs, and help the homeless reintegrate into society and lead productive lives" (Stein, 2005). Critics contend that they are another example of judicial overreach into social service domains (Quirouette, 2015). This chapter compares and contrasts court-based strategies and programs that serve homeless populations by reviewing the scholarly literature and other available information on their structures, operations, missions, goals, efficacy, and appropriateness. The chapter concludes with thoughts on the future of these courts and their place in the larger problem-solving court movement.

## HISTORY OF HOMELESSNESS

People have faced housing insecurity and homelessness for longer than societies have existed (Ault & Nevett, 2011). Causes of homelessness throughout history and up to the present include destitution, war, and natural disasters (Jones, 2016). However, the modern history and contemporary approaches to mitigating homelessness reflect broader understandings of interactions among race, mental health, geography, the economy, civil society, and the justice system (NLCHP, 2015), which has led to extensive research on the efficacy of alternative sentencing for homeless, nonviolent offenders.

Proper analysis of the contemporary history of homelessness requires a basic understanding of the economic crises that defined much of the United States in the 1970s and 1980s. Rapid changes in interest rates, inflation, and skyrocketing unemployment rocked society as policymakers and the Federal Reserve responded piecemeal to each crisis (Bryan, 2013). By 1974, inflation had reached 9 percent (The Econ Review, 2013). That same year, due to the OPEC oil embargo, oil reached $11.65 per barrel, up from $2.90/barrel in the previous year (Amadeo, 2020). The collapse of the savings and loans industry, Housing and Urban Development (HUD) budget cuts, deindustrialization of American cities, and the mass deinstitutionalization of asylum patients, all contributed to the homelessness crisis (Wolch, 2007). Deindustrialization consisted of a dying manufacturing sector and the shift toward a service sector economy, which had a role to play in growing poverty. In January 1980, there were 19.3 million manufacturing jobs in the United States. By 2000, two million had disappeared, and by January 2010, there were only 11.5 million jobs (Scott, 2015). Such jobs were the livelihoods and means of social mobility for many Americans. Once the majority of jobs shifted to professions that required an expensive college degree, more people found themselves struggling to survive. Between 1950 and 2000, the percentage of college-educated workers increased from 15 percent to over 60 percent.

During the same period, the wages of college graduates rose from 25 percent more than high school graduates to over 100 percent more than those with only a high school diploma (Buera & Kaboski, 2012). Between 1980 and 1990, the number of Americans receiving public assistance increased from 4.6 percent to 10.1 percent (NCES, 2011). As Americans' savings became devalued by inflation, mortgage originators prioritized short-term profits and pushed many to insolvency (U.S. GAO, 1996). At the same time, changes to the economic landscape made it even harder for the average American worker. Economic inequality within the United States has grown in the past fifty years. Wages and benefits of the working class have fallen since the 1970s, while the top 1 percent own 44 percent of the world's wealth (1 percent own more than the bottom 90 percent) (Hardoon, 2015). Notably, a large percentage of homeless people work, but they are unable to afford housing, medical care, or the cost of participation in the criminal justice system, including the indirect cost of time in court, the employment implications of convictions, lost wages due to incarceration and direct costs associated with fines, penalties, and fees (Binde, 2012; Natapoff, 2014).

Governmental support for housing also evaporated during the latter part of the twentieth century. President Reagan cut Section 8 housing aid shortly after taking office (Shashaty, 1981). In 1976, the public housing program supported 517,000 units. By 1982, the number of units dropped to about 150,000 units (Shashaty, 1981). In 2001 dollars, the 1976 HUD budget was approximately $75 billion; by 1989, it was $18.9 billion on the same scale (Dolbeare, 2001). In 1978, housing subsidies were 7 percent of the federal budget. By the late 1980s, they accounted for only 0.7 percent. In California specifically, the supply of affordable housing (housing costing less than 30 percent of an individual's income) shrunk rapidly, from 35 percent of the total stock in 1974 to 16 percent during the 1980s (Wolch, 2007).

Finally, the deinstitutionalization of persons with mental illness rounded out the trifecta that underlay the growing homeless crises (Ventriglio, Mari, Bellomo, & Bhugra, 2015). Today, between 20 percent and 25 percent of America's homeless have severe mental illnesses. In the general population, only 6 percent suffer similarly (NCH, 2009). This trend dates back to the 1950s. The number of patients in asylums and psychiatric hospitals dropped from 558,239 in 1955, to 71,619 in 1994 (Torrey, 1998). Many of these people wound up in jails and prisons, some for behaviors associated with being homeless (Torrey, 1998). The prison population increased sharply by 216 percent, from 501,886 total inmates in 1980 to 1,587,791 in 1995 (Torrey, 1998). The general population only increased 16 percent during this time (Torrey, 1998). Subsequently, a pipeline developed from state hospitals to the streets, and then jails and prisons. Approximately 50,000 people annually go straight to homeless shelters right after being released from prison (Mitchell, 2018). These numbers reinforce the sentiment that "society has a limited tolerance of mentally disordered behavior" (Lamb, 1984, p. 905). Because of the desire to remove certain disruptive elements from societal view, involuntary hospitalization and treatment wound up replaced by arrest and incarceration as options and social services for persons with mental illnesses dwindled.

Current data paints a grim picture. At the HUD's Point-in-Time count for its Annual Homeless Assessment Report (AHAR) on a single night in January 2019, a total of 567,715 people were homeless in the United States. Of these, 37 percent were without access to shelter (HUD, 2020, p. 8). The overall homeless population since 2016 has increased by 17,787, and the unsheltered population has increased by 34,936 (HUD, 2020, p. 8). In 2019 alone, the unsheltered homeless population increased by 16,826, or 8.7 percent (HUD, 2020, p. 9). In the same year, the number of homeless in major cities increased 13,778 (5 percent) and by 2,332 (7 percent) in other urban areas (HUD, 2020, p. 17).

As the number of homeless persons continues to rise, many traditional governmental responses exacerbate the problem. Most jurisdictions still criminalize homelessness in some fashion. Of the 187 cities surveyed for the 2019 Housing Not Handcuffs report, 72 percent have at least one law restricting camping in public, and 57 percent have one or more laws prohibiting camping in particular public areas (NLCHP, 2019, p. 38). Fifty-one percent have at least one law prohibiting sleeping in public (NLCHP, 2019, p. 41), and 50 percent, or ninety-three cities, have laws restricting living in one's vehicle (NLCHP, 2019, p. 43). Finally, 83 percent of the 187 cities have at least one law restricting begging in public, with 65 percent having one or more laws prohibiting begging in particular public places (NLCHP, 2019, p. 44).

There are some ameliorative initiatives, however. Born of necessity in response to the coronavirus pandemic, local governments are expanding outreach programs, increasing the number of temporary shelters, suspending enforcement of anti-sleeping laws, and increasing housing subsidies to name a few (see, e.g., National Alliance to End Homelessness, 2020). The recent Supreme Court decision in *City of Boise v. Martin* and its progeny bode well for the decriminalization movement, as well. Finally, localities continue to develop homeless and housing courts to respond to myriad housing and related needs. The homeless court movement, the brainchild of Steve Binder and Vietnam veterans in San Diego, offers support to homeless persons and those who hope to help them.

## DEVELOPMENT OF HOMELESS COURT MODEL

Beginning in the late 1970s and partially in response to an alarming rate of homelessness among Vietnam and other veterans, nonprofit and faith-based organizations began developing intervention programs for persons who were homeless (Lewin, 1987). Many of these programs focused exclusively on homeless or at-risk veterans (ABA &NCHV, 2006). These programs flourished and demonstrated some success in reducing homelessness, responding to veterans' mental health needs, and reducing recidivism (Finigan & Carey, 2007).

Building on that knowledge, the first homeless court began in San Diego, California, with the Stand Down Program (ABA & NCHV, 2006). It may have been the first problem-solving court in the United States and the Nation's first collaborative treatment court addressing criminal cases of veterans. The Miami-Dade drug court usually receives recognition as the first problem-solving court (Goldkamp & Weiland, 1993). However, that title should be shared with the Stand Down program that was taking a similar, therapeutic approach on the west coast. Today, at least twenty states have one or more specialty court programs dedicated to serving homeless persons.

## Stand Down and the First Homeless Court

The Stand Down court, so named because military personnel "stands down" when they are in friendly territory and can thus relax, started in 1988 to respond to veterans' needs as observed among founders Robert Van Keuren and Dr. Jon Nachison (ABA & NCHV, 2006; Binder, 2002). Both Vietnam veterans created a three-day tent community with services where homeless veterans could pause their battle with the streets and stand down. At this first gathering, they distributed a Veterans Administration (VA) survey that revealed that for 116 of 500 homeless veterans, their greatest need was to resolve outstanding bench warrants (ABA &NCHV, 2006, p. 5). In response, the San Diego Superior Court set up a court station at the event's next annual meeting in 1989: The court at Stand Down. Within three years, it had resolved 4,895 cases for 942 homeless veterans (ABA & NCHV, 2006, p. 5). In 1990, it expanded its services to battered and homeless women. It broadened its scope again in 1994 to nonveteran residents of the city-sponsored, cold weather shelter. In 1995, it became available to the general homeless population (ABA & NCHV, 2006, p. 12). The need for services far exceeded the capacity of this one court that only met annually. Therefore, with a grant from the Department of Justice's Bureau of Justice Assistance, it commenced quarterly, then monthly, operations (ABA & NCHV, 2006). Today, these occur, on an alternating basis, at a Vietnam Veterans of San Diego location and the St. Vincent de Paul Church (Binder & Horton-Newell, 2013, p. 36; ABA & NCHV, 2006, p. 63).

The court at Stand Down became a model for other cities nationwide. The Board of Governors of the American Bar Association (ABA) promoted its replication (ABA & NCHV, 2006, p. 7). In 1991, the Board of Governors of the ABA established the Commission on Homelessness and Poverty, charged with educating the Bar and public on unique legal impediments faced by homeless persons and poor communities. Today, the ABA encourages courts to adopt its Homeless Court Policy and follow it "to the extent appropriate for each jurisdiction" (ABA & NCHV, 2006, p. 9). Given that, it makes sense that one of its current priorities is the creation of homeless courts.

So just what is the formula for this program's success? How do these courts operate? Moreover, how does the court at Stand Down, and all other homeless courts, measure success? The following summarizes existing data to respond to these queries.

## Court Operations

Homeless court programs usually operate as a partnership among multiple entities. Of the thirty-seven courts investigated for this chapter, twenty-eight are combined public/private ventures. The government oversees the legal and more formal proceedings, and community-based nonprofit organizations provide more personalized services such as AA meetings and job training. The nonprofits are essential to the rehabilitation process as a bridge between homeless persons and the community. They oversee treatment and administer a wide array of services that become the basis for whatever alternative sentences the court might impose. For example, in Maricopa County, Arizona, twenty-seven qualified charities provide homeless transitional care programs such as the Salvation Army and Central Arizona Shelter Services (Boehm, 2019). They encourage participation in the program and advocate for their homeless defendants, like the court in Contra Costa, California, where C.O.R.E. (Coordinated Outreach Referral, Engagement) teams find unsheltered homeless people, assess their needs, and facilitate connection to shelters and services (Weilenman, 2018). Finally, they give people the resources and support they need to comply with court orders. The Orange County court even provides legal aid for civil matters, in addition to vocational training and assistance accessing government benefits (Orange County Public Defender, 2020) (table 5.1).

## Homeless Courts Overview and Key Components

The ABA, which has served as a leading figure in efforts to standardize homeless courts, describes them as court-based programs that "combine a progressive plea bargain system, alternative sentencing structure, assurance of 'no custody,' and proof of program activities, to address a full range of offenses" (ABAb, 2018, p. 1). Participation is voluntary, and court personnel avoid any practices that might appear coercive (ABAa, 2018). These programs operate much like other problem-solving courts: Teams of legal and social service personnel provide wrap-around services to respond to the sequelae of issues that often lead people into homelessness (Cantil-Sakauye & Depner, 2020, p. 12).

**Table 5.1    Homeless Court Client Identification Processes and Goals**

| | Public/Private Partnership | Alternative Sentencing |
|---|---|---|
| Birmingham, AL | Yes | Yes |
| Maricopa County, AZ | Yes | Yes |
| Alameda County, CA | Yes | Yes |
| Contra Costa, CA | Yes | N/A |
| Fresno County, CA | Yes | Yes |
| Los Angeles, CA | Yes | Yes |
| Orange County, CA | Yes | Yes |
| San Bernardino, CA | Yes | N/A |
| San Diego, CA | Yes | Yes |
| San Joaquin, CA | Yes | Yes |
| Sonoma County, CA | Yes | Yes |
| Ventura County, CA | Yes | Yes |
| Denver, CO | Yes | N/A |
| Sarasota, FL | N/A | Yes |
| Atlanta, GA | N/A | N/A |
| Oahu, HI | N/A | Yes |
| Chicago, IL | N/A | N/A |
| Louisville, KY | N/A | N/A |
| New Orleans, LA | Yes | Yes |
| Boston, MA | Yes | Yes |
| Baltimore, MD | Yes | Yes |
| Ann Arbor, MI | Yes | Yes |
| Detroit, MI | Yes | Yes |
| Hennepin County, MN | N/A | Yes |
| Springfield, MO | Yes | N/A |
| St. Joseph City, MO | N/A | Yes |
| Bernalillo County, NM | Yes | Yes |
| Las Vegas, NV | Yes | Yes |
| Charleston, SC | Yes | Yes |
| Columbia, SC | Yes | Yes |
| Florence, SC | N/A | Yes |
| Myrtle Beach, SC | Yes | Yes |
| Spartanburg, SC | Yes | Yes |
| Houston, TX | Yes | Yes |
| Salt Lake City, UT | Yes | N/A |
| Manhattan, NY | N/A | Yes |
| Harlem, NY | Yes | Yes |

*Sources*: Authors.

However, many of the procedures followed by these courts are quite different from other problem-solving courts, as discussed below. The underlying charge is tangential to the program; usually, the criminal charges are dismissed so long as participants conform to expectations (Wilson, 2016, p. 12). According to the ABA, all legal matters are typically handled in just one hearing, and over 90 percent of participants see their charges dismissed (ABAa, 2018, p. 1).

Homeless courts have not adopted the ten Key Components of drug courts, veterans courts, and other problem-solving courts. Instead, in 2006, the ABA promulgated standards for these courts and endorsed them as an effective means to mitigating homelessness and related problems (ABAb, 2018). The standards are as follows:

• Prosecutors, defense counsel, and the court should agree on which offenses may be resolved in the Homeless Court Program, and approve the criteria for individual participation, recognizing that defendant participation in Homeless Court Programs shall be voluntary.
• Community-based service providers should establish criteria for individual participation in the Homeless Court Program and screen individuals pursuant to these criteria.
• The Homeless Court Program shall not require defendants to waive any protections afforded by due process of law.
• All Homeless Court Program participants shall have time for meaningful review of the cases and issues prior to disposition.
• The Homeless Court Program process and any disposition therein should recognize homeless participants' voluntary efforts to improve their lives and move from the streets toward self-sufficiency, including participation in community-based treatment or services.
• Participation in community-based treatment or services shall replace traditional sanctions such as fines, public work service and custody.
• Defendants who have completed appropriate treatment or services prior to appearing before the Homeless Court shall have minor charges dismissed, and, where appropriate, may have more serious misdemeanor charges before the court reduced or dismissed. Where charges are dismissed, public access to the record should be limited.

(ABA(a), 2018, p. 1). Notably, these guiding principles emphasize voluntariness; they do not require any particular treatments. The participants bear a great deal of responsibility for seeking treatment and demonstrating to the court that they accomplished and documented certain program activities as they move from the streets to self-sufficiency. Homeless courts empower participants to work with program staff, make the most of services, and extricate themselves from the streets. The traditional court modality of conviction defining the problem and sentencing solving the problem with fines, public work service and custody, does not address the underlying cause(s) of homelessness. The service providers and participants work to address individuals' needs to overcome the condition of homelessness, to lead a healthy, law abiding life.

It appears that most homeless courts roughly follow these guidelines. Some courts, such as the one in Bernalillo County, New Mexico, actually cite the

ABA's seven guiding principles. Many seek to replicate the original court in San Diego. Chief Municipal Judge Dana Turner in Columbia, South Carolina, formed the state's first homeless court in 2014 after visiting the original court in San Diego and became convinced of its effectiveness (LeBlanc, 2014). The court in Springfield, Missouri, also was modeled after the one in San Diego (Rehwald, 2015). Many more broadly follow the recipe of working with community partners, requiring informed consent, promoting self-sufficiency, and alternative sentencing.

## Service Partnerships

Like most problem-solving courts, homeless courts leverage interagency partnerships or community working groups to provide a panoply of services for homeless persons (Pope-Sussman, 2015). However, service provision is less centralized than in other specialized courts, and much of the onus of crafting treatment plans fall to shelter workers and the homeless people themselves (Buenaventura, 2018, p. 3). In other problem-solving courts, formal channels for referrals and streamlined social service plans make the courts the center of control for clients' cases. Homeless courts disperse operations across multiple organizations and multiple geographic locations. They usually establish "entry criteria," the goals and objectives that participants will accomplish before they are referred to homeless courts. Service providers share these criteria with all the collaborative partners. Practitioners recognize that homeless service agencies often specialize in certain populations (e.g., veterans, women, youth, mental health, workforce development) and that homeless individuals present different needs, traumas, and conditions for services. Accordingly, they specialize and tailor their services.

Once service providers identify homeless persons' needs, they usually create individualized action plans detailing exactly what the homeless person must do to successfully complete the program (Farole, et al, 2005, p. 63). Service providers document proof of the individuals' accomplishments in letters, certificates, and meeting slips. For example, the Downtown Austin (Texas) Community Court, which deploys community court officers with police into the streets to identify homeless people to educate those living in the streets about the availability of services through the courts and their partners (Pope-Sussman, 2015). As another example, New York's Midtown Community Court offers offenders opportunities to confer with social service counselors before arraignment. During intake, the counselors screen for housing insecurity and arrange for community-based support as appropriate (Pope-Sussman, 2015).

The same is true for actual court proceedings, which often occur in community locations rather than courthouses. For instance, the San Diego

Homeless Court Program conducts hearings at local homeless service agency facilities to meet participants where they can capitalize on the trust these agencies develop with participants to the court and to signal that these providers' services address and solve the myriad of problems that lead to homelessness. At least one study demonstrates that the San Diego program improves homeless persons' perception of procedural justice and increases their likelihood of attending court hearings (Burke, 2001; Gonsalves, 2020).

Similarly, the Denver, Colorado, homeless court sessions previously were held at City Hall. Transportation to City Hall was challenging for many homeless people for financial and logistical reasons (McGhee, 2017). Many homeless people depended on the Denver Rescue Mission for basic needs like food, water, and shelter, and they were visiting the Rescue Mission frequently, and sometimes daily (McGhee, 2017). Therefore, to serve their specific demographic better, they began holding sessions at the Rescue Mission, a nonprofit, Christian organization. It made a big difference in the court's ability to handle cases. In 2015, the homeless court at City Hall handled 131 cases. By January 18, 2017, four sessions (eight weeks) after its creation, the outreach court at the Mission had already heard seventy-eight. The court soon began operating exclusively at the Mission, with previous cases transferred. The familiar setting, less intimidating atmosphere, and decreased transportation cost all increased the likelihood that homeless persons will show up on their court date. Furthermore, the charity itself, with workers whom homeless people know and trust, could encourage participation and assuage fears of being arrested. Thus, community-based court sessions appeared to respond to concerns about homeless persons' failure to appear for court sessions or mandated appointments (Brand-Williams, 2018).

## Eligibility

All homeless courts accept homeless people who face at least one nonviolent, misdemeanor charge. However, other than that baseline for eligibility, other criteria vary broadly among courts. Eligibility most often hinges on the type of offense. Homeless persons typically face misdemeanor charges for violations of ordinances against panhandling, trespassing, sleeping, urinating, loitering, eating, or bathing in public (Almodovar & McNally, 2007), and most of the homeless courts limit their jurisdiction to these types of offenses (Hennick, 2017). Twenty out of thirty-seven explicitly exclude violent offenses (table 5.2). Most also require demonstrable willingness on the part of the homeless person to improve their psychosocial health. For example, the Maricopa County Regional Homeless Court in Arizona accepts only nonviolent homeless offenders who are expressly trying to secure income (employment or benefits),

**Table 5.2   Homeless Court Utilization of Public/Private Partnerships and Alternative Sentencing**

|  | Inception | Eligibility |
|---|---|---|
| Birmingham, AL | N/A | Homeless and convicted of a minor violation/misdemeanor |
| Maricopa County, AZ | 2006 | Defendant must be homeless, lack serious offenses, be trying to secure income, and enrolled in a program with a qualified provider. They must also be in regular contact with their case manager. |
| Alameda County, CA | 2004 | Homeless with minor, nonviolent offenses. |
| Contra Costa, CA | N/A | 90 days of satisfactory participation in a self-help program and referral by case manager. |
| Fresno County, CA | 2002 | Homeless with only minor offenses, and be clean and sober for 60 days. |
| Los Angeles, CA | 2006 | Homeless, and must not have any open felony cases or outstanding warrants in felony/misdemeanor matters. |
| Orange County, CA | 2008 | Homeless with a low-level misdemeanor or outstanding warrant. |
| San Bernardino, CA | 2017 | Homeless with no worse than a misdemeanor. |
| San Diego, CA | 1989 | Full range of misdemeanor offenses. |
| San Joaquin, CA | 2006 | Homeless with minor traffic or moral offenses. As well as fines and bench warrants. |
| Sonoma County, CA | 2016 | Homeless and cited with infractions. |
| Ventura County, CA | N/A | Homeless and has already completed community service. |
| Denver, CO | 2005 | N/A |
| Sarasota, FL | 2019 | Homeless and charged with a minor offense. |
| Atlanta, GA | 2019 | N/A |
| Oahu, HI | 2017 | Homeless with nonviolent, low level offenses. |
| Chicago, IL | 2017 | Homeless and charged with a minor offense. |
| Louisville, KY | 2018 | N/A |
| New Orleans, LA | 2010 | N/A |
| Boston, MA | 2011 | Homeless with a misdemeanor or nonviolent felony. Warrant must be in state |
| Baltimore, MD | 2013 | Homeless with an outstanding warrant or nonviolent misdemeanor. |
| Ann Arbor, MI | N/A | Defendant must be homeless, have civil infractions or a nonviolent misdemeanor, and consent to a voluntary action plan. |
| Detroit, MI | 2012 | N/A |
| Hennepin County, MN | 2013 | Homeless with no more than a misdemeanor. |
| Springfield, MO | 2010 | N/A |

*(Continued)*

**Table 5.2   Homeless Court Utilization of Public/Private Partnerships and Alternative Sentencing** (*Continued*)

|  | Inception | Eligibility |
|---|---|---|
| St. Joseph City, MO | 2018 | Homeless and not convicted of violent crimes. |
| Bernalillo County, NM | N/A | Determined by community advocates. |
| Las Vegas, NV | N/A | Low-level misdemeanor cases. |
| Charleston, SC | 2015 | Homeless and cooperative with a personalized program. |
| Columbia, SC | 2014 | Homeless with a victimless misdemeanor offense. |
| Florence, SC | 2019 | Determined by the office of the 12th Circuit Solicitor. |
| Myrtle Beach, SC | 2019 | N/A |
| Spartanburg, SC | 2019 | 7th Circuit Solicitor's Office determines what qualifies. No worse than a nonviolent offense with a penalty of 30 days in jail. |
| Houston, TX | 2006 | Homeless with a class C misdemeanor. |
| Salt Lake City, UT | N/A | N/A |
| Manhattan, NY | 1993 | Homeless with not more than a low-level offense. |
| Harlem, NY | N/A | N/A |

*Sources:* Authors.

enroll in a program with a qualified social services provider (e.g., mental health and substance abuse), and have regular contact with their case managers.

These requirements are not so different from other problem-solving courts. In homeless courts, the homeless person usually must arrange for satisfaction of the prerequisites before going to court (Kerry & Pennell, 2001, p. 18). The Santa Monica, California, court focuses on "vulnerable, chronically homeless individuals who have been in Santa Monica for several years (generally, five or more) and who have had multiple contacts with the criminal justice system arising from their homeless status" (Buenaventura, 2018, p. 5). In sum, eligibility criteria are court-dependent and established by the individual court's task force or team (Cantil-Sakauye & Depner, 2020, p. 14).

## Screening

Before or upon acceptance into the program, most homeless courts either screen participants for mental health and substance use needs and risk of violence or self-harm. Some courts conduct the screenings in house, while many, like the Bernalillo County Metropolitan homeless court in New Mexico, rely upon external community partners (Hennick, 2017). These screenings serve two purposes: either to (1) establish what the homeless persons' needs are and help them identify service providers, or (2) to "screen" to see if the homeless person has complied with prior service planning as a precondition to attending the "pure discharge" hearing.

The former type of screening often occurs in courts that follow a therapeutic jurisprudence model and the latter in the courts that are more focused on community justice (Buenaventura, 2018). As an example of the latter, Boston's Homeless Court requires that potential clients must prove that they have completed all substance abuse, mental health treatment, and job training programs as recommended by their homeless shelters (SAMHSA, 2020). This approach contradicts the federally endorsed Housing First policy, under which homeless and housing insecure persons first receive housing assistance so that they literally and proverbially have a "home base" from which to pursue social and job services (NAEH, 2020). It is an interesting twist on the homeless court approach. As the District Attorney for the Boston Homeless Court explained, they "already have to be on track to self-sufficiency" before they can even be considered for the judicially monitored program (SAMHSA, 2020). The San Diego Homeless Court and many others recognize federal Housing First programs and related state-level initiatives and accept referrals from them (Binder & Wechter, 2020). Homeless persons work with their program to establish a documented list of accomplishments for their referral to Homeless Court. This does not preclude access to housing or utilization of other programs (Binder & Wechter, 2020).

## Formal Court Proceedings

Compared to community, drug, and veterans courts, homeless courts are a bit more informal and often involve much less formal court contact. Many homeless courts conduct business in shelters or community centers, not courtrooms, and they often follow the "pure dismissal" model that is quite different from other problem-solving courts' approaches (Binder & Horton-Newell, 2013; Center for Families, Children, and the Courts, 2020; Pope-Sussman, 2015). In a typical court that follows this model:

> Defendants are referred to the court by an application process completed by a social service agency. Sponsoring agencies to complete an action plan with defendants, outlining treatment recommendations, and resources promoting community self-sufficiency. If the defendant complies with this action plan, court fines and fees are waived, and the defendant is not taken into custody. The court promotes recovery and a pathway out of homelessness through self-sufficiency and improving the quality of life of homeless persons. (Hennick, 2017, p. 38, describing Ann Arbor, Michigan's Street Outreach Court)

Exceptions exist. The Santa Monica, California, court follows a more traditional therapeutic jurisprudence approach under which participants regularly meet with court personnel to ensure compliance with treatment protocols and other obligations (Buenaventura, 2018, p. 15). The court may meet weekly, biweekly, or monthly (Brand-Williams, 2018; Buenaventura, 2018, p. 2; Rehwald, 2015), which suggests a high case clearance rate considering that the majority of these courts hold only one hearing for each case.

The "pure dismissal" model suffers from criticism for its lack of oversight or involvement in the rehabilitation process (Buenaventura, 2018, p. 14). First, critics who prefer the Santa Monica model described earlier in the chapter raise due process concerns: If courts leave programming and oversight to private partners, inconsistencies can arise, from court to court and from case to case, in what participants need to do to earn dismissal of their charges (Buenaventura, 2018, p. 28). Also, such extensive, out-of-court involvement of private entities may jeopardize client privacy. By bringing in organizations such as the New Directions shelter in Myrtle Beach, South Carolina (WMBF News Staff, 2019), or Pine Street Inn in Boston, Massachusetts (Baskin, 2020), municipalities are banking on private citizens to preserve clients' confidential personal and legal information. While these nonprofits are still bound by HIPAA rules (45 CFR Part 160), the very collection of such data can be seen as a risk by those already wary of the criminal justice system. It is worth mentioning, however, that the San Diego Homeless Court has never had a breach of security in its more than thirty years of hearings at Stand Down or monthly hearings (Binder & Wechter, 2020).

Most recently, homeless individuals have been concerned about the new policy of temperature checks due to coronavirus. If they appear ill, they may be diverted to other "dedicated shelters" full of sick people (Baskin, 2020), which appears to be discouraging homeless people from using the shelters. This last point is not a critique so much as an observation. Coronavirus complicates homeless persons' ability, or inclination, to comply with the plans that are prerequisites to having their charges dismissed. Accordingly, courts need to be more flexible during this perilous public health crisis, particularly when the one-and-done model gives homeless people only one chance to appear in court and prove that they deserve to have their charges dismissed.

On the other hand, the pure dismissal model might suit jurisdictions concerned about costs, judicial overreach, and politics behind social services for homeless persons (Coyle & Ellis, 2019). No studies have examined the relative costs of homeless courts versus other problem-solving courts. However, it makes sense that homeless courts cost less to run than other types of specialized courts because of the back-end approach and heavy reliance upon nonprofit organizations. Veterans courts, drug courts, human trafficking courts, and others hold periodic team meetings and periodic formal court proceedings, for months, and sometimes years (see, e.g., Douds & Ahlin, 2018; Farole, Puffett, Rempel, & Byrne, 2005, p. 64).

For example, Dauphin County, Pennsylvania, veterans court teams, which, on average, include nine criminal justice professionals, meet weekly at 10:00 am on Fridays for at least an hour. Then they hold formal court for some portion of the veterans in their program. Court often runs into the afternoon, meaning that veterans court consumes at least half of every Friday. Evidence indicates that this program effectively reduces recidivism among its veteran clients and improves veterans' quality of life (Richards, 2017). The community accepts the cost as necessary to rehabilitating its veterans. However, more cost-averse communities might prefer more low-profile judicial involvement. Of the thirty-seven courts investigated for this chapter, six courts list saving money as a program goal (table 5.3). By ceding some outreach, oversight, rehabilitation management, and specialized client work to nonprofits, they save tax money. This approach may make homeless courts more viable and incentivize their use (NCHV, 2006, p. 14).

Intensive problem-solving court programs, with their court-run mentoring programs and court-based social services coordinators, also receive criticism for alleged usurpation of the traditional roles of courts (Thompson, 2002, p. 65). Critics contend that courts should not concern themselves so heavily with offender rehabilitation and should leave social service provision to the private sector (Hodulik, 2001, p. 1074).

Finally, courts that provide alternatives for offenders sometimes incite political pushback from segments of society that tend to blame offenders for their criminogenic problems. The majority of the public support problem-solving courts in theory (Thielo et al., 2019), but critics object to subsets of offenders receiving special treatment (McCormick-Goodhart, 2013, p. 920). In communities with less of an appetite for funding criminal justice reform, or in areas where it is not politically palatable to run judicially based programs for special populations, the homeless court "pure dismissal" model might pass political muster in light of its low cost and relatively low profile involvement with oversight and monitoring of homeless persons' rehabilitation (Coyle, 2019).

## Sentencing and Rehabilitation

Under the ABA model adopted by most homeless courts, homeless persons are sentenced under a "credit for time served model" in which participants engage in activities at their homeless shelters instead of incarceration, community service, or fines. "These activities include life-skills, chemical dependency or AA/NA meetings, computer and literacy classes, training or searching for employment, medical care (physical and mental), counseling,

**Table 5.3   Homeless Court Inception and Client Eligibility Standards**

| | Client Identification | Goals |
|---|---|---|
| Birmingham, AL | N/A | Transition back into society, address root causes |
| Maricopa County, AZ | NGO providers encourage participation. | Help those that want to help themselves transition from being homeless. |
| Alameda County, CA | Good candidates are identified through a consortium of local service providers. | Address legal barriers confronting the homeless. |
| Contra Costa, CA | Referral by case manager. | Clearing of fines. |
| Fresno County, CA | Referral by civil society. | Improving access to justice for the homeless. |
| Los Angeles, CA | Those who qualify can fill out a form. | Help homeless resolve legal barriers to self-sufficiency. |
| Orange County, CA | N/A | Resolve low-level legal impediments and provide homeless people with links to crucial services. |
| San Bernardino, CA | Local shelters and advocates refer participants who need to resolve cases, settle fines, restore benefits, or have a block on license lifted. | N/A |
| San Diego, CA | Participants sign up through their local homeless service agency. | Address underlying causes of homelessness and recognize defendant's efforts to improve their life. |
| San Joaquin, CA | People can sign up at any homeless shelter in San Joaquin. | N/A |
| Sonoma County, CA | N/A | Remove hurdles that keep people from finding permanent housing. |
| Ventura County, CA | Referral by social service agency case worker. | Reduce recidivism and build trust in justice system, as well as reducing court and jail costs. |
| Denver, CO | N/A | Be more humane and save money. |
| Sarasota, FL | N/A | Address root causes of chronic homelessness. |
| Atlanta, GA | N/A | N/A |
| Oahu, HI | N/A | Help those unable to stop committing "quality of life offenses." Also to reduce court congestion. |
| Chicago, IL | N/A | N/A |
| Louisville, KY | N/A | N/A |
| New Orleans, LA | A homeless court coordinator filters viable participants forwarded by shelter directors. | Remove legal impediments to employment and housing. |

*(Continued)*

**Table 5.3   Homeless Court Inception and Client Eligibility Standards** (*Continued*)

| | Client Identification | Goals |
|---|---|---|
| Boston, MA | N/A | Address root causes of homelessness. |
| Baltimore, MD | Participants volunteer to get on the DHP (docket for homeless persons). | Address root causes of homelessness, and save money. |
| Ann Arbor, MI | N/A | Address root causes of homelessness. |
| Detroit, MI | N/A | Save money, clear dockets, and address root causes. |
| Hennepin County, MN | N/A | Assist defendant in securing housing, as well as saving money on jail expenses. |
| Springfield, MO | Referral from probation/police officer, municipal court judge, prosecuting attorney, or homeless service agency. | Secure housing, benefits, and employment for participants. |
| St. Joseph City, MO | Referral by either law enforcement, the prosecutor, or their social worker. | Help client gain stability. |
| Bernalillo County, NM | Homeless people receiving services from charities can be referred if they have misdemeanors. | Address root causes, and help homeless people develop self-sufficiency. |
| Las Vegas, NV | N/A | Improving personal circumstances and reducing risk of re-offending. |
| Charleston, SC | Referral by judge or prosecutor. | N/A |
| Columbia, SC | Homeless defendants are screened by a team. | Link repeat offenders with services to help them become self-sufficient. |
| Florence, SC | N/A | Treat and rehabilitate qualified homeless participants. |
| Myrtle Beach, SC | N/A | N/A |
| Spartanburg, SC | Applications can be sent to the Public Defender or 7th Circuit Solicitor. | Encourage participants to receive and complete treatment and rehab programs. |
| Houston, TX | Participants request the service from a local homeless service provider. | Reintegration into society, as well as saving money. |
| Salt Lake City, UT | N/A | N/A |
| Manhattan, NY | N/A | Reduce crime and incarceration, improve public trust in justice, and seek sentences that are restorative to the victim, defendant, and community. |

*(Continued)*

Table 5.3   Homeless Court Inception and Client Eligibility Standards (Continued)

| | Client Identification | Goals |
|---|---|---|
| Harlem, NY | N/A | Help youth minimize contact with the justice system. Reduce recidivism, and help those released from prison reenter society on stable footing. |

Source: Authors.

and volunteer work" (ABAc, 2018, p. 1). Twenty-nine of the thirty-seven homeless courts currently in operation employ alternative sentencing. However, sentencing practices in these courts are far from standardized. The model calls for waiver of fines and community service, but many jurisdictions still impose some traditional sanctions. In Florida, at least one county requires homeless persons to perform community service but "pays" them $10.00 per hour as an offset against their fines and penalties (see Almodovar & McNally, 2007, for discussion).

Interestingly, the ABA insists that homeless courts "are not coercive or punitive in nature" (ABAc, 2018). However, that optimistic assessment ignores literature suggesting that all problem-solving courts implicitly involve some degree of coercion. Perhaps the real issue is whether the benefit of receiving services and avoiding criminal charges outweigh the due process cost of coercion. It is also worth comparing such a program to the traditional justice system, which is arguably far more coercive.

Ultimately, homeless courts primarily pursue rehabilitative processes with the end goal of reintegrating participants into society. Of the thirty-seven homeless courts studied, ten expressly seek to address the root causes of a defendant's homelessness, and twelve state that their goal is to promote clients' self-sufficiency and transition to housing security from homelessness (table 5.3).

## Outcomes and Impacts

Ostensibly, all homeless court programs, regardless of whether they explicate the goal, uplift homeless people. But do they achieve their goals? Evidence suggests that they do. In a 2000 San Diego study, researchers interviewed homeless court participants on a variety of measures. Their study, which enjoyed a 61 percent voluntary participation rate, found that the experience in the homeless court improved participants' "overall satisfaction with the court process" (97 percent) (Kerry & Pennell, 2001, p. 53). Almost all participants also responded positively to all seven metrics of satisfaction with court personnel. Also, 75 percent said that the experience had reduced their fear of police (Kerry & Pennell, 2001, p. 53). A plurality of participants was more likely to seek permanent housing (46 percent); apply for a job (38 percent); and apply for a driver's license (39 percent) (Kerry & Pennell, 2001, p. 54). However, the program did not reduce the number of "no shows" for court appearances long term. When the court began operations, 76 percent of participants appeared for their scheduled court dates. However, within months, that rate dropped to just over 50 percent (Pennell & Kerry, 2001).

Drop-offs in successful outcomes also occurred in a Pinellas County, Florida, Homeless Outreach Program. They reported 100 percent compliance with program requirements among participants in its early years. However, a subsequent study revealed a 21 percent noncompliance rate (Almodovar & McNally, 2007, p. 201). It is difficult to interpret whether 79 percent compliance indicates a successful program without comparison data, but on its face, the numbers would indicate a successful program.

More recently, Buenaventura employed propensity scoring to analyze housing usage changes among homeless court participants in Santa Monica, California. Over a 24-month follow-up period, she observed "an increase of 123.7 days in permanent housing usage and an increase of 43.3 days in transitional housing usage by graduates" (Buenaventura, 2018, p. iii). Notably, the same court has only a 61 percent graduation rate (Buenaventura, 2018, p. 6). A handful of studies that look at outcomes in homeless courts provide a promising foundation upon which to build future studies.

## CRITICAL EVALUATION AND POLICY RECOMMENDATIONS

Critical consideration must be given to all problem-solving courts, regardless of the population or problem they seek to serve. Homeless courts, in particular, have not enjoyed much scholarly attention, and the time is ripe to examine them more closely (Naito, 2019). Privacy, due process, equity, and cost-benefit concerns all deserve continued discussion. There also are valid concerns about judicial overreach and net-widening, or undue expansion of the criminal justice system's reach (Quirouette, 2015). However, there are a few challenges unique to homeless courts that can and should be addressed as more jurisdictions move toward using this court model. First, these courts rely heavily upon community partners to identify potential participants. Anecdotal evidence indicates that these community partners may receive training on how to identify potential clients, but there is no standardization within or among states. A national organization should consider developing and sharing education and training programs for organizations that may work with homeless courts on unconscious biases, appropriate communication techniques, information sharing, and personal safety. The development of such a standard should refer to the San Diego Homeless Service Provider Toolkit and Homeless Service Provider Network, which were designed to address these issues and ongoing concerns.

Community partners not only identify participants; they also screen them for needs and compliance. Needs assessments are well within the skill sets of many community organizations. They often employ well-established protocols and evidence-based tools to screen for mental health and substance abuse needs. Those scientific approaches should be encouraged through a national advisory body, and courts should document how community partners are screening and what techniques they use. Compliance monitoring presents more challenges. Courts that intervene at the end of the rehabilitative process (those that are "pure dismissal" or some hybridized version thereof) do not issue any orders until after a period of monitoring by community partners. So, there are no judicially documented expectations. Compliance monitoring falls to the community partners, who have varying degrees of knowledge and experience. Participants do not necessarily interact with the same community partners, and they are not subject to the same standards for compliance, giving rise to equity issues. There also are more significant opportunities for prejudice and bias to infiltrate highly decentralized compliance monitoring systems across multiple organizations. Homeless courts could adopt a checklist of expectations for compliance, and legal organizations (e.g., bar associations) could provide education on best practices for compliance monitoring.

Communication challenges plague all organizations. The dispersed nature of homeless court partnerships exacerbates those challenges. Likewise, with any public-private partnership, misunderstandings arise about stakeholders' respective roles and their scope of responsibilities. Homeless court programs that are court-based or prosecutor-based may help avoid one common pitfall in which homeless shelters promise "legal assistance" rather than "assistance with criminal charges." In at least one court, homeless shelters advertised free legal assistance, which led to a flood of requests at legal aid societies that were not equipped to respond to the demand (Almodovar & McNally, 2007). Stakeholders can manage these types of problems through training, frequent reviews of procedures, and better communication.

Homeless courts also have been criticized for being a Band-Aid on a bullet wound, too little treatment, and minimally responsive to the complex problem of homelessness. Homelessness reflects a "wider structural, systemic, and sociopolitical problem" (Quirouette, 2015). The same could apply to any of the problems that specialized courts seek to redress. Addiction, veterans' challenges with reintegration into society, domestic violence, among others, all reflect much larger social ills. Homeless courts are not a panacea, but they are a viable approach.

## CONCLUSION

The National Law Center on Homelessness and Poverty defines the criminalization of homelessness as the "punishing of life sustaining conduct" (NLCHP, 2019, p. 37) for those without a home. This is a recognition that the homeless suffer disproportionately from certain laws. It is harder for them to remain innocent of aptly named quality-of-life offenses consisting of nonviolent misdemeanors and minor offenses like public intoxication and trespassing. The criminal record that can be gained simply by having no other place to be makes it harder for them to secure housing, a job, government benefits, and more. This antagonistic approach impedes the success of and disenfranchises a struggling populace whose primary offense is arguably destitution. Homeless courts are an experimental alternative. They allow nonviolent misdemeanors to be resolved without jail time or fines through a collaboration of public and private institutions. In lieu of traditional sentencing, participants receive credit for time served for completing assigned activities. These usually consist of either community service or taking measurable steps toward self-sufficiency. The latter can take many forms such as AA meetings, job training, literacy classes, seeking employment, and more. This eliminates a huge barrier to the upward mobility of the homeless while at the same time promoting self-sufficiency. Participants do not need money, or time in jail, to pay their debt to society. If they demonstrate commitment to making permanent lifestyle changes toward ending their homelessness (and the offense(s) entailed), then they are offered a hand to help them do just that. That said, issues regarding privacy and judicial overreach still exist.

## REFERENCES

American Bar Association (a). (2018). About homeless courts. Retrieved from https ://www.americanbar.org/groups/public_interest/homelessness_poverty/initiatives/ homeless-courts/about-homeless-courts/

American Bar Association (b). (2018). Homeless courts facts & best practices. Retrieved from https://www.americanbar.org/content/dam/aba/administrative/h omelessness_poverty/homeless-courts/hlc-best-practices.pdf#

American Bar Association (c). (2018). Sentencing structure. Retrieved from https:// www.americanbar.org/groups/public_interest/homelessness_poverty/initiatives/h omeless-courts/sentencing_structure/

ABA & NCHV. (2006). Taking the court to stand down. Retrieved from http://www
.nchv.org/images/uploads/HCP_Stand_Down_Training_Book1_final.pdf.

Almodovar, L. A., & McNally, S. S. (2007). Are you worried about going to jail? The public defender's Office Homeless Outreach Program. *Stetson Law Review, 36,* 183–205.

Amadeo, K. (2020). The truth about the 1973 Arab oil crisis. Retrieved from https://
www.thebalance.com/opec-oil-embargo-causes-and-effects-of-the-crisis-3305806

Ault, B. A., & Nevett, L. C. (2011). *Ancient Greek houses and households chrono-
logical, regional, and social diversity.* University of Pennsylvania Press.

Baskin, K. (2020, April 2). How the Pine Street Inn feeds Boston's frightened homeless. *Boston Globe.* Retrieved from https://www.bostonglobe.com/2020/04/02/l
ifestyle/how-pine-street-inn-feeds-bostons-frightened-homeless/

Binder, S. (2002). The Homeless Court Program: Taking the Court to the Streets.
*Federal Probation, 65*(1), 14–17.

Binder, S., & Horton-Newell, A. (2013). Returning home to homelessness; San
Diego's Homeless Court Program models ways to help. *Experience, 23*(3), p. 36.

Binder, S., & Wechter, M. (2020, July 9). Homeless courts: Recognizing progress
and resolving legal issues that often accompany homelessness (United States,
Interagency Council on Homelessness, USICH). Retrieved from https://www
.usich.gov/news/homeless-courts-recognizing-progress-and-resolving-legal-issues
-that-often-accompany-homelessness

Boehm, J. (2019, May 8). There are 6,614 people experiencing homelessness in
Maricopa County. Here's how to help. *The Republic.* Retrieved from https://ww
w.azcentral.com/story/news/local/phoenix/2019/05/08/homelessness-rising-pho
enix-maricopa-county-how-help/1126862001/

Brand-Williams, O. (2018, March 13). 'Homeless Court' provides second chance.
Retrieved from https://www.chicagolawbulletin.com/archives/2018/03/13/homel
ess-court-3-13-18

Bryan, Michael. "The Great Inflation." *Federal Reserve History*, 22 Nov. 2013, www
.federalreservehistory.org/essays/great_inflation

Buenaventura, M. (2018). Treatment not custody: Process and impact evaluation of
the Santa Monica homeless community court (Unpublished doctoral dissertation).
*Pardee RAND Graduate School.* Retrieved from https://www.rand.org/pubs/rgs_
dissertations/RGSD418.html

Buera, F., & Kaboski, J. (2012). The rise of the service economy. *American Economic
Review, 102*(6), 2540–2569.

Burke, C. (2001). *SANDAG 2001 Report, San Diego Homeless Court Program: A
process and impact evaluation.* San Diego Association of Governments.

Cantil-Sakauye, T. G., & Depner, C. (2020, January). Homeless and community
court blueprint (United States, Judicial Council of California, Center for Families,
Children & the Courts). Retrieved from https://www.courts.ca.gov/documents/
homeless-community-court-blueprint.pdf

Cava, M., Fritze, J., & Chandler, M. (2019, September 11). Trump officials look
to fix California homeless problem, state officials say back off. Retrieved from
https://www.usatoday.com/story/news/nation/2019/09/10/trump-attacks-california
-homeless-crisis-picking-new-fight-state/2279231001/

Coyle, D. J., & Ellis, R. J. (2019). *Politics, policy, and culture*. Routledge.

Dolbeare, C. N. (2001). *Changing priorities: The federal budget and housing assistance, 1976–2002*. National Low Income Housing Coalition.

Douds, A. S., & Ahlin, E. M. (2018). *The veterans treatment court movement: Striving to serve those who served*. Routledge.

Farole, D. J., Jr., Puffett, N., Rempel, M., & Byrne, F. (2005). Applying problem-solving principles in mainstream courts: Lessons for state courts. *Justice System Journal, 26*(1), 57–75.

Finigan, M. W., & Carey, S. M. (2007, April). *Impact of a mature drug court over 10 years of operation: Recidivism and costs (Final Report)*. Retrieved, from https://www.ncjrs.gov/pdffiles1/nij/grants/219225.pdf

Goldkamp, J. S., & Weiland, D. (1993). *Assessing the impact of Dade County's felony drug court*. Washington, DC: Crime and Justice Research Institute. Retrieved from https://www.ncjrs.gov/pdffiles1/nij/145302.pdf

Gonsalves, J. J. (2020). *The progression of California's collaborative courts* (Doctoral dissertation, California State University, Sacramento).

Hardoon, D. (2015, January 19). Wealth: Having it all and wanting more. Retrieved from https://policy-practice.oxfam.org.uk/publications/wealth-having-it-all-and-wanting-more-338125

Hennick, E. E. (2017). *The Homeless Court in Salt Lake City, Utah: Access to justice and mercy for a disenfranchised population* (Unpublished doctoral dissertation, The University of Utah.)

Henry, M., Watt, R., Mahathey, A., Ouellette, J., & Sitler, A. (2020, January). *The 2019 Annual Homeless Assessment Report (AHAR) to Congress (United States, Housing and Urban Development, Office of Community Planning and Development)*. Retrieved from https://files.hudexchange.info/resources/documents/2019-AHAR-Part-1.pdf

Hodulik, J. (2001). Drug court model as a response to broken windows criminal justice for the homeless mentally ill. *Journal of Criminal Law and Criminology, 91*(4), 1073–1100.

Iovino, N. (2020, May 28). Residents sue to block homeless camp in San Francisco's Haight Ashbury. Retrieved from https://www.courthousenews.com/residents-sue-to-block-homeless-camp-in-san-franciscos-haight-ashbury/

Jones, S. (2016, May 10). Homeless at home: Most displaced people found in Syria, Yemen and Iraq. *The Guardian*. Retrieved from https://www.theguardian.com/global-development/2016/may/11/homeless-at-home-most-displaced-people-found-in-syria-yemen-and-iraq

Kerry, N., & Pennell, S. (2001). *San Diego Homeless Court Program: A process and impact evaluation* (United States, San Diego, CA, San Diego Association of Governments).

Lamb, H. R. (1984). Deinstitutionalization and the homeless mentally ill. *Hospital & Community Psychiatry, 35*(9), 899–907.

LeBlanc, C. (2014, October 5). Columbia set to open S.C.'s first Homeless Court. Retrieved, from https://www.thestate.com/news/local/article13894424.html

Lewin, T. (1987, December 30). Nation's Homeless Veterans Battle a New Foe: Defeatism. *The New York Times*. Retrieved from https://www.nytimes.com/1987/1 2/30/us/nation-s-homeless-veterans-battle-a-new-foe-defeatism.html

McCormick-Goodhart, M. A. (2013). Leaving no veteran behind: Policies and perspectives on Combat Trauma, Veterans Courts, and the Rehabilitative Approach to Criminal Behavior. *Penn State Law Review, 117,* 895–926.

McGhee, T. (2017, April 27). New homeless Outreach Court meets people where they are—At Denver Rescue Mission. Retrieved from https://www.denverpost.com/201 7/01/27/homeless-outreach-court-denver-rescue-mission/.

Mitchell, M. (2018, March 29). Homelessness and Incarceration Are Intimately Linked. New Federal Funding is Available to Reduce the Harm of Both. [Web log post]. Retrieved from https://endhomelessness.org/homelessness-incarceration-intimately-linked-new-federal-funding-available-reduce-harm/

NAEH. (2020). State of Homelessness: 2020 Edition (Publication). Retrieved from https://endhomelessness.org/homelessness-in-america/homelessness-statistics/stat e-of-homelessness-2020/

Naito, M. E. (2019). The future of drug, homeless, and veterans courts. *The Lower Criminal Courts*, Chapter 14: 141–152.

Natapoff, A. (2014). Gideon's servants and the criminalization of Poverty. *Ohio State Journal of Criminal Law, 12,* 445.

National Center for Education Statistics. (NCES). "Youth Indicators 2011; America. Retrieved from http://nces.ed.gov/pubs2012/2012026/tables/table_32.asp.

NCH. (2009, July). Mental Illness and Homelessness (Publication). Retrieved from https://www.nationalhomeless.org/factsheets/Mental_Illness.pdf

NLCHP. (2015, January). Homelessness in America: Overview of data and causes. Retrieved from https://nlchp.org/wp-content/uploads/2018/10/Homeless_Stats_ Fact_Sheet.pdf

NLCHP. (2019, December). Housing Not Handcuffs 2019. Retrieved from http://nlc hp.org/wp-content/uploads/2019/12/HOUSING-NOT-HANDCUFFS-2019-FINA L.pdf.

Orange County Public Defender. (2020). http://www.pubdef.ocgov.com/programs/ homeless_outreach_court.htm

Pollak, J. B. (2019, December 26). Trump slams Gavin Newsom over homelessness in Christmas Tweet. Retrieved from https://www.breitbart.com/politics/2019/12/25 /trump-slams-gavin-newsom-over-homelessness-in-christmas-tweet/

Pope-Sussman, R. (2015). *Responding to homelessness: 11 ideas for the justice system.* Center for Court Innovation.

Quirouette, M., Hannah-Moffat, K., & Maurutto, P. (2016). 'A precarious place': Housing and clients of specialized courts. *British Journal of Criminology, 56*(2), 370–388.

Rehwald, J. (2015, July 12). Homeless Court success stories graduate. Retrieved from https://www.news-leader.com/story/news/local/ozarks/2015/07/11/springf ield-homeless-court-programs-first-success-stories-graduate/30037135/.

Richards, A. (2017, May 02). Institutions that work: Dauphin County veterans court. Retrieved from https://www.abc27.com/news/institutions-that-work-dauphin-co unty-veterans-court/

SAMHSA. (2020, April 30). *Boston's Homeless Court provides legal assistance.* United States, Department of Health and Human Services, Substance Abuse and Mental Health Services Administration.

Scott, R. E. Manufacturing job loss: Trade, not productivity, is the culprit. *Economic Policy Institute.* Retrieved from www.epi.org/publication/manufacturing-job-loss -trade-not-productivity-is-the-culprit.

Shashaty, A. (1981, October 18). U.S. cuts back and shifts course on housing aid. Retrieved from https://www.nytimes.com/1981/10/18/realestate/us-cuts-back-and -shifts-course-on-housing-aid.html

Stein, J., & Rucker, P. (2019, September 18). Trump: Homeless people hurt the 'prestige' of Los Angeles, San Francisco. Retrieved from https://www.washingtonpos t.com/politics/trump-homeless-people-hurt-the-prestige-of-los-angeles-san-franci sco/2019/09/17/71e71b9e-d982-11e9-ac63-3016711543fe_story.html

Stein, R. A. (2005, July 28). Paving the way for justice. Retrieved from https://www .abajournal.com/magazine/article/paving_the_way_for_justice

The Econ Review. (2013). President Nixon imposes wage and price controls. Retrieved from www.econreview.com/events/wageprice1971b.htm.

Thielo, A. J., Cullen, F. T., Burton, A. L., Moon, M. M., & Burton, Jr, V. S. (2019). Prisons or problem-solving: Does the public support specialty courts?. *Victims & Offenders, 14*(3), 267–282.

Thompson, A. C. (2002). Courting disorder: Some thoughts on community courts. *Washington University Journal of Law and Policy, 10,* 63-100.

Torrey, E. F. (1998). *Out of the shadows: Confronting America's mental illness crisis.* Wiley.

U.S. General Accounting Office. (1996). *Resolution Trust Corporation's 1995 and 1994 Financial Statements.* Author.

Weilenman, D. (2018, May 23). CORE teams striving to help homeless in Martinez. *Martinez News-Gazette.* Retrieved from https://martinezgazette.com/core-teams-s triving-to-help-homeless-in-martinez/

Wilson, A. (2016). A new beginning for Milwaukee's Homeless: Addressing homelessness through the homeless court system. *International Journal of Therapeutic Jurisprudence.* Retrieved from https://papers.ssrn.com/sol3/papers.cfm?abstract_i d=2742902

WMBF News Staff. (2019, March 13). Myrtle Beach homeless court gives second chance to those in need. Retrieved from https://www.wmbfnews.com/2019/03/13/ myrtle-beach-homeless-court-gives-second-chance-those-need/

Wolch, J. et al. (2007). *Ending homelessness in Los Angeles.* Inter-University Consortium Against Homelessness.

Worrall, J. L., & Nugent-Borakove, M. E. (2008). *The changing role of the American prosecutor.* State University of New York Press.

Ventriglio, A., Mari, M., Bellomo, A., & Bhugra, D. (2015). Homelessness and mental health: A challenge. *International Journal of Social Psychiatry, 61*(7), 621–622.

## Section II

# COURTS BASED ON INDIVIDUAL CHARACTERISTICS

Criminogenic needs were the initial impetus behind problem-solving courts. The problem-solving court movement evolved such that new courts addressing demographic similarities developed. These courts catapulted onto the problem-solving court scene by embracing the concept of therapeutic jurisprudence promoted by drug courts. However, they lack a clear connection to any specific or cluster of criminogenic or therapeutic needs. These courts instead created separate court dockets by focusing on a common demographic characteristic of justice-involved individuals.

Demographics include characteristics such as age, neighborhood, employment status, disability, individuals who were previously incarcerated, race, and ethnicity. Some of these defining attributes lend themselves to a natural extension of drug courts and other criminogenic problem-solving courts. For example, teen courts—an age-based court—address criminal offenses committed by young persons. This unifying factor brings together similarly situated youth who are adjudicated by their peers. Reentry courts are another form of problem-solving court based on a demographic characteristic. These courts strictly work with a demographic of people recently released from jail or prison. They aim is to support offender reintegration after a completed carceral sentence. The common demographic characteristic is the reason participants in these courts are grouped for case processing.

One interesting aspect of these courts is how they appear, on the surface, to focus on one or more demographic features common to participants. However, people are complex, and they often require a holistic approach when involved in the criminal justice system. The courts examined in Section II of this book appear to unite participants based on offender characteristics. This birds-eye view overshadows the courts' incorporation of treatments and other social services to meet participants' criminogenic needs. It is this overlap between criminogenic courts and those courts that highlight common individual characteristics where the original drug court model begins to branch out beyond the original intent of specialty courts.

Chapter 6, "Juvenile Dependency Courts: Goals and Challenges of the Adoption and Safe Families Act of 1997," is written by Mitra Z. Honardoost and Eileen M. Ahlin. This problem-solving court focuses on ensuring permanent housing situations for children whose parents are involved in the criminal justice system. Their discussion focuses on the Adoption and Safe Families Act (ASFA) policy surrounding permanency decisions and the pressure to place a child as quickly as possible. Expediency helps provide children with stability. However, the ASFA policy provides for the termination of parental rights for children who have been in out-of-home care for fifteen of the last twenty-two months. Their chapter thoughtfully considers whether this timeframe is reasonable for substance-using parents, the most common reason for removing children from their homes.

In chapter 7, "Community Courts: Restoring the Community One Case at a Time," Tyrell Connor methodically outlines the reasons behind community courts' development. Readers will note that these courts handle cases that are committed by a range of offenders. Their common feature is the location of participants' crimes. Connor describes how community courts seek to make whole the community, which was aggrieved by the criminal offense. These courts' focus is not changing criminal behavior by addressing criminogenic needs (like the courts described in Section I). However, many of them provide access to social services such as substance abuse treatment and housing support.

In chapter 8, "A Trifecta of Challenges for Veterans Treatment Courts," Jared A. Michaels and Anne S. Douds highlight essential questions about how these courts are meeting intended goals. They focus on three elements of veterans treatment courts that suggest before more courts are created, there is a need to pause and reflect on their implementation. This chapter acknowledges as important and presently unclear in current practice, the rights and roles of victims in the veterans treatment court process; what mentoring programs should entail and how they should operate for participants and the court; and the lack of data to support the effectiveness of problem-solving courts.

In chapter 9, "Tribal Healing to Wellness Courts," Elyshia D. Aseltine and Joan Lobo Antunes examine how problem-solving courts are applied in Native American communities. Such wellness courts, as they are typically called, approach treatment holistically by embracing cultural traditions that emphasize the communal nature of native populations. The individual participant needs are not the only focus in these courts; it is also understood that spiritual and cultural practices are essential to the well-being of the tribal community. The authors expertly describe how this adherence to traditional practices is not adopted readily by all community members suggesting that wellness courts may struggle to achieve their goals while representing the diversity inherent in first nations.

Section II describes some of the problem-solving court models built on commonalities among persons involved in the criminal justice system. These demographic or trait characteristics are not the only reason participants in these courts are brought together. However, there are enough similarities to suggest between the subgroup of participants and sufficient differences from the problem-solving courts based purely on criminogenic needs to drive a new formula in these alternatives to traditional court case processing and correctional options. The chapters in this section clearly identify a need to better understand how courts premised on offender characteristics differ from criminogenic based problem-solving courts. Is it culture? Is it a shared experience? At the same time, it is essential to understand what components in these court models are the same. The best example of congruence is treatment. If some type of treatment is provided to all problem-solving court participants, the differences become much more important when trying to justify the different models.

*Chapter 6*

# Juvenile Dependency Courts

## *Goals and Challenges of the Adoption and Safe Families Act of 1997*

Mitra Z. Honardoost and Eileen M. Ahlin

## INTRODUCTION

When parents become involved in the criminal justice system, they often encounter the child welfare system where parental custody may become an issue. To address custody issues among justice-involved adults, there are more than 300 juvenile dependency courts operating across the United States (Children and Families Futures, 2015). These specialty courts handle adult court cases involving children who were removed from their homes due to parental neglect or abuse. As a type of problem-solving court, juvenile dependency courts combine judicial supervision and frequent court contact with needed alcohol and drug therapies, mental health care, and other social services. Juvenile dependency courts are a more focused version of family wellness courts and family drug courts, which emphasize parental counseling and treatment as well as parenting skills training, though the labeling of such courts is often muddled. While juvenile dependency courts aim to provide social support services to parents involved with the criminal justice system, their main goal focuses on child welfare by supporting safe and permanent placement through reunification with parents or adoption. Some children never achieve reunification or adoption. They may remain in kinship care with a relative until they are an adult or stay in foster care. Child custody is equally, if not more, prominent than the needs of the justice-involved parents, as any amount of time spent outside of permanent custody placement can be detrimental to child development. Therefore, dependency courts prioritize and expedite permanent placement.

  In this chapter, we discuss the federal government's efforts through the Adoption and Safe Families Act (ASFA) of 1997 to expedite child custody and stability through parent-child reunification or adoption among families in juvenile dependency courts. We begin by highlighting alcohol and drug use as common factors associated with out-of-home placements and describe the court process when a child welfare case comes to the court's attention. Next, we examine the emergence and intentions behind the ASFA and what challenges this initiative places on parents striving to achieve sobriety and regain custody of their children. In conclusion, we focus on key themes that emerge as juvenile dependency courts push to achieve two competing goals.

## JUVENILE DEPENDENCY COURT PROCESS

The juvenile dependency court process begins with formal allegations of child maltreatment, including all forms of child abuse and neglect. These courts handle four main types of abuse: physical, sexual, neglect, and emotional. Anything considered non-accidental physical injury caused to a child by the child's parents or legal guardian is physical abuse. This can include shaking, slapping, punching, beating, kicking, burning, or biting. Acts including, touching, fondling, and penetration fall into the sexual abuse category. Failure by caretakers to provide for children's basic needs is considered neglect. This would include inattention to anything from the child's housing, food, clothing, medical, and educational needs. Emotional abuse, which is often the most difficult abuse to identify, includes verbal harassment of a child, shaming, threat, and ridicule (Ventrell, 1998).

Using Pennsylvania as a case study, we outline how a family comes to the attention of the juvenile dependency court system following a report of child abuse and neglect. Identification of cases usually begins with reports to state-level intake services, followed by referral to county-level social service offices where investigations are initiated. Private citizens may report suspected child abuse through ChildLine, a state-run hotline, and mandated reporters must report suspected child abuse to the state, through a report to their designated representative or a call to ChildLine, in accordance with their institutions' or organizations' policies (Child Protective Services Law, 1975; Kenny et al., 2017). Child-serving professionals such as schoolteachers and health care professionals, among others, typically are mandated reporters (Child Protective Services Law, 1975).

### Agency-Level Procedures

Once an agency receives a report, it makes an initial assessment and categorizes either as possibly indicating either a need for general protective services (GPS) for cases that do not appear to involve abuse or child protective services (CPS) for cases possibly involving child abuse, as seen in

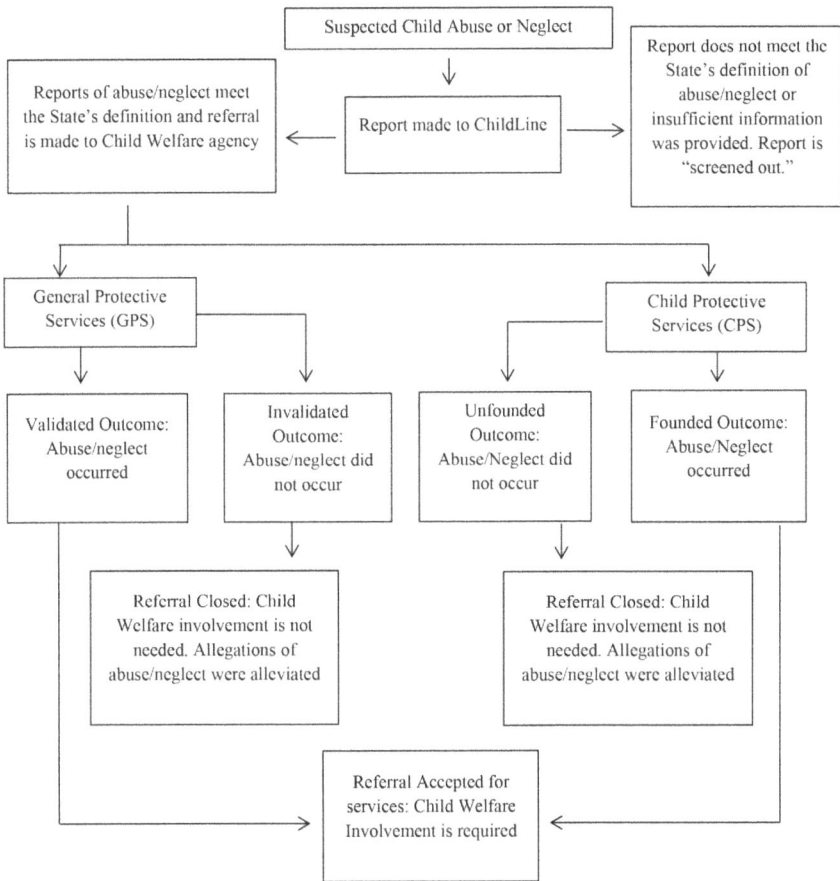

**Figure 6.1    Child Welfare Process for a Referral.** *Source*: Created by authors based on Dependency Court procedures in York County, Pennsylvania.

figure 6.1. Examples of GPS include, but are not limited to, truancy, child behavioral problems, and drug usage by parents or children (see, e.g., Mifflin County, 2020). This initial determination may change as the investigation progresses. CPS are generally more serious and can include sexual, physical, and emotional abuse reports. Once child welfare agencies receive reports of child maltreatment and decide whether to pursue it as a GPS or CPS case, caseworkers investigate the allegations (55 PA. Code CHS. 3480 and 3490; 29 Pa.B. 3513). Ultimately, and usually within a few days, caseworkers determine whether a case is "founded" or validated or "unfounded" or not validated (23 PA Code 6337).

"Unfounded" means that the report did not have enough substantiation to warrant further inquiry or was found to be untrue. Unfounded cases do not receive any further action, but the case is kept on file. If the case is founded, then the caseworker must decide whether the family should receive services. If a case is accepted for services, caseworkers next must decide whether it is possible to keep the child within their home or if an emergency petition to remove the child from the home should be filed (§§ 3130.61; 3130.67; Barth, 1996). If a child is placed under emergency custody of the state, the family automatically receives services, and the matter moves into the courts for an emergency hearing. Figure 6.1 displays a detailed outline of the child welfare process in Pennsylvania, highlighting what occurs from the point of report to social services until the case is either accepted or not accepted for services.

Following the initial determination about services, the case transfers to one of two departments within the child welfare agency as seen in figure 6.2. If the child goes into out-of-home care (e.g., foster care), the case moves to the reunification and permanency unit. In this unit, the child welfare caseworker attempts to reunify the child with their parents, if and when appropriate. If a child remains in the home of their parents, under protective supervision, the case moves to the family preservation unit. The child welfare caseworker within the unit must provide services to the family to assure the safety of the child within the care of their parents. If it is determined that the child is no longer safe within the home, the child welfare caseworker petitions the courts for placement into out-of-home care.

Under federal mandate, child welfare agencies must offer and provide services to families before removing a child from the home (Sagatun-Edwards & Saylor, 2000) except in the case of emergency placement into foster care. If services are not helpful or if the family denies services, with or without court supervision, the child is at higher risk of being placed outside of the home. There are often instances when a child can only be protected if removed from the custody of the parents and placed elsewhere. Out-of-home care is often referred to as foster care, a term used to refer to kinship, non-kinship, group homes, shelters, detention centers, and residential treatment facilities (Barth, 1996).

## Court Involvement

An emergency placement hearing must be scheduled within seventy-two hours of removing children from their homes (23 Pa. § 6315(d)). All parties receive notice of this hearing, and the hearing officer determines whether longer-term out-of-home placement is necessary. The court also decides whether the agency made reasonable efforts to avoid out-of-home placements, and this issue may be raised again at the adjudication hearing (Hardin, 1996). "Reasonable efforts" to prevent out-of-home placement could include

Child is placed in Out-of-home Care and case is passed to the Permanency and Reunification Unit (ASFA Begins)

Periodic Court Hearings are held to Review family's progress:

Shelter Care Hearings - Occur within 72 hrs of when a child is placed into care to assure agency made reasonable efforts to prevent placement.

*Adjudication of Dependency Hearings: Held once when a Child is noted to be without proper parental care or control and supervision is needed by the courts to assure safety. Child can be in out-of-home placement or under protective supervision

* Permanency Review/Case Review Hearings: Occurs every 6 months of the adjudication of dependency hearing. Child can be in out-of-home placement or under protective supervision

*Status Hearings: Held every three months after the most recent Permanency or Case Review

Referral Accepted for services: Child Welfare Involvement is required

Safety Plan is created to assure safety of child and to prevent placement of child in out-of-home care

Safety Plan Hearing is held to assure family entered plan willingly

Safety Plan is valid for 60 days. At or prior to the 60 days, ending Child Welfare Agency determines if child may remain at home, or if placement of child is needed.

If safety plan is violated at any time during the 60 days, the child is automatically placed in out-of-home care.

Termination of Parental Rights

Adoption

Other

Guardianship transferred

Case closed due to alleviated concerns

Child remains at home in the care of their parents and the case is passed to the Family Preservation Unit

Services are court ordered for the family under protective supervision and periodic court reviews are held*

Case closed due to alleviated concerns

Child placed into out-of-home care due to ongoing concerns of abuse/neglect

Child is reunified home

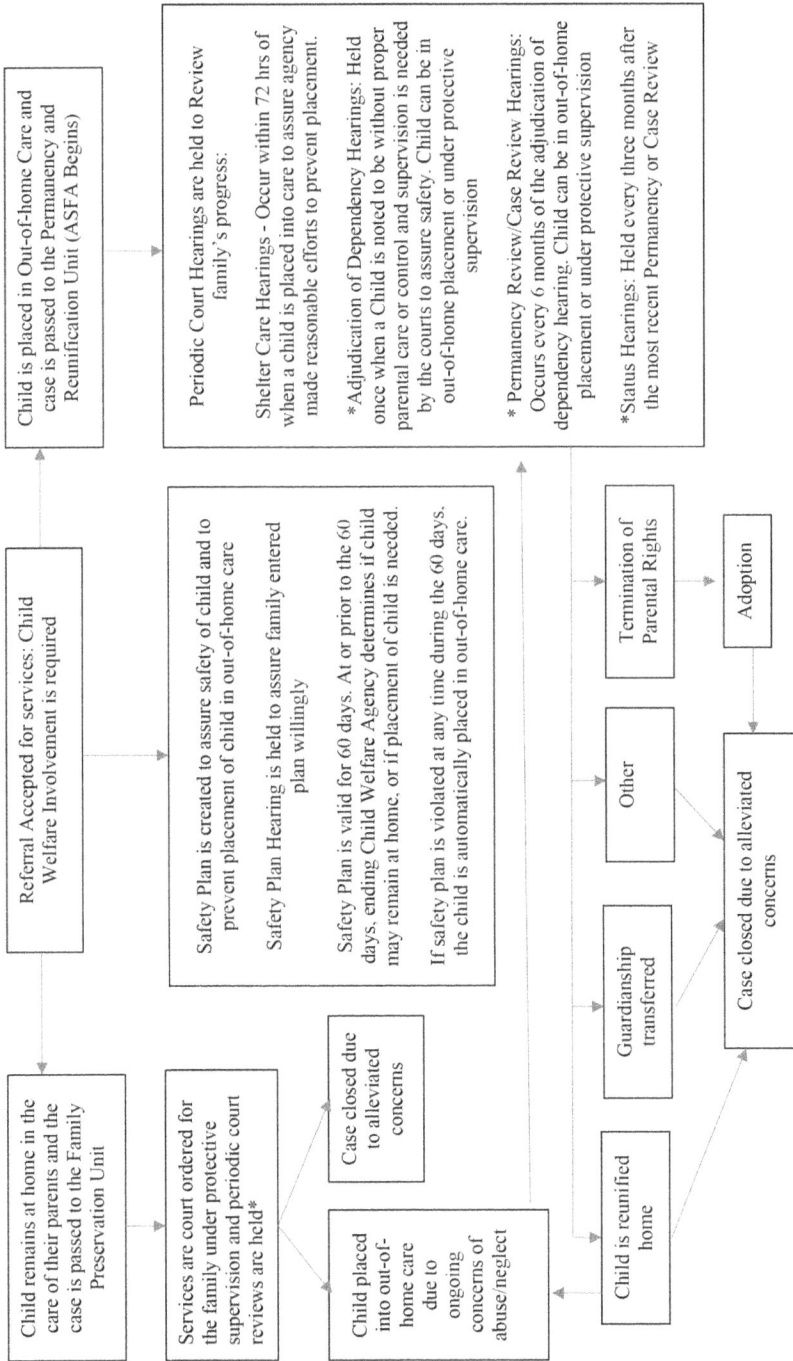

**Figure 6.2 Child Welfare Process for an Accepted Case.** *Source:* Created by authors based on Dependency Court procedures in York County, Pennsylvania.

removing the abuser from the home or safety planning with the family (Cons. Stat. Tit. 23, § 6373; Tit. 42, § 6351).

If the child remains in the home, the court may hold a safety plan hearing instead of an emergency hearing. The safety plan hearing does not have to occur within seventy-two hours, but the courts attempt to schedule them as quickly as possible. Cases frequently go this way when parents voluntarily allow the child to reside elsewhere or when a parent removes the alleged perpetrator from the home.

Next, there is an adjudication hearing to determine whether the child is "dependent" and who should have custody of the child. A dependent child is defined as one who is without proper parental support or care and is in the custody of the state (42 Pa.C.S. Chapter 63; Ventrell, 1998). Courts hold periodic reviews to monitor families' progress in receiving appropriate child placement and referral to appropriate services. Hearing officers hold disposition hearings every three months, and judges conduct six-month reviews (Hardin, 1996). Figure 6.2 outlines what happens once a family is accepted for services.

## PARENTAL SUBSTANCE USE AND OUT-OF-HOME PLACEMENTS DURING JUVENILE DEPENDENCY COURT PROCESS

Juvenile dependency courts determine whether children should be removed from their homes while their justice-involved parent receives social services (Hardin, 1996). Children may be placed in out-of-home care for a variety of reasons, including parent substance abuse, parent or child mental health issues, parent incarceration, and lack of overall family stability (Lloyd, Akin, & Brook, 2017; Nicholson, 2006). The most common reason for out-of-home placement is parental substance use. Many cases of child maltreatment in the United States involve parental substance use and estimates vary. Eleven to 14 percent of cases investigated through child welfare, 18–24 percent of cases substantiated through child welfare, 24–56 percent of family preservation cases in child welfare, and 50–79 percent of foster care cases involve parental substance abuse (Chuang, Moore, Barrett, & Young, 2012; Testa & Smith, 2009). According to Young (2016), the percentage of children placed into foster care due to parental substance use rose from 22.1 percent in 2009 to 29.7 percent in 2014; a larger escalation than any other factor contributing to out-of-home placement. Clearly, parental substance use substantially impacts likelihood of contact with social services, more so than any other concern, and it continues to grow in prominence.

Youth removed from their homes due to parental substance use implicates secondary risks. Children involved within the juvenile dependency court system, who also have a parent with a substance use disorder, are at higher risk of experiencing extended time in out-of-home placements, recurrent involvement with both the child welfare and juvenile dependency court systems, and lower rates of family reunification (He, Traube, & Young, 2014). There are also long-term adverse consequences. For example, children raised by substance using caregivers run a higher risk of perpetrating child abuse and neglect against their own children compared to those who are raised in families without substance use disorders (Sagatun-Edwards & Saylor, 2000).

Out-of-home placements can also negatively impact early childhood development. Children begin to form attachments with their parents from birth, and these bonds increase in strength over time (Bowlby, 1982; Woolgar, 2020). Separating children from their parents and placing them into foster care can contribute to poor mental health for the children (Lowenthal, 1999; McWey & Mullis, 2004). Children may feel that they have lost a part of themselves when separated from their parents (Littner, 1975). This is damaging to their self-esteem and to their ability to relate to others (Littner, 1975). Bowlby (1982) asserted that children who experience the loss of an attachment figure will exhibit distress even if the attachment figure is replaced with a capable caretaker. Whether the attachment is secure or insecure, separation will likely be distressing and anxiety-provoking (Howe, Brandon, Hinings, & Schofield, 1999). This distress can manifest in problematic behaviors, such as aggression, delinquency, and depression (Kaplan, Pelcovitz, & Labruna, 1999).

Roberts (2002) stressed that disruption of the parent-child relationship could cause youth to feel like they are being disloyal to their parents. Even if the parent-child relationship is not entirely positive, some scholars contend that continued contact allows youth to have a more realistic view of their parents (Fahlberg, 2012), and can help to preserve family relationships (Hess, 1987; Hess & Proch, 1988). For families involved with social services systems, children's removal from home does not necessarily represent a clear-cut and final exit from the family, possibly resulting in a high degree of boundary ambiguity. In fact, Jones and Kruk (2005) found many children in foster care reported they do not feel like they are part of any family. This ambiguity can lead to feelings such as hopelessness and depression (Boss, 2004).

Due to these potential negative consequences, courts consider their decisions on removing children from their homes very seriously. Once the court decides that children must be removed, courts must make another weighty decision on where to place children. Choices are on a continuum, ranging from the least restrictive setting and becoming more restrictive depending on risk levels within the family situation. Foster care with an emergency caretaker is the least restrictive setting for a child placed in out-of-home care. Foster care can include residing with relatives, which is known as kinship foster care, or with nonrelative foster parents. Placement into a shelter/detention center is the next least restrictive out-of-home placement followed by group homes. A residential treatment facility is the most restrictive setting for out-of-home placement.


## PERMANENCY DECISIONS AFTER JUVENILE DEPENDENCY COURT PROCESS COMPLETED

### Family Reunification

If the court finds it necessary to remove the child from the home, then another legal matter arises. Eventually, the court must make a permanency decision regarding parental rights and custody. Juvenile dependency courts strive to achieve permanent placement as quickly as possible, and they prefer reunification with the family whenever possible. Akin (2011) determined that overall, reunification with parent is the most common permanency outcome. The decision to reunify a child with their biological parent(s), or to pursue alternative permanency options, is a major decision as it can affect the lives of children and their families (Jedwab, Chatterjee, & Shaw, 2018).

Reunification of a child with his or her parents typically occurs once juvenile dependency courts determine it is appropriate and safe to do so, and the court relies upon input from child welfare agencies. Reunification is measured by a parent's progress during periodically held juvenile dependency court hearings. For a child to be reunified to their biological parents, the parents must convince the courts that they have made enough progress with their goals and that the risk for neglect or abuse has been lowered substantially. Parents must comply with state-mandated child welfare policies. These policies include allowing the child welfare agency to conduct both announced and unannounced visits to the home. Home visits are used to assure that the family continues to reside in a home that is fit for a child. Inspectors check for stable electricity, running water, and proper/appropriate sleeping arrangements. Parents must maintain communication with child welfare agencies and notify the child welfare caseworker of any sudden change in household member, phone number, or address. A parent's failure to cooperate with child welfare policies can negatively impact the chances of reunification. In addition, a parent must provide proof of stable housing and income and show interest in wanting reunification by participating in visitations on a regular basis. It would be contrary to the child's best interest if the child were to return home prior to successful completion or progress in goals.

Prospects of reunification may also be negatively affected when families are economically disadvantaged (Thomlison, Maluccio, & Abramczyk, 1996; Westat, 1995), when a child is from a one-parent family (McDonald, Poertner, & Jennings, 2007; Rockhill, Green, & Furrer, 2007), or when a parent has a drug or alcohol problem (Brook & McDonald, 2007; Fein & Staff, 1993; Harris, 1999; Mapp & Steinberg, 2007; Shaw, 2006; Wade, Biehal, Farrelly, & Sinclair, 2010). A child's reunification can also depend on the reason why children were placed into out-of-home care in the first place.

Parental behavior once a child enters out-of-home placement can also negatively or positively impact reunification (Bullock, Little, & Millham, 1993). Quick access and use of services by parents are a major component of successful reunification (Cheng & Li, 2012; Murphy & Fairtlough, 2015). Foster children are much more likely to achieve permanency when their families receive services that match their actual family needs (Cheng, 2010). Targeted services might include housing and cash assistance (Cheng & Li, 2012), substance abuse treatment (Choi & Ryan, 2007), mental health counseling (Marsh, Ryan, Choi, & Testa, 2006), in-home child welfare services (Lee, Jonson-Reid, & Drake, 2012), and frequent home visits to the parent's home by the child welfare caseworker (Talbot, 2008). Regularly held visits between the child and their parents can also increase the chances of reunification, as it improves relationships and helps monitor the parent's progress (Carnochan Rizik-Baer, & Austin, 2013; Chambers, Brocato, Fatemi, & Rodriguez, 2016; Fanshel & Shinn, 1978; Perkins, 1997).

## Out-of-Home Permanency and Termination of Parental Rights

Family reunification is the preferred permanency outcome, though it is not common for a subset of youth. Just as parental substance use is the most common reason for out-of-home placement, it is also the leading factor associated with the termination of parental rights in juvenile dependency courts. Substance abuse–related problems are often combined with mental health issues, poor physical health, poverty, and a general lack of resources and human capital. This constellation of unfavorable circumstances and a general lack of sufficient housing, dearth of money, lack of treatment options, and single-parenting in conjunction with parent substance use often inhibits good parenting and custody termination may be the best option for the family (see also Lopez, del Valle, Monstserrate, & Bravo, 2013). When reunification fails and parental rights are terminated, there are several permanency options available. Prior work by Wattenberg, Kelley, and Kim (2001) identified four permanency options: kinship adoption, nonrelative adoption, long-term family foster care (for children who are still in placement), and transfer of legal custody/legal guardianship.

All juvenile dependency court cases must follow the same child welfare policies, and parental substance abuse cases must also adhere to additional requirements to ensure successful reunification of the family. For cases involving parent substance abuse, a parent must show that they have remained substance free, for a consistent period, by providing random drug tests. Courts require proof of commitment to drug and alcohol counseling, rehabilitation or any additional drug and alcohol services. In parental substance abuse cases, failure to obtain any drug and alcohol evaluations and failure to follow through with recommendations provided by drug and alcohol evaluations (i.e., individual and group counseling) may also lead to children remaining in out-of-home placement for extended periods or even permanently. A parent's refusal to submit to random drug tests may also be viewed as suspicious, and drug-positive specimens may further extend the length of time children remain in out-of-home placements.

Permanency options for young children removed from their parents' custody due to parental drug use often take two different trajectories. First, children aged ten and younger are more likely to be adopted than older children, leading juvenile dependency courts to have a higher sense of comfort in terminating parental rights among families with younger children (Akin, 2011; Connell, Katz, Staunders, & Tebes, 2006). The second trajectory suggests younger children removed from their parents due to parental drug use are less likely to return home, and, if they do return home, they do so more slowly (Green, Rockhill, & Burrus, 2008; Green, Rockhill, & Furrer, 2007). Work by Green and colleagues (2007, 2008) indicates that being older and placement outside of the home via juvenile dependent courts due to parental alcohol use were significant predictors of number of days in out-of-home placement. For every year increase in age, a youth was 5 percent less likely to receive a permanency outcome (e.g., reunification, adoption) during the three-year study period. Youth in out-of-home placements via juvenile dependency court because of their parent's alcohol and drug use were 33 percent times less likely to receive a permanent care placement. Interestingly, the chances of parent-child reunification were significantly less likely if the child was placed in out-of-home care due to parental substance use alone and was not related to parental drug use.

To examine how parental substance use impedes permanency, Lloyd, Akin, and Brook (2017) asked three main questions. Firstly, do young children ages zero to three with parental drug removals exit foster care to reunification at different rates as compared to older children with parental drug removals and to other younger children without parental drug removals? Secondly, do young children ages zero to three with parental drug removals exit foster care to adoption at different rates compared to older children with parental drug removals and to other young children without parental drug removals? And, thirdly, do young children ages zero to three with parental drug removals exit foster care to guardianship at different rates as compared to older children with parental drug removals and to other young children without parental drug removals? Using administrative child welfare data from a Midwestern state over a ten-year period, Lloyd et al. (2017) showed that parental drug use was a barrier to parent-child reunification. However, the effects of parental drug use on permanency exits such as adoption and guardianship were mixed.

## THE DEVELOPMENT OF ADOPTION
## AND SAFE FAMILIES ACT

Children are often in limbo during the juvenile dependency court process, and the outcome has great implications on their lives. As such, these courts emphasize speedy permanency decisions. The ASFA of 1997 corrected prior legislation in order to increase timeliness of permanency decisions. Before ASFA, the Adoption and Assistance and Child Welfare Act of the 1980 emphasized placing the child with their own parents to avoid the need for out-of-home placements. ASFA amended the Adoption and Assistance and Child Welfare Act and shifted the emphasis of juvenile dependency courts from family reunification to the child's overall safety and well-being. As such, ASFA decreases the length of time children spend in out-of-home placements, prevents possible future abuse from biological parents by promoting adoptions, and promotes timely permanency outcome decisions. ASFA also requires states to exercise reasonable efforts to avoid placement of a child out of the care of their parents.

ASFA requires that both the courts and the child welfare agency develop a permanency goal for children who are removed from their parents. Permanency goals can include reunification back with parents, adoption, or independent living. A permanency plan is developed and used as a roadmap for all parties involved to ensure the success of the permanency goal. The court reviews the permanency plan at a permanency hearing within twelve months of out-of-home placement. If the court determines little progress has been made toward the permanency goals, it can change the goal from reunification to adoption.

In 1998, just after ASFA passed, the termination of parental rights rate was 10.7 percent, which increased to 16.2 percent a decade later. This increase in parental rights termination arises from the ASFA requirement that juvenile dependency courts move to terminate parental rights for children who have been in out-of-home care for fifteen out of the past twenty-two months. This fifteen-month deadline encourages child welfare agencies to work efficiently to find alternative permanency options for a child before reunification efforts fail. This directive also leaves parents as few as 15 months to demonstrate that they are substantially improving the conditions that led to the removal of their child.

Scholars have identified that the sobriety process is not always the easiest or quickest when struggling with a substance abuse addiction. Harris-McKoy, Meyer, McWey, and Henderson (2014) suggest that ASFA's shortened time emphasis may be of significant concern for parents struggling with substance abuse, impacting most of the juvenile dependency court cases. Parents often seek drugs to escape reality, and when they become ready to fight their addiction, they encounter difficulties along the way (Hannett, 2007). Access to and compliance with treatment may be affected by several factors such as insurance approvals, lack of treatment facilities and resources, and poverty, (Harris-McKoy et al., 2014). Parents with substance abuse concerns face inevitable delays as they wait for an open treatment spot.

One portion of the recovery process is obtaining quick access to drug and alcohol treatment. Those racing the ASFA clock must not only seek treatment in a timely fashion, they must also maintain their sobriety. The path to sobriety varies and depends on drug choice and length of drug use. Sobriety can take years to achieve. Detoxification is widely considered to be the first step in drug treatment but is often not enough to maintain sobriety (Guide to Drug Detox, n.d.). The amount of time in treatment is also an important factor. There is a direct correlation between the length of time in treatment and rate of relapse (Sack, 2012), and ASFA puts a boundary on the amount of time allowed for substance use recovery.

Treatment success also depends on several factors that may create additional burdens for parents with substance abuse concerns who are racing the ASFA clock. The type of substance used, severity of use at intake, type of treatment received, and the definition of what is meant by a successful outcome all influence success. To be effective, treatment length may be extensive for substance using parents. In general, it takes at least ninety days and up to one year for maximum improvement in residential and outpatient care for methadone users. This time frame reinforces the urgency to secure a treatment spot.

When a child enters out-of-home placement, juvenile dependency courts, with the help of child welfare agencies, can order parents to comply with services to assure sobriety. Judges can order parents to obtain level-of-care assessments, obtain a drug and alcohol evaluation, comply with drug and alcohol counseling, and submit to random drug tests. Caseworkers monitor parents' compliance by obtaining evaluations and reports from drug and alcohol providers. Legal counsel and the judge receive summaries of these reports, and the judge reviews progress during hearings.

Reunification requirements include successful recovery from addiction and maintaining sobriety. Quick and easy access into treatment programs and successful completion of at least one program can increase the likelihood of reunification. In return, the amount of time a child spends in out-of-home placements decreases (He, Traube, & Young, 2014); a desirable outcome for family and the various social agencies involved. If reunification requirements are not done within this timeframe, parents risk termination of their parental rights.

Termination of parental rights is the permanent, formal severing of the legal bond between the child and their parents. Under ASFA, caregivers have as little as fifteen months to comply with reunification requirements (Wattenberg, Kelley, & Kim, 2001). When making the determination to pursue termination of parental rights, judges within juvenile dependency courts must reflect on both clear and convincing evidence, as well as, what is in the best interest of the child (Meyer, McWey, McKendrick & Henderson, 2010). Juvenile dependency court judges may reflect on a parent's ability to maintain and obtain sobriety (Meyer, McWey, & Henderson, 2010), a parent's stability (e.g., income and housing), the bond between the child and parent, and past history or involvement with child welfare agencies as evidence to help determine whether termination of parental rights is in the best interest of the child. Additional factors weigh on the decision to terminate parental rights, such as mental illness (Meyer, McWey, & Henderson, 2010), domestic violence, involvement with the criminal justice system (Wattenberg, Kelley, & Kim, 2001), and incarceration (Meyer, McWey, & Henderson, 2010).

ASFA reduced the length of time a youth spends in out-of-home placement (Nicholson, 2006) by expediting the route to permanency. ASFA obligates states to begin termination of parental rights proceedings when a child has been in out-of-home care for fifteen of the past twenty months. It allows concurrent planning to occur in which efforts at family reunification proceed simultaneously with attempts to achieve alternative permanency such as legal guardianship or adoption (Hort, 2001).

ASFA requires reasonable efforts at reunification by children and youth caseworkers and it provides financial inducements to states that accomplish a successful foster care adoption. All states are granted a base number for the estimated amount of foster care adoptions they should have within the fiscal year. A state is awarded $4,000 for each additional foster child that is adopted and receives an additional incentive for placing a foster care child up for adoption. For a state to receive the incentives, ASFA requires the state to file a petition to terminate the natural parents' rights if reunification has not been successful within fifteen months. With these financial incentives in play, Lercara (2016) points out that state agencies may put their own interests before the best interest of a child. The subjective nature of the "reasonable efforts" standard, coupled with the financial incentives provided to states placing children into adoptive homes, effectively undermines the goal of reunification (Lercara, 2016).

Lercara (2016) outlines the many flaws in the ASFA and provides examples of how it inappropriately encourages adoption to limit the child's time in out of care placement. The author proposes amendments to ASFA to put more emphasis on reuniting children with their parents. Lercara also proposes changes to ASFA to replace the term "reasonable efforts" with the term "best efforts." Having a best efforts standard would increase the child welfare agency's obligation to work toward permanency goals and reunification of the family. Moye and Rinker (2002) also outline how ASFA can ultimately set parents up for failure. They note that, if a family is receiving any Temporary Assistance for Needy Families (TANF) benefits, those benefits cease when a child enters out-of-home placement. Most families who enter the child welfare system depend on welfare, case assistance, and food stamps. Without TANF benefits, most are left without adequate housing, food, and proper clothing. Access to Medicaid benefits for families also evaporates when a child enters placement, which prevents most parents from receiving substance abuse treatment or proper medical care. To make matters more complicated, most child welfare agencies require parents to have stable and appropriate housing and a proper source of income prior to reunification. Parents in some cases may also have to pay for child support when their children are in foster care (Moye & Rinker, 2002).

## CONCLUSION

Juvenile dependency courts developed to help protect children of all ages from experiencing abuse and neglect (Ventrell, 1998). Although ASFA attempts to promote timely permanency placements for children in the child welfare system, existing data have said little about whether ASFA is meeting its intended goals. For some parents, beating the ASFA clock and obtaining quick access to drug and alcohol treatment can be difficult. The recovery from addiction is not a straightforward, quick and easy, process. Lack of appropriate services for families poses a significant barrier to reunification, and families with substance abuse issues face additional challenges under ASFA given time constraints on the treatment process. For those parents who are offered and provided substance abuse services, research has demonstrated that it often takes longer than twelve months to overcome their addictions (Moye & Rinker, 2002). On average, it takes almost three months for women to access substance abuse services even after the implementation of ASFA (Rockhill, Green, & Furrer, 2007). ASFA's fifteen-month time limit may prove too short for parents to locate and utilize services for such problems as comorbidity of substance abuse and mental illness. Research has established that parents with substance abuse issues had lower rates of reunification, and ASFA made it less likely that parents in need of substance abuse treatment will be able to receive treatment before their children are placed into permanency homes (Moye & Rinker, 2002).

Despite the well-intentioned efforts of ASFA, persons struggling with substance use disorders and ancillary issues surrounding their involvement in the criminal justice system may be unable to redirect their lives within the required timeframe. Juvenile dependency courts take seriously the effects of this experience on children of parents engaged in the multifaceted recovery process. Children who are placed in foster care during the juvenile dependency court process experience uncertainty, and family unit insecurity, as they await a placement determination. If their parent becomes sober and regains custody, their life will return to the trajectory it was following prior to their involvement with the juvenile dependency court; with the intention that the environment has been improved because their parent has addressed their substance use issue. If the parent involved in the juvenile dependency court process is unable to reach sobriety, the child faces a turning point and the prospect of being adopted, possibly by a foster family. These very real possibilities are contingent on the parent achieving goals set by the court and within the AFSA timeframe. However, sobriety and adherence are rarely well-planned or bounded by time frames often leading to a state of ambiguity for the child. This uncertainty became a concern to the federal government as many children were lingering in foster care as they awaited potential reunification with their parent. The passage of AFSA may create an unfair setback for parents struggling with substance use disorders, making reunification a forsaken dream.

## REFERENCES

Akin, B. A. (2011). Predictors of foster care exits to permanency: A competing risks analysis of reunification, guardianship, and adoption. *Children and Youth Services Review, 33*(6), 999–1011.

Barth, R. P. (1996). The juvenile court and dependency cases. *The Future of Children,* 6(3), 100–110.

Boss, P. (2004). Ambiguous loss research, theory, and practice: Reflections after 9/11. *Journal of Marriage and Family, 66*(3), 551–566.

Bowlby, J. (1982). Attachment and loss: Retrospect and prospect. *The American Journal of Orthopsychiatry, 52*(4), 664–678.

Brook, J., & McDonald, T. P. (2007). Evaluating the effects of comprehensive substance abuse intervention on successful reunification. *Research on Social Work Practice, 17*(6), 664–673.

Bullock, R., Little, M., & Millham, S. L. (1993). *Going home: The return of children separated from their families*. Dartmouth.

Carnochan, S., Rizik-Baer, D., & Austin, M. J. (2013). Preventing re-entry to foster care. *Journal of Evidence-Based Social Work, 10*(3), 196–209.

Chambers, R. M., Brocato, J., Fatemi, M., & Rodriguez, A. Y. (2016). An innovative child welfare pilot initiative: Results and outcomes. *Children and Youth Services Review, 70*, 143–151.

Cheng, T. C. (2010). Factors associated with reunification: A longitudinal analysis of long-term foster care. *Children and Youth Services Review, 32*(10), 1311–1316.

Cheng, T. C., & Li, A. X. (2012). Maltreatment and families' receipt of services: Associations with reunification, kinship care, and adoption. *Families in Society, 93*(3), 189–195.

Children and Families Futures. (2013 rev 2015). *Guidance to states: Recommendations for developing family drug court guidelines*. Office of Juvenile Justice and Delinquency Prevention (OJJDP) Office of Justice Programs. Retrieved from: http://www.cffutures.org/files/publications/FDC-Guidelines.pdf

Child Protective Services Law. (1975). *23 Pa.C.S. Chapter 63. Child Protective Services*. Juvenile Court Judges' Commission.

Choi, S., & Ryan, J. P. (2007). Co-occurring problems for substance abusing mothers in child welfare: Matching services to improve family reunification. *Children and Youth Services Review, 29*(11), 1395–1410.

Chuang, E., Moore, K., Barrett, B., & Young, M. S. (2012). Effect of an integrated family dependency treatment court on child welfare reunification, time to permanency and re-entry rates. *Children and Youth Services Review, 34*(9), 1896–1902.

Connell, C. M., Katz, K. H., Saunders, L., & Tebes, J. K. (2006). Leaving foster care—the influence of child and case characteristics on foster care exit rates. *Children and Youth Services Review, 28*(7), 780–798.

Fahlberg, V. (2012). *A child's journey through placement*. Jessica Kingsley Publishers.

Fanshel, D., & Shinn, E. B. (1978). *Children in foster care: A longitudinal investigation*. Columbia University Press.

Fein, E., & Staff, I. (1993). Last best chance: Findings from a reunification services program. *Child Welfare, 72*(1), 25–40.

Green, B. L., Rockhill, A., & Burrus, S. (2008). The role of interagency collaboration for substance-abusing families involved with child welfare. *Child Welfare, 87*(1), 29–61.

Green, B. L., Rockhill, A., & Furrer, C. (2007). Does substance abuse treatment make a difference for child welfare case outcomes? A statewide longitudinal analysis. *Children and Youth Services Review, 29*(4), 460–473.

Guide to Drug Detox. (n.d.). *The guide to detox: Taking you through the detox process*. Retrieved from: https://www.dualdiagnosis.org/guide-drug-detox/

Hannett, M. (2007). Lessening the sting of ASFA: The rehabilitation-relapse dilemma brought about by drug addiction and termination of parental rights. *Family Court Review, 45*(3), 524–537.

Hardin, M. (1996). Responsibilities and effectiveness of the juvenile court in handling dependency cases. *The Future of Children, 6*(3), 111–125.

Harris, M. S. (1999). Comparing mothers of children in kinship foster care: Reunification vs. remaining in care. In J. Gleeson & C. F. Hairston (Eds.), Kinship care: Improving practice through research (pp. 145–166). Child Welfare League of America.

Harris-McKoy, D., Meyer, A. S., McWey, L. M., & Henderson, T. L. (2014). Substance use policy, and foster care. *Journal of Family Issues, 35*(10), 1298–1321.

He, A. S., Traube, D. E., & Young, N. K. (2014). Perceptions of parental substance use disorders in cross-system collaboration among child welfare, alcohol and other drugs, and dependency court organizations. *Child Abuse & Neglect, 38*(5), 939.

Hess, P. M. (1987). Parental visiting of children in foster care: Current knowledge and research agenda. *Children and Youth Services Review, 9*(1), 29–50.

Hess, P. M., & Proch, K. O. (1988). *Parental visiting in out-of-home care: A guide to practice*. Child Welfare League of America.

Hort, K. (2001). Is twenty-two months beyond the best interest of the child? AFSA's guidelines for the termination of parental rights. *Fordham Urban Law Journal, 28*, 1879–1921.

Howe, D., Brandon, M., Hinings, H., & Schofield, G. (1999). *Attachment theory, child maltreatment and family support*. Macmillan.

Jedwab, M., Chatterjee, A., & Shaw, T. V. (2018). Caseworkers' insights and experiences with successful reunification. *Children and Youth Services Review, 86*, 56–63.

Jones, L., & Kruk, E. (2005). Life in government care: The connection of youth to family. *Child and Youth Care Forum, 34*(6), 405–421.

Kaplan, S. J., Pelcovitz, D., & Labruna, V. (1999). Child and adolescent abuse and neglect research: A review of the past 10 years. Part I: Physical and emotional abuse and neglect. *Journal of the American Academy of Child & Adolescent Psychiatry, 38*(10), 1214–1222.

Kenny, M. C., Abreu, R. L., Marchena, M. T., Helpingstine, C., Lopez-Griman, A., & Mathews, B. (2017). Legal and clinical guidelines for making a child maltreatment report. *Professional Psychology: Research and Practice, 48*(6), 469–480.

Lee, S., Jonson-Reid, M., & Drake, B. (2012). Foster care re-entry: Exploring the role of foster care characteristics, in-home child welfare services and cross-sector services. *Children and Youth Services Review, 34*(9), 1825–1833.

Lercara, B. (2016). The adoption and safe families act: Proposing a "Best efforts" standard to eliminate the ultimate obstacle for family reunification. *Family Court Review, 54*(4), 657–670.

Littner, N. (1975). The importance of the natural parents to the child in placement. *Child Welfare, 54*(3), 175–181.

Lloyd, M. H., Akin, B. A., & Brook, J. (2017). Parental drug use and permanency for young children in foster care: A competing risks analysis of reunification, guardianship, and adoption. *Children and Youth Services Review, 77*, 177–187.

López, M., del Valle, J. F., Montserrat, C., & Bravo, A. (2013). Factors associated with family reunification for children in foster care. *Child & Family Social Work, 18*(2), 226–236.

Lowenthal B. (1999). Effects of child maltreatment and ways to promote children's resiliency. *Childhood Education, 75*(4), 204–209.

Mapp, S. C., & Steinberg, C. (2007) Birth families as permanency resources for children in long term foster care. *Child Welfare, 86*, 29–51.

Marsh, J. C., Ryan, J. P., Choi, S., & Testa, M. F. (2006). Integrated services for families with multiple problems: Obstacles to family reunification. *Children and Youth Services Review, 28*(9), 1074–1087.

McDonald, T. P., Poertner, J., & Jennings, M. A. (2007) Permanency for children in foster care: a competing risks analysis. *Journal of Social Service Research, 33*, 45–56.

McWey, L. M., & Mullis, A. K. (2004). Improving the lives of children in foster care: The impact of supervised visitation. *Family Relations, 53*(3), 293–300.

Meyer, A. S., McWey, L. M., McKendrick, W., & Henderson, T. L. (2010). Substance using parents, foster care, and termination of parental rights: The importance of risk factors for legal outcomes. *Children and Youth Services Review, 32*(5), 639–649.

Mifflin County. (2020). *What are general protective services?* Retrieved from: http://www.co.mifflin.pa.us/dept/CY/Pages/General-Protective-Services.aspx

Moye, J., & Rinker, R. (2002). It's a hard knock life: Does the adoption and safe families act of 1997 adequately address problems in the child welfare system? *Harvard Journal on Legislation, 39*(2), 375–394.

Murphy, E., & Fairtlough, A. (2015). The successful reunification of abused and neglected looked after children with their families: A case-file audit. *British Journal of Social Work, 45*(8), 2261–2280.

Nicholson, E. K. (2006). Racing against the ASFA clock: How incarcerated parents lose more than freedom. *Duquesne Law Review, 45*(1), 83–96.

Perkins, D. F. (1997) *Family visitation centre study: A final report.* Cooperative Extension Service, Institute of Food and Agricultural Services, University of Florida-Gainesville.

Roberts, D. (2002). *Shattered bonds: The color of child welfare.* Civitas Books.

Rockhill, A., Green, B. L., & Furrer, C. (2007). Is the adoption and safe families act influencing child welfare outcomes for families with substance abuse issues? *Child Maltreatment, 12*(1), 7–19.

Sack, D. (2012). How long does addiction recovery take? *Psych Central*. Retrieved from  https://blogs.psychcentral.com/addiction-recovery/2012/01/how-long-addiction-recovery/

Sagatun-Edwards, I., & Saylor, C. (2000). A coordinated approach to improving outcomes for Substance-Abusing families in juvenile dependency court. *Juvenile and Family Court Journal, 51*(4), 1–16.

Shaw, T. V. (2006). Reentry into the foster care system after reunification. *Children and Youth Services Review, 28*(11), 1375–1390.

Talbot, E. P. (2008). Successful family reunification: Looking at the decision-making process. *Social Work & Christianity, 35*(1), 48–72.

Testa, M. F., & Smith, B. (2009). Prevention and drug treatment. *The Future of Children, 19*(2), 147–168.

Thomlison, B., Maluccio, A. N., & Abramczyk, L. W. (1996). The theory, policy, and practice context of family reunification: An integrated research perspective. *Children and Youth Services Review, 18*(4), 473–488.

Ventrell, M. (1998). Evolution of the dependency component of the juvenile court. *Juvenile & Family Court Journal, 49*(4), 17–37.

Wade, J., Biehal, N., Farrelly, N., & Sinclair, I. (2010) *Maltreated children in the looked after system: a comparison of outcomes for those who go home and those who do not.* University of York.

Wattenberg, E., Kelley, M., & Kim, H. (2001). When the rehabilitation ideal fails: A study of parental rights termination. *Child Welfare, 80*(4), 405–431.

Westat. (1995). *A review of family preservation and family reunification programs.* U.S. Department of Health and Human Services. Retrieved from: http://aspe.hhs.gov/hsp/cyp/fpprogs.htm (accessed 25 February 2019).

Woolgar, M. (2019). Attachment theory. In S. Hupp & J. D. Jewell (Eds.), *The Encyclopedia of Child and Adolescent Development* (pp. 1–10). Wiley & Sons.

Young, N. K. (2016). *Examining the impact of the opioid epidemic.* Written Testimony, U.S. Senate Committee on Homeland Security and Governmental Affairs. Retrieved from: http://www.cffutures.org/files/Young_Homeland%20Security%20and%20Governmental%20Affairs%20Final.pdf.

*Chapter 7*

# Community Courts

## *Restoring the Community One Case at a Time*

### Tyrell Connor

## INTRODUCTION

In the early 1990s, New York City law enforcement noticed an increase in criminal offenses throughout the city (De Blasio & Shea, 2020). Violent crime was at an all-time high and misdemeanor arrests began to increase (Friedman et al., 2017; Patten et al., 2018). Midtown Manhattan, which is home to most of the city's top attractions such as Times Square, began to struggle economically. The visible deterioration and prostitution deterred patrons from local businesses in the area. Local business owners grew frustrated and demanded answers from local officials.

New York City courts centralized operations across the five boroughs in the 1960s, which led to increased caseloads and processing. Although these courts succeeded in establishing a uniformed and standardized judicial system, they no longer focused on community needs. Notably, due to the increase of cases, courts began to prioritize serious offenses over low-level offenses. Quality of life offenses, such as prostitution, shoplifting public urination, disorderly conduct, and small possession of marijuana, was virtually ignored within these centralized courts.

Quality of life offenses impacted Midtown's community the most. This area in Manhattan, between 34th Street and 59th Street is home to a mix of office buildings in its large central business district, residential apartments, and prominent landmarks, including Grand Central Station, the Empire State Building, and Broadway making it one of the most populated sectors of New York City. Residents, business leaders, judges, the Center for Court Innovation, and the Mayor's office began planning on how to fix it. After three years of planning, in 1993, the nation's first community court, Midtown Community Court, was established. This court was developed to respond to the concerns of residents and specifically targeted offenses ignored in the central court. People who were arrested for low-level offenses and misdemeanors were now arraigned in Midtown Community Court. Although prosecutors and defense attorneys expressed skepticism about the inception of this new court, many believed in the court's promise (Hoffman, 1993).

Midtown Community Court diverged from the central court in a few ways. This court had a dedicated judge to handle all cases. Social services, such as onsite group counseling, drug treatment, and prostitution and shoplifting diversion programs, were on-site to assist defendants who needed resources for situations such as prostitution, substance abuse, and homelessness. Additionally, instead of just receiving a fine or jail time, sanctions in this court would usually mandate some form of social service and community service to be performed in Midtown. For example, a defendant may be mandated to attend an anti-shoplifting course or quality-of-life course and to participate in community service to clean up nearby graffiti or parks.

The National Center for State Courts evaluated the court's progress by comparing the court's conventional outcome measures with the centralized downtown court. After the first eighteen months in operation, Midtown community court, compared to the centralized downtown court, had more than twice as many community service and social service sentences for drug and petty larceny charges. They had three times as many community and social service mandates for theft and illegal vending and four times for prostitution charges. There was a reduction in the use of outcomes such as "time served" and "conditional discharge" compared to the downtown court for prostitution, drug offenses, petty larceny, turnstile jumping, and illegal vending. The use of jail sentences was less than the downtown court for prostitution (73 percent), petty larceny (50 percent), and turnstile jumping (29 percent). The Midtown community court increased caseload while reducing burden on institutional corrections. Additionally, compliance rates for community service mandates were higher for Midtown than the downtown court (75 percent compared to 50 percent, respectively) (Sviridoff, Rottman, Ostrom, & Curtis 2001).

Midtown also succeeded in improving the quality-of-life conditions within the community. Within the first three years of inception, between 1993 and 1996, arrests for prostitution dropped by 56 percent, and illegal vending fell 24 percent (Sviridoff, Rottman, Ostrom, & Curtis 2001). Community attitudes also changed. Community leaders and residents had more favorable attitudes of the court, and most acknowledged the community court was responsible for the visible reduction of low-level offenses and public restitution. Police officers initially had negative views about the court, but after the first eighteen months, they became vocal advocates and supporters of the community court. The success of the Midtown Community Court eventually sparked a movement for community courts around the world (Lee & Martinez, 1998).

## COMMUNITY COURTS

As of 2020, there were about forty community courts in the United States. According to Lang (2011), community courts ask a set of critical questions that seek to shed light on the role a court can play within a community. Lang asks, "What can a court do to solve neighborhood problems? Is it possible to forge new and creative responses to low-level offending instead of relying on incarceration as a default setting? What roles can community residents, businesses, and service providers play in improving justice? And how can the answers to those questions be applied beyond the community court itself to the wider court system?" (Lang, 2011, pg. 1). Community courts often apply these questions as the framework for program development.

### How Are Community Courts Different from Other Problem-Solving Courts?

Most problem-solving courts to date aim to address criminogenic needs (see section I) or have an offense-specific focus (see section III). For example, many problem-solving courts primarily focus on drugs, DUIs, domestic violence, or mental health issues. Others address types of crimes such as human trafficking or domestic violence. Community courts diverge from these other problem-solving courts because of its focus on neighborhood dynamics and their needs (Reno et al., 2000; Center for Court Innovation, 2005). Instead of focusing on just one primary type of offense or offender, their goal is to restore community trust by addressing offenses that may damage the community. As a result, community courts use a broader focus in their courts' programming such that they can have a positive impact and reach more people than other problem-solving courts.

Community courts also have daily court proceedings similar to conventional municipal-level courts. Many other problem-solving courts, such as reentry and drug courts, meet with participants biweekly or monthly in a phased approach. Other problem-solving courts also typically have resources for a finite number of spots for court participants. Due to the nature of low-level and "quality-of-life" offenses, community courts have higher caseloads and reach more people than other problem-solving courts. Broken windows philosophy, emphasizing the detrimental impact of visible signs of antisocial behaviors and signs of crime such as graffiti and prostitution, drives these courts to focus on low-level offenses and misdemeanors (Wilson & Kelling, 1982). Therefore, the higher levels of contact with residents can lead to increased court legitimacy and potential net-widening effects that will be discussed later in the chapter.

Community courts also can provide social service resources to populations that may be overlooked in conventional courts. For example, the Midtown Community Court offers many resources and assistance for individuals arrested for prostitution. This includes a five- or ten-session onsite group counseling program titled Women's Independence, Safety and Empowerment (WISE), TransWomen Empowerment, and "John" School. Red Hook Community Court offers GED courses and job readiness programs for its participants. Newark's Community Court holds many group sessions for mental health, lifestyle, and substance abuse onsite for various demographics. Furthermore, many community court programs have youth court and youth programs onsite to address behaviors among the younger demographic and serve as a resource for local youth. Many judges in community courts encourage participants and others to return to the court if they need assistance and assert that getting arrested is not the only way to access court resources.

## Community Court Essentials

Community courts have not been researched to the extent of drug courts. Henry and Kralstein (2011) conducted a comprehensive review of research literature on nineteen community courts. Findings from these studies were relatively positive and found value in the use of community courts.

### *Community Court Staff*

Community courts have staff members that are a combination of traditional courtroom staff and social service staff. Most community courts have a dedicated judge and defense attorneys that handle the majority of the cases. Community court prosecutors usually rotate their court assignments and may only spend a few months each year handling cases. Parole or probation officers are sometimes also assigned to a community court to assist in specific cases that may include parole or probation violations.

In addition to the courtroom staff, social service staff are also present. On staff, there is usually a combination of licensed clinical social workers; resource coordinators; a youth coordinator; community service coordinators; and a series of specialists focusing on community service, intake, alternative sanctions, job readiness, and community outreach. It is also not uncommon to find resident volunteers in community courts to assist with programming for the youth or defendants. The collaboration between traditional courtroom staff and the social service sector creates a space for comprehensive assessment and resources and mirrors the holistic intent of problem-solving courts. This combination of services in one court setting expands the services offered and adds more options for judges and attorneys than conventional courts.

## Enhanced Information and Individualized Justice

Community courts train their staff to better understand many of the social issues their participants may experience. It is not uncommon for community court staff to attend training on mental illness, drug addiction, and sex trafficking. A well-trained staff means that they will be able to better identify issues with defendants and guide them to the appropriate resources more accurately. Team meetings are also used for essential stakeholders like judges, attorneys, social workers, and specialists to come together and discuss each open case. This information is used to find the best and most appropriate incentives and sanctions for each case. Individualized justice allows team members to view each case independently and tailor a treatment plan that should have the most effective outcomes. For example, sometimes a person is arrested for aggressive panhandling due to homelessness and unemployment because of mental illness. The team can address all matters in the meeting, and the judge can assign a mandate that includes mental health treatment combined with a job readiness program and temporary housing. Therefore, addressing the individualized needs of the participant that led to their involvement with the criminal justice system, the team decreases the odds of recidivism or re-offending. This ability to address the root causes of crime is one of the significant distinctions between community courts and conventional courtroom practices. Beyond addressing the needs of the offender, community courts actively work to change community perceptions. Community courts create outreach initiatives to support local programs and raise awareness. For example, Red Hook's Community Court worked alongside community leaders to clean up Coffey Park, which was known as "Needle Park," due to the strong presence of drug use and dealing. Additionally, Red Hook developed a court-sponsored baseball league to engage the local youth. Community engagement is a core value of community courts that makes them unique compared to other problem-solving courts.

## Community Engagement

Community courts are created due to community needs. Residential surveys are often used to measure the most pressing issues within a community. That information is used in the planning of community courts. For example, Hahn (2014) found that Newark residents expressed that unemployment, drug selling, guns, gang activity, and homelessness were some of the "big issues" plaguing the community. Newark Community Solutions responded by implementing job readiness programs and building relationships with local employers to increase employment opportunities for court participants. Newark's community court also established a program called NuAv, which was a community outreach service meant to identify local gang members and victims of gun violence and offer services to help decrease the impact of trauma and exposure. In a similar vein, Red Hook's Community Court judge established a youth softball league and solicited the help of local law enforcement and court staff to help coach the teams. This type of community engagement shows community residents that community courts are not just about punishment but are meant to be a part of the community and restoration.

## Alternative Sanctions

Like other problem-solving courts, community courts offer alternative sanctions to avoid incarceration (Kaiser & Holtfreter, 2016). Because community courts rely on restorative justice principles, they implement sanctions meant to repair and heal the relationship between offender and community rather than focus on punishment and removal from the community. Community courts accomplish this by offering sanctions that assist the offender and intently heal the community. For example, Hakuta et al. (2008) and Katz (2009) found that the community courts studied increased alternative sanctions offered and reduced jail sentences and jail days served. Most, if not all, community courts mandate community service as part of their sanctions. Mahoney and Carlson (2007) found that community services were included in all sentences. When observing a Philadelphia community court, it was found that community service hours increased by 50,000 between 2002 and 2007 and was included in all sentencing (Durkin et al., 2009). The use of alternative sanctions reduces the burden on the criminal justice system by incarcerating fewer people and restoring communities. Across the street from Red Hook Community Justice Center is a park that is known as Needle Park because of the excessive amount of drug use that happened there. Due to the court's presence and community service mandates, the park has now been fully restored and is now a clean outdoor space where residents can enjoy this community resource. In fact, Red Hook's judge has been known to host softball tournaments for the community at the park.

## Cost-Effectiveness

The potential to save money in local budgets provides incentives for communities to be fiscally responsible. Some studies have found that community courts are cost-effective. Sviridoff et al. (2001) analyzed the Midtown Community Court and found that the court saved the community roughly $1.4 million. Ross et al. (2009) found that a community court in

Australia also saved the community money. Generally, community courts can introduce cost-savings for local communities. This may be imperative for state budgets that seek to relieve financial pressures by reducing spending on criminal justice practices.

## THEORETICAL FOUNDATIONS

Similar to other problem-solving courts, community courts are grounded on a few theoretical principles. Many community courts use broken windows theory, therapeutic jurisprudence, and restorative justice as guiding principles.

### Broken Windows

The overarching philosophy that drives the targeting of low-level offenses stems from broken windows theory developed by Wilson and Kelling (1982). They argued that vandalism and community breakdown could lower community control and create a platform for serious and violent crime to flourish. They asserted that reducing the effects of "urban decay" would substantially reduce or remove serious crime.

The use of this theory helped establish a rationale as to why community courts should be developed. Due to the increased caseloads within centralized courts, particularly from minor offenses that were believed to contribute to "urban decay," there needed to be a space to focus on these offenses. The development of community courts allowed criminal justice practitioners to solely focus on low-level offenses, which simultaneously easing the burden on centralized courts. This new model was an overall benefit to the court system. Centralized courts can now remove low-level offenses from their dockets by sending these cases to community court. This would then give centralized courts more time to focus its resources on more serious crimes.

Community courts view most offenses as harming the community. This is because many of the offenses observed in these courts are "victimless" crimes. Therefore, crimes committed in this manner are taken seriously by community courts with the belief that it will restore order to the community and prevent an escalation in criminal offending. The introduction of broken windows theory in the early 1980s, which highlights the need to demonstrate that lower level offenses are taken seriously by police and the courts, led to increased enforcement of low-level offenses and increased attention in the courts. This new attention to minor crime led to an overburdened court system. With the introduction of community courts, instead of the court process as a punishment for low-level offenses, there are now consistent and legitimate means to address minor offenses in the courts.

## Restorative Justice

Most problem-solving courts embrace the ideology of restorative justice. According to Braithwaite (1989), restorative justice involves all parties of an injustice having opportunities to discuss the ramifications of the harm that occurred. The restorative justice process suggests that extensive involvement by the offender, victim, family, friends, and a representative from the community is critical to achieving effective change. Braithwaite believed that communities can potentially lower crime rates if they communicate shame about crime effectively, known as reintegrative shaming. He claims that an open conversation about shaming could be a useful tool in correcting behavior. Braithwaite was careful to recognize that shaming can have adverse effects, especially in the form of stigmatization, if not performed effectively. He argued that there must be a combination of community shaming joined with respect for the offender. By this, he meant that people must treat the offender as a good person who just committed a bad deed instead of a bad person who committed a bad deed. Through this perspective, he viewed stigmatization as being something in which offenders and society view as unforgiving, whereas the reintegrative shaming is received as a forgiving act. In summary, Braithwaite (2002) concluded, "Societies that are forgiving and respectful while taking crime seriously have low crime rates; societies that degrade and humiliate criminals have higher crime rates" (Braithwaite, 2002, p. 258).

Community courts operate within the guiding principles of restorative justice and collaborate with various stakeholders from the community to effectively handle low-level offenses. Although, many of the crimes presented within community courts may be perceived and labeled as "victimless" crimes such as turnstile hopping, being at a park after hours, or public intoxication, these courts view the community as the "victim." Many offenders may view their minor offenses as "not hurting anyone," but community courts demonstrate to defendants how their behavior may harm the community. In turn, most mandates are coupled with a social service sanction to help improve or inform the offender and community service assignments. The community service mandates serve as a mechanism to illustrate that the offender is restoring or making right the damage caused by his or her actions. When offenders are cleaning parks, graffiti, serving food, and tending to gardens, it legitimizes the court and attempts to reverse any damage committed.

These practices also contribute to reducing the stigma of offenders by promoting reintegrative shaming. In other words, community courts purposefully stay away from actions and labels that stigmatize individuals. Many community courts practice this by calling defendants "clients" or "participants" instead of "defendants" or "offenders." Additionally, after completing program mandates, it is not uncommon for judges to encourage a round of applause for participants and give ceremonial certificates and praise (Berman & Gold, 2012). Restorative justice approaches allow community courts to reduce labeling effects and the possibility of recidivism.

## Therapeutic Jurisprudence

Potentially one of the most distinctive features of problem-solving courts is the use of therapeutic jurisprudence. Wexler and Winick (1996) assert that therapeutic jurisprudence allows legal practitioners to execute forms of justice in a therapeutic fashion that is used to help the offender and the community by striving for successful rehabilitation. This framework gives courtroom practitioners the ability to be more interactive and engaged with defendants. Most problem-solving court literature claims that this enhances the judge's ability not only to be better informed when making decisions but also to have a direct influence on the defendant's behavior and outcomes (Berman & Fox, 2010). Building a rapport with defendants is key to this process, as it is within any therapeutic setting. Attorneys, judges, clerks, court officers, and social service staff actively seek to build rapport with defendants.

This is possible and common because most community courts have one dedicated judge. Therefore, the judge that regularly meets participants can encourage and build a rapport to increase compliance rates. The judges are the most critical factor when applying therapeutic jurisprudence (Winick, 2003). The goal is to provide context to individual cases and provide a plan to reduce the chances of future offending. Judges will consider employment, family, mental and physical health, substance abuse, and other factors when deciding the outcomes of cases, emphasizing the holistic nature of problem-solving courts. Judges in problem-solving courts are usually viewed more positively than judges in conventional courts, and their ability to apply therapeutic jurisprudence principles might be the reason (Winick, 2003).

## Procedural Fairness and Legitimacy

Increasing the legitimacy of local courts is more likely to happen when community residents and defendants view the court as fair and just. Most research on community courts shows that defendants and community residents view the courts more positively than traditional court processing (Moore, 2004; Frazer, 2006; McKenna, 2007). For example, Frazer (2006) found that defendants had more positive perceptions of the judges in the Red Hook Community Court compared to those on the downtown court bench. Furthermore, McKenna (2007) found that both staff and defendants viewed the overall impact of the court as positive and useful.

Recent research has begun to highlight how community courts attempt to actively increase legitimacy. Connor (2018) found that community court judges use the significant elements of procedural justice (voice, respect, trustworthiness, and neutrality) to build a rapport with defendants to increase compliance. Zozula (2019) describes how community courts' organizational model gives them the flexibility to increase legitimacy to multiple audiences. In other words, community courts' ability to punish low-level crimes appeases the concerns of conservative audiences while offering alternative sanctions appeals to liberal audiences. Overall, community courts create an opportunity to rebuild trust and legitimacy in communities that may need it.

## WEAKNESSES

Community courts have been widely praised since the inception of Midtown's Community Court. However, over time, researchers have highlighted some limitations and concerns about community courts. There has been concern about how effective community courts are at reducing rearrest and recidivism compared to conventional courts. This is primarily due to the way community courts measure success by documenting compliance rates. Finally, similar to other problem-solving courts, community courts do not address or document racial outcomes effectively.

### Compliance versus Recidivism

One of the biggest critiques of community courts is their negligence of documenting recidivism. Community courts usually measure success by observing compliance rates, focusing on the positive outcomes. For example, when a participant completes all required mandates, that individual is marked as compliant in the court's database. However, if that same individual returns for another violation or rearrest and again completes the community court mandates, it is documented as another successful case. The rearrest is not documented or included in the measure of compliance. Therefore, this practice gives the illusion that community courts are successful because most defendants complete their assigned mandates or sanctions. Karafin (2008) surveyed thirty-five community courts around the globe and found that the average community service compliance rate was 82 percent. The average social service compliance rate was 68 percent, but only four courts were able to report re-offending rates. Karafin concluded that community courts need to expand and improve their ability to monitor and measure a variety of outcome data.

## Rearrest Rates (mixed results)

A few studies have attempted to observe how effective community courts are at reducing crime and re-offending. Overall, the results are mixed, with more studies showing no impact on reconviction rates. Study by Ross et al. (2009) is the only one that observed how the Neighbourhood Justice Centre in Melbourne, Australia, impacted local crime rates. They found a reduction in burglaries and motor vehicle theft within two years of the court's inception. They also found that 34 percent of community court participants re-offended within eighteen months compared to 41 percent for the downtown court defendants. Similarly, Sviridoff et al. (2001) found reduced prostitution and illegal vending arrests in Midtown. In some cases, a community court's presence also increased perceptions of safety in local neighborhoods (Moore, 2004).

Beyond these few studies, most research indicates no significant difference in re-offending between community courts and conventional courts (Sviridoff et al., 2001; Karafin, 2008; Jolliffe & Farrington, 2009; Nugent-Borakove, 2009). Community courts appear to be more effective at court procedure and defendant compliance, but not more effective at reducing recidivism. Although community courts may reduce costs and increase legitimacy, they may not be the ideal method for reducing crime. More research is needed to understand why community courts may not reduce re-offending more than conventional courts.

## Community Court Punishment

Similar to most problem-solving courts, community courts use incarceration as the final (or last resort) method of punishment. Community courts usually give participants alternative sanctions in order to avoid jail time and fines. However, some cases inevitably result in incarceration. Zozula (2019) described community courts as institutions that rely on what she calls "ambivalent justice." This is the process in which courts sort defendants into moral categories. In other words, they identify deserving and undeserving participants based on how well they respond to court sanctions. If a participant fails treatment or other mandates, then they are viewed as undeserving. Zozula states that this is problematic because "jail time was imposed as a punishment for defendants' moral failing to display accountability and responsibility, not for the crimes they had committed" (p. 102). Therefore, punishing the so-called undeserving allows community courts to increase their legitimacy in conservative or law-and-order spaces. In a comprehensive study of Red Hook Community Justice Center, Lee et al. (2013) found that although Red Hook uses jail 10 percent less than the downtown court, it was more punitive. On average, a jail sentence from Red Hook was sixty-four days versus fifteen days for the downtown court. In the Midtown Community Court, someone who committed petty larceny would receive an average of seventy-nine days in jail but a similar defendant would receive an average of forty-nine days at the downtown court for the same offense (Sviridoff, Rottman, Ostrom, & Curtis, 1997).

## Lack of Racial Analysis and Impact

One of the most significant limitations of community courts is the lack of attention to racial dynamics and outcomes. Current research on drug courts has begun to expose the racial disparities in their outcomes (Dannerbek et al., 2006; McKean & Warren-Gordon, 2011; Marlowe, 2013; Ho, Carey, & Malsch, 2018; Breitenbucher et al., 2018; Shannon et al., 2018; Marlowe et al., 2018). Overall, studies suggest that non-white participants are far less successful than their white counterparts. Marlowe, Hardin, and Fox (2016) found that drug court participants have a graduation rate of 39 percent compared to 70 percent of white participants.

There are some explanations as to why racial disparities exist within problem-solving courts. Baker et al. (2014, 2015) find that defendants are more likely to view the court as fair when they share the same racial identity as courtroom actors. Generally, defendants find problem-solving courts to be fairer; however, non-white participants have different perspectives (Cresswell, 2001; Frazer, 2006; Gallagher, 2013; Gallagher & Nordberg, 2018). For example, Gallagher and Nordberg (2018) interviewed seventy African American drug court participants. They found that the participants viewed interactions with the judge to be favorable but had negative feelings toward other court and treatment staff. Recently, Atkin-Plunk, Peck, and Armstrong (2019) found that non-white defendants in problem-solving courts had lower perceptions of procedural justice and fairness.

According to the psychological literature, it is within therapeutic practices and settings that race should be recognized and addressed (Sue & Sue, 2008). Black clients are more likely to terminate counseling prematurely and find it more challenging to build a rapport with counselors who are white (Andrews & Bonta, 2010; Constantine, 2007; Sue & Sue, 2012; Terrell & Terrell, 1984; Thompson & Jenal, 1994; Vasquez, 2007; Wiezbicki & Pekarik, 1993). Some evidence suggest that problem-solving courts that are aware of these racial dynamics yielded better outcomes for non-white participants (Hickert, Boyle, & Tollefson, 2009; Gallagher, Nordberg, & Dibley, 2017; Roll et al., 2005; Wolf, Sowards, & Wolf, 2003). For example, Roll et al. (2005) found that because the counseling and judicial staffs were non-white, which represented the racial makeup of many participants, it led to better outcomes for non-white participants.

Investigating racial outcomes in problem-solving courts should be a priority for all specialized courts. Community courts and other innovative forms of justice have an opportunity to rectify, or at least address, generations of racial malpractice. Failing to recognize and address any racial disparities continues the racist practices observed in traditional forms of justice. This is especially true for community courts because more people have contact in these courts compared to other problem-solving courts. Community courts have dockets similar to most conventional municipal courts. Their focus on low-level offenses broadens the reach of community courts, which leads to higher daily caseloads compared other problem-solving courts. Drug courts have begun to make efforts to reduce racial inequalities with national programs like the National Association of Drug Court Professionals. However, outside of drug court programs, focus on equity and inclusion is mostly neglected within specialized courts.

## COMMUNITY COURT PROFILES

Community courts are present in every region of the United States. This section is dedicated to highlighting three community courts located in different U.S. regions. Red Hook Community Justice, the largest community court in the country, is located in Red Hook, Brooklyn, New York. South Dallas Community Court was the first of three community courts to open in Dallas, Texas. Finally, the Seattle Community Court, which covers the entire city of Seattle, implemented unique offense selection criteria for entrance into the court.

### Red Hook Community Justice Center

Red Hook resides in an old shipping port district that is physically and socially isolated from the larger city because of an elevated expressway and the substantial loss of public transportation (Lee et al., 2013). Today, Red Hook is home to one of the most significant housing developments in the nation. About 70 percent of the neighborhood's residents live in public housing. The neighborhood of Red Hook comprises over 90 percent black and Hispanic residents. However, in order for the court to have a consistent and sufficient number of cases, they expanded the catchment area to neighboring areas as well. Even though Red Hook has a population of over 11,000, the court covers a population of about 100,000 (Lee et al., 2013). The expansion of jurisdiction increases the potential number of white defendants by encompassing predominately white areas. Within the Red Hook neighborhood, 30 percent of the neighborhood's working-aged men are unemployed, and more than 78 percent of children are raised by a single-parent home. Also, only 6 percent of adults have college degrees (Lee et al., 2013).

In 1992, Red Hook made national headlines when a local school principal was shot and killed in the crossfire of two drug groups while he was searching the public housing development for a missing student. It was during this time that the problem-solving court movement had been experiencing increasing momentum, and the Midtown Community Court had just been established. The death of the local principal propelled the District Attorney to begin planning a community court in the Red Hook community. The District Attorney had already been brainstorming areas where he can place a new community court, and the death of the principal led him to Red Hook.

The Red Hook community court's development instantly became unique and attractive because it addressed the criticisms and weaknesses of its predecessor, the Midtown Community Court. Gordon (1994) had asserted that the Midtown Community Court was not a community court. He believed that the purpose of this court, because it did not lie within a residential community, was to benefit the businesses of affluent white owners while scapegoating and exploiting the poor. Midtown also did not have a set demographic to serve because it is a commuter and business district, and many of its clientele came from outside the area, especially concerning prostitution. What made Red Hook an ideal community court location was that it provided services for a poor community had large-scale public housing with predominately minority inhabitants, and also lacked a core local economy.

After identifying Red Hook as an ideal location to build a community court, the District Attorney began to assemble a team and speak with community members, similar to the process at Midtown. Focus groups, surveys, and town hall meetings were used to understand the needs of the community and garner stakeholder input and support. The results of the discussion with community members showed that residents of Red Hook had a deep distrust for government officials and police, mainly due to the elevated expressway. The court system had high levels of distrust as well because offenders continued to offend. The public housing units had a plethora of gang involvement and violence, which resulted in residents fearing to go outside.

The residents in the community also had a stake in deciding where the building should be located. They decided on a vacant parochial school on the border and in the center of the community (Berman, 2005). Even the design of the building was carefully considered and well planned. For example, the judge's bench was placed lower than usual so that the judge could be eye level with the parties to reduce intimidation. They wanted to make the experience humane and welcoming so much of the building uses natural light. Even those in custody have a separate entrance to the building so that they are not seen walking throughout the building in handcuffs, which can be a shameful experience (Berman, 2005). After seven years of planning, developing, and renovating, the Red Hook community court opened in June of 2000.

Since the development of the community court, it has had beneficial impacts on the surrounding area. The community court had sought to decrease the use of jail and increase the use of alternative sanctions. About 50 percent of convicted cases receive a community or social service sentence and effectively reduces jail use for misdemeanor offenses. According to the Center for Court Innovation, the Red Hook Community Court also contributes roughly 70,000 hours of community service to Red Hook, which is worth about $500,500 worth of labor based on minimum wage.

## South Dallas Community Court

The South Dallas Community Court opened in October 2004 and was the first of three Dallas community courts. This court began as Dallas City Attorney's Office initiative between community prosecution and the municipal court. The success of this initiative eventually led to the permanent implementation of a community court. This court is housed in the Martin Luther King Jr. Community Center, which had already been open twenty years before the court moved in. The community center was a local staple in the community that residents visited for many community programs, including a public library, making it an ideal location.

This court serves cases that include quality-of-life offenses, assaults, prostitution, possession of drug paraphernalia, illegal dumping, hazardous building conditions, and overgrown vegetation. Additionally, this court operates a weekly drug court docket (Community Court, n.d.). The South Dallas Community Court has partnerships with local organizations such as streets and sanitation, Office of Community Services, Mayor's office and City Council, Grow South Initiative, Neighborhood Plus, and many other local programs. Collaborating with local organizations expands court resources and allows court participants to get assistance with a wide range of matters. For example, the court will assess the risk/needs of participants, and those who need substance abuse treatment will be given resources and assistance to combat addiction.

The South Dallas Community Court is heavily integrated and involved in the local community. In 2017, the community court completed 16,478 hours of community service and completed 1,116 community service projects (Casto et al., 2017). The court also had an 83 percent compliance rate for all mandates, with 752 defendants completing the program. In addition to court mandates, the court also participated in local community events such as National Night Out and Community Court Career Fairs. Furthermore, the South Dallas Community Court created in-house initiatives such as Prostitution Diversion, GANG initiative, and "Night" Court, to address the specific needs of the community.

The success of the South Dallas Community Court eventually led to national recognition and leadership. In 2008, 2014, and 2018, the South Dallas Community Court was selected as one of three courts in the nation by the U.S. Department of Justice's Bureau of Justice Assistance to be a National Mentor Court for community courts across the globe. The court works alongside the Center for Court Innovation to host site visits from jurisdictions around the world, seeking to establish their community courts (Center for Court Innovation, n.d.).

## Seattle Community Court

The Seattle Community Court was established in 2005 and, in 2007, expanded its jurisdiction to cover the entire city of Seattle. Multiple factors led to the development of Seattle's first community court. First, local business leaders wanted to address the homeless population because it interfered with a local business. Aggressive panhandling, theft, and disorderly conduct would deter patrons from entering local businesses, and employers wanted the city to address this issue. Secondly, local justice leaders were aware of the innovation of community courts. They realized that traditional methods of dealing with minor offenses were not working and wanted to diverge from old ways. Third, the city's jails were overpopulated. City officials did not want to spend money on a new jail and sought new ideas to handle low-level offenses. Finally, many local criminal justice leaders began to recognize how criminogenic needs and psychosocial conditions of defendants converged, and they wanted a more comprehensive method to address social issues such as homelessness, substance abuse, mental illness, and unemployment. All of these factors led to the planning and development of Seattle's first community court.

After several visits to Portland's Community Court, Seattle put together a planning committee that included a judge, attorneys, a chief clerk, and a member of the court administrator's senior staff. They received assistance from the Center of Court Innovation and local agencies and leaders to establish the court. Similar to other community courts, Seattle's court focused on quality-of-life offenses. One interesting criterion of Seattle's court was that first-time offenders were not eligible for participation. The court wanted to provide its resources to people with high needs and repetitive minor offenses. Additionally, the city's prosecutors were instructed to assess *the current risk* of defendants and public safety. This meant that people who might have had past violent or robbery convictions can still be eligible for the program if the offenses occurred long ago, and the defendant is currently a low-risk for public safety. The exclusion of first-time offenders and inclusion of past, more serious, offenses made Seattle's community court more distinct from other courts.

Seattle's Community Court proved to be effective in several ways. The court included community service as a sanction for all sentences. Two local community organizations, Street Outreach Services, and the Metropolitan Improvement District were used for about 90 percent of community service assignments. It was also found that successful cases were linked with about three services on average. The Seattle Community Court was also successful in reducing re-offending, establishing more efficient court processing, and reduced jail space use, saving the city roughly $370,000 in 2007 (Mahoney & Carlson, 2007).

Similar to the South Dallas Community Court, in 2009, Seattle's Community Court was selected as a Mentor court (Community Court, 2019). In 2009, the Justice Management Institute evaluated Seattle's court and found the community court group committed 66 percent fewer offenses while the control group had an increase of 50 percent during the same period. The Seattle Mayor's Office also estimated that the court saved the city roughly $1.5 million during their first three years of operation (Schweig, n.d.). Overall, Seattle's Community Court embraced the community court model by partnering with over twenty-five community organizations and leading with evidenced-based practices.

## CONCLUSION

Community courts are a promising new wave of innovative justice. Their ability to connect the community with the criminal justice system is a significant distinction from other problem-solving courts. Additionally, the amount of people who have contact with community courts is more expansive than other specialized courts. These courts, although not perfect, create a unique opportunity to rebuild, reinforce, and retain residents. Currently, many citizens have been losing trust in the court system due to the increasing evidence of pervasive injustices. Community courts may be a solution to repairing the trust and rectifying injustices. These courts change the perceptions of courts as a place of punishment and burden to an institution of uplift and resources. It is with great hope that as community courts continue to grow that their core value of compassionate justice positively influences the lives of all those within reach.

# REFERENCES

Andrews, D. A., & Bonta, J. (2010). Rehabilitating criminal justice policy and practice. *Psychology, Public Policy, and Law, 16*(1), 39–55.

Atkin-Plunk, C. A., Peck, J. H., & Armstrong, G. S. (2019). Do race and ethnicity matter? An examination of racial/ethnic differences in perceptions of procedural justice and recidivism among problem-solving court clients. *Race and Justice, 9*(2), 151–179.

Berman, G. (2005). *Good courts: The case for problem-solving justice.* New Press.

Berman, G., & Fox, A. (2010). The future of problem-solving justice: An international perspective. *University of Maryland Law Journal of Race, Religion, Gender & Class, 10*, 1–24.

Berman, G., & Gold, E. (2012). Procedural justice from the bench: How judges can improve the effectiveness of criminal courts. *The Judges' Journal, 51*(2), 20–22.

Braithwaite, J. (1989). *Crime, shame, and reintegration.* Cambridge University Press.

Braithwaite, J. (2002). Setting standards for restorative justice. *British Journal of Criminology, 42*, 563–577.

Breitenbucher, P., Bermejo, R., Killian, C. M., Young, N. K., Duong, L., & DeCerchio, K. (2018). Exploring racial and ethnic disproportionalities and disparities in family treatment courts: Findings from the regional partnership grant program. *Journal of Advancing Justice, 1*, 35–62.

Casto, L., Caso, C., & Gibson, D. (2017). *Overview of Dallas community courts. Government Performance and Financial Management Presentation: City of Dallas.* City of Dallas: Dallas, TX.

Center for Court Innovation. (2005). *Community court research: A literature review.* Center for Court Innovation.

Center for Court Innovation. (n.d.). South Dallas community court brochure. Retrieved from: http://www.courtinnovation.org/sites/default/files/documents/Dall asBrochure.pdf

Community Courts Put Rehabilitation First. (2019). The Seattle Times. Retrieved from: https://www.seattletimes.com/opinion/editorials/community-courts-put-reh abilitation-first/

Community Courts: Restorative and Swift Justice. (n.d.). Dallas city attorney office. Retrieved from: http://www.dallascityattorney.com/Community_Courts.html

Connor, T. A. (2018). Legitimation in action: An examination of community courts and procedural justice. *Journal of Crime and Justice, 42*(2), 161–183.

Constantine, M. G. (2007). Racial microaggressions against African American clients in cross-racial counseling relationships. *Journal of Counseling Psychology, 54*(1), 1–16.

Cresswell, L. (2001). Minority and non-minority perceptions of drug court program severity and effectiveness. *Journal of Drug Issues, 31*(1), 259–292.

Dannerbeck, A., Harris, G., Sundet, P., & Lloyd, K. (2006). Understanding and responding to racial differences in drug court outcomes. *Journal of Ethnicity in Substance Abuse, 5*(2), 1–22.

De Blasio, B., & Shea, D. (2020). *Police department city of New York*. Compstat.

Durkin, M., Cheesman, F., Maggard, S., Rottman, D., Sohoni, T., & Rubio, D. (2009). *Process evaluation of the Philadelphia community court*. National Center for State Courts.

Frazer, M. S. (2006). *The impact of the community court model on defendant perceptions of fairness*. Center for Court Innovation.

Freidman, M., Grawert, A. C., & Cullen, J. (2017). *Crime trends: 1990-2016. Brennan Center for Justice*. New York University Law School.

Gallagher, J. R. (2013). African American participants' views on racial disparities in drug court outcomes. *Journal of Social Work Practice in the Addictions*, *13*(2), 143–162.

Gallagher, J. R., & Nordberg, A. (2018). African American participants' suggestions for eliminating racial disparities in graduation rates: Implications for drug court practice. *Journal for Advancing Justice, 1*, 89–108.

Gallagher, J. R., Nordberg, A., & Dibley, A. R. (2017). Improving graduation rates for African Americans in drug court: Importance of human relationships and barriers to gaining and sustaining employment. *Journal of Ethnicity in Substance Abuse*, *18*(3), 1–15.

Gordon, M. (1994). Street justice. *New York*, *27*(48), 46.

Hahn, J. W. (2014). *Community perceptions of Newark: Neighborhood quality of life, safety, and the justice system*. Center for Court Innovation.

Hakuta, J., Soroushian, V., & Kralstein, D. (2008). *Do community courts transform the justice response to misdemeanor crime? Testing the impact of the Midtown Community court*. Center for Court Innovation.

Henry, K., & Kralstein, D. (2011). *Community courts: The research literature: A review of findings*. Center for Court Innovation.

Hickert, A. O., Boyle, S. W., & Tollefson, D. R. (2009). Factors that predict drug court completion and drop out: Findings from an evaluation of Salt Lake County's adult felony drug court. *Journal of Social Service Research*, *35*(2), 149–162.

Ho, T., Carey, S. M., & Malsch, A. M. (2018). Racial and gender disparities in treatment courts: Do they exist and is there anything we can do to change them? *Journal for Advancing Justice, 1*, 5–34.

Hoffman, J. (1993). A user-friendly experiment in justice; Community court aims at saving time and money in dealing with minor offenses. *The New York Times*, B1.

Jolliffe, D., & Farrington, D. P. (2009). *The effects on offending of the community justice initiatives in Liverpool and Salford*. Ministry of Justice.

Kaiser, K. A., & Holtfreter, K. (2016). An integrated theory of specialized court programs: Using procedural justice and therapeutic jurisprudence to promote offender compliance and rehabilitation. *Criminal Justice and Behavior*, *43*(1), 45–62.

Karafin, D. L. (2008). *Community courts across the globe: A survey of goals, performance measures and operations*. Center for Court Innovation.

Katz, S. (2009). *Expanding the community court model: Testing community court principles in the Bronx centralized courthouse*. Center for Court Innovation.

Lang, J. (2011). *What is a community court?* Center for Court Innovation.

Lee, E., & Martinez, J. (1998). *How it works: A summary of case flow and interventions at the midtown community court.* Center for Court Innovation.

Lee, C. G., Cheesman, F., Rottman, D., Swaner, R., Lambson, S., Rempel, M., & Curtis, R. (2013). *A community court grows in Brooklyn: A comprehensive evaluation of the Red Hook (Community Justice Center Final Report).* National Center for State Courts.

Mahoney, B., & Carlson, A. (2007). *The Seattle community court: Start-up, initial implementation, and recommendations concerning future development.* The Justice Management Institute.

Marlowe, D. B. (2013). Achieving racial and ethnic fairness in drug courts. *Court Review, 49*(1), 47.

Marlowe, D. B., Hardin, C. D., & Fox, C. L. (2016). *Painting the current picture: A national report on drug courts and other problem-solving courts in the United States.* National Drug Court Institute.

Marlowe, D. B., Shannon, L. M., Ray, B., Turpin, D. P., Wheeler, G. A., Newell, J., & Lawson, S. G. (2018). Developing a culturally proficient intervention for young African American men in drug court: Examining feasibility and estimating an effect size for habilation empowerment accountability therapy (HEAT). *Journal for Advancing Justice, 1,* 109-130.

McKean, J., & Warren-Gordon, K. (2011). Racial differences in graduation rates from adult drug treatment courts. *Journal of Ethnicity in Criminal Justice, 9*(1), 41–55.

McKenna, K. (2007). *Evaluation of the North Liverpool community justice centre.* Ministry of Justice Research Series.

Moore, K. (2004). *Op Data, 2001: Red Hook, Brooklyn.* Center for Court Innovation.

Nugent-Borakove, E. (2009). *Seattle municipal community court: Outcome evaluation final report.* Justice Management Institute.

Patten, M., Hood, Q.O., Low-Weiner, C., Lu, O., Bond, E., Hatten, D., & Chauhan, P. (2018). *Trends in misdemeanor arrests in New York 1980 to 2017: A report of the misdemeanor justice project.* John Jay College of Criminal Justice.

Reno, J., Marcus, D., Leary, M. L., & Gist, N. E. (2000). *Community courts: An evolving model.* Center for Court Innovation.

Roll, J. M., Prendergast, M., Richardson, K., Burdon, W., & Ramirez, A. (2005). Identifying predictors of treatment outcome in a drug court program. *The American Journal of Drug and Alcohol Abuse, 31*(4), 641–656.

Schweig, S. (n.d.). *Seattle community court supplies creative solutions for high-impact, low-level crime.* Center for Court Innovation.

Shannon, L. M., Jackson Jones, A., Nash, S., Newell, J., & Payne, C. M. (2018). Examining racial disparities in program completion and post-program recidivism rates: Comparing Caucasian and Non-Caucasian treatment court participants. *Journal for Advancing Justice, 1,* 63–88.

Sue, D. W., & Sue, D. (2012). *Counseling the culturally diverse: Theory and practice* (6th ed.). John Wiley & Sons, Inc.

Sviridoff, M., Rottman, D., Ostrom, B., & Curtis, R. (2001). *Dispensing justice locally: The implementation and effects of the midtown community court.* Center for Court Innovation.

Terrell, F., & Terrell, S. (1984). Race of counselor, client sex, cultural mistrust level, and premature termination from counseling among Black clients. *Journal of Counseling Psychology, 31*(3), 371–375.

Thompson, C. E., & Jenal, S. T. (1994). Interracial and intraracial quasi-counseling interactions when counselors avoid discussing race. *Journal of Counseling Psychology, 41*(4), 484–491.

Vasquez, M. J. T. (2007). Cultural difference and the therapeutic alliance: An evidence-based analysis. (Report). *The American Psychologist, 62*(8), 878–885.

Wexler, D. B., & Winick, B. J. (1996). *Law in a therapeutic key: Developments in therapeutic jurisprudence.* Carolina Academic Press.

Wierzbicki, M., & Pekarik, G. (1993). A meta-analysis of psychotherapy dropout. *Professional Psychology: Research and Practice, 24*(2), 190–195.

Wilson, J., & Kelling, G. (1982). Broken windows. *Atlantic, 249*(3), 29.

Winick, B. J. (2003). Therapeutic jurisprudence and problem-solving courts. (Special Series: Problem Solving Courts and Therapeutic Jurisprudence). *Fordham Urban Law Journal, 30*(3), 1055.

Wolf, E. M., Sowards, K. A., & Wolf, D. A. (2003). Predicting retention of drug court participants using event history analysis. *Journal of Offender Rehabilitation, 37*(3–4), 139–162.

Zozula, C. (2019). *Courting the community: Legitimacy and punishment in a community court.* Temple University Press.

*Chapter 8*

# A Trifecta of Challenges for Veterans Treatment Courts

Jared A. Michaels and Anne S. Douds

## INTRODUCTION

Veterans treatment courts (VTCs) premiered in the problem-solving court arena in the mid-2000s in Buffalo, New York, and Anchorage, Alaska (Smith, 2012). Since then, advocates have celebrated them as a judicial extension of the "no warrior left behind" ethos (Russell, 2009), and by scholars as responsive to veterans' criminogenic and service-related needs (Cavanaugh, 2011; Johnson et al., 2015). Most of the research on VTCs in the early years focused on process evaluation and theoretical benefits of the programs (National Center for State Courts, n.d.). However, researchers are beginning to consider some of the knottier policies and practices in VTCs (see, e.g., Benner, 2019; Douds & Hummer, 2019; Hartley & Baldwin, 2019). Three of the most pressing concerns represent a trifecta of challenges that have the potential to deny victims' rights, undermine uniformity and consistency across mentoring programs, and create confusion concerning the efficacy of these courts. On the other hand, if these issues can be addressed, VTCs can continue to grow into robust mechanisms for the legal redemption of eligible veterans. This chapter begins with a synopsis of the evolution of VTCs, then moves through three sections of inquiry on (1) the rights and roles of victims in VTCs; (2) challenges surrounding mentoring programs in VTCs; and (3) the dearth of data on outcomes and cost-benefit analysis in VTCs. Each section concludes with policy recommendations.

## BACKGROUND

More than 460 VTCs operate in the United States, and no two are exactly the same (Flatley et al., 2017). Some of those differences are by design; the

VTC movement prides itself on community responsivity and individualized justice. Founded in therapeutic jurisprudence (Howlett & Stein, 2016), VTCs are one form of problem-solving court that divert eligible criminal defendant/ veterans from traditional criminal courts to needs-based programs. Many problem-solving courts focus on a specific crime,[1] such as domestic violence (Campie & Francis, 2019; Regoeczi & Hubbard, 2018), or a specific condition,[2] such as addiction (Haskins, 2019; Walker et al., 2016). Problem-solving courts utilize restorative justice and procedural justice models to handle cases holistically and ensure all parties feel the result of the case is fair and reduce the potential of future recidivism (Berman & Feinblatt, 2001; Braithwaite, 1999; Boone & Langbroek, 2018).

VTCs, as indicated by their name, focus on a type of offender: people who have served, or are serving, in the United States military (Rowen, 2020; Russell, 2009). Many VTCs limit their services to veterans who have committed a crime stemming from their time in service, such as substance abuse or conduct related to trauma or posttraumatic stress (Cavanaugh, 2011; Douds & Ahlin, 2017). Other eligibility criteria can vary. While some VTCs accept only nonviolent participants, others accept those facing charges involving violence (Cavanaugh, 2011; Douds & Ahlin, 2017). Similarly, VTCs generally do not accept veterans who were dishonorably discharged (Baldwin, 2015).

The VTC movement grew from judges' concerns that traditional criminal court processes are ill-suited to respond to veterans' unique needs (Cavanaugh, 2011; Russell, 2009; Smith, 2012). Unfortunately, VTCs did not develop empirically from systematic evaluation of veterans' criminogenic needs or investigation into how best to serve those needs to reduce offending (Baldwin & Brooke, 2019). Instead, VTCs arose in part due to societal perceptions that veterans deserve special treatment due to their service and in part due to misperceptions about veterans' risk of offending (Rowen, 2020; see also Bronson et al., 2015). VTCs' emergence coincided with an intense phase of the Global War on Terror, and public opinion largely favored military personnel (Kleykamp et al., 2018; Pew Research Center, 2011). Scholars continue to debate the propriety and equity of treating some part of the offending population differently, an issue for many problem-solving courts (Berman & Feinblatt, 2015; Hartley & Baldwin, 2019; Lucas & Hanrahan, 2016; Rowen, 2020).

Nevertheless, there is a rational argument for providing "special" or "extra" services for veterans. Post-traumatic stress (PTS), depression, and traumatic brain injuries (TBIs) are tragic signatures of the current wars. Many veterans in VTCs suffer from either or both conditions (Smee et al., 2013). Moreover, veterans may suffer from military sexual trauma (MST), which makes them more likely to suffer from comorbid issues such as PTSD

(Kintzle et al., 2015) Conversely, PTSD-afflicted veterans might suffer from similarly comorbid issues such as depression or substance abuse (Reisman, 2016). While the data are clear that, proportionally, veterans are less likely than nonveterans to be incarcerated for criminal offenses (Bronson et al., 2015), the data also are clear that veterans with untreated mental health issues are at higher risk for committing certain crimes (Finlay et al., 2017; Yerramsetti et al., 2017). To the extent that their increased risk for offending relates to injuries they sustained in service to the Nation, it makes sense to provide government-funded interventions for their service-related conditions and related criminal justice needs. Analogous to workers compensation, injuries suffered in the course of military service should be compensable by government.

VTCs pull from community-based resources and the Veterans Administration's Veteran Justice Outreach (VJO) program to offer a larger swath of specialized resources than traditional trial courts often cannot access on their own (Cavanaugh, 2011). VTC culture also contributes to their efficacy (Ahlin & Douds, 2018; Vaughan et al., 2019), and mentor programs appear to contribute to veterans' successful completion of VTC programs (Knudsen & Wingenfeld, 2016; Slattery et al., 2013). Finally, VTCs facilitate invaluable substance abuse treatment, employment services, and streamlined access to federal and state resources and benefits (Johnson, 2016; Tsai et al., 2018).

Problem-solving courts, including VTCs, continue to enjoy broad spectrum public support (Thielo et al., 2019). Opinion research suggests that communities value the potential upside of rehabilitative models and discount potential threats to due process inherent to problem-solving court models (Thielo et al., 2019; Tsai et al., 2017). Historic concerns about coerciveness and due process remain (Mitchell, 2018). But VTCs suffer from three additional challenges that, if not resolved, may threaten their public support and empirical value. Specifically, VTCs must examine their practices (or lack thereof) related to victims; the appropriate extent of mentor involvement in VTCs; and more consistent measures of effectiveness.

## VICTIMS IN VTCS

VTCs handle cases involving victims, and many accept cases of domestic violence and crimes of interpersonal violence (Bronson et al., 2015; Douds et al., 2017; Gourley, 2016; Kravetz, 2012; Taft et al., 2009).[3] There is robust debate among scholars about whether VTCs should accept cases involving crimes that include any form of victimization, and even more heated disagreement about the propriety of handling domestic violence cases in veteran-centric settings.[4] While that theoretical discussion is beyond the scope of this chapter, it deserves thoughtful attention and should inform policy going forward. As of now, however, the horse has left the stable; policy must deal with the reality that VTCs take cases involving victims.

## Victims' Rights

VTCs grew from drug courts that purportedly handle only "victimless crimes" (Hodulik, 2001; Robinson & Tate, 2016) and that, generally, do not accept cases involving violent crimes or other crimes commonly associated with victimization (King & Pasquarella, 2009). Perhaps early VTC advocates simply did not think about victims' rights. Unfortunately, as the VTC movement grew, there was not concomitant growth in attention to victims in VTCs.

All states, the federal government, the District of Columbia, many Native American tribes, and most U.S. territories recognize a handful of victims' rights. In general, federal law provides a baseline for victims' rights that courts must honor (34 U.S.C. § 20141 [2018]). Those fundamental rights include descriptions of services available to victims, reasonable protection from their offenders, notice of certain court proceedings, separate waiting areas during court sessions, general information about criminal justice processes, and the opportunity to give a victim impact statement either prior to or during sentencing (34 U.S.C. § 20141 [2018]). Most states provide additional rights, and thirty-three states establish victims' rights in the language of their constitutions, with corresponding adjustments in court system policy (Glassberg & Dodd, 2008). Those additional rights include the right to participate in plea negotiations, the right to consult with the prosecutor, and the right to be present during all formal proceedings (U.S. Department of Justice, Office for Victims of Crime, 2002).

While traditional courts appear to do a reasonably good job of honoring those rights, (Boateng & Abess, 2017; Cassell, 2017), the same cannot be said for most problem-solving courts (Binder, 2020; Glassberg & Dodd, 2008). For example, many VTCs require that prosecuting attorneys confer with victims as part of the pre-admission screening process, but there is no consistency among practices after that initial consultation (Luna & Redlich, 2020; see e.g., state statutes in Louisiana, LA Rev Stat § 13:5366 [2018], New Jersey, NJ Rev Stat § 2C:43-26 [2019], and Florida, FL Stat § 948.08 [2019]).[5] In a study that the second author currently is finalizing, Douds and her research team found that only a handful of 22 VTCs in a mid-Atlantic state had any documented policies related to victims. Those anemic policies require consultation with victims prior to admission to VTC, and one gives veto power to victims over their veteran/offenders' admission. Interview data in that same study revealed that, in practice, other counties also give victims voice in admissions decisions, but those courts do not have any documented or consistent policies. None of the courts honored all legally mandated victims' rights.

## Victim Advocates

Victim advocates do as their title indicates—they advocate for victims. There are more than 12,000 victims' services offices operating across all fifty states (Oudekerk et al., 2019). Most are local-level, nonprofit organizations that train volunteers and employees to advocate for victims' rights and needs. Perhaps VTCs could improve their responsiveness and achieve some efficiencies by including victim advocates in their operational teams.

The typical VTC team includes a judge, a district attorney, a defense attorney, a dedicated probation officer, a Veterans Justice Outreach (VJO) specialist, and a mentor coordinator (McCall et al., 2019). They often also include mental health or drug-treatment specialists (McCall et al., 2019). Typical hearings involve a judge, the veteran offender, a probation officer, a volunteer mentor, and a defense attorney (Rowen, 2020). Notably, none of the literature says that VTC teams usually, or even occasionally, involve a victim advocate.[6]

Victim advocates serve several purposes. They provide a constant reminder that courts must pay attention to victims' needs (Durfee, 2019). They help combat potentially coercive forces during the process of the case (Lemon, 2006; Pinchevsky, 2017; Zegveld, 2018), particularly in domestic violence cases that, by nature, are fraught with problematic power dynamics (Fialk & Mitchel, 2004). They provide agency or voice for victims throughout the legal process, and they bring depth of knowledge about victims' needs and victims' services to a team that otherwise may not have any expertise on victims' issues (Fialk & Mitchel, 2004; Kravetz, 2012). Moreover, because victim advocates work at the community level, they can reinforce VTCs' efforts to remain responsive to communities' needs. Finally, independent victim advocates (those not linked with the prosecutor's office) are best suited to protect victims' confidences and promote their best interests (Bakht, 2005).[7]

## Bottom Line for Victims in Veterans Courts

Federal legislation such as 34 U.S.C. § 20141 (2018) establishes a floor for court procedure, and VTCs are not meeting even these minimum standards. Some scholars suggest that problem-solving courts are exempt from these requirements as a sort of gray area (Casey, 2004; Spinak, 2010). Why? And even if legally they are not required to provide services, should they not do so as part of their therapeutic mission? Intersections among victims' rights legislation and VTC policies must be explored more thoroughly. Moreover, state legislatures should consider establishing binding schema for preserving victims' rights. As of now, only ten states provide for victims' rights in their VTC legislation.[8] Among these state laws, the language and concerns differed. While Colorado's statute signaled intent to "restore victims of crime" and make sure the defendant will "pay restitution to victims of crime," Connecticut's statute included language similar to a Crime Victim Act or Victims Bill of Rights, about providing "notice" and making sure the victim "has an opportunity to be heard by the court on the matter." Regardless of whether states have legislation specific for VTCs or more general laws governing problem-solving courts, all VTCs should amend their policies and procedures to incorporate their states' crime victims' rights law and other applicable law, and they should coordinate with their local victim advocacy organizations to develop meaningful, local-level programming and procedures.

## MENTORS IN VTCS

Unlike other problem-solving courts, many VTCs have mentor programs or are in the process of creating them. Of the 461 VTCs Flatley and colleagues reviewed in 2017, 68.8 percent had operational mentoring programs, and 9.5 percent had one under development. Mentor programs commonly define mentors as "coach, guide, role model, advocate, and a support person for the individual veteran participant with whom he/she is working" (Johnson, 2016, p. 45). Others define their role more in military jargon, as "battle buddies" to help with "substance abuse, PTSD, mental illness or whatever issues landed them in the court system" (Michigan Judiciary, 2019, p. 4). These broad definitions leave significant room for interpretation, and there is variation across the country as to who may be a mentor and what they are supposed to do.

### Eligibility to Be a Mentor

VTCs typically form their mentor policies internally; thus, there are no uniform standards for eligibility or other criteria. Broadly speaking, mentors are veterans who volunteer and pass certain background checks and screening criteria.[9] Additionally, some courts exclude mentors who are homeless or housing insecure (Buncombe County VTC, n.d.), and other programs exclude active law enforcement officers and others who may have a conflict of interest (Montgomery County VTC, n.d.). All must complete some form of training before working with VTC participants.

## Training

The nature, scope, and content of training vary from court to court. Justice for Vets offers mentor training on a national scale that covers some aspects of mentoring, but it does not address thorny issues such as privilege/confidentiality, due process, and mandated reporting (Justice for Vets, n.d.). Local-level policies include in-house mentor training (Pierce County VTC, 2011);[10] clinical and legal training sessions; communication; navigating the VA; boundary setting; and issue-specific sessions on conditions such as PTSD and TBI (Judicial Branch, n.d.; Montgomery County VTC, n.d.; Tennessee Association of Recovery Court Professionals [TARCP], n.d.).

## Roles and Responsibilities

At the most basic level, mentors help court staff refer veterans to needed services, and provide nonclinical support (Buncombe County VTC, n.d.; TARCP, n.d.). They serve as role models under the theory that "social relationships with other law-abiding individuals and groups are a primary factor in desistance from crime" (Johnstone & Van Ness, 2007, p. 234). They are listeners, "force multipliers," and advocates, but they are not supposed to help veterans solve their legal or personal problems. Nevertheless, many do. Some stories shared by mentors belie their detached objectivity and indicate that mentors, perhaps understandably, become attached to their mentors and embroiled in their issues (Lucas, 2018; Moore, 2012). Anecdotal evidence illustrates inconsistencies within and among VTCs. For example, one Idaho county encourages mentors to do anything they can to assist veterans, including giving them rides (Venkatraj, 2017), while another county in the state admonishes veterans that "your mentor should not be a crutch. He or she is not allowed to give you rides, money, or other things of value" (Comal County VTC, 2020).

## Confidentiality

Some programs mandate that mentors maintain confidences; others require that they report anything that mentees report that violates court rules or the law (Douds & Ahlin, 2017; Lucas, 2018; Pierce, 2011). Mentors are also expected to call upon the necessary authorities when the participant or someone else from the program is put at risk (VTC of Dane County, n.d.; Comal County VTC, n.d.), but as Moore (2012) describes, it can be hard for a mentor to establish a direct connection between risky activity and threat of harm, while moreover, mentors can have some confusion as to whether they should report such behavior.

Nonetheless, mentors are intended to be perceived as a trustworthy figure for the participant mentee. Asserting the independence of the mentors, the Buncombe County VTC does not see mentors as part of the VTC team (Buncombe County VTC, n.d.), falling in line with the general trend that while mentors should offer suggestions and general guidance to participants, their input is not widely taken into account for participant progression through the VTC process. This was a repeated comment brought up during the Lucas (2018) study where some mentors experienced frustration as a result of this disconnect, while others found the separation to be justified due to the level of professional specialization that members of the VTC treatment team provide.

As Lucas (2018) notes, not all courts order a specific mentor/mentee pairing. But most are asked to commit to a minimum of a year of involvement, which reflects the approximate time required for many veterans' cases to process through courts (Charleston County VTC, 2018). In situations when a specific pairing occurs, a mentor/mentee pair can be based on the time period they served, branch of service, and rank (Hawai'i VTC, n.d.) or whether they had combat experience, matching, branch of service, "specific skill of a peer mentor matched to the need of a veteran participant," and based on similar age, gender, and ethnicity (Fifth Judicial District VTC, 2015).

Mentor programs seek to better veteran participants' lives. While many jurisdictions work toward this goal in different ways, it appears that mentor programs do contribute to their intended purpose. VTCs that are considering implementing mentor programs should analyze how they will operate on a logistical level and consider tracking data and incorporating measures of success. Thus far, there have been only a handful of evaluations of VTC mentor programs, and all of those have been case studies. More data would be very helpful as these programs continue to grow. Moreover, VTCs should strive to recruit new mentors to stave off mentor burnout, all the while considering their training standards and what resources the program provides mentors.

## Strengths of Mentor Programs

The limited data on the impact of mentor programs is "suggestive [of] evidence that establishing a mentor-mentee relationship promotes success for Veterans Court participants" (Johnson, 2016, p. 53; see also Cartwright, 2011; Slattery et al., 2013). Mentor programs seem to work best when combined with trauma-specific treatment and medication (Knudsen et al., 2016). As noted earlier, little is known about the mechanisms by which VTC mentor programs achieve success, but it likely relates to their obvious role in recreating a semblance of military culture. Mentors literally embody the warrior ethos and "no one left behind" mentality that has sustained service members through perilous duty stations and challenging reintegration experiences (Ahlin & Douds, 2018; Douds & Ahlin, 2017; Lucas, 2018). They also provide another link to veteran-specific resources such as VA offices, local veterans service offices, and other support agencies.

## Weaknesses of Mentor Programs

Mentor programs frequently fail to function as intended (Johnson, 2016), and they often suffer from confusion about what mentors should do (and should not do) vis-a-vis their mentees (Lucas, 2018; Moore, 2012). Mentors' roles are not defined well, and mentors in the same court have as many as four different understandings of their rights and obligations (Lucas, 2018). Moreover, despite being one of the closest persons to the veteran participant, the VTCs examined by Lennon (2019) do not require any reporting from mentors. The mentor role contributes more to the veteran participants' well-being than to the legal process of the VTC. "He or she is in a unique role, someone who can speak to court personnel and the justice-involved veteran without legal ramifications" (Lennon, 2019, p. 12). The relationship between mentor, prosecutor, and other court personnel is tentative at best; it is informal and with relatively infrequent extensive communication between the mentor and VTC. Herein lays a troubling ambiguity. It is not clear if mentors fail to follow the mission of the VTC as their role has not been sufficiently described. While volunteer mentors are hailed as a critical component of VTCs, the position is also susceptible to the scattered rules, regulations, and practice experienced by VTCs around the country.

## DEARTH OF DATA

As critical consideration of VTCs grows, so too does the rigor of research on outcomes for participants, court systems, and communities. Several scholars offer a variety of outcome analyses, but Lucas and Hanrahan (2016) concur with the authors that the research community needs more robust outcome evaluations, particularly longitudinal outcomes for veterans, to provide more holistic understandings of the impacts of VTCs. At present, no states have mechanisms for tracking statewide performance measures for VTCs or other specialized courts (see, e.g., Gonsalves, 2020).

To begin to build a base for future research, the authors searched five databases for the terms "veterans court" and "outcomes," which led them to identify twenty-eight discreet veterans/participant outcomes discussed in relation to VTCs. The authors then searched those same five databases again, using the search terms "veterans court" and each of those twenty-eight outcomes. Table 8.1 summarizes and provides examples from the results of that research.

## Graduation rates

Most VTCs track graduation/completion rates, which are simple counts of numbers of veterans who complete programs. Graduation requires successful completion of all prescribed programming, but it does not require linear progressions through that programming. In other words, participants may have setbacks, fail required drug test, or miss mandatory appointments and still graduate from the program. This is congruent with the problem-solving court model (see chapter 1). Participants achieve graduation when VTC court personnel determine that they have met the requirement. Therefore, this metric is not consistent across courts, and it may mask some incidents of what otherwise would be called recidivism, such as failing a drug test. However, it could be meaningful to compare graduation rates among specialized courts to examine relative effectiveness of different court models and other issues.

Studies that examine graduation rates find that VTCs' outcomes "appear at least as favorable as those of other specialized treatment courts" (Holbrook & Anderson, 2011, p. 5). Fourteen respondent courts hosted 465 total participants over approximately two years, including fifty-nine graduated, twenty-one terminated, and eight withdrew (Holbrook & Anderson, 2011, p. 31). They note that one veteran recidivated after graduation. The authors highlight an alleged 98 percent graduation rate. But when examined more closely, these numbers indicate a less than 50 percent graduation rate. The authors confound graduation with recidivism and report a 2 percent recidivism rate without accounting for the twenty-nine who terminated and, presumably, were not tracked for recidivism after leaving the program. This study highlights the need for definitional accuracy and consistency as the research community attempts to track graduation rates, and all other outcomes, in VTCs. At this point, there is no consistent metric for graduation across courts.

## Recidivism Rates

Comparison and analysis of recidivism rates also can be problematic. Recidivism measures have been defined in a variety of ways, generally involving arrest for a new crime during VTC participation or within a pre-set number of years following graduation from VTC (Himes, 2019) (after entry); Knudsen & Wingenfeld, 2016 (in-program, six months, and twelve months); Johnson et al., 2015 (following graduation); Caron, 2013 (at six

**Table 8.1  Panoply of Participant Outcome Measures and Related Studies**

| Outcome Measure | Study Authors and Year |
| --- | --- |
| Graduation | Holbrook and Anderson, 2011 |
| | Johnson, 2016 |
| Recidivism *(breakdown in Table Three)* | Caron, 2013 |
| | Erickson, 2016 |
| | Frederick, 2014 |
| | Hartley and Baldwin, 2019 |
| | Himes, 2019 |
| | Holbrook and Anderson, 2011 |
| | Johnson et al., 2017 |
| | Johnson, 2016 |
| | Johnson et al., 2015 |
| | Knudsen and Wingenfeld, 2016 |
| | Shannon et al., 2017 |
| | Slattery et al., 2013 |
| | Smith, 2012 |
| | Tsai et al., 2018 |
| | Tsai et al., 2017 |
| Sobriety | Caron, 2013 |
| | Derrick et al., 2018 (using DAST-10 and AUDIT-C) |
| | Himes, 2019 |
| | Johnson et al., 2017 |
| | Shannon et al., 2017 |
| | Slattery et al., 2013 |
| | Stainbrook et al., 2015 (using CAGE) |
| Participation in specific treatment programs | Caron, 2013 |
| | Himes, 2019 |
| | Johnson et al., 2017 |
| Participation in domestic violence treatment | Caron, 2013 |
| Procedural Justice | Dollar et al., 2018 |
| VA benefits connectedness | Caron, 2013 |
| | Johnson, 2016 |
| | Tsai et al., 2018 |
| | Tsai et al., 2017 |
| Employment/Income | Caron, 2013 |
| | Himes, 2019 |
| | Johnson, 2016 |
| | Shannon et al., 2017 |
| | Tsai et al., 2018 |
| | Tsai et al., 2017 |
| Education | Johnson, 2016 |
| | Shannon et al., 2017 |
| Physical Health | Knudsen & Wingenfeld, 2016 |
| | Tsai et al., 2018 |

*(Continued)*

**Table 8.1   Panoply of Participant Outcome Measures and Related Studies** (*Continued*)

| Outcome Measure | Study Authors and Year |
| --- | --- |
| Housing | Caron, 2013 |
| | Himes, 2019 |
| | Johnson et al., 2017 |
| | Tsai et al., 2018 |
| | Tsai et al., 2017 |
| PTSD | Derrick et al., 2018 |
| | Larsen, 2014 |
| | Knudsen and Wingenfeld, 2016 |
| | Slattery et al. 2013 |
| | Stainbrook et al., 2015 |
| BASIS 24 (mental health and substance abuse) | Knudsen and Wingenfeld, 2016 |
| | Slattery et al., 2013 |
| | Stainbrook et al., 2015 |
| PHQ Depression | Derrick et al., 2018 |
| | Larsen, 2014 |
| Trauma History (THS) | Larsen, 2014 |
| Combat Exposure Scale (CES) | Larsen, 2014 |
| Addiction Survey Index (ASI) | Himes, 2019 |
| | Larsen, 2014 |
| Mental Health Statistics Improvement Program (MHSIP) | Knudsen and Wingenfeld, 2016 |
| Quality of Life (SF-36) and Related Measures | Knudsen and Wingenfeld, 2016 |
| Recovery Markers Questionnaire | Knudsen and Wingenfeld, 2016 |
| Hours of Sleep | Knudsen and Wingenfeld, 2016 |
| Family Functioning | Knudsen and Wingenfeld, 2016 |
| Aggression – Modified Overt Aggression Scale (MOAS) | Derrick et al., 2018 |
| Prosocial activities and relationships | Johnson 2016 |
| Mentor program participation[i] | Johnson, 2016 |
| Mental health diagnoses; at entry and end | Johnson 2016 |
| Days in program | Tsai et al., 2017 |
| Judicial interaction | Himes, 2019 |
| | Shannon et al., 2017 |
| Characteristics of military service | Derrick et al., 2018 |

[i] This measure is included in the table but not discussed in the test because most VTCs require that veterans work with a mentor (Flatley, 2017). Therefore, this measure may not be useful to most VTCs.
*Source:* Compiled by authors.

months, twelve months, eighteen months, and twenty-four months after entry); Slattery et al., 2013 (one year); Smith, 2012 (three years).[11] These definitional differences, as well as variations in interpretation and implementation among various courts, may account for the somewhat conflicting data from the extant literature. The following table showcases studies based on comparisons between participant and non-participants (of both veteran

Table 8.2    Recidivism Breakdown

| Outcome Measure | Study Authors and Year |
|---|---|
| Studies comparing participants and non-participants (general population) | Erickson, 2016<br>Frederick, 2014<br>Smith, 2012 |
| Studies comparing participants and non-participants (veterans) | Erickson, 2016<br>Hartley and Baldwin, 2019<br>Johnson, 2016<br>Smith, 2012<br>Tsai et al., 2017 |
| Studies comparing graduates and non-graduates | Caron, 2013<br>Hartley and Baldwin, 2019<br>Himes, 2019<br>Johnson, 2016 |
| Studies analyzing participant recidivism over time | Caron, 2013<br>Hartley and Baldwin, 2019<br>Johnson et al., 2017<br>Johnson, 2016<br>Johnson et al., 2015<br>Knudsen and Wingenfeld, 2016<br>Shannon et al., 2017<br>Slattery et al., 2013<br>Tsai et al., 2018 |

*Source:* Compiled by authors.

and general population demographics), between program graduates and non-graduates, and a general assessment of recidivism data over time or within a specific point in time for a program (table 8.2).

In the Smith (2012) study, 45 percent of veterans who graduated from VTCs recidivated compared with the overall state recidivism rate of 50.4 percent. Interestingly, in this study, recidivism rates were lower among veterans who terminated early from the VTC program. Only 36 percent of those who left early committed a subsequent crime. Forty-one percent of veterans who opted not to participate in VTC ended up recidivating (Smith, 2012). In contrast, Hartley and Baldwin (2019) found that VTC graduates were least likely to recidivate at a statistically significant level. Johnson and colleagues (2015) similarly "found arrests following separation from the veterans' court program, was inversely associated with length of stay in the program," and Johnson's 2016 study found that only 9 percent of veterans recidivated while in the VTC program and only 6 percent recidivated "eventually" (Johnson, 2016, p. 39). Himes (2019) saw a relatively higher recidivism rate at 36.2 percent for the two counties reviewed by the study. Frederick (2014) recorded a 2 percent recidivism rate for the Buffalo VTC, less than 2 percent for eleven of the then fourteen, 2011 VTCs, and a roughly 2.9 percent recidivism rate for the Anchorage VTC graduates from 2004 to 2006. Erickson (2016) reviewed two other VTCs in addition to the Anchorage locale covered by Smith (2012), noting a 3 percent recidivism rate for one and "very low" for the other. Erickson (2016) nonetheless cautions interpretation of positive results regarding inflated metrics and false positives. Moreover, at least one study found increased recidivism among VTC participants in comparison to veterans who do not engage in VTC programming (Tsai et al., 2017)

Courts define what constitutes "recidivism" so differently within and among jurisdictions that it is impossible to perform apples-to-apples comparisons at this point (Arno, 2014; Erickson, 2016). Moreover, the studies discussed here define recidivism as a new "arrest," not as a new offense. If a veteran uses illegal drugs but does not get arrested for that use, then the court does not necessarily consider that recidivism. A positive drug test in traditional court would count as recidivism, but a positive drug test in VTC might not. Similarly, Johnson (2016) notes that courts may count as recidivism a participant being charged with a crime, despite situations when the judge may not find the participant defendant guilty, invalidating the principle of innocent until proven guilty. For this and other reasons, it is difficult to compare outcomes between traditional and problem-solving courts. Comparisons among various types of problem-solving courts might be more practical, as mentioned earlier.

The methodological, definitional, and interpretive differences among these studies highlight the need for further evaluation of confounding and contributing factors associated with successful completion of VTC programs (see McCall et al., 2018). Practitioners and the research community should work together to craft consistent definitions of both terms in order to promote meaningful comparisons and analysis.

## Treatment Participation and Completion

In addition to tracking data in relation to time of entry and time of exit through graduation and recidivism data, some studies measure VTC program duration, or how long the program lasts (Tsai et al., 2017),[12] specific treatment duration (Derrick et al., 2018; Hartley & Baldwin, 2019; Johnson, 2016), treatment frequency (Himes, 2019), and treatment completion rates for specific programs in addition to graduation rates (Caron, 2013) as they relate to recidivism. Himes (2019) notes a statistically significant relationship between participants completing treatment sessions and program completion. These measures help parse the efficacy of treatment type and treatment intensity. Overall, it appears from the limited literature that the longer the programming, the more successful the veteran is on a variety of measures.

Veterans who do not commence or complete treatment are more likely to recidivate (Johnson et al., 2017). Almost all courts refer veterans to in-program and post-program treatment, but follow-up and enforcement are weak and inconsistent (Johnson et al., 2017). Some of these studies are longitudinal, and others provide a point-in-time snapshot of whether veterans engaged in their prescribed treatment plans, ranging from substance abuse counseling to employment assistance. VTCs and veterans benefit from tracking length of participation; the longer veterans stay in VTC programs, the less likely they are to recidivate (Johnson, 2016). Three studies helpfully examine outcomes, duration, and demographics. Tsai and colleagues (2018) and Johnson (2016) both examine outcomes in relation to a variety of demographic characteristics. Himes (2019, p. 69) breaks down treatment completion, graduation, and recidivism by gender, age, race/ethnicity, marital status, drug-of-choice, housing status, employment status, and history of combat service. Her sample size was small, but her model deserves attention. Similarly, Johnson and colleagues (2017) examined relationships among housing status and a variety of other factors and in-program recidivism. In an ideal world, VTCs could all track these data and run similar analyses to even better tailor services to need.

## Sobriety

Abstinence from alcohol or substance use are part and parcel to treatment participation and completion. At least four published studies examined sobriety as a unit of analysis, and some break down those measures into numbers of tests administered, frequency of testing, and tests for substance use (Johnson, 2016). Sobriety is positively associated with desistence from offending, indicating an obvious point of intervention with multiple prosocial implication (Johnson et al., 2017). Spotty drug testing practices and non-standardized approaches to screening "contravene the standards and best practices of treatment courts per the NADCP, which stipulate testing all participants on a truly random basis" (Johnson, 2016, p. 33). It appears that all VTCs require proof of sobriety as a condition of participation (Douds & Ahlin, 2017). Therefore, it stands to reason that tracking sobriety outcomes flows naturally from standard VTC operations. Increasing test numbers and frequency will allow VTCs to better understand the scope of sobriety problems among their veterans and craft more suitable interventions for their participants. If VTCs were to agree, as a matter of policy, to use certain measures of sobriety such as DAST-10, AUDIT-C, or CAGE (Derrick et al., 2018; Stainbrook et al., 2015), then VTCs would be better prepared to compare data and develop nationwide, standardized practices founded in data.

## Aggression

Derrick and colleagues uniquely measured aggression and mitigating treatment. They found a "statistically significant reduction in aggressive behaviors among" VTC participants (Derrick et al., 2018, p. 178). They also found that outcomes related to aggression depended in part on the nature of veterans' military service, shining light on this critical but grossly under-studied factor. Treatment providers need to understand the influence of lengthy deployments, combat, trauma, loss of loved ones, and problems with reintegration have on veterans' responsibility to treatment. VTCs could help immensely with this aspect by gathering this information at intake to asking mentors to assist by making notes as they get to know their mentees and explore these sensitive topics.

## PTSD Evaluation

There are well-established connections among PTSD, hyper-arousal, and aggression (Elbogen et al., 2016; Rodenberg et al., 2015). However, there is far less evidence that PTSD actually increases offending (Sreenevasan et al., 2013). Some courts use formal PTSD assessment tools to develop treatment plans for their veterans, a practice that could prove invaluable as researchers continue to parse the relationships among mental health and offending. Slattery and colleagues (2013) assessed preliminary results of veterans with PTSD and TBI in a pilot VTC program, measuring participants through baseline, six-month, and twelve-month 200 item interviews including the PTSD Checklist-Civilian version (PCL-C). They do not explain why they did not use the PCL-M screening tool that targets military personnel rather than the PCL-C version that focuses more on civilians (Yarvis et al., 2012). The distinctions are not dramatic, and future research will not need to choose because the new PCL-5 does not distinguish between military and civilian (Weathers et al., 2013). Perhaps VTCs could agree to all use PCL-5 to facilitate meaningful comparisons going forward. Higher PCL-C scores indicate higher morbidity. PCL-C scores decreased over time, with longer participation in VTC programs associated with decreased symptoms. The Stainbrook et al. (2015) study also noted a net reduction in PCL-C scores. It is crucial that VTCs increase the attention they pay to PTSD evaluation and tracking of offending to better ascertain the nature of the relationship. Study of PTSD among VTC participants is a critical area of expansion as more VTCs are created and as a more holistic understanding of PTSD is reached.

## Mental and Behavioral Health (Other than PTSD)

Much has been made of veterans' alleged fragile mental health (Frederick, 2014). Larsen's comprehensive study among forty VTC participants between

November 2011 and April 2013 and using five established screening tools and semi-structured interviews paints a different picture. Using the Depression Patient Health Questionnaire (PHQ), Trauma History Screen (THS), Combat Exposure Scale (CES), PCL, and Addiction Severity Index (ASI), she found no significant differences between veterans and non-veterans on scores for psychiatric problems. However, she found that veterans are at significantly higher risk for lifetime drug and alcohol abuse (Larsen, 2014). Larsen's study did not focus specifically on VTCs, but her work could serve as a model for intake and periodic assessments within VTCs. Therefore, it is included here for informational purposes.

Johnson's 2016 study suggests that veterans are amenable to treatment and willing to do the work necessary to recover. In that study, 91.5 percent of veterans successfully completed treatment (Johnson, 2016). Slattery and colleagues (2013) also employed the twenty-four-item Behavior and Symptom Identification Scale (BASIS-24) and collected self-report data on alcohol and substance use and substance-related behaviors. BASIS-24 scores decreased over time, suggesting a positive relationship between time spent in the VTC and symptoms experienced. Stainbrook and colleagues (2015) also used BASIS-24 and noted improvements in behavioral health outcomes. Self-reported substance use decreased but participants also reported that sometimes they hid their hiding drinking or drug use and notably the reported times veteran participants had problems from drinking or drug use increased (Slattery et al., 2013). One takeaway from this is that VTC proceedings helped dissolve the warrior mentality and destigmatize veterans reporting when they are experiencing issues or difficulty. Moving forward, VTCs must recognize obstacles that may be in place and act to better understand how to interpret data obtained despite discreet challenges. Similar to the sobriety category, VTCs may want to decide on standardized metrics to record, although as a larger category there will be more tests necessary to gain a holistic understanding of the mental and behavioral health state of participants.

## Procedural Justice

Procedural justice is known for its focus on all stakeholders in judicial proceedings, especially regarding participant satisfaction, thereby increasing likelihood of program completion (Kopelovich et al., 2013). However, procedural justice also notably does not affect court outcomes (Atkin-Plunk & Armstrong, 2016). Dollar and colleagues (2018) found that their "results indicate that individuals reporting increases in perceptions of procedural justice with the judge during their first 3 months were more likely to successfully complete the court process" (Dollar et al., 2018, p. 42). Gottfredson, Kearley, Najaka, and Rocha (2007) found that attending drug court's mandated judicial hearings increased perceptions of procedural justice, which decreased criminal activity. In the largest study to date, Rossman et al. (2011) compared defendants in twenty-three drug courts with defendants in six comparable traditional courts. Relying on survey data from defendants collected at baseline, six months, and eighteen months, this Multi-Site Adult Drug Court Evaluation (MADCE) concluded that perceptions of procedural justice are greater in the problem-solving court context and that higher levels of procedural justice are associated with compliance and reduced crime at follow-up. Interestingly, the MADCE data also revealed that perceptions of procedural justice did not vary over time but did vary from court to court. While studies reveal the judge as the most likely person to convey procedural justice (Marlowe et al., 2005; Marlowe et al., 2004; Wales et al., 2010), other mental health court team members (case workers, probation, legal representatives) are also vital in forming defendant perceptions. Canada and Watson (2013) examined defendant perceptions of procedural justice with judges and other mental health court staff. Their data suggest that defendants feel a strong sense of procedural justice when interacting with court team members. Interestingly, however, in-depth interviews revealed differing degrees of procedural justice between judges and other court team members. For example, although there were variations by court, participants consistently reported that they felt heard and validated by the judge but expressed less validation and respect in their interactions with case managers (Dollar et al., 2018). It is imperative that VTCs consider the perceptions of all stakeholders in order to truly understand ways to tailor treatment and reinforce prospects of procedural justice in proceedings to best achieve intended outcomes.

## Access and Use of Veterans Administration (VA) Benefits

VA benefits provide eligible veterans with educational benefits such as the GI Bill, VA-backed home loans, life insurance, and other time-sensitive services such as educational and career counseling, healthcare, and service-connected disability benefits (U.S. Department of Veterans Affairs, n.d.). VTC participation may increase the likelihood that veterans will access those benefits. In one study, almost half of veteran participants increased their VA connectedness (Johnson, 2016). The VJO is critical to this connection, and state and local courts have incentives to connect veterans with federally funded programs that decrease cost burdens on community level providers; 29 percent started receiving VA benefits after exiting the VTC program (Tsai et al., 2018). VTCs are in a relatively unique position between the criminal justice system and the VA that should prove immensely useful for facilitating participants' use of eligible benefits. Future studies on VA benefit access in

VTCs can further investigate how this system may be optimally utilized, and it is recommended more VTCs record VA benefit data.

## Judicial Contacts

Himes (2019) did not find a statistically significant relationship between judicial interactions and completion rate of the program or recidivism rate following program participation. Most studies only nod at judicial contacts as a positive factor that contributes to veterans' success, estimating frequency but not tracking actual frequency or duration with any consistency (Shannon et al., 2017). If interactions with judges do, in fact, improve veterans' outcomes, it would be relatively simple for a court administrator to track the number of times each veteran appears in court and interacts with a judge, and perhaps supplement this tracking with interviews with veterans about the impact of those interactions.

## Employment/Income

Among the few studies that look at relationships between VTC completion and employment, all find a positive relationship: completing VTC programming increased the likelihood that a veteran will either gain or improve employment or income, and improvements in employment decreases recidivism (Tsai et al., 2017). Over half of VTC graduates improved their employment status. In contrast, veterans who did not graduate were more likely to be in a worse employment position than when they started (Johnson, 2016, p. 49). Some qualitative studies with small sample sizes may not be ripe for generalization, but they helpfully reinforce the value of assessing such outcomes as employment, education, and housing (Shannon et al., 2017). Almost 47 percent more veterans were employed by the time they left the VTC program (Tsai et al., 2018). Employment can be viewed as participant contributions toward society, possibly interpreted as a sign of re-adjustment to civilian life and therefore worth measuring to apply in future studies.

## Housing

Much like employment, veterans who participate in VTCs are more likely than others to obtain stable housing and, in turn, to desist from offending (Tsai et al., 2017). As noted earlier, stable housing appears to mitigate recidivism (Johnson, 2016). Veterans in a Hennepin County VTC saw a 6.7 percent reduction in homelessness and 66.5 percent increased their housing stability, with VTC graduates being more likely than others to improve their housing status (Johnson, 2016, p. 46). Tsai and colleagues (2018) found that 39 percent more veterans lived in their own housing after completing VTC. Knudsen and Wingenfeld (2016) demonstrated that more than half of VTC participant saw no change in housing status; 11.6 percent suffered increased housing instability, and 31.4 percent improved their housing stability. Johnson and colleagues (2017) concluded that stably housed veterans were at lower risk of incarceration compared with non-stably housed participants following program participation. Therefore, it is important that VTCs strive to aid veteran participants in obtaining stable housing while within the program, to better prepare the participants following graduation.

## Education

VTC graduates were more likely than others to improve their educational status between time of entry to VTC and exit from VTC (Johnson, 2016). Shannon and colleagues (2017) noted one of the two VTCs examined had one veteran participant's individual accomplishments recorded as educational pursuit, literacy classes, and two individuals went to vocational school. The impact of VTC programs on education will likely shift over time as less veterans of the Vietnam conflict are seen in VTCs and more from conflicts such as the OEF/OIF and even OND (Operation New Dawn) abroad come home. The current eligibility criteria to join the military require that individuals have either a high school diploma or GED (USA.gov, 2020). However, veterans of the Vietnam war may not have been required to have such educational requirements as part of the draft (Bell & Cocke, 2004). Therefore, VTCs would have experienced different needs in the past than future participants will have for fostering educational development. Nonetheless, education presents itself as a beneficial opportunity for VTCs to implement helpful change in veteran participants' lives, with tangible goals, measurable progress, and meaningful results.

## Prosocial Relationships and Activities

Knudsen and Wingenfeld (2016) analyzed VTC participants' family functioning before and after mental health intervention, noting a significant increase in family functioning score from the baseline pre-treatment to twelve months. Johnson (2016) also showed similar benefits from VTCs regarding prosocial relationships and activities, where approximately 80 percent of participants either sustained or improved their prosocial relationships and activities. It may be beneficial for VTCs to consider utilizing these sorts of metrics to further understand the life of their veteran participants and analyze both improvements and deterioration, all the while collecting analyzable data.

## Nature of Service

Derrick and colleagues (2018) found that characteristics of service can be important predictors of mental health consequences and therefore should be considered when developing treatment plans for court participants. Variables such as branch of service, duration of service, whether participants were involved in combat, and whether they received awards during their service can be later applied to assess risk factors and possibly even preempted on the side of the military pre-discharge. Service members and veterans who spent longer in the service were at increased risk for negative measures of trauma and stress (Derrick et al., 2018). The researchers note "Veterans who had received an honorable discharge were more likely to demonstrate improvement on the drug use scale throughout participation in the treatment court" and although this might indicate "good" behavior, they also theorize that one possible reason for the discrepancy is that "veterans who received an other-than honorable (OTH) discharge were already experiencing symptoms of mental health or substance use that contributed to their discharge" and that "honorably discharged veterans have access to the full range of health care at the VA while veterans with an OTH discharge do not" (Derrick et al., 2018, p. 179). As such, there may be a massive equity issue with VTCs that do not accept veterans with OTH discharges, who may be in even more trouble than veterans who had been honorably discharged and treated properly after their discharge.

## LOOKING FORWARD

VTCs can improve by integrating new technologies as they appear. Technology acquisitions can create opportunities for more robust data analysis and cost-cutting measures that prove to be more efficient. "Therefore, cloud, open-source, and shared services are the strategies that the treatment courts need to employ to lower costs" (McMillan, 2020, p. 27). One such example espoused by Jim McMillan, a Principal Court Management Consultant, National Center for State Courts, is the description of cloud-based NoSQL/MongoDB as a low cost "game changer" for treatment coordination in specialized courts (McMillan, 2020). According to McMillan, some key features of the cloud-based system include instant retrieval, relational and non-relational functionalities for data "cards" and the ability to provide audit tracking of card modification. VTCs should utilize and benefit from new technologies as they appear but should always consider the implications of systemic changes especially as they relate to data privacy, security, and fostering understanding of new systems.

Implementation of data recording practices and analysis is one relatively easy and important change that can be made to VTCs to enact some sense of standardization in practices across the country, although there will always be differences in what measures are focused on and how policy is implemented based on that data. As time passes, more and more information will be able to be teased out of VTCs and fed into the larger understanding of the institution. Similarly, any potential federal attempts to standardize VTCs will prove to bring additional pros and cons. The availability of longitudinal data on graduates of VTC programs similarly will support further understanding and research of VTCs and as such should be utilized to its fullest in order to make VTCs the best they can be.

## NOTES

1. Please see chapter 10 on domestic violence courts, chapter 11 on human trafficking courts, chapter 12 on sex offender courts, and chapter 13 on opioid courts.

2. Please see, for example, chapter 1 on drug courts, chapter 2 on mental health courts, and chapter 3 on DWI courts.

3. Tsai and colleagues (2017) reported that, of 8,083 VTC participants in VA-associated sites enrolled in the VJO program from July 2010 to November 2015, 21.5 percent had charges for violent offenses, 15.7 percent for domestic disputes, 5.5 percent related to child support issues, 14.4 percent for property offenses, 22.9 percent for drug offenses, 35 percent for public order offenses, 6.6 percent for probation or parole violation, 31.4 percent DUI offenses and 8.5 percent for other offenses. Assuming no one was injured as a result of the drug, DUI, property, public order, probation/parole violation, or other offenses, 42.7 percent, or 377, cases would have still involved victims. Despite this, the study does not specifically mention victim involvement in these VTCs. Another study completed by Timko and colleagues (2016) including data from 2012 (*n* = 173), 2013 (*n* = 266), and 2014 (*n* = 351) saw 79.7 percent VTCs surveyed in 2014 indicate they accepted felony defendants, 81.9 percent accept misdemeanor, 61.6 percent accepted both felony and misdemeanor, while 21.8 percent accepted domestic violence cases and 5.2 percent accepted violent offenses.

4. Kravetz and colleagues (2012) contend that VTCs are ill-suited to handle violent crimes due to their lack of access to qualified professionals specializing in combat-related trauma and domestic violence dynamics, and that trying intimate partner violence cases in the docket sends a mixed message about the VTC's role. Hawkins (2010) echoes those concerns and says that domestic violence often involves repeated, escalating offenses, while VTCs are more likely to handle one-off cases. Russell (2015) qualifies this concern by describing the Buffalo, New York, VTC as making an eligibility distinction between those who are charged with domestic violence before entering the armed forces and those who developed such behaviors in relation to a service-related issue. Baldwin and Rukus (2015) highlight VTC's lack of fidelity to restorative justice models, also noting that victims rarely attend proceedings, even when invited. Finally, Fresneda (2013) notes, the process that

seeks to bring together offender and victim to produce socially positive results can become a danger for victims of domestic violence. On the other hand, Gover et al. (2007) note that some characteristics unique to the DVC offer a better structure of procedural justice than a traditional court, by way of added accountability to the perpetrator, through fining perpetrators of domestic violence in a majority of the cases and increasing perpetrator time spent in jail before trial.

5. Some courts do better than others with victims' rights. For example, Maine Co-Occurring Disorders and Veterans Court (CODVC) indicates that it may exclude a defendant who the court deems to present a substantial danger to their victim or the surrounding community (Maine Judicial Branch, n.d.). In practice, some VTCs do more for victims than indicated by their documented policies. For example, in one west coast court, although there are not written policies concerning victims, veterans must escrow funds for restitution to cover victims' losses (Binder, 2020). The Eighth Judicial District Court mandates veteran participants in its VTC component for felony DUI participants must attend a victim impact panel before completing the program (Eighth Judicial District Court, 2018). Similarly, the Ingham County, Michigan, VTC requires participants to attend a MADD victim impact panel during their second "treatment" phase of VTC operations, in addition to paying restitution for crime victims' rights services (Ingham County VTC, 2014). The King County District Court Regional Veterans Court considers victims in providing a "courtroom environment that is supportive of the veteran and the victim" while also maintaining a victim advocate on its team (King County Regional Veterans Court, 2019). One east coast court invites victims to give impact statements in open court, and another includes a victim advocate in its VTC team (Douds & Schultz, under review).

6. Other problem-solving courts such as domestic violence courts always include victim advocates (Gover et al., 2007).

7. "The independent victim advocates have a greater flexibility to keep information confidential. This arrangement is seen as taking advantage of the strengths of both systems without sacrificing the confidentiality of complainants" (Bakht, 2005, p. 236).

8. Alabama (AL Code § 12-17-226.3 [2014]), Colorado (CO Rev Stat § 18-1.3-101 [2018]), Connecticut (CT Gen Stat § 54-56l [2012]), Florida (FL Stat § 948.08 [2019]), Kansas (KS Stat § 12-4415 [2018]), Louisiana (LA Rev Stat § 13:5366 [2018]), Michigan (MCL 600.1208 [2012]), Nevada (NV Rev Stat § 176.015 [2019]), New Jersey (NJ Rev Stat § 2C:43-26 [2019]), and Utah (UT ST § 78A-5-307 [2020]).

9. See, for example, Pierce County Veterans Treatment Court (VTC), 2011; Eleventh Judicial Court Veterans Court Mentor Program, 2018; Buncombe County VTC, n.d.; Montgomery County VTC, n.d.; Michigan Judiciary, 2019; Charleston County VTC, 2018. But see Colorado, n.d. which allows non-veterans to serve as mentors.

10. For example, a Idaho VTC requires that mentors "observe several court sessions," "shadow three peer mentoring sessions with three different peer mentors," lead three sessions while under observation, discussing the sessions and corresponding observation forms, and completing individual supervision with the mentor coordinator (Fifth Judicial District VTC, 2015).

11. For example, Alaska researchers define recidivism for veterans in VTCs as "a new criminal offense or a formal petition to revoke probation within one to three years of: (1) graduation from Veterans Court; (2) failure to complete Veterans Court; or (3) electing not to enter Veterans Court" (Smith, 2012, p. 107).

12. Also, VTCs often have "tracks" or "levels," pursuant to which veterans are placed on short (six month or so), intermediate (one year or so), or long term (two or more years) plans, depending on their needs and the nature of their offense.

## REFERENCES

Arno, C. (2014). Proportional Response: The Need for More-and More Standardized-Veterans' Court. *University of Michigan Journal of Law Reform, 48*(4), 1039–1072.

Atkin-Plunk, C. A., & Armstrong, G. S. (2016). An Examination of the Impact of Drug Court Clients' Perceptions of Procedural Justice on Graduation Rates and Recidivism. *Journal of Offender Rehabilitation, 55*(8), 525–547.

Bakht, N. (2005). Problem Solving Courts As Agents Of Change. *Criminal Law Quarterly, 50*, 224.

Baldwin, J., & Brooke, E. (2019). Pausing in the Wake of Rapid Adoption: A Call to Critically Examine the Veterans Treatment Court Concept. *Journal of Offender Rehabilitation, 58*(1), 1–29. DOI: 10.1080/10509674.2018.1549181.

Baldwin, J., & Rukus, J. (2015). Healing the Wounds: An Examination of Veterans Treatment Courts in the Context of Restorative Justice. *Criminal Justice Policy Review, 26*(2), 183–207.

Baldwin, J. M. (2015). Investigating the Programmatic Attack: A National Survey of Veterans Treatment Courts. *The Journal of Criminal Law and Criminology, 105*, 705–751.

Bell, W.G., & Cocke, K.E. (Eds.) (2004). VI. Personnel. *Department of the Army Historical Summary: Fiscal Year 1973*. 1977. Washington, DC: Office of the Chief of Military History, Dept. of the Army.

Benner, S. (2019). *The Influence of Veteran Identity on Progress in the Veteran Treatment Court of Kalamazoo, Michigan: A Proposed Evaluation* (Doctoral dissertation).

Berman, G., & Feinblatt, J. (2001). Problem-solving courts: A brief primer. *Law & Policy, 23*(2), 125–140.

Berman, G., & Feinblatt, J. (2015). *Good courts: The Case for Problem-Solving Justice* (Vol. 8). Quid Pro Books.

Binder, S. (June 16, 2020). Personal Communication. Deputy Public Defender, cofounder Homeless Court Program at Office of the Public Defender, County of San Diego.

Boateng, F. D., & Abess, G. (2017). Victims' Role in the Criminal Justice System: A Statutory Analysis of Victims' Rights in US. *International Journal of Police Science & Management, 19*(4), 221–228.

Boone, M., & Langbroek, P. (2018). Problem-solving Justice: European approaches. *Utrecht Law Review 14*(3), 1–6.

Braithwaite, J. (1999). Restorative Justice: Assessing Optimistic and Pessimistic Accounts. In M. Tonry (Ed.), *Crime and Justice: A Review of Research* (Vol. 25, pp. 1–127). University of Chicago Press.

Bronson, J., Carson, A., Noonan, M., & Berzofsky, M. (2015). Veterans in Prison and Jail, 2011–12. Retrieved from http://www.bjs.gov/index.cfm?ty=pbdetail&iid=5479.

Buncombe County Veterans Treatment Court. (n.d.). Buncombe County Veterans Treatment Court - Become a Mentor. https://www.buncombeveteranscourt.com/become-a-mentor

Campie, P., & Francis, K. B. (2019). Domestic/Family Violence Courts. In Bernat F., Frailing K., Gelsthorpe L., Kethineni S., Pasko, L. (eds) *The Encyclopedia of Women and Crime 1* Hoboken, NJ: Wiley.

Canada, K., & Watson, A. (2013). "Cause Everybody Likes to be Treated Good:" Perceptions of Procedural Justice Among Mental Health Court Participants. *American Behavioral Scientist, 57*, 209–230.

Casey, T. (2004). When Good Intentions Are Not Enough: Problem-Solving Courts and the Impending Crisis of Legitimacy. *SMU Law Review, 57*(4), 1459–1520.

Caron, A. (2013). *Fourth Judicial District Veterans Court—Two Year Review: July 2010—June 2012*. Minneapolis, MN: Judicial Branch Minnesota. Retrieved from http://www.mncourts.gov/Documents/4/Public/Research/Veterans_Court_Two_Year_Review.pdf

Cassell, P. (2017). Crime Victims' Rights. *University of Utah College of Law Research Paper No. 224*, 1–20.

Cartwright, T. (2011). To Care For Him Who Shall Have Borne the Battle: The Recent Development of Veterans Treatment Courts in America. *Stanford Law & Policy Review, 22*, 295.

Cavanaugh, J. M. (2011). Helping Those Who Serve: Veterans Treatment Courts Foster Rehabilitation and Reduce Recidivism for Offending Combat Veterans. *New England Law Review, 45*, 463–488.

Charleston County Veterans Treatment Court. (2018). *Charles County Veterans Treatment Court Mentor Guide*. Charleston: Charleston County Probate Court.

Colorado Judicial Branch. (n.d.). *Colorado Veterans Treatment Court Peer Mentor Application*. Denver, CO: Colorado Judicial Branch.

Colorado Judicial Branch. (n.d.). Veterans Court Mentor Program. Retrieved from https://www.courts.state.co.us/Administration/Custom.cfm?Unit=prbsolcrt&Page_ID=742

Comal County Veterans Treatment Court. (2020). *Veterans Treatment Court Participant Handbook*. New Braunfels, TX: Comal County Court at Law #2.

Derrick, R., Callahan, L., Vesselinov, R., Krauel, R., Litzenberger, J., & Camp, L. (2018). Serving Those Who Served: Outcomes from the San Diego Veterans Treatment Review Calendar (SDVTRC) Pilot Program. *Psychological Injury and Law, 11*(2), 171–183.

Dollar, C. B., Ray, B., Hudson, M. K., & Hood, B. J. (2018). Examining Changes in Procedural Justice and Their Influence on Problem-Solving Court Outcomes. *Behavioral Sciences & the Law, 36*(1), 32–45.

Douds, A. S., & Ahlin, E. M. (2018). *The Veterans Treatment Court Movement: Striving to Serve Those Who Served.* Routledge.

Douds, A. S., & Hummer, D. (2019). When a Veterans' Treatment Court Fails: Lessons Learned from a Qualitative Evaluation. *Victims & Offenders, 14*(3), 322–343.

Douds, A., Ahlin, E., Howard, D., & Stigerwalt, S. (2017). Varieties of Veterans' Courts: A Statewide Assessment of Veterans' Treatment Court Components. *Criminal Justice Policy Review, 28*(8), 740–769.

Durfee, A. (2019). *Gender, Victimization, and Victim Service Needs Among Community Court Defendants: A Research-to Practice Fellowship Project.* Mesa, AZ: Arizona State University School of Social Transformation.

Eighth Judicial District. (2018). *Veterans Treatment Court Program Participant Handbook.* Las Vegas, NV: Eighth Judicial District Court Specialty Courts Division.

Elbogen, E. B., Dennis, P. A., & Johnson, S. C. (2016). Beyond Mental Illness: Targeting Stronger and More Direct Pathways to Violence. *Clinical Psychological Science, 4*(5), 747–759.

Eleventh Judicial Court Veterans Court Mentor Program. (2018). *Illinois 11th Judicial Circuit Veterans Court Program Mentor Guide.* Bloomington, IL: McClean County Illinois Government.

Erickson Jr, J. W. (2016). Veterans Treatment Courts: A Case Study of Their Efficacy for Veterans' Needs. *International Journal of Law and Psychiatry, 49*, 221–225.

Fialk, R. & Mitchel, T. (2004). Jurisprudence: Due Process Concerns for the Underrepresented Domestic Violence Victim. *Buffalo Women's Law Journal, 13*(8), 171–218.

Fifth Judicial District Veterans Treatment Court. (2015). *5th Judicial District Veterans Treatment Court Mentor Handbook 2015.* Twin Falls, ID: Fifth Judicial District.

Flatley, B., Clark, S., Rosenthal, J., & Blue-Howells, J. (2017). *Veterans Court Inventory 2016 Update: Characteristics of and VA involvement in Veterans Treatment Courts and other Veteran-focused court programs from the Veterans Justice Outreach Specialist Perspective.* Washington, DC: US Department of Veterans Affairs, Veterans Health Administration.

Frederick, A. (2014). Veterans Treatment Courts: Analysis and Recommendations. *Law & Psychology Review, 38*, 211–230.

Fresneda, L. J. (2013). The Aftermath of International Conflicts: Veterans Domestic Violence Cases and Veterans Treatment Courts. *Nova Law Review, 37*(3), 630–656.

Glassberg, H., & Dodd, E. (2008). *A Guide to the Role of Crime Victims in Mental Health Courts.* New York, NY: The Council of State Governments Justice Center.

Gonsalves, J. J. (2020). *The Progression of California's Collaborative Courts* (Doctoral dissertation, California State University, Sacramento).

Gottfredson, D. C., Kearley, B. W., Najaka, S. S., & Rocha, C. M. (2007). How Drug Treatment Courts Work: An Analysis of Mediators. *Journal of Research in Crime and Delinquency, 44*(1), 3–35.

Gourley, S. (2016). Possible Causes of Increased Domestic Violence Among Military Veterans: PTSD or Mefloquine Toxicity? *Montview Liberty University Journal of Undergraduate Research, 2*(1), 1–24.

Gover, A., Brank, E., & Macdonald, J. (2007). A Specialized Domestic Violence Court in South Carolina: An Example of Procedural Justice for Victims and Defendants. *Violence Against Women, 13*(6), 603–626.

Hartley, R., & Baldwin, J. (2019). Waging War on Recidivism Among Justice-Involved Veterans: An Impact Evaluation of a Large Urban Veterans Treatment Court. *Criminal Justice Policy Review, 30*(1), 52–78.

Haskins, P. A. (2019). Problem-Solving Courts: Fighting Crime by Treating the Offender. *NIJ Journal,* 281 (9), 71–79.

Hawai'i Veterans Treatment Court. (2020). *Hawai'i Veterans Treatment Court Mentor Handbook.* Honolulu, HI: The Judiciary, State of Hawai'i Circuit Court of the First Circuit.

Hawkins, M. D. (2010). Coming home: Accommodating the special needs of military veterans to the criminal justice system. *Ohio State Journal of Criminal Law, 7,* 563.

Himes, M. L. (2019). Veterans' Treatment Courts in Kentucky: Examining How Personal Characteristics and During-Program Occurrences Influence Program Completion and Criminal Recidivism. *Theses and Dissertations – Social Work.* Retrieved from https://uknowledge.uky.edu/csw_etds/24

Hodulik, J. (2001). Drug Court Model as a Response to Broken Windows Criminal Justice for the Homeless Mentally Ill. *Journal of Criminal Law & Criminology, 91*(4), 1073–1100.

Holbrook, J., & Anderson, S. (2011). Veterans Courts: Early Outcomes and Key Indicators for Success. *Widener Law School Legal Studies*, Research Paper No. 11-25.

Howlett J. R., & Stein, M. B. (2016). Post-Traumatic Stress Disorder: Relationship to Traumatic Brain Injury and Approach to Treatment. In D. Laskowitz, & G. Grant (Eds.), *Translational Research in Traumatic Brain Injury.* CRC Press/Taylor and Francis Group; 2016. Chapter 16. Retrieved from https://www.ncbi.nlm.nih.gov/books/NBK326723/

Ingham County Veterans Treatment Court. (2014). *Participant Handbook.* East Lansing, MI: 54b District Court.

Finlay, A. K., Stimmel, M., Blue-Howells, J., Rosenthal, J., McGuire, J., Binswanger, I., Smelson, D., Harris, A. H., Frayne, S. M., Bowe, T., & Timko, C. (2017). Use of Veterans Health Administration Mental Health and Substance Use Disorder Treatment After Exiting Prison: The Health Care for Reentry Veterans Program. *Administration and Policy in Mental Health, 44*(2), 177–187.

Johnson, M. (2016). *Hennepin County Veterans Court Evaluation.* Minneapolis, MN: Fourth Judicial District Minnesota. Retrieved from http://www.mncourts.gov/mncourtsgov/media/fourth_district/documents/Research/Veterans-Court-Evaluation-FINAL.pdf.

Johnson, R. S., Stolar, A. G., McGuire, J. F., Mittakanti, K., Clark, S., Coonan, L. A., & Graham, D. P. (2017). Predictors of Incarceration of Veterans Participating in US Veterans' Courts. *Psychiatric Services, 68*(2), 144–150.

Johnson, R., Stolar, A., Wu, E., Coonan, L., & Graham, D. (2015). An Analysis of Successful Outcomes and Associated Contributing Factors in Veterans' Court. *Bulletin of the Menninger Clinic, 79*(2), 166–173.

Johnstone, G., & Van Ness, D. W. (2007). *Handbook of Restorative Justice.* Taylor & Francis.

Justice for Vets (n.d.). Mentor Corps: Professional Development. *Justice for Vets.* Retrieved from https://justiceforvets.org/mentorcorps/resources/

King County Regional Veterans Court. (2019). *Regional Veterans Court.* https://www.kingcounty.gov/courts/district-court/regional-veterans-court.aspx

King, R. S., & Pasquarella, J. (2009). D*rug Courts: A Review of the Evidence.* The Sentencing Project. Retrieved from https://www.sentencingproject.org/wp-content/uploads/2016/01/Drug-Courts-A-Review-of-the-Evidence.pdf

Kintzle, S., Schuyler, A., Ray-Letourneau, D., Ozuna, S., Munch, C., Xintarianos, E., Hasson, A., & Castro, C. (2015). Sexual trauma in the military: Exploring PTSD and mental health care utilization in female veterans. *Psychological Services, 12*(4), 394–401.

Kleykamp, M., Hipes, C., & Maclean, A. (2018). Who Supports U.S. Veterans and Who Exaggerates Their Support? *Armed Forces & Society, 44*(1), 92–115.

Kopelovich, S., Yanos, P., Pratt, C., & Koerner, J. (2013). Procedural justice in mental health courts: judicial practices, participant perceptions, and outcomes related to mental health recovery. *International Journal of Law and Psychiatry, 36*(2), 113–120.

Knudsen, K., & Wingenfeld, S. (2016). A Specialized Treatment Court for Veterans with Trauma Exposure: Implications for the Field. *Community Mental Health Journal, 52*(2), 127–135.

Kravetz, P. (2012). Way off base: An argument against intimate partner violence cases in veterans treatment courts. *Veterans Law Review, 4*, 162.

Larsen, J. (2014). Trauma and the Justice-Involved Veteran. eScholarship, University of California. Retrieved from https://escholarship.org/uc/item/3d86x7vx

Lemon, N. K. D. (2006). Access to Justice: Can Domestic Violence Courts Better Address the Needs of Non-English Speaking Victims of Domestic Violence? *Berkeley Journal of Gender, Law & Justice, 21*, 38–254.

Lennon, C. (2020). The Growth and Need for Veterans Treatment Courts. *Touro Law Review 35, 4*(5), 1170–1194.

Lucas, P. A. (2018). An Exploratory Study of Veterans Treatment Court Peer Mentors: Roles, Experiences, and Expectations. *Drug Court Review, 1*, 59–85.

Lucas, P. A., & Hanrahan, K. J. (2016). No Soldier Left Behind: The Veterans Court Solution. *International Journal of Law and Psychiatry, 45*, 52–59.

Luna, S., & Redlich, A. D. (2020). A National Survey of Veterans Treatment Court Actors. *Criminal Justice Policy Review.* Retrieved from https://doi.org/10.1177/0887403420911414

Maine Judicial Branch. (n.d.). *Maine Co-Occurring Disorders and Veterans Court.* Augusta, ME: State of Maine Judicial Branch.

Marlowe, D. B., Festinger, D. S., Dugosh, K. L., & Lee, P. A. (2005). Are Judicial Status Hearings a "Key Component" of Drug Court? Six and Twelve Months Outcomes. *Drug and Alcohol Dependence, 79*(2), 145–155.

Marlowe, D. B., Festinger, D. S., Lee, P. A., Dugosh, K. L., & Benasutti, K. M. (2006). Matching Judicial Supervision to Clients' Risk Status in Drug Court. *Crime & Delinquency, 52*(1), 52–76.

McCall, J. D., Rodriguez, K. L., Barnisin-Lange, D., & Gordon, A. J. (2019). A Qualitative Examination of the Experiences of Veterans Treatment Court Graduates in Allegheny County, Pennsylvania. *International Journal of Offender Therapy and Comparative Criminology, 63*(3), 339–356.

McCall, J. D., Tsai, J., & Gordon, A. J. (2018). Veterans Treatment Court research: Participant Characteristics, Outcomes, and Gaps in the Literature. *Journal of Offender Rehabilitation, 57*(6), 384–401.

McMillan, J. A. (2020). A New Data Systems Approach for Drug and Treatment Courts. In C. Campbell & J. Holtzclaw (Eds.), *Trends in State Courts 2020* (pp. 26–29). National Center for State Courts.

Michigan Judiciary. (2019). *Veterans Treatment Courts in Michigan: A Manual for Mentors & Mentor Coordinators.* Retrieved from https://courts.michigan.gov/ Administration/admin/op/problem-solving-courts/Documents/Veteran%20Treat ment%20Courts%20-%20A%20Manual%20for%20Mentors%20and%20Mentor %20Coordinators_FINAL.pdf

Mitchell, O. (2018). Judging Addicts: Drug Courts and Coercion in the Justice System. *Journal of Criminal Justice Education, 30*(2), 313–316.

Montgomery County Veterans Treatment Court. (n.d.). *The Montgomery County Veterans Treatment Court Handbook.* Clarksville, TN: Montgomery County Veterans Treatment Court.

Moore, E. C. (2012). *A Mentor in Combat Veterans Court: Observations and Challenges.* Williamsburg, VA: National Center for State Courts.

National Center for State Courts. (n.d.). Veterans Courts Resource Guide. Retrieved from https://www.ncsc.org/topics/alternative-dockets/problem-solving-courts/vete rans-court/resource-guide

Oudekerk, B., Warnken, H., & Langton, L. (2019). Victim Services Providers in the United States, 2017. U.S. Department of Justice – Bureau of Justice Statistics. Retrieved from https://www.bjs.gov/content/pub/pdf/vspus17.pdf.

Pew Research Center. (2011). *Chapter 5: The Public and the Military.* Pew Research Center.

Pierce County Veterans Treatment Court. (2011). *Mentor Program Handbook.* Ellsworth, WI: Pierce County Government.

Pinchevsky, G. M. (2017). Understanding Decision-making in Specialized Domestic Violence Courts: Can Contemporary Theoretical Frameworks Help Guide These Decisions? *Violence Against Women, 23*(6), 749–771.

Regoeczi, W. C., & Hubbard, D. J. (2018). The Impact of Specialized Domestic Violence Units on Case Processing. *American Journal of Criminal Justice, 43*(3), 570–590.

Reisman, M. (2016). PTSD Treatment for Veterans: What's Working, What's New, and What's Next. *Pharmacy and Therapeutics, 41*(10), 623.

Robinson, J., & Tate, C. (2016). Veterans Endeavor for Treatment and Support: The Role the Army Judge Advocate General's Corps Should Play in Establishing

Federal Veterans Treatment Courts in and around Major Army Installations. *The Army Lawyer*, 23–36.

Rodenburg, J., Heesink, L., & Drožđek, B. (2015). PTSD, Anger and Aggression: Epidemiology, Aetiology and Clinical Practice. In Martin C., Preedy V., Patel V. (eds) *Comprehensive Guide to Post-Traumatic Stress Disorder*. Springer, Cham. 17.

Rossman, S. B., Rempel, M., Roman, J. K., Zweig, J. M., Lindquist, C. H., Green, M., Downey, P. M., Yahner, J., Bhati, A. S., Farole Jr., D. J. (2011). *The Multi-Site Adult Drug Court Evaluation: The Impact of Drug Courts*, Volume 4. Retrieved from https://www.ncjrs.gov/pdffiles1/nij/grants/237112.pdf

Rowen, J. (2020). Worthy of Justice: A Veterans Treatment Court in Practice. *Law & Policy*, *42*(1), 78–100.

Russell, R. T. (2015) Veteran Treatment Courts. *Touro Law Review, 31*(8), 385–401.

Russell, R. T. (2009). Veterans Treatment Court: A Proactive Approach. *New England Journal on Criminal and Civil Confinement, 35,* 357–364.

Shannon, L. M., Birdwhistell, S., Hulbig, S. K., Jones, A. J., Newell, J., & Payne, C. (2017). Examining Implementation and Preliminary Performance Indicators of Veterans Treatment Courts: The Kentucky Experience. *Evaluation and Program Planning*, *63*, 54–66.

Slattery, M., Dugger, M., Lamb, T., & Williams, L. (2013). Catch, Treat, and Release: Veteran Treatment Courts Address the Challenges of Returning Home. *Substance Use & Misuse*, *48*(10), 922–932.

Smee, D. E., McGuire, J., Garrick, T., Sreenivasan, S., Dow, D., & Woehl, D. (2013). Critical Concerns in Iraq/Afghanistan War Veteran-Forensic Interface: Veterans Treatment Court as Diversion in Rural Communities. *The Journal of the American Academy of Psychiatry and the Law*, *41*(2), 256–262.

Smith, J. (2012). The Anchorage, Alaska Veterans Court and Recidivism: July 6, 2004–December 31, 2010. *Alaska Law Review*, 29. Retrieved from https://scholarship.law.duke. edu/cgi/viewcontent.cgi?article=1175&context=alr

Spinak, J. M. (2010). A Conversation About Problem-Solving Courts: Take 2. *University of Maryland Law Journal of Race, Religion, Gender & Class, 10*, 113–136.

Sreenivasan, S., Garrick, T., McGuire, J., Smee, D. E., Dow, D., & Woehl, D. (2013). Critical concerns in Iraq/Afghanistan war veteran-forensic interface: Combat-related postdeployment criminal violence. *Journal of the American Academy of Psychiatry and the Law Online*, *41*(2), 263–273.

Stainbrook, K., Penney, D., & Elwyn, L. (2015). The Opportunities and Challenges of Multi-Site Evaluations: Lessons from the Jail Diversion and Trauma Recovery National Cross-Site Evaluation. *Evaluation and Program Planning*, *50*, 26–35.

Taft, C. T., Weatherill, R. P., Woodward, H. E., Pinto, L. A., Watkins, L. E., Miller, M. W., & Dekel, R. (2009). Intimate Partner and General Aggression Perpetration Among Combat Veterans Presenting to a Posttraumatic Stress Disorder Clinic. *The American Journal of Orthopsychiatry*, *79*(4), 461–468.

Tennessee Association of Recovery Court Professionals (n.d.). *Veteran Treatment Court Mentoring*. Tennessee Association of Recovery Court Professionals. Retrieved from https://tarcp.org/veterans-treatment-courts/veteran-treatment-court-mentoring

Thielo, A., Cullen, F., Burton, A., Moon, M., & Burton, V. (2019). Prisons or Problem-Solving: Does the Public Support Specialty Courts? *Victims & Offenders, 14*(3), 267–282.

Tsai, J., Finlay, A., Flatley, B., Kasprow, W., & Clark, S. (2018). A National Study of Veterans Treatment Court Participants: Who Benefits and Who Recidivates. *Administration and Policy in Mental Health and Mental Health Services Research, 45*(2), 236–244.

Tsai, J., Flatley, B., Kasprow, W. J., Clark, S., & Finlay, A. (2017). Diversion of Veterans With Criminal Justice Involvement to Treatment Courts: Participant Characteristics and Outcomes. *Psychiatric Services, 68*(4), 375–383.

USA.gov. (2020). *Join the Military.* Retrieved from https://www.usa.gov/join-military

U.S. Department of Justice, Office for Victims of Crime. (2002). *Victim Input into Plea Agreements.* Retrieved from https://www.ncjrs.gov/ovc_archives/bulletins/legalseries/bulletin7/welcome.html

U.S. Department of Veterans Affairs. (n.d.). *VA benefits for service members.* Retrieved from https://www.va.gov/service-member-benefits/

Vaughan, T., Bell Holleran, L., & Brooks, R. (2019). Exploring Therapeutic and Militaristic Contexts in a Veteran Treatment Court. *Criminal Justice Policy Review, 30*(1), 79–101.

Venkatraj, K. A. (2017). Colorado's About Face: Mechanics, Progress, and Challenges Facing Veterans Trauma Courts in Colorado. *University of Colorado Law Review, 88*(2), 385–428.

Veterans Treatment Court of Dane County. (n.d.). *Mentor Application Packet.* Madison, WI: Dane County Veterans Treatment Court, Branch 11.

Wales, H. W., Hiday, V. A., & Ray, B. (2010). Procedural justice and the mental health court judge's role in reducing recidivism. *International Journal of Law and Psychiatry, 33*(4), 265–271.

Walker, L. E., Pann, J. M., Shapiro, D. L., & Van Hasselt, V. B. (2016). Problem-Solving Courts. In Best Practices for the Mentally Ill in the Criminal Justice System (pp. 19–49). Springer.

Weathers, F. W., Litz, B. T., Keane, T. M., Palmieri, P. A., Marx, B. P., & Schnurr, P. P. (2013). The PTSD Checklist for *DSM-5* (PCL-5). Scale available from the National Center for PTSD at www.ptsd.va.gov.

Yarvis, J. S., Yoon, E., Ameuke, M., Simien-Turner, S., & Landers, G. (2012). Assessment of PTSD in Older Veterans: The Posttraumatic Stress Disorder Checklist: Military Version (PCL-M). *Advances in Social Work, 13*(1), 185–202.

Yerramsetti, A., Simons, D., Coonan, L., & Stolar, A. (2017). Veteran treatment courts: A promising solution. *Behavioral Sciences & the Law, 35*(5–6), 512–522.

Zegveld, L. (2018). Victims as a Third Party: Empowerment of Victims? *International Criminal Law Review, 1*(aop), 1–25.

*Chapter 9*

# Tribal Healing to Wellness Courts

Elyshia D. Aseltine and Maria João Lobo Antunes

## INTRODUCTION

There is a common assertion in the substance abuse literature that Native Americans have higher rates of alcohol consumption compared to other racial/ethnic groups (Indian Health Service, 2015; Lane & Simmons, 2011; Tribal Law and Policy Institute, 1999). "Statements about pronounced alcohol use among Native Americans are centuries old" emerging in as early as the late 1700s (Cunningham, Solomon, & Muramoto, 2016, p. 65). Explanations of the elevated use of alcohol by Native Americans often describe such consumption patterns as a consequence of colonization, structural disadvantage, or biological/genetic predisposition to problem drinking (i.e., the "firewater myth") (Gonzalez, Bravo, & Crouch, 2019). Despite the long history of such claims, there is a growing contemporary debate about the veracity of differential use claims. Recent research suggests that Native American "adults have some of the highest alcohol abstinence rates compared to the overall U.S. population" (Burduli et al., 2018, p. 588). In addition, researchers describe a great variation in patterns of alcohol consumption in Native American communities both across and within geographic areas (Spicer et al., 2003; Whitesell, 2006), thus demonstrating that higher rates of consumption is not a universal characteristic of Native American communities. Finally, using national-level data, Cunningham, Solomon, and Muramoto (2016) argue that Native Americans' alcohol misuse is comparable to that of whites.

Though data about higher consumption by Native Americans is mixed, this does not negate a need for prevention and treatment services for Native Americans. Health consequences of alcohol abuse, including alcohol-related mortality, are often more severe for Native Americans than for whites (Moon, Yang, Barritt, Bataller, & Peery, 2020). It is likely that at least some of the more dire health consequences of alcohol abuse for Native Americans are due to exacerbating factors such as "environmental pollution, poor nutrition, relatively high unemployment, educational challenges, and limited access to health care" (Cunningham, Solomon, & Muramoto, 2016, p. 73).

In 1953, the United States repealed federal legislation prohibiting alcohol in Native American communities, and tribal nations were free to determine for themselves how they would regulate alcohol possession, sales, and consumption. About one-third of nations maintained complete prohibition while the remaining adopted partial restrictions (Lee et al., 2018). Subsequent changes in federal law (i.e., the Indian Alcohol Substance Abuse Prevention and Treatment Act of 1986 and the 2010 amendments) have increased the severity of punishments allowed tribal justice systems. For example, alcohol-related offenses are now punishable with up to three years of incarceration or fines of $15,000 or both (Owens, 2012). Since the passage of these laws, Native Americans have been "overrepresented in the justice system for alcohol-related arrests" (Feldstein, Venner, & May, 2006, p. 2). In fact, in some communities, Native Americans are more likely to experience incarceration in response to drinking behavior than they are to receive treatment (Feldstein, Venner, & May, 2006).

In response to long-standing concerns over substance abuse and the increasingly prominent role that the criminal justice system has played in responding to problem drinking, several tribal nations have adopted a drug court model as an alternative to incarcerating substance use-involved defendants. Tribal Healing to Wellness Courts (referred to as Wellness Courts in the remaining text) are therapeutic substance abuse courts that have been adapted to better serve the unique cultural and social needs of Native American people. Such courts "apply traditional Native American healing and communal practices" as a means for addressing substance abuse believed to be at the root of criminal behavior or child abuse/neglect (National Drug Court Initiative, 2016, p. 12). Similar to other therapeutic courts, Wellness Courts emphasize a holistic approach designed to "get to the emotions, thoughts and feelings" of participants as means of "healing wounds" (Lam, 2014, p. 18). Wellness Court participants' wounds are not only personal (i.e., caused by the hardships and challenges individual participants may have experienced), they are also communal. The wounds are the "lingering symptoms of conquest" (Flies-Away & Garrow, 2013, p. 406) that have left Native American people disconnected from their rich spiritual and cultural histories and divested them of their rightful economic and social resources. The focus on incorporating Native American spiritual and cultural practices as well as the explicit attention paid to addressing long-standing subjugation makes Wellness Courts unique among other types of therapeutic courts. For advocates of Wellness Courts, working to undo the psychic impacts of U.S. colonialism by reconnecting

Native American people to their cultural histories and practices holds promise not just for improving the lives of individual court participants, their families, and their communities but also for advancing the larger project of tribal nation-building (Flies-Away & Garrow, 2013).

In the remaining sections of this chapter, we briefly describe the creation and funding of Wellness Courts as well as their ideal structure and operations, as described by proponents and in training materials. Finally, we review the limited evaluative research that exists on Wellness Courts and outline several of the challenges and critiques of Wellness Court implementation and use.

## CREATION AND FUNDING OF TRIBAL HEALING TO WELLNESS COURTS

There are more than 560 federally recognized Native American tribes in the United States (Cobb & Mullins, 2010). Though each of these tribes is sovereign and has its own constitution (Lam, 2014), a number of them do not have the resources to manage independent tribal criminal justice processes and facilities, including criminal courts. As such, some nations rely on federal or surrounding local/state governments to administer criminal justice within their communities. It is difficult to find current data on the number of courts operated by tribal authorities. According to a report published by the Bureau of Justice Assistance, approximately 330 tribal courts were in operation in 2010—this figure captures all types of tribal courts, including Wellness Courts (Cobb & Mullins, 2010). The U.S. government limits the types of cases that are eligible for processing by tribal courts, including Wellness Courts: civil cases (including family law) involving Native Americans, as well as misdemeanors and felonies as defined by tribal law committed by Native American juveniles and adults. U.S. federal courts retain jurisdiction over violations of federal felony laws even when the accused is Native American.

While U.S. drug courts first emerged in the 1980s, they were not adopted by Indian Nations until the late 1990s. Initial funding for a Native American version of drug courts was provided by the Office of Justice Program's Drug Courts Program Office (DCPO). In 1997, the DCPO established the Tribal Drug Courts Initiative. The DCPO contracted with the National Association of Drug Court Professionals (NADCP) to create an advisory board for the initiative in addition to a training program. The first training sessions for what would ultimately be called "Tribal Healing to Wellness Courts" began in September 1997 (Tribal Law and Policy Institute, 1999).

Early advocates of what would become Wellness Courts identify the opening up of federal drug court funding in the late 1990s as a pivotal moment in Native American jurisprudence: "it represented a reversal of past federal Indian policies that sought to destroy traditional dispute resolution methods" (Johnny, 2001, p. 262). For many Native Americans, "tribal justice systems are the most important visible manifestation of tribal sovereignty" (Tribal Law and Policy Institute, 1999, p. 3). Though debate among advocates about whether accepting federal funding to implement Wellness Courts is truly advantageous for Native American communities (Johnny, 2001), the expansion of funding for drug courts in tribal communities clearly resulted in the increased adoption of such courts by tribal leaders.

There were twenty-two nations funded to form Wellness Courts in the first phase of the Tribal Drug Courts Initiative. Due in part to funding challenges (discussed later) the continual operation of these courts has been difficult and, over the years, the number of Wellness Courts in operation has varied significantly. In 1999, there were twelve Wellness Courts in operation (Johnny, 2001), which increased to 89 by 2009 and then to 138 by 2014 (National Drug Court Initiative 2016, p. 35). According to the most recent directory published on the Tribal Law and Policy Institute's Tribal Healing to Wellness Courts website, there are currently ninety-four Wellness Courts in operation in twenty-five states with Arizona, New Mexico, and Washington states having the most.

Though some courts have opted to forgo federal funding in order to retain full autonomy (Johnny, 2001), most Wellness Courts rely on federal funding or partnerships with local and state government agencies in order to operate. The scarcity of tribal resources often necessitates external funding and partnerships (Flies-Away & Garrow, 2013). Federal funding has been sporadic. In 2015, the U.S. Senate introduced legislation to provide additional federal grant funding to support further development of Wellness Courts. However, the bill was not brought to a vote before the closing of the congressional session (Office for State, Tribal, Local and Territorial Support, 2016).

## THE IDEAL STRUCTURE AND OPERATIONS OF
## TRIBAL WELLNESS TO HEALING COURTS

Wellness Courts have adopted a modified version of the drug court model's ten Key Components (Flies-Away & Garrow, 2013). Similar to the drug court principles, the ten Key Components that guide Wellness Courts include directions for Wellness Courts to: maintain a team approach (Key Component #1); create multiple points of referral (Key Component #2); engage in early identification and screening of eligible participants (Key Component #3); provide holistic treatment (Key Component #4) and intensive supervision of participants (Key Component #5); dispense both incentives and sanctions

(Key Component #6); maintain active judicial involvement (Key Component #7); administer regular monitoring of program performance measures (Key Component #8); support ongoing professional development of court staff (Key Component #9); and maintain regular communication between court team members and community stakeholders (Key Component #10). (For more detailed descriptions of the key components, see Flies Away, Garrow, & Sekaquaptewa, 2014.) The key core components of the drug court model are "strikingly similar to traditional methods of resolving disputes" (Johnny, 2001, p. 262) in Native American communities. As such, proponents believe that there is great potential in the drug court model as it allows for the melding of drug court principles with traditional dispute resolution practices and culturally specific traditions (Tribal Law and Policy Institute, 1999). The incorporation of Native American healing and wellness techniques and the unique linguistic and cultural practices of tribal groups are integral to Wellness Court operations. As such, the Tribal Key Components "are specifically crafted to serve the needs of tribal communities and integrate basic community and nation building concepts" (Flies-Away & Garrow 2013, p. 412).

The ideal Wellness Court is restorative and diversionary. There is a dual emphasis on repairing harms done by the misbehavior (including harms done to the community) and providing participants with an alternative to incarceration (Tribal Law and Policy Institute, 2003). While Wellness Court proponents acknowledge that the law has been broken, they believe that substance abuse is at the root of the misbehavior; misbehavior rooted in substance abuse warrants an alternative to incarceration centered on the provision of comprehensive and holistic treatment (Armstrong, 2016).

Wellness Court actors adopt a collaborative rather than an adversarial approach to working with each other (Tribal Law and Policy Institute, 2003). The core group of Wellness Court actors includes the judge, prosecutor, public defender (when available), probation officer, and substance abuse treatment provider/mental health worker. However, the Wellness Court team may incorporate any stakeholders committed to the Wellness Court clients' well-being and success, including representatives from law enforcement, social services, and schools, as well as employers, traditional healers, and community elders (Tribal Law and Policy Institute, 2003). While Wellness Court judges are generally identified as the most important actor in the Wellness Court (Flies-Away & Garrow, 2013; Gottlieb, 2010; Lam, 2014; Wahwassuck, Smith, & Hawkinson, 2010), the ability of the entire court team to work collaboratively is essential. "A major facet of a wellness court's personality and healing potential depends on how well the team works to not only solicit and connect with treatment and other useful resources, but also to support and supervise the components of participant treatment plans" (Flies-Away & Garrow 2013, p. 413).

The typical Wellness Court processes drug and alcohol-related offenses (e.g., drug possession, driving under the influence, public intoxication, etc.), offenses believed to be caused by underlying substance abuse issues (e.g., disorderly conduct), and/or child abuse/neglect cases. Each tribal jurisdiction has the autonomy to stipulate the conditions necessary for a referral (Flies-Away & Garrow, 2013). In general, judges, prosecutors, and defense attorneys make referrals to the program; in some cases, different stakeholders, including criminal justice practitioners, social workers, and mental health counselors, can also submit referrals. Referrals are subject to further legal and clinical screening procedures to ensure that the Wellness Court has jurisdiction and that the potential participant is a good candidate for the Wellness Court.

Referral to Wellness Courts can occur at various stages of the court process. Participants referred during the pre-trial/pre-adjudication phase often must sign a statement of facts or a plea agreement (McGill, 2019)—ideally after conferring with an attorney who will inform them of their due process rights and of any legal ramifications of agreeing to participate in the program—prior to participation in the Wellness Court. Such consultation is important because, should the participant fail to complete the Wellness Court requirements, the statement of facts may be used in future prosecutorial efforts, at the discretion of the prosecutor. In cases where a participant has signed a plea agreement, they may be required to serve the original sentence they would have received had they not chosen to participate in the Wellness Court. For clients referred post-adjudication, Wellness Court judges have the power to set aside or vacate sentences if the participant successfully completes the requirements of the program. Successful completion of Wellness Court programs often includes the expungement of a participant's criminal record—this may prove useful in expanding their future employment opportunities (McGill, 2019).

Participants sign contracts with the Wellness Court in which they agree to intensive supervision (which may include home visits), random drug testing, treatment, and counseling (e.g., AA meetings, outpatient treatment, and mental health counseling) and any other program demands of the Wellness Court. Additionally, drug court participants may be expected to abstain from legal drugs, (including cigarettes, over-the-counter cold medication, and prescriptions [Flies-Away & Garrow, 2013]); comply with curfews; participate in life skills training, anger management classes, educational programs, general health programs (e.g., basketball games, gym, and pool workouts [McGill, 2019]), and cultural activities (e.g., sweat lodges, square dances, open mic events, powwows, basketball games [McGill, 2019]). Finally, their family members may also be expected to participate in treatment/counseling efforts.

Wellness Court programming is divided into phases, usually four phases in total. Participants must meet the particular therapeutic and self-improvement milestones for each phase before they proceed to the next phase; phases are designed to progressively address the challenges faced by the client. The first phase tends to be the most intensive, "as participants have obligations almost every day of the week and the weekend" (Flies-Away & Garrow, 2013, p. 414). Participation in the Wellness Court is not for the weary: "Drug and wellness court participation is not easy. There are many requirements, expectations, and responsibilities involved in court compliance. Much time and focus is [*sic*] needed to maintain the busy schedule these processes expect of participants" (Flies-Away & Garrow, 2013, p. 414). Participants also agree to be subjected to a graduated system of incentives and punishments for (un) successful completion of court requirements. Importantly, failing to meet a court requirement (e.g., failing a urinalysis) could result in a short period of incarceration. Successful completion of all phases of the Wellness Court can take anywhere from eighteen months to several years (Flies-Away & Garrow, 2013). Ideally, Wellness Courts should provide aftercare for those who have successfully completed all phases of the program (Johnny, 2001).

## EVALUATIONS OF WELLNESS COURTS

Though program monitoring and evaluation is an important part of the ideal Wellness Court's operations (see Key Component #8), empirical research about their effectiveness is scant. There is very little literature from which to draw conclusions about participant outcomes and or cost-savings. "Evaluations of problem-solving courts have not kept pace with their rapid growth" (Hornick, Kluz, & Bertrand, 2011, p. 7). Studies that do exist tend to be limited in scope, involve the use of non-randomized comparison groups, illustrate selection bias, and rely heavily on qualitative rather than quantitative data (Hornick, Kluz, & Bertrand, 2011). In addition, existing evaluations are of courts that may not strictly adhere to the Wellness Court model, that is, they include non-Native American participants or do not specifically incorporate Native American cultural practices as part of the approach.

We can draw conclusions from three studies. The first study is an evaluation of four of the earliest first Wellness Courts in the United States (Gottleib, 2010). All four courts were created under the Tribal Drug Court Initiative: the Blackfeet Alternative Court (adult) and the Fort Peck Community Wellness Court (juvenile) in Montana; the Hualapai Wellness Court (adult and juvenile) in Arizona; and Poarch Band of Creek Indians Drug Court (adult) in Alabama (Gottlieb, 2005). According to Gottleib (2010), "Graduates are as likely to reoffend as non-graduates [and] adult participants tend to fare better than juveniles—the recidivism rate for adults ranged from 50–64% but was over 90% in the juvenile courts" (Gottleib, 2010, p. ii). In addition, "adult participants have fewer post-program alcohol and drug arrests than pre-program arrests for the same length of time" (Gottleib, 2010, p. x). Most of the post-program arrests are for public intoxication or disorderly conduct. Though Gottleib was able to draw some conclusions about outcomes of participants in these early courts, she notes significant challenges associated with the lack of data maintained by the courts she studied.

The second study focuses on the Cass County/Leech Lake Band of Ojibwe Wellness Court (CCDWI), established in April 2006. CCDWI is a multi-jurisdictional court (i.e., a circuit judge and a tribal court judge oversee the court proceedings) that targets chronic DWI offenders. Overall, the results of the outcome analysis for the CCDWI are positive. Compared to those who experienced traditional court processes, CCDWI participants had 60 percent fewer rearrests one year after program entry, and 33 percent fewer rearrests two years after program entry. Most rearrests were for low-level crimes—there were no new felony arrests two years after program entry—and it took longer for participants to be rearrested compared to the comparison group (twenty-two months versus eighteen months, respectively) (Zil et al., 2014, p. III). The average graduation rate for the CCDWI program was 65 percent (Zil et al., 2014, p. III). Researchers also conducted a cost-benefit analysis of the court. They find that it would take about five years for taxpayers to real-ize the cost savings associated with this type of court (Zil et al., 2013, p. IV). It is important to note that this court services tribal and non-tribal members (Wahwassuck, Smith, & Hawkinson, 2010) thereby limiting our understand-ing of its implications for tribal members.

The third study focuses on the Anchorage Wellness Court (Roman et al., 2013). Researchers find that participation in the Anchorage Wellness Court resulted in significantly reduced recidivism and reconviction for those who opted into the Court's treatment program. In addition, the court demonstrated "large and significant benefits to the criminal justice system and crime vic-tims, returning over three dollars in benefits for each dollar in program costs" (Roman et al., 2013, p. vi). Similar to the aforementioned study, this court does not limit itself to Native American defendants. It is also unclear how Native American cultural practices are incorporated into the court's program-ming model, or if they are incorporated at all.

The overarching goal of Tribal Wellness Courts is to offer a holistic, culturally specific approach to the treatment of substance abuse for Native Americans. The scant research that is available does suggest that participa-tion in the courts decreases recidivism, primarily for adult clients; however, because of a lack of extensive and rigorous evaluation, it is difficult to describe with confidence any consistent benefits Wellness Courts confer to clients. Further, there are no existing studies of the inner workings of Wellness Courts. We have little information, beyond that provided by training manuals and advocates about how treatment is provided, whether standards of care are uniform, or whether Wellness Courts are maintaining fidelity to the ten key components. These are all important considerations for determining the utility and potential of Wellness Courts. As important, current studies that do exist do not specify if, or how, Native American cultural practices are incorporated into court processes, much less the added benefit of their incorporation. Existing studies of Wellness Courts include non-Native American clients, but it is not clear how results may vary across groups and whether Tribal practices impart benefits to all participants. The question remains whether access to Wellness court should be restricted to Native American clients and if not, how the holistic practices can help heal all those who take part in treatment.

## CHALLENGES AND CRITIQUES
## OF WELLNESS COURTS

While Wellness Courts share challenges like those of other drug courts, there are several challenges that these courts face that other drug courts do not. In addition, though there are strong advocates for the Wellness Court model both inside and out of Native American communities, these courts are not without critics.

Maintaining funding of the Wellness Courts has been a challenge since their inception. Many Wellness Courts rely on initial grants from the U.S. federal government. The ideal model is for Wellness Court budgets to be absorbed by tribal funding sources once the federal grants end. The reality is that many of the Wellness Courts are unable to secure the necessary funding and thereby cease to operate once federal grants are no longer available or a funding fiscal cycle ends. This was the case for three of the four earliest Wellness Courts in operation (Gottleib, 2010) and continues to be a pressing issue for the sustainability of more recent Wellness Courts (McGill, 2019).

Wellness Courts (like many drug courts) are typically the result of collaborative efforts involving a number of social service agencies and government entities. Inter-agency participation in drug courts is essential in keeping with a multidisciplinary "team" emphasis as outlined in the Key Components of drug courts (discussed earlier). Alternatively, if some of the services of the court could be provided by outside entities with separate funding streams, it also could prove to be a useful strategy for reducing the costs of running a Wellness Court.

While it may alleviate some fiscal woes, inter-agency cooperation raises some additional challenges, especially in the context of Wellness Courts. Wellness Courts often operate in communities that are already lacking sufficient tribal resources to address residents varied social, economic, and criminal justice needs (Joe et al., 2008). Wellness Court practitioners often note the additional needs of court participants that are unable to be addressed by the court or its partners, including treatment, transitional housing, employment, and family counseling (Everett, Mason Dosik, & Cohn, 2009; Joe et al., 2008; McGill, 2019). Interagency efforts require that agencies supporting Wellness Court objectives are themselves sustainable and that they will continue to support the Wellness Court's activities. Should such supporting agencies collapse (Johnny, 2001) or relationships become strained (Everett, Mason Dosik, & Cohn, 2009), Wellness Courts may be left unable to continue their operations. In addition, Wellness Courts that seek support from non-tribal social service agencies may encounter personnel or programs that are culturally insensitive or discriminatory toward Native Americans (Joe et al., 2008).

An inter-agency challenge unique to Wellness Courts is the "checkerboard" jurisdictional and legal landscape that such courts must navigate. In some cases, as with the Cass County/Leech Lake Band of Ojibwe Wellness Court discussed earlier, the Circuit Court and the Tribal Court may share jurisdiction over cases. Depending on location and its funding sources, Wellness Courts may be subject to additional competing jurisdictional claims or legal requirements from the federal government, from the local state, from the local county, and the local tribal authority (Joe et al., 2008, p. 10–11). In addition, most tribal nations do not operate independent tribal criminal justice systems (including law enforcement, probationary services, or detention facilities). Reliance on external governmental entities to provide these services undoubtedly brings a host of additional expectations and complications.

A diverse number of agencies involved in Wellness Courts also pose significant problems for inter-agency information sharing, as agency practices regarding record-keeping may be inconsistent or incompatible, especially if some agencies' records are automated and others' are not. The lack of information-sharing poses significant problems for comprehensive evaluations of Wellness Courts' effectiveness in reducing crime and recidivism or generating fiscal savings (Joe et al., 2008). Perhaps more important, it likely poses problems for case management and tracking the therapeutic services and outcomes of court participants (Garrow, Cordero, & van Schilfgaarde, 2018).

The high degree of inter-agency collaboration also poses potential problems for protecting Wellness Court participants' privacy rights. Court participants often "must agree to allow a ream of persons to have access to their information" (Flies-Away & Garrow, 2013, p. 421). Standards and capacities with respect to cultural competency, security for record-keeping, and rigor of privacy protections could vary significantly from agency to agency. This tension between necessary communication for therapeutic purposes and protection of privacy rights is not unique to Wellness Courts. However, given the complex landscapes of jurisdiction and oversight, the challenges to maintaining privacy rights across partners in the collaborative court effort are likely more pronounced than in other drug court contexts. While advocates argue that due process rights should not trump therapeutic goals, because of lack of study, it is unclear how such priorities are upheld in practice (Flies-Away & Garrow, 2013).

Concerns around privacy protections are enhanced by the reality that Wellness Courts often operate without the active and on-going participation of defense attorneys (Gottleib, 2010). Again, this is not a problem that is unique to Wellness Courts; it is not unusual for lower criminal courts across the country to operate without effective or even consistent defense counsel (Bach, 2010). As is the case in these other lower-level criminal courts, this reality raises concerns about how voluntary participation in such courts is as well as about how well-informed potential participants are of the range of legal options they may have to resolve their charges (Gottleib, 2010). Some of the lack of participation of defense counsel in Wellness Courts is due to the fact that participants often must sign a plea agreement in order to participate and that much of court programming takes place post-conviction. In general, there are limited legal requirements or supports for continued participation of defense counsel post-conviction.

Several specific concerns have been raised about the absence of defense counsel in Wellness Courts. As mentioned previously, some jurisdictions in which Wellness Courts operate are unable to provide the full range of resources needed to make the court, and its attendant therapeutic supports, function smoothly. In one study, court participants "complain[ed] of hearsay evidence on noncompliant behavior being allowed" (Gottleib, 2010, p. viii) because of the inability of the court to closely monitor court participants. In another, lawyers noted participants "being sanctioned without a full trial" (Lam, 2014, p. 19). Noncompliant behavior could result in a range of punitive sanctions, including termination from the program or incarceration or both. As mentioned earlier, participants can be involved with the Wellness Courts for eighteen months or more before they graduate—this may be more time than they would have spent if they had opted to serve their original sentence in detention (Gottleib, 2010). In addition, participants may spend substantial amounts of time trying to comply with Wellness Court requirements while they are involved in the program (Flies-Away & Garrow, 2013). Typically, the time spent in Wellness Court programming does not count toward an unsuccessful participant's time served. As a result of signing the original plea agreement, the unsuccessful court participant could be required to serve their entirety of what would have been their original criminal sentence all without further legal recourse, even if they were near completing the Wellness Court requirements (Flies-Away & Garrow, 2013).

Even if a participant is not ejected from the program for noncompliance, they may still be subjected to incarceration. Wellness Court judges can, and do, use incarceration as a punishment for participants failing to meet court expectations. Gotttleib (2010) notes in three of the four courts she studies, incarceration was often too readily used as a sanction. Zil et al. (2013) also note the frequent use of short jail sanctions for all positive drug tests, even in the Wellness Court's early phases. The ready use of incarceration as a punishment is not only antithetical to therapeutic goals but also ironic, given that many Wellness Court participants chose to participate in this court as a means of avoiding incarceration (Gottleib, 2010).

Another significant concern raised around the Wellness Courts is the courts' ability to be responsive to the religious/spiritual diversity within Native American communities (Garroutte et al., 2014; Gottleib, 2010). While Wellness Courts, by definition, incorporate aspects of local tribal culture and spirituality, this is not always welcomed by court participants or by the broader Native American community. Local buy-in is an important component of the Wellness Court model (Flies-Away & Garrow, 2013) but in some Native American communities "many people no longer practice the traditional ways" (Gottleib, 2010, p. viii) either because of lack of awareness or because such ways are perceived as "un-Christian" (Joe, 2008). Adopting approaches that assume, or try to impose, cultural and spiritual homogeneity within Native American communities may diminish local support and individual participation in the Wellness Court.

A final concern about Wellness Courts is with the degree that such courts can actually achieve the lofty expectations of some of their advocates. One such advocate argues:

> [Wellness Courts] help heal and mend human depressions and decay that hinder tribal community and nation building . . . [They] are vital to the visions and hopes of indigenous futures as they cause the lost to become found, the disconnected to become linked, and the disinterested person to become a vibrant citizen who can reinvest himself back into his family, her community, and his or her nation in useful and productive ways. (Flies-Away & Garrow 2013, p. 407, p. 409)

It is difficult to imagine any institution, much less a criminal court, that could achieve the twin goals of individual healing and nation building. It is unlikely that Wellness Courts, however effective they might be in treating substance abuse and preventing future criminality, can serve as a panacea for the complicated social problems Native American communities face. It is more likely that substance abuse in the United States has become a catchall explanation for deeply entrenched and long-standing economic, political, and social problems that are rooted in historical and contemporary colonialism. Flies Away and Garrow (2013, p. 406) note that Wellness Courts are part of a spiritual revolution aimed at ridding the "indigenous psyche of the remaining symptoms common to a conquered and cowed people . . . [including] substance abuse and addiction, and the attendant devastating crime, delinquency, child abuse and neglect, and other misconduct." The root of the problem with Wellness Courts may very well be that they aim to treat the problem's symptoms rather than the cause.

## REFERENCES

Armstrong, B. (2016). Therapeutic courts in the Alaska Court System. *Alaska Justice Forum, 33*(2–3), 2–6.

Bach, A. (2010). *Ordinary injustice: How America holds court.* Metropolitan Books/ Henry Holt & Co.

Burduli, E., Skalisky, J., Hirchak, K., Orr, M. F., Foote, A., Granbois, A., Ries, R., et al. (2018). Contingency management intervention targeting co-addiction of alcohol and drugs among American Indian adults: Design, methodology, and baseline data. *Clinical Trials, 15*(6), 587–599.

Cobb, K., & Mullins, T. (2010). *Tribal probation: An overview for Tribal Court Judges.* Bureau of Justice Assistance. Retrieved from: https://www.appa-net.org/ eweb/docs/appa/pubs/TPOTCJ.pdf

Cunningham, J., Solomona, T., & Muramotoa, M. (2016). Alcohol use among Native Americans compared to Whites: Examining the veracity of the 'Native American elevated alcohol consumption' belief. *Drug and Alcohol Dependence, 160,* 65–75.

Everett, R., Mason Dosik, S., & Cohn, L. (2009). *Transferability of the Anchorage Wellness Court Model.* U.S. Department of Justice. Retrieved from: http://citeseer x.ist.psu.edu/viewdoc/download?doi=10.1.1.216.4893&rep=rep1&type=pdf

Feldstein, S. W., Venner, K. L., & May, P. A. (2006). American Indian/Alaska Native alcohol-related incarceration and treatment. *American Indian and Alaska Native Mental Health Research (Online), 13*(3), 1–22.

Flies-Away, J. T., & Garrow, C. (2013). Healing to Wellness Courts: Therapeutic jurisprudence. *Michigan State Law Review, 43*(2), 403–450.

Flies-Away, J. T., Garrow, C., & Sekaquaptewa, P. (2014). *Tribal Healing to Wellness Courts: The Key Components* (2nd Edition). *Tribal Law and Policy Institute.* Retrieved from: http://www.wellnesscourts.org/files/Tribal%20Healing %20to%20Wellness%20Courts%20The%20Key%20Components.pdf

Garroutte, E. M., Beals, J., Anderson, H. O., Henderson, J. A., Nez-Henderson, P., Thomas, J., Croy, C., Manson, S. M., & AI-SUPERPFP Team. (2014).

Religio-spiritual participation in two American Indian populations. *Journal for the Scientific Study of Religion, 53*(1), 17-37.

Garrow, C., Cordero, K., & van Schilfgaarde, L. (2018). *Tribal Healing to Wellness Courts: Case management.* Office of Justice Programs. Retrieved from: http://wel lnesscourts.org/files/HTWC%20Case%20Management.pdf

Gottleib, K. (2010). *Process and outcome evaluations in four Tribal Wellness Courts.* U.S. Department of Justice. Retrieved from: https://www.ncjrs.gov/pdffiles1/nij/ grants/231167.pdf

Joe, J., Chong, J., Young, R., Lopez, D., Jones, B. J., & Gaikowski, G. (2008). *Final report: Participatory evaluation of the Sisseton Wahpeton Oyate IASAP demonstration project.* U.S. Department of Justice. Retrieved from: https://www.ncjrs.go v/pdffiles1/nij/grants/222740.pdf

Johnny, R. E. (2001). The Duckwater Shoshone Drug Court, 1997–2000: Melding traditional dispute resolution with due process. *American Indian Law Review, 26*(2), 261–286.

Hornick, J. P., Kluz, K., & Bertrand, L. D. (2011). *An evaluation of Yukon's Community Wellness Court. Calgary.* The Canadian Research Institute for Law and the Family. Retrieved from: https://prism.ucalgary.ca/handle/1880/107424

Indian Health Service. (2015). *Behavioral health fact sheet.* US Department of Human and Health Services. Retrieved from: http://www.ihs.gov/newsroom/fa ctsheets/behavioralhealth/

Lam, M. (2014). Courts that heal. *Law Society Journal, 52*(1), 18–19.

Lee, J. P., Pagano, A., Moore, R. S., Tilsen, N., Henderson, J. A., Shell, A. I., . . . & Gruenewald, P. (2018). Impacts of alcohol availability on Tribal lands where alcohol is prohibited: A community-partnered qualitative investigation. *International Journal of Drug Policy, 54,* 77–86.

Marlowe, D., Hardin, C., & Fox, C. (2016). *Painting the current picture: A national report on Drug Courts and other Problem-Solving Courts in the United States.* National Drug Court Initiative. Retrieved from: https://www.ndci.org/wp-content/ uploads/2016/05/Painting-the-Current-Picture-2016.pdf

McGill, J. (2019, April 10). Blackfeet healing to Wellness Court offers alternatives to prison sentence. *Glacier Reporter.* Retrieved from: http://www.cutbankpioneer press.com/glacier_reporter/news/article_a8f500f4-5b17-11e9-9118-97d03ca84a5 0.html

Moon, A. M., Yang, J. Y., Barritt IV, A. S., Bataller, R., & Peery, A. F. (2020). Rising mortality from alcohol-associated liver disease in the United States in the 21st Century. *American Journal of Gastroenterology, 115*(1), 79–87.

Office for State, Tribal, Local and Territorial Support. (2016). Senators Introduce Bill on Tribal Healing to Wellness Courts. Centers for Disease Control and Prevention. Retrieved from: https://www.cdc.gov/phlp/docs/bill-tribalhealing .pdf

Owens, J. (2012). Historic in a bad way: How the tribal law and order act continues the American tradition of providing inadequate protection to American Indian and Alaska native rape victims. *Journal of Criminal Law & Criminology, 102,* 497–528.

Roman, J., Chalfin, A., Reid, J., & Reid, S. (2008). Impact and cost-benefit analysis of the Anchorage Wellness Court. *Urban Institute*. Retrieved from: https://www.urb an.org/sites/default/files/publication/31971/411746-Impact-and-Cost-Benefit-Anal ysis-of-the-Anchorage-Wellness-Court.PDF

Rossman, S., Rempel, M., Roman, J., Zweig, J., Lindquist, C., Green, N., Downey, M., & Yahner, J. (2011). The multi-site adult drug court evaluation: The impact of drug courts. *U.S. Department of Justice*. Retrieved from: https://www.ncjrs.gov /pdffiles1/nij/grants/237112.pdf

"S. 2205—114th Congress: Tribal Healing to Wellness Courts Act of 2015." www .GovTrack.us. 2015. July 13, 2020. Retrieved from: https://www.govtrack.us/c ongress/bills/114/s2205

Sovereign Nation of the Kenaitze. (2020). *Henu Community Wellness Court*. Retrieved from: https://www.kenaitze.org/tribal-government/tribal-court/henu -community-wellness-court/

Spicer, P., Beals, J., Croy, C. D., Mitchell, C. M., Novins, D. K., Moore, L., Manson, S. M., & American Indian Service Utilization, Psychiatric Epidemiology, Risk and Protective Factors Project Team. (2003). The Prevalence of DSM-III-R Alcohol Dependence in two American Indian populations. *Alcoholism: Clinical and Experimental Research, 27*(11), 1785–1797.

Tribal Law and Policy Institute. (1999). *Healing to Wellness Courts: A preliminary overview of Tribal Drug Courts*. Bureau of Justice Assistance, Office of Justice Programs, U.S. Department of Justice. Retrieved from: https://www.tribal-institute .org/download/heal.pdf

Tribal Law and Policy Institute. (2003). *Tribal Healing to Wellness Courts: The key components*. Bureau of Justice Assistance, Office of Justice Programs, U.S. Department of Justice. Retrieved from: https://www.ncjrs.gov/pdffiles1/bja/1881 54.pdf

Wahwassuck, K., Smith, J. P., & Hawkinson, J. R. Building a legacy of hope: Perspectives on joint tribal-state jurisdiction. *William Mitchell Law Review, 36*(2), 859–897.

Whitesell, N. R., Beals, J., Mitchell, C. M., Novins, D. K., Spicer, P., Manson, S. M., & AI-SuperPFP Team. (2006). Latent class analysis of substance use: Comparison of two American Indian reservation populations and a national sample. *Journal of Studies on Alcohol, 67*(1), 32–43.

Zil, C. E., Waller, M. S., Johnson, A. J., Harrison, P. M., & Carey, S. M. (2014). *Cass County/Leech Lake Band of Ojibwe Wellness Court, Walker, MN: Process, out- come, and cost evaluation report*. NPC Research. Retrieved from: http://npcresea rch.com/wp-content/uploads/Cass-County-Wellness-Court-Process-Outcome-and -Cost-Evaluation-FINAL-FOR-OTS.pdf

## *Section III*

# COURTS BASED ON OFFENSE CHARACTERISTICS

As noted in prior sections, criminogenic needs originally inspired problem-solving courts, presuming a direct relationship between the underlying risk factor and potential for offending. These courts operated, and continue to operate, on the logic that, if underlying needs are resolved, offending will not occur. In many instances, this makes sense. Drug courts treat the underlying addiction that compels users of illicit substances to violate laws that prohibit their use or reduce their capacity to make decisions that reduce their likelihood of committing an offense. Deterrence through criminalization is not sufficient to discourage addicts who are neuro-biologically compelled to use illicit substances or have become ensnared in the cycle of addiction. More attenuated relationships exist, as well, in criminogenic-based courts. Mental health courts try to ameliorate adverse consequences of mental conditions that diminish impulse control or exacerbate rage. If people living with mental health issues receive treatment that helps them manage their conditions or attendant behaviors, they are less likely to come into contact with the criminal justice system.

But some courts are based not only on criminogenic need but also on offense-specific characteristics, usually arising from socially constructed aspect of the offenses. These offense-based courts, many of which relate to crimes involving sex or drugs, add a layer of intersectionality that make them both theoretically and operationally more problematic. Social stigma and bias surrounds many of the cases and these courts. They cut across race and class, and the courts involving sex crimes inherently implicate gender issues. These courts pay great attention, perhaps more than other problem-solving courts, to the social context of their work. Participants' needs and reduction of offending remain paramount, but they work in ever-evolving environments that are influenced by changing the social construction of the offense types they handle. For example, domestic violence courts arguably promote increased punitiveness toward offenders and more compassion for victims; others might offer that both offenders and victims in domestic violence court are caught in a dangerous waltz of co-dependence and enabling behaviors. Sex offense and human trafficking courts attempt to inject more compassion, humanity, and therapy into what have been, for decades, highly stigmatized criminal behaviors. Finally, opioid courts, that some may classify as drug courts, struggle with social and class stigmas surrounding types of drugs that have cut epidemic swaths of loss across segments of society. These four types of courts reflect some of the most complex efforts by court-based programs to remediate stigmatized social ills that interact with criminalized conduct.

In chapter 10, "Seeking Safety & Accountability through Domestic Violence Courts," Amanda B. Cissner and Rebecca Thomforde Hauser discuss domestic violence courts that promote purposes of victim safety and offender accountability. They recognize that a complex web of psychological and sociocultural factors contributes to domestic violence. Over the years, domestic violence moved from being normalized to tolerated to criminalized, concurrent with rapidly evolving media and criminal justice responses. Farrah Fawcett's made-for-tv movie *The Burning Bed (1984)* brought national attention to the cycle of violence documented in Faith McNulty's nonfiction account of domestic battering. Those works signaled a seismic shift in societal understandings of domestic violence and ushered in an era of reform. Domestic violence courts emerged over the next decade, as did public awareness campaigns and mandatory arrest laws. Evolving understanding of gender dynamics informed the public response to domestic violence, as well. Although many early initiatives failed, domestic violence courts continued to grow and refine their efforts. This chapter provides an up-to-the-minute analysis of these important courts as they enter their third decade.

In chapter 11, "Restoring Humanity through Human Trafficking Courts," Anne S. Douds, Ella R. Warburton, and Kealy A. Cassidy consider another type of court that similarly tackles an intractable social problem complicated by issues of sex and gender. Human trafficking courts, which at this point more often deal with sex crimes than labor trafficking, suffer from a lack of theoretical foundations in that they often do not address the coercion/consent debate. But perhaps they are not intended to grapple with whether any prostitution is consensual. Instead, they look at characteristics of people who engage in sex trades and set about providing interventions that respond to those characteristics. Thus, it could be argued that this chapter belongs in the section on offender characteristics. But we chose to place this chapter here to highlight the complexities of running courts premised upon responding to a certain type of crime—sex crimes—but that actually attempts to treat a convoluted constellation of criminogenic and social welfare needs. These courts identify people who have violated laws about selling sex as a gateway to accessing services that help them with underlying issues that, if resolved, will give them greater autonomy, greater power, and maybe greater choice in whether to continue working in sex trades in violation of criminal laws.

In chapter 12, "Sex Offense Courts: A Historical and International Overview," Ashley Kilmer and Amanda Emmert survey sex offense courts in three nations and provide differential analysis of their origins, laws, and policies. Unlike the courts in South Africa and Canada, sex offense courts in the United States take a therapeutic approach, which grounds them solidly in problem-solving court jurisprudence. The authors note that, despite differences in historic development, sex offense courts all strive to improve efficiency and effectiveness among sex offense prosecutions. Notably, this chapter could be read in conjunction with chapter 11 to provide scholarly foundation for consideration of how persons who purchase sex and persons who broker sex trades should be handled. Conversations surrounding the meaning of rape and sexual assault also must be considered. But it may be worth considering how these courts could interact, particularly with respect to victim services.

In chapter 13: "Opioid Intervention Courts," Lisa Shannon, Monica Himes, Shondrah Nash, and Jennifer Newell offer insights into why new opioid courts deserve attention as one of the most recent innovations in the problem-solving court model. They call for more research on these emerging courts that, thus far, do not appear to follow an identifiable model that is distinguishable from other substance abuse courts. Perhaps the social construction of opioid use sets them apart sufficient to justify a separate court. The authors also examine soon-to-be-released standards and suggest program evaluations on courts that adopt new standardized protocols. Because opioid courts are so new and have yet to coalesce around a mission, there is room to consider race, class, and gender as these courts undergo their first rounds of empirical evaluation.

We hope that this third section of the book provides food for thought and fodder for future analysis. Courts in this section emphasize that, while problem-solving courts are innovative and modern, they remain mired in social stigmas and historic prejudices that should be considered as all of them are subjected to increasingly rigorous evaluation.

*Chapter 10*

# Seeking Safety and Accountability through Domestic Violence Courts

Amanda B. Cissner and Rebecca Thomforde Hauser

## INTRODUCTION

Prior to the late 1970s, conventional wisdom viewed domestic violence as a private matter by players in the criminal justice system, marked by police hesitant to make domestic violence arrests and prosecutors who declined to pursue cases or dismissed cases for lack of victim cooperation.[1] Victim service agencies were few and far between, and courts lacked effective mechanisms for holding offenders accountable.

Since that time, in response to battered women's and victim's rights movements (Horowitz, 2003; Schechter, 1982), an array of new initiatives has emerged, seeking to use the mechanisms afforded the criminal justice system to promote victim safety and hold offenders accountable. Pro-arrest policies, evidence-based prosecution—a method in which prosecutors rely on material evidence to prosecute a case, thus removing victims from prosecutorial decision-making—and specialized prosecution units were early methods for bringing domestic violence out of the private domain (Rebovich, 1996; Sherman, 1992). The 1994 Violence against Women Act created national support for these efforts, establishing funding for victim services and research as well as *federal* pro-arrest legislation (Buzawa & Buzawa, 1996; Hanna, 1996).

Following implementation of these efforts, courts nationwide were overwhelmed by a massive influx of domestic violence cases. This caseload crisis, coupled with an onslaught of new local and federal legislation pertaining to domestic violence, set the stage for the rise of specialized domestic violence courts in the 1990s and early 2000s. Such courts typically bring all or most of the domestic violence cases in a single jurisdiction before a dedicated, specially trained judge (or judges) during a calendar dedicated to such cases. Domestic violence courts thus seek to create informed responses to the unique and personal issues presented by cases of domestic violence.

Specialized domestic violence courts were informed by a broader problem-solving court movement, including drug, mental health, community, and reentry courts (Berman & Feinblatt, 2005; Casey & Rottman, 2003). This movement initially was driven by a focus on the improved efficiencies offered by specialization (McCoy, 2003), but increasingly gained support based on more substantive goals achieved through specialization (e.g., less problematic drug use, improved mental health, greater access to community resources, and reduced recidivism). Accordingly, the perceived impetus for domestic violence courts soon shifted beyond merely addressing the onslaught of new court cases to the unique characteristics of domestic violence itself.

Domestic violence courts seek to have a positive impact on the lives of individual victims and on a culture that for too long tolerated violence between domestic partners. A 2009 national survey of more than 200 criminal domestic violence courts and victim advocates detected broad agreement in identifying the primary goals of domestic violence courts as victim safety and offender accountability (Labriola et al., 2009, see figure 10.1). More than 200 dedicated criminal domestic violence courts across at least twenty-seven states have been established across the United States since the mid-1990s. Such courts have gained momentum internationally; Canada was home to more than 50 domestic violence courts by 2008, and the United Kingdom was home to more than 100 courts by 2013. Jurisdictions across the country have sought to expand their scope to incorporate civil cases in integrated domestic

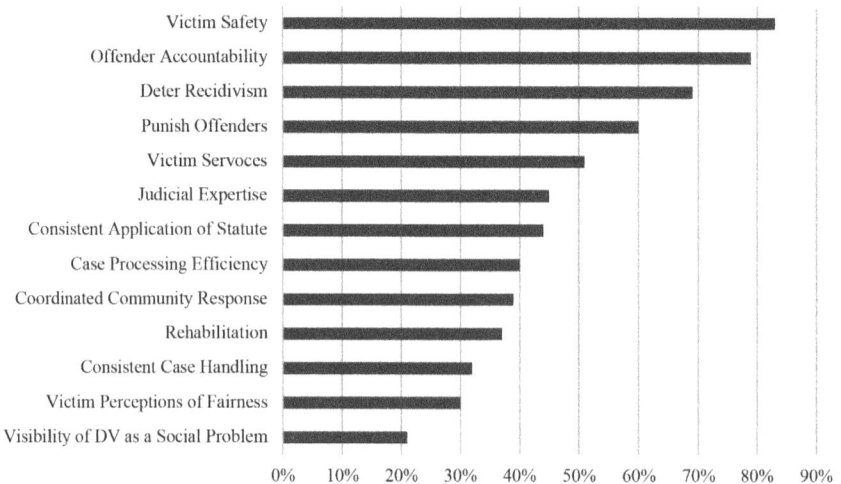

Figure 10.1 *Percentage of Court Respondents Reporting Goal Was "Extremely Important." Source*: Labriola et al., 2009.

violence courts, based on the idea of bringing all of a family's interrelated cases before a single judge (Goldkamp, 1996; Sack, 2002; Steketee et al., 2001).

This chapter describes the various models of domestic violence courts, reviews the underlying principles behind the courts, and then provides an overview of the research on domestic violence courts. Examples in the form of notes from the field are offered throughout the chapter to elucidate some of the noteworthy mechanisms courts across the country have adopted.

## MODELS

Earliest domestic violence courts predominately were seated in the criminal court context. Such courts bring misdemeanor or felony cases (or both, depending on jurisdiction) before a dedicated judge (or judges) on a dedicated court calendar. Common eligible criminal charges include assault, harassment, menacing, stalking, and criminal violation of a protective (restraining) order; some jurisdictions include specific "domestic violence" charges in their penal codes. Eligible relationships likewise vary by jurisdiction, with many courts limiting eligibility to those who have (or previously had) an intimate relationship—including those who are (or previously were) married, living together, or have children in common; in many jurisdictions, a dating relationship is sufficient (Labriola et al., 2009).

Many criminal domestic violence courts further employ a compliance calendar to bring those charged with domestic violence back to court on a regular basis to verify and motivate compliance with court orders. These judicial status hearings may be implemented by either the original sentencing judge or another judicial officer, typically also with specialized training.

Both dedicated civil protective order dockets and integrated dockets address civil issues where there is an underlying issue of domestic violence. Integrated domestic violence courts operate under a one family/one judge model to bring all of a family's interrelated cases before a single judge. This judge thus gains a comprehensive picture of the issues and dynamics at play within the family and, ideally, can make better-informed decisions. The specific cases eligible for such courts vary by jurisdiction, but may include criminal domestic violence charges, civil protective orders, criminal violations of protective orders, child custody and visitation, abuse and neglect, and divorce proceedings. Dedicated civil protective order dockets are more limited, but similarly rely on a judge (or judges) with special training to hear all requests for civil protection (restraining) orders during a dedicated court calendar. Some such courts additionally handle enforcement of such protective orders, including civil or criminal violations, depending on the jurisdiction (Sack, 2002).

## KEY COMPONENTS

Domestic violence courts are not regulated by a national trade organization or a nationally recognized set of core components, unlike drug treatment courts. Since 2013, the Department of Justice's Office on Violence against Women has provided funding to well-established domestic violence across the country as part of its Mentor Court Initiative (Department of Justice, Office of Public Affairs, 2013). This funding enables the mentor courts to provide support to communities interested in implementing specialized domestic violence courts or enhancing their community's response to domestic violence cases, primarily by hosting site visits and sharing materials and lessons learned from their experiences.[2] Despite no codified key components, domestic violence courts are generally designed to promote victim safety; defendant[3] accountability and engagement; informed judicial decision-making; consistent handling of all domestic violence matters; efficient case processing; procedural fairness; and holistic services for victims (Mazur & Aldrich, 2002; Sack, 2002). Toward these ends, domestic violence courts commonly implement the following components:

(1) Dedicated Court or Docket for all Domestic Violence Cases: One or more dedicated judge hears all domestic violence matters—depending on the court, this might include criminal or civil cases. A dedicated judge presiding over all such cases is believed to promote consistency. Moreover, specialized training on the dynamics of domestic violence enables the judge to make better informed decisions when it comes to, for instance, imposing criminal and civil protective orders, bail conditions, treatment and other program mandates, and sanctions for noncompliance. In the integrated model, a single judge is able to access comprehensive information across civil and criminal cases and utilize that information to make consistent and informed decisions.

Scheduling all domestic violence cases during a single dedicated docket further enables specialized courts to incorporate enhanced courthouse safety protocols. Strategies such as separate waiting areas and seating for victims and their children; court officers to monitor court hallways, entrances, and parking lots; staggered arrival and departure times for litigants; and in-court advocates to update victims who prefer not to attend court proceedings in person are commonly implemented to promote safety in domestic violence courts.

(2) Comprehensive Resources for Families: Domestic violence courts may provide referrals to all individuals affected by the violence, including both victims and defendants; such referrals are commonly managed by a resource coordinator or other specialized staff member. In addition to supportive services for adult and child victims, resource coordinators may draw from a wide range of programs for defendants, such as abusive partner intervention programs (APIP, also commonly referred to as batterer programs), substance use programs, parenting after violence classes, mental health services, and other treatment for issues co-occurring with the intimate partner violence. More recently, domestic violence courts are seeking to address defendants' other criminogenic needs through referrals to workforce development or job training. To address the complex needs of defendants with substance use issues, some jurisdictions have created hybrid domestic violence drug courts.

Compliance with services and programs mandated through criminal courts is often confirmed through ongoing judicial status hearings; supervised visitation centers may ensure timely referrals and responses in civil and integrated courts. In the context of civil cases, courts frequently strive to enhance litigant access to civil legal services, having attorneys on-site for immediate referral for both parties. Domestic violence courts further seek to increase access to justice by reflecting the cultures of the community the court serves, creating culturally responsive options, such as those described in Notes from the Field: Creating Culturally-Responsive Courts.

*Notes from the Field: Creating Culturally Responsive Courts*

In order to create a welcoming environment to litigants from Red Lake and Leech Lake Bands of Objibwe, the *Beltrami County (MN) Domestic Violence Court* has signs in Ojibwe displayed throughout the court. There is room for litigants to perform a smudging ritual before or after their court hearing and the flags of both tribes are flown in front of the courthouse. The court has worked with its community partners to create abusive partner intervention programming with additional culturally specific components based on Native values and culture, as directed by The Duluth Model and Mending the Sacred Hoop. Referrals can also be made to culturally specific, tribally run abusive partner intervention programs.

The *Tucson Domestic Violence Court* has worked to create access to justice for the Deaf community. The local community-based victim service agency has the appropriate resources to enable victims to communicate with advocates, family and friends, and court personnel. Advocates are trained in Deaf culture, and they co-staff cases with Deaf service agencies.

The court provides separate interpreters for victims of domestic violence with hearing loss in court hearings, outreach, education, and advocacy. [4]

(3) Compliance Monitoring: Criminal domestic violence courts frequently rely on judicial status hearings during a regular compliance calendar to monitor ongoing compliance with court orders. During these reviews, the compliance judge typically receives updated information from service providers, victim advocates, probation, and prosecutors—provided either in-person or via a report submitted to the court. Such coordination is intended to improve defendant accountability and enables the judge to respond swiftly and consistently to any reported noncompliance. In the integrated and civil court contexts, judges may also monitor compliance with civil protective orders, child support payments, supervised visitation, and parenting-time plans.

Possible responses to noncompliance might include more frequent court appearances or probation reporting; modified protective, visitation, or support orders; probation revocations; or even jail time.

(4) Advocacy for Victims: Promoting victim safety is a central aim of domestic violence courts. Accordingly, these courts generally work closely with victim service providers who provide victims with safety planning, counseling, and access to coordinated services. Domestic violence courts promote coordinated access to advocacy services, working with both community-based and system-based (e.g., through the prosecutor's office) advocates. Frequently, an advocate or advocates are present during court sessions, either to provide support to victims who are also present or to report back to victims who prefer not to attend court in person. Advocates may also escort victims to meetings with the prosecutor or other social service agencies as requested. In addition, civil and integrated courts often work with community agencies to provide free civil legal services to victims filing for orders of protection and parenting time plans.

*Notes from the Field: Providing Legal Services to Victims*

The *Stearns County (MN) Repeat Felony Domestic Violence Court* handles serious repeat felony offenders and staffs a full-time legal aid attorney who provides representation to victims of intimate partner violence. The legal aid attorney handles matters related to child support, child custody, protective orders, housing, consumer credit, disability/health care, and others as needed. There is no fee required and no time limit on the services. Legal Aid coordinates with the court's victim assistance coordinator and community-based advocates to ensure each victim's needs are addressed holistically.

*The 17th Circuit Court of Illinois* has created a series of YouTube videos that provide guidance on obtaining and modifying protective orders, including remote filing for emergency orders.[5]

(5) Specialized Training: Training provided to domestic violence court judges may include operational and legal matters, dynamics of domestic violence, and impacts of domestic violence on children. Toward ensuring that all individuals working in the court are sensitive to the unique dynamics of domestic violence, other court personnel (e.g., clerks, security officers) may also receive specialized training.

(6) Community Partner Involvement: Research suggests that a strong multi-disciplinary collaborative team promotes better implementation of criminal justice programs; such collaboration requires ongoing dialogue and work across participating stakeholder agencies (Labriola et al., 2013). Domestic violence courts must work closely with a network of stakeholders, including prosecutors, defense counsel, civil attorneys, children's attorneys, victim service agencies, law enforcement, probation, and a wide range of service providers (e.g., abusive partner intervention programs, mental health services, and substance use treatment). Courts frequently bring diverse stakeholders together for ongoing communication through regular meetings, intended to encourage collaboration, build community, address conflicts or gaps in a timely manner, and provide a forum for ongoing training and education. Some courts engage in ongoing self-assessment to evaluate implementation of best practices in domestic violence courts.

(7) Data Collection: In order to provide continuous assessment, document effectiveness, and encourage improvement of court operations, courts are encouraged to engage in ongoing data collection and analysis. Such documentation need not meet the standards of rigorous program evaluation, but may include relatively simple measures of court outcomes, processes, costs, and benefits. Sharing such information publicly can be a valuable tool for public accountability.

## NEW AND EMERGING TRENDS

Some domestic violence courts seeking to incorporate broader research and best practices have developed promising new strategies that have yet to be widely applied. While more research is needed to identify how these practices specifically impact outcomes in domestic violence cases, it is clear that domestic violence courts can learn from the growing body of research and strengthen their policies to better serve victims and defendants.

Several domestic violence courts are creating trauma-informed courthouses, where court policies and processes—as well as those of related agencies, such as prosecutors' offices and law enforcement—are reviewed and revised, incorporating contemporary understandings of the neurobiology of trauma. Courts may also identify trauma-informed programming for defendants as well as holistic services that foster resiliency for victims and children, including the use of restorative circles for high-risk defendants.

Building on a model pioneered in Miami-Dade County, the domestic violence court in Kansas City, Missouri, created a domestic violence-drug court to better address the needs of defendants with substance use issues (Wachal, 2019). These courts work with both substance use treatment providers and abusive partner intervention programs to create specialized treatment plans and sanctioning matrices responsive to the unique needs of the target population.

Other courts seek to include more risk-needs-responsivity principles into their processes, for example, by implementing validated domestic violence risk assessments to inform the intensity of programming and judicial monitoring, create firearms surrender procedures and monitor compliance, and link high-risk victims to civil legal and other services on-site at the court.

Findings from the Family Court Enhancement Project, funded by the Office on Violence against Women, are influencing civil court responses to domestic violence cases through the development of guiding principles in how to address domestic violence in custody and related issues.[6] Each of four enhancement sites identified challenges to access to justice for litigants in family courts with domestic violence issues. This project takes many lessons learned from the specialized domestic violence court movement and applies them to the broader family court system in an attempt to develop guiding principles to enhance the handling of domestic violence cases across diverse communities.

Finally, jurisdictions across the country recently have begun to pilot the use of restorative approaches to respond to intimate partner violence. Restorative approaches generally seek to promote the agency of those harmed, address the harms and their causes, and provide a framework for accountability and an opportunity for healing. The use of restorative approaches in cases involving domestic violence is not without controversy, with some worrying that such approaches may unduly emphasize consensus or risk undermining the needs of victims. However, a recent national study of restorative approaches to intimate partner violence found that criminal courts were the most common source of referrals across the programs surveyed, suggesting that these approaches may have a role in court settings (Cissner et al., 2019). One such program is highlighted in *Notes from the Field: Restorative Approaches to Domestic Violence.*

*Notes from the Field: Restorative Approaches to Domestic Violence*

The *Domestic Violence Restorative Circles program* is offered through Men as Peacemakers, a nonprofit in Duluth, Minnesota. Those harmed and those who have caused harm do not come together in a face-to-face process. Instead, those who have been harmed are invited to participate in support circles, where they meet with support persons and community members in a safe space to discuss past violence, healing, and growth. Those who have caused harm opt to enter transition circles through the court as part of a plea agreement or a condition of probation. These circles include the participant, circle keepers, and trained community members, including an advocate to represent the "survivor voice." The final step of the transition circles includes a contract, which outlines the steps the participant will take to ensure the safety and well-being of themselves, others, and the community, and to safely repair harm if possible.

## RESEARCH ON DOMESTIC VIOLENCE COURTS

The research to date is mixed on the impacts of domestic violence courts. The most widely studied model by far is the criminal domestic violence court model. Outcome evaluations have examined a range of criminal justice outcomes, including recidivism, case processing, dispositions, and sentences.

### Impact on Recidivism

Overall, rigorous quasi-experimental studies have found mixed results in terms of court impacts on recidivism. At least eleven quality evaluations (including one meta-analysis) test the impact of domestic violence courts on recidivism (see table 10.1). Of these, three produced small to significant reductions in rearrests across most measures analyzed: San Diego, California (Angene, 2000); Lexington County, South Carolina (Gover et al., 2003); and Dorchester, Massachusetts (Harrell et al., 2007). Four sites produced null or negative findings: Shelby, Tennessee (Henning and Kesges, 1999), Brooklyn (Newmark et al., 2001), Manhattan (Peterson, 2004), and Ann Arbor, Michigan (Harrell et al., 2007). Two studies of the Milwaukee domestic violence court produced mixed results (Davis et al. 2001; Harrell et al., 2006; details ahead). Likewise, a study of domestic violence courts across New York state produced mixed results (Cissner et al., 2013), as did a study of the Minneapolis domestic violence court (Eckberg & Podkopacz, 2004). These different results may simply reflect inconsistencies in research methodology, but another possibility is that they reflect real differences in the effectiveness of the various domestic violence court models.

**Table 10.1 Summary of DV Court Impacts on Recidivism and Accountability, Select Impact Studies**

| Authors | Site | Recidivism | Accountability | |
|---|---|---|---|---|
| | | | Conviction | Sentencing |
| Angene (2000) | San Diego, CA | New police contact (DV): Decrease | No significant change | Incarceration sentences: Decrease; Sentence length: Increase |
| Cissner, Labriola, & Rempel (2013) | New York State (Mix) | Post-conviction DV rearrest: Decrease; All rearrest: No significant change | No significant change | Incarceration sentences: Increase [NS] |
| Davis, Smith, & Rabbitt (2001) | Milwaukee, WI (Mix) | Victim report: Decrease; Felony rearrest: Decrease [NS]; Misd rearrest: Increase [NS] | Increase | Jail sentences: Decrease |
| Eckberg & Podkopacz (2002) | Minneapolis, MN (Mix) | Pretrial rearrest: No significant change; New domestic assault: Decrease | Increase | |
| Gover (2003) | Lexington County, SC | DV rearrest: Decrease | | |
| Gutierrez, Blais, and Bourgon (2017) | Meta-analysis | General rearrest: Decrease; DV rearrest: Decrease | | |
| Harrell, Newmark, & Visher (2007) | Dorchester, MA | Victim report: Decrease; Rearrest: Decrease [NS] | Increase | Sentence severity: Increase |
| | Ann Arbor, MI | Victim report: No significant change; Rearrest: Increase [NS] | | No significant change |
| Harrell, Schaffer, DeStefano, & Castro (2006) | Milwaukee, WI | DV rearrest: Decrease (because they were more likely to be incarcerated) | | Time in Jail: Decrease |

| | | | | |
|---|---|---|---|---|
| Newmark, Rempel, Diffily, & Kane (2001) | Brooklyn, NY | Rearrest: Increase | No significant change | No significant change |
| Peterson (2004) | New York, NY | DV rearrest: Increase [NS] | No significant change | Jail sentences: Decrease<br>Sentence time: Decrease |
| Quann (2006) | Ontario, Canada | Re-conviction: No significant change | | Sentence severity: Increase |

[NS] Finding does not reach statistical significance.
*Source:* Adapted from Cissner et al., 2013.

In a particularly revealing evaluation, Harrell et al. (2006) found that the Milwaukee domestic violence court *did* reduce the one-year rearrest rate; however, the reduction arose not because the defendants were less likely to commit new crimes when the opportunity arose, but because they were more closely supervised and hence more likely to be taken off the street and put in jail on probation revocations. In effect, the Milwaukee court's positive impact on offender accountability mediated the relationship between the court and recidivism.

Finally, a 2016 meta-analysis synthesizing the results of twenty domestic violence court studies found small but significant impacts on recidivism; those whose cases were heard in the domestic violence courts had 5 percent lower rates of general recidivism and just under 3 percent lower rates of domestic violence recidivism. However, study quality was generally rated low and, among those studies with the highest methodological rigor, there were no net significant domestic violence court impacts on recidivism (Gutierrez et al., 2016).

The limited available research on integrated courts is similarly mixed. Three studies covering a total of 11 New York integrated courts found more new criminal contempt charges for violating a protective order in the integrated courts—possibly due to greater monitoring or more protective orders issued under the specialized model. However, general recidivism was not significantly different between the integrated and traditional models (Cissner et al., 2011; Katz & Rempel, 2011; Picard-Fritsche et al., 2011).

## Impact on Accountability

In practice, accountability can be defined as holding defendants responsible for their actions. Accountability can be operationalized in a number of ways: prosecution of a higher percentage of domestic violence arrests; a higher conviction rate; more severe sentences such as jail, prison, or intensive probation; or the imposition of swift and certain sanctions for initial noncompliance with court orders (see Frank, 2006; Harrell et al., 2007; Labriola et al., 2007). The following notes from the field offer examples of accountability measures undertaken by two courts.

### Notes from the Field: Establishing Accountability

The *Ada County (ID) Domestic Violence Court* worked closely with the local abusive partner intervention programs to create compliance reports that reflect each program's curriculum and both the court and program compliance expectations. That information is shared electronically through a shared database, allowing the court immediate compliance status reports.

Criminal and family court coordinators in the *Winnebago County (IL) Domestic Violence Coordinated Court* share compliance information to ensure that both judges are aware of any noncompliance. The courts created compliance forms for abusive partner intervention programs and probation and created protocols regarding regular reporting. The Court Coordinator meets with both domestic violence court judges prior to the compliance calendar to review cases and identify any additional information needed to ensure the judge is fully informed regarding compliance.[7]

## Criminal Convictions

Results on the impact of domestic violence courts on criminal convictions are far from definitive. Multiple studies have linked the implementation of specialized domestic violence courts to increased conviction rates (Davis et al., 2001; Eckberg & Podkopacz, 2004; Harper et al., 2010; Harrell et al., 2007). Other studies found no significant difference in conviction rates between domestic violence court and traditional court processing (Angene, 2000; Cissner et al., 2013; Newmark et al., 2001; Peterson, 2004).

## Criminal Sentences

Impact on criminal sentencing is likewise unclear, with studies finding both greater (Quann, 2006; Visher et al., 2008) and lesser (Angene, 2000; Davis et al., 2001; Peterson, 2004) use of jail sentences in domestic violence courts. Again, conflicting results may be due to differences in study designs or real differences in policies and practices across different jurisdictions.

## Special Conditions

In contrast, there is considerable evidence across studies that domestic violence courts are more likely than non-specialized courts to mandate defendants to a wide range of special conditions, such as abusive partner intervention programs, substance use treatment, special bail conditions, intensive probation supervision, and ongoing judicial status hearings to document compliance with conditions (Angene, 2000; Gondolf, 1998; Harper et al., 2010; Harrell et al., 2007; Newmark et al., 2001).

Typically held during a dedicated compliance calendar on a designated day and time, judicial status hearings draw on the collaborative model to bring relevant compliance information before the dedicated judicial officer. Coordination between the court and mandated programs, prosecutors, victim advocates (with victim consent), probation, police, and others means that the judicial officer has up to date information on program attendance, new arrests, and any violations of protective orders during these court appearances. As with other problem-solving court models, ongoing compliance may be met with less frequent court appearances, while noncompli-ance can lead to swift sanctions (e.g., increase in compliance reporting, amended court orders, jail time). The Urban Institute's Judicial Oversight Demonstration found that such ongoing judicial monitoring increased both the likelihood and severity of sanctions for noncompliance (e.g., missing mandated program sessions, failure to meet with probation officers; Harrell et al., 2006; Harrell et al., 2007). Likewise, studies of domestic violence courts in Brooklyn and San Diego found that increased judicial monitoring resulted in greater likelihood and severity of penalties for noncompliance (Angene, 2000; Harrell et al., 2006; Harrell et al., 2007; Newmark et al., 2001). A randomized control trial testing the impact of judicial monitoring in the Rochester, New York, domestic violence court found less consis-tent application of penalties in response to noncompliance, with differ-ent judges applying monitoring and penalties differently (Labriola et al., 2012).

The Judicial Oversight Demonstration additionally examined the impact of intensive probation monitoring in coordination with domestic violence courts and found such probation was associated with reduced re-offense. However, the authors attribute this reduction to the increased incarceration—and consequent incapacitation—brought about by increased probation revocations among those monitored more intensely (Harrell et al., 2006). A study of an intensive specialized probation unit in Rhode Island found reduced re-offense and lengthier arrest-free periods; the reductions were attributed to frequent contact with victims and probationers and enhanced ability to respond to technical violations (Klein et al., 2008).

Numerous studies have examined the effectiveness of abusive partner intervention programs at reducing re-offense (e.g., Davis et al., 2000; Dunford, 2000; Feder & Dugan, 2002; Feder & Wilson, 2005; Gondolf, 2005; Harrell, 1991; Labriola et al., 2005; Palmer et al., 1992). Two meta-analyses assessed the two most commonly implemented approaches: the Duluth model and cognitive behavioral therapy (Babcock et al., 2004). The first of these found small but significant impacts of Duluth-based programs across five randomized trials, with those who participated in such interventions less likely to have a new arrest. Similarly, partners of those who participated in Duluth-based programs were less likely to report new violence across five additional studies. In contrast, neither official rearrest or victim report showed significant changes in re-offense among those participating in programs employing cognitive behavioral therapy (Babcock et al., 2004).

Despite modest impacts on re-offense documented in much of the research, many courts continue to utilize abusive partner intervention programs as a mechanism of accountability. By one estimate, as many as 80 percent of abusive partner intervention program participants are court mandated (Healy et al., 1998), and, in many courts, such programs are one of the most readily available options for accountability.

## Accountability in Integrated Courts

As noted earlier, integrated courts were found to result in more mutually favorable family court outcomes and to detect more violations of protective orders. In a finding attributed primarily to greater victim participation in integrated courts (where, in contrast to stand-alone criminal courts, victims frequently have ongoing civil matters compelling them to return), criminal cases in one integrated court were more likely to result in a conviction. Among cases ending in conviction, cases in this court also resulted in more severe convictions than business as usual (Picard-Fritsche et al., 2011). However, two other studies of the New York integrated model did not replicate this impact.

## Impact on Case Processing

Results with regard to case processing efficiency have been more conclusive, with several rigorous studies finding that criminal domestic violence courts speed case processing. Analyses of misdemeanor domestic violence courts in Milwaukee, Minneapolis, Manhattan, San Diego, and Boise suggest that these courts do speed up case processing time (Angene, 2000; Davis et al., 2001; Eckberg & Podkpacz, 2004; Harper et al., 2010; Peterson, 2004). For example, in San Diego, research documented a 74 percent reduction in the median number of days to disposition in a domestic violence court—from fifty-seven to fifteen days (Angene, 2000). Following the inception of the domestic violence court in Minneapolis, the average time to case resolution was reduced by nearly a week (Eckberg & Podkpacz, 2004). In Manhattan, prior to the implementation of the domestic violence court, only 14 percent of domestic violence cases were resolved within five weeks, compared with a quarter of cases once the domestic violence court was implemented (Peterson, 2004). A study of twenty-four specialized courts across New York state found that cases in domestic violence courts were resolved two months faster than those processed in traditional courts (Cissner et al., 2013).[8]

Conversely, results from the Brooklyn felony court indicate that case processing increased after the specialized court opened, a finding the authors attribute to the increased severity of indictment charges in the post-implementation period and the greater attention paid to each of these cases under the specialized model (Newmark et al., 2001).

A series of evaluations of the New York state integrated model also found that, due to same-day scheduling of cases, integrated courts reduced the number of trips to court litigants were required to make, though individual cases generally took longer to reach resolution in the specialized courts (Cissner et al., 2011; Katz & Rempel, 2011; Picard-Fritsche et al., 2011). Other findings from the New York courts were mixed. An integrated court in Vermont produced shorter case processing time and fewer new convictions (Schlueter et al., 2011). In general, the limited research on integrated models is fraught with methodological issues, suggesting more research on such courts is needed before firm conclusions can be drawn.

## Impact on Victim Safety

Victim safety was the most highly valued goal reported across sites responding to a 2009 policy survey (see figure 10.1). Stakeholders interviewed as a part of the study were asked to identify primary means for achieving victim safety. Protective orders, rigorous defendant monitoring, courthouse safety measures, and victim services were the key mechanisms identified (Labriola et al., 2009).

Many domestic violence courts work closely with community-based victim advocates to provide support and updates throughout the court process, safety planning, and linkages to service providers (Bell & Goodman, 2001; Gover, 2007; Mazur & Aldrich, 2002; Newmark et al., 2001). For victims who do not wish to attend court in person, advocates may also act as liaisons with the court.

Domestic violence courts have been shown to be more likely than non-specialized courts to connect victims to services (Harrell et al., 2007; Henning & Klesges, 1999; Newmark et al., 2001). The literature also suggests that victims have more positive perceptions of domestic violence courts than traditional courts (Eckberg & Podkopacz, 2004; Gover, 2007; Gover et al., 2003; Hotaling & Buzawa, 2003; and for the one study not finding such an effect, see Davis et al., 2001). In particular, positive experiences reflected a belief that they were treated fairly in the domestic violence court (Eckberg & Podkopacz, 2004; Harrell et al., 2007; Henning & Klesges, 1999); perceptions that the judge cared about and understood their situation (Eckberg & Podkopacz, 2004; Harrell et al., 2007); and satisfaction with advocates (Harrell et al., 2007; Hotaling & Buzawa, 2003).

Victim satisfaction with domestic violence courts is not universal and is likely a function of the quality and breadth of services to which they are linked. A study of specialized courts across Michigan, Wisconsin, and Massachusetts did not find differences between victims who received services and those who did not. The authors conclude that this was likely due to unmet service needs across both groups—in particular, employment assistance, crisis services, and services designed to build victims' social networks (Visher et al., 2008).

## Impact on Procedural Justice

Procedural justice refers to the fairness of justice procedures and interpersonal treatment of litigants. Some research suggests that higher perceptions of procedural fairness lead to better acceptance of court decisions, a more positive view of individual courts and the justice system, and greater compliance with court orders (e.g., Tyler & Huo, 2002). Examples of specific strategies undertaken to enhance procedural justice in domestic violence courts across the country are included in *Notes from the Field: Improving Procedural Fairness*.

An evaluation of the domestic violence court in Clay County, Minnesota, included measures of defendant and victim perceptions of procedural justice. Defendants reported the following: nearly all felt that the abusive partner intervention program was assisting them in resolving their violence issues and issues with their partners; all defendants reported that the court held them accountable for the conduct that led to their court involvement; and despite feeling that the court was biased toward victims, almost all defendants felt that the outcome in their case was fair and just. Victims nearly universally rated the court's handling of their case positively and reported enhanced perceptions of safety. However, a disconnect between victims' and prosecutors' priorities resulted in some confusion and frustration among victims (Thompson, 2014).

Victims at the Yonkers Integrated Domestic Violence Court generally rated their experience more positively than defendants. Nonetheless, half of all those surveyed (59 percent of victims, 44 percent of defendants) agreed that the court had treated their case fairly (Picard-Fritsche, 2011)

Finally, the Minnesota Family Court fairness study found that domestic violence litigants who received a full explanation from a judicial officer reported fair treatment and were more likely to comply with court orders, even if the outcome was unfavorable (Eckberg & Podkopacz, 2004).

## Notes from the Field: Improving Procedural Fairness

*Multnomah County (OR)* created the position of a court navigator to identify self-represented litigants experiencing domestic violence, refer them to additional services and resources, and provide information about the court process and family law forms in order to mitigate user confusion about the court process.

To help self-represented litigants, the *California court system* developed and posted a series of factsheets for individuals thinking about filing a domestic violence protective order as well as those with an order filed against them. The factsheets use plain language and illustrate the protective order process, including relevant court forms, related family law issues, and interaction with law enforcement and other agencies.

In *Bemidji (MN)*, the domestic violence court created a defendant handbook that outline probation conditions, compliance court dates, and programming and treatment appointments.

Domestic violence courts in *Kansas City (MO)* and *Moorhead (MN)* have created sanctioning matrices that are shared with defendants to improve transparency. These matrices give defendants a better idea of what they can expect if they are not compliant with court orders.[9]

## Coordination

Drawing on a model of coordinated community response, many domestic violence courts seek to bring a diverse, multidisciplinary team of stakeholders to the table during planning (Eckberg & Podkopacz, 2004; Steketee et al., 2000) and ongoing court operations (e.g., Harrell et al., 2007; Henning & Klesges, 1999; Newmark et al., 2001). Such collaboration has been linked to greater access to victim services, better informed decision making by judges, and improved prosecutorial practice (Gover, 2007; Harrell et al., 2007; Henning & Klesges, 1999; Newmark et al., 2001; Weber, 2000), as well as greater stakeholder buy-in (Cissner, 2005; Steketee et al., 2000). Collaboration also promotes specialized training across diverse stakeholder agencies (Harrell et al., 2007; Newmark et al., 2001).

## CONCLUSION

Over nearly three decades, domestic violence courts have made great strides to better reach their goals of enhancing victim safety and offender accountability. Despite these efforts, research paints an equivocal picture of these courts' impacts on future violence. Likewise, impacts on case resolutions and sentences are mixed. More promising are the findings with regard to the use of special conditions, reduced case processing time, linkages to victim services, and user satisfaction.

More recently, these courts have begun to incorporate the growing body of research regarding what works with general criminal justice populations, applying such evidence-based practices as domestic violence risk assessments to inform court mandated conditions, supervision, protective orders, and parenting-time plans. Courts are also exploring mechanisms for incorporating trauma-informed care and restorative approaches to improve the court experience and promote healing in families impacted by domestic violence.

## NOTES

1. With permission from the authors, themes similar to those included herein were previously discussed in Cissner, A., Labriola, M., and Thomforde Hauser, R. (2019.) "Domestic violence courts." pp. 380–385 in *The Sage encyclopedia of criminal psychology, Volume I*, edited by Robert D. Morgan. Thousand Oaks, CA: SAGE Publications, Inc., as well as across several Center for Court Innovation publications (Gender & Justice Initiatives Staff, 2011a, 2011b, 2011c; Moore, 2009).

2. Many of the examples throughout this chapter come from the mentor courts.

3. In the family/integrated model, individuals alleged to have committed violence against an intimate partner would more accurately be referred to as "respondents." In the interest of streamlining, the term "defendant" is used consistently throughout this chapter, regardless of the type of court being discussed.

4. Source: Center for Court Innovation Gender & Family Justice Programs staff, 2020.

5. Source: Center for Court Innovation Gender & Family Justice Programs staff, 2020.

6. See https://familycourtenhancementproject.org/ for more information.

7. Source: Center for Court Innovation Gender & Family Justice Programs staff, 2020.

8. Eighteen of the twenty-four domestic violence courts included in the study are misdemeanor courts, one handles both misdemeanors and felonies, and the remaining five are felony courts.

9. Source: Center for Court Innovation Gender & Family Justice Programs staff, 2020.

## REFERENCES

Angene, L. (2000). *Evaluation report for the San Diego County domestic violence courts*. San Diego Superior Court.

Babcock, J. C., Green, C. E., & Robie, C. (2004). Does batterers' treatment work? A Meta-analytic review of domestic violence treatment. *Clinical Psychology Review,* 23(8), 1023–1053.

Bell, M. E., & Goodman, L. A. (2001). Supporting battered women involved with the court system: An evaluation of a law-school based advocacy intervention. *Violence Against Women*, 7(12), 1377–1404.

Berman, G., & Feinblatt, J. (2005). *Good courts: The case for problem-solving justice*. The New Press.

Buzawa, E., & Buzawa, C. (1996). *Domestic violence: The criminal justice response* (2nd ed.). Sage Publications.

Casey, P., & Rottman, D. (2005). Problem-solving courts: models and trends. *Justice System Journal,* 26(1), 35–56.

Center for Court Innovation, Gender & Justice Initiatives Staff. (2011a). *Criminal domestic violence courts: Key principles*. Center for Court Innovation.

———. (2011b). *Integrated domestic violence courts: Key principles.* Center for Court Innovation.

———. (2011c). *Civil domestic violence courts: Key principles.* Center for Court Innovation.

Cissner, A. (2005). *Process evaluation of the Brooklyn youthful offender domestic violence court.* Center for Court Innovation.

Cissner, A. B., Labriola, M., & Rempel, M. (2013). *Testing the effects of New York's domestic violence courts: A statewide impact evaluation.* Center for Court Innovation.

Cissner, A. B., Picard-Fritsche, S., & Rempel, M. (2014). New York state's integrated domestic violence court model: Results from four recent studies. *Domestic Violence Report,* April/May 2014, 51–63.

Cissner, A., Sasson, E., Thomforde Hauser, R., Packer, H., Pennel, J., Smith, E. L., Desmarais, S., & Burford, G. (2019). *National portrait of restorative approaches to intimate partner violence: Pathways to safety, accountability, healing, and well-being.* Center for Court Innovation.

Davis, R., Smith, B. E., & Rabbitt, C. (2001). Increasing convictions in domestic violence cases: A field test in Milwaukee. *The Justice System Journal, 22*(1), 62–72.

Davis, R., Taylor, B. G., & Maxwell, C. D. (2000). *Prosecuting domestic violence cases with reluctant victims: Assessing two novel approaches in Milwaukee.* Final report submitted to the U.S. Department of Justice, National Institute of Justice.

Department of Justice, Office of Public Affairs. (2013, March 28). *Justice Department selects three domestic violence courts to serve as resources to specialized courts nationwide* [Press release]. Retrieved from: https://www.justice.gov/opa/pr/just ice-department-selects-three-domestic-violence-courts-serve-resources-specialize d-courts.

Dunford, F. (2000). The San Diego Navy Experiment: An Assessment of Interventions for Men Who Assault Their Wives. *Journal of Consulting and Clinical Psychology, 68*(3), 468–475.

Eckberg, D., & Podkopacz, M. (2004). *Family Court Fairness Study.* Fourth Judicial District of the State of Minnesota, Fourth Judicial District Research Division.

Feder, L. R., & Dugan, L. (2002). A test of the efficacy of court-mandated counseling for domestic violence offenders: The Broward County experiment." *Justice Quarterly*, 19(2), 343–375.

Feder, L. R., & Wilson, D. B. 2005. A meta-analytic review of court-mandated batterer intervention programs: Can courts affect abusers' behavior? *Journal of Experimental Criminology, 1*(2), 239–262.

Frank, P. B. (2006). *Top ten reasons why the NY model for batterer programs does not treat, fix, cure, rehabilitate, or otherwise get individual men to stop abusing women.* Retrieved from: http://www.nymbp.org/principles.htm.

Goldkamp, J. (1996). *The role of drug and alcohol abuse in domestic violence and its treatment: Dade County's domestic violence court experiment.* U.S. Department of Justice, National Institute of Justice.

Gondolf, E. W. (2005). *Culturally focused batterer counseling for African American men*. National Institute of Justice.

Gover, A.R. (2007). Specialized domestic violence court in South Carolina: An example of procedural justice for victims and defendants. *Violence Against Women, 13*(6), 603–626.

Gover, A. R., MacDonald, J. M., & Alpert, G. P. (2003). Combating domestic violence: Findings from an evaluation of a local domestic violence court. *Criminology and Public Policy, 3*(1), 109–132.

Gutierrez, L., Blais, J., & Bourgon, G. (2017). Do domestic violence courts work? A meta-analytic review examining treatment and study quality. *Justice Research and Policy, 17*(2), 75–99.

Hanna, C. (1996). No right to choose: Mandated victim participation in domestic violence prosecutions. *Harvard Law Review, 109*(8), 1850–1910.

Harper, C. J., Parry, C. F., & Grossman, N. (2010). *Ada county domestic violence court: Program evaluation report, qualitative and quantitative findings*. Report prepared for the Idaho Supreme Court.

Harrell, A. (1991). *Evaluation of court-ordered treatment for domestic violence offenders: Final report*. Washington, DC: Institute for Social Analysis.

Harrell, A., Newmark, L., & Visher, C. (2007). *Final report on the evaluation of the judicial oversight demonstration, volume 2: Findings and lessons on implementation*. Final report for the National Institute of Justice. National Institute of Justice.

Harrell, A., Schaffer, M., DeStefano, C., & Castro, J. (2006). *Evaluation of Milwaukee's judicial oversight demonstration*. Urban Institute.

Healey, K., Smith, C., & O'Sullivan, C. (1998). *Batterer intervention: Program approaches and criminal justice strategies*. National Institute of Justice.

Henning, K., & Klesges, L. M. (1999). *Evaluation of the Shelby County domestic violence court: Final report*. Shelby County: TN.

Hotaling, G., & Buzawa, E. (2003). *Victim satisfaction with criminal justice case processing in a model court setting*. National Institute of Justice.

Horowitz, E. (2003). *Institutionalized Feminism? The case of a domestic violence court*. Unpublished Ph.D. dissertation, Department of Sociology, Yale University, New Haven, CT.

Klein, A. R., Wilson, D., Crowe, A. H., & DeMichele, M. (2008). *Evaluation of the Rhode Island probation specialized domestic violence supervision unit*. National Institute of Justice.

Labriola, M., Bradley, S., O'Sullivan, C. S., Rempel, M., & Moore, S. (2009). *A national portrait of domestic violence courts*. Center for Court Innovation.

Labriola, M., Cissner, A., Davis, R. C., & Rempel, M. (2012). *Testing the efficacy of judicial monitoring: A randomized trial at the Rochester, New York domestic violence courts*. Center for Court Innovation.

Labriola, M., Gold, E., & Kohn, J. (2013). *Innovation in the criminal justice system: A national survey of criminal justice leaders*. Center for Court Innovation.

Labriola, M., Rempel, M., O'Sullivan, C. S., Frank, P., McDowell, J., & Finkelstein, R. (2007). *Court responses to batterer program noncompliance: A national perspective*. Center for Court Innovation.

Labriola, M., Rempel, M., & Davis, R. (2005). Do batterer programs reduce recidivism? Results from a randomized trial in the Bronx. *Justice Quarterly, 25*(2), 252–282.

Mazur, R., & Aldrich, L. (2003). What makes a domestic violence court work? Lessons from New York. *American Bar Association, 2*(42), 5–42.

Moore, S. (2009). *Two decades of specialized domestic violence courts: A review of the literature.* Center for Court Innovation.

McCoy, C. (2003). The politics of problem solving: An overview of the origins and development of therapeutic courts. *American Criminal Law Review, 40*(4), 1513–1534.

Newmark, L., Rempel, M., Diffily, K., & Kane, K. M. (2001). *Specialized felony domestic violence courts: Lessons on implementation and impact from the Kings County experience.* Urban Institute.

Palmer, S., Brown, R., & Barerra, M. (1992). Group treatment program for abusive husbands. *American Journal of Orthopsychiatry, 62*(2), 276–283.

Peterson, R. R. (2004). *The Impact of Manhattan's specialized domestic violence court.* New York City Criminal Justice Agency, Inc.

Peterson, R. R. (2014). *Case processing in Brooklyn's integrated domestic violence court.* New York City Criminal Justice Agency, Inc.

Picard-Fritsche, S., Cissner, A., & Puffett, N. (2011). *The Erie County Integrated Domestic Violence Court: Policies, practices, and impacts.* Center for Court Innovation.

Quann, N. (2006). *Offender profile and recidivism among domestic violence offenders in Ontario, Canada.* Department of Justice, Research and Statistics Division.

Rebovich, D. J. (1996). Prosecution response to domestic violence: Results of a survey of large jurisdictions. In E. S. Buzawa & C. G. Buzawa (Eds.), *Do arrest and restraining orders work?* (pp. 176–191). Sage Publications.

Sack, E. (2002). *Creating a domestic violence court: Guidelines and best practices.* Family Prevention Fund.

Schechter, S. (1982). *Women and male violence.* South End Press.

Schlueter, M., Wicklund, P., Adler, R., Owen, J., & Halvorsen, T. (2011). *Bennington County Integrated Domestic Violence Docket project: Outcome evaluation.* Final report submitted to the Vermont Court Administrator's Office and the Vermont Center for Crime Victim Services.

Sherman, L. W. (1992). *Policing domestic violence: Experiments and dilemmas.* Free Press.

Steketee, M., Levey, L., & Keilitz, S. (2000). *Implementing an integrated domestic violence court: Systemic change in the District of Columbia.* National Center for State Courts.

Thompson, K. (2014). *A study of the Clay County Domestic Violence Court: Offender and victim perceptions of procedural justice.* North Dakota State University.

Tyler, T., & Huo, Y. J. (2002). *Trust in the Law: Encouraging Public Cooperation with the Police and Courts.* Russell Sage Foundation.

Visher, A., Harrell, A., Newmark, L., & Yahner, J. (2008). Reducing intimate partner violence: An evaluation of a comprehensive justice system-community collaboration. *Criminology and Public Policy*, 7(4), 495–523.

Wachal, C. (2019). "Spotlight: Kansas City's DV drug court program." *Justice for Families: Technical Assistance Newsletter*, 8(2), 5.

Weber, J. (2000). Domestic violence courts: Components and considerations. *Journal of the Center for Families, Children and the Courts, 2,* 23–36.

*Chapter 11*

# Restoring Humanity through Human Trafficking Courts?

Anne S. Douds, Ella R. Warburton,
and Kealy A. Cassidy

## INTRODUCTION

Human trafficking represents one of the most pernicious and entrenched threats to human rights in the United States (Goodman & Mazur, 2014). Federal law in the United States recognizes two main types of human trafficking: labor trafficking and sex trafficking (Trafficking Victims Protection Act [TVPA], 2000). Labor trafficking involves "the recruitment, harboring, transporting, supplying, or obtaining a person for labor or services through the use of force, fraud, or coercion for the purpose of involuntary servitude or slavery," and sex trafficking occurs when "a commercial sex act is induced by force, fraud, or coercion, or in which the person induced to perform sex acts is under 18 years of age" (Logan et al., 2009, p. 4, summarizing the TVPA, 2000). The word "trafficking" in the TVPA has been misinterpreted to mean that persons must be physically transported against their will; the law does not require forced physical transportation (Clawson et al., 2009). Instead, trafficking laws focus on coercion, requiring inquiry into whether victims have been compelled to engage in labor or sex by force, threat, or duress (TVPA, 2000). Originally conceived as an international issue, modern law and policy now recognize that human trafficking occurs within the borders of the United States and among United States citizens. Although Congress has been creating federal programs for trafficking victims at a prolific rate, most of the day-to-day work falls on local-level entities.

Human trafficking courts (HTCs)[1] are one of the latest, local-level efforts to respond to human trafficking, and they are one of the newer versions of what have become known as "problem-solving courts," "treatment courts," or "specialized courts"—courts that provide alternatives to traditional criminal justice processes based either on offense or offender types (Kendis, 2019; National Institute of Justice [NIJ], 2020). This chapter synthesizes existing research on HTCs, beginning with consideration of the populations they serve, their missions and goals, and their components. The chapter then reviews existing studies on their processes and outcomes, and then ends with thoughts on areas for future research in these courts that seek to inject humanity and trauma-informed care into programming that is sensitive to the coercive cycle of victimization inherent to trafficking.

## LEGAL BACKGROUND OF HTCS

HTCs find statutory support in the TVPA, which has been reauthorized nine times. Its latest iteration pays enhanced attention to coercion of victims/ offenders through "threats of serious harm to or physical restraint against any person; any scheme, plan, or pattern intended to cause a person to believe that failure to perform an act would result in serious harm to or physical restraint against any person; or the abuse or threatened abuse of the legal process" (TVPA, 2000, Section 7012; *see also* Polaris Project, 2018). At least forty-three states have similar state-level legislation (Barnhart, 2009). The Justice for Victims of Trafficking Act (JVTA) of 2015 amended the TVPA to improve services for victims; increase offense level for buyers of commercial sex from victims of trafficking to high-level felonies; de-emphasize criminal liability for victims/offenders; decrease the prosecutions' burden of proof for proving someone has been trafficked; add training requirements for first responders; increase fines; and create a domestic trafficking victim's fund to support victim assistance programs (JVTA, 2015). Most states have added similar legislation to their state codes (see, e.g., 18 Pa. C.S. § 3011 *et seq.*). These important changes reflect advocates' efforts to reverse past legal patterns that often disproportionately punished the person being trafficked, particularly those who were being trafficked in the sex trade, which effectively perpetuated the cycle of victimization (Goodman & Mazur, 2014). The JVTA also created a survivor-led U.S. Advisory Council on Human Trafficking (US Department of State, 2020). Most relevant to this chapter, federal funds first became available for development of specialized courts to serve eligible victims/offenders in 2015 Section 103 of the JVTA (2015).

The TVPA and JVTA have been refined and expanded through clarifying legislation and federal agency action. Federal law now provides a comprehensive framework for responding to human trafficking in the United States (Logan et al., 2009). The Department of Health and Human Services (HHS), the Office for Victims of Crime (OVC), and the Department of Justice (DOJ) run programs for identifying, "certifying," and assisting international victims of trafficking (HHS, 2009). Certified trafficking victims are eligible for federal food, housing, medical, and shelter assistance programs, such as Medicaid and Temporary Assistance for Needy Families (TANF), to name a few (TVPA, 2000). Domestic trafficking victims do not need to be certified; they can receive assistance and services upon identification (HHS, 2009). However, they must pursue their claims for services through their state of residence (Clawson et al., 2009). Multiple federal agencies continue to develop initiatives with respect to human trafficking, with increasing attention on victims' needs (see, e.g., Department of Homeland Security [DHS], 2020).

The federal, top-down approach described earlier scaffolds responses to trafficking victims' needs, but most of the programs and services for domestic adult victims derive from state law and local programs (Crank, 2014; Mueller, 2013; National Conference of State Legislatures [NCSL], 2018). It is not clear why, but more of the community-level efforts focus on sex trafficking rather than labor trafficking. Researchers propose several hypotheses to explain the emphasis on sex trafficking. First, victims of labor trafficking may be less visible, performing forced labor inside peoples' homes or businesses (Logan, 2009). Relatedly, communities often can see people buying and selling sex, and they do not like the negative impacts that visible sex trafficking has on property values and public safety (Logan, 2009). Prostitution crimes also are easier for law enforcement to investigate, as they often involve publicly visible transactions between sex sellers and sex buyers. Finally, sex trafficking historically has received greater media attention (Logan, 2009). All four of these suppositions suggest that communities concentrate their time, resources, and funding on problems that are more visible and more salient.

While sex trafficking programs may resonate more with communities, they also are more fraught with internal and external biases and prejudices that render service provision to sex trafficking victims more complex, as discussed in detail further (Blakey, 2018). Confusion concerning who is a "victim" and who is a "criminal" underlies these biases, and critics question that fundamental appropriateness of providing a "work around" for people who violate prostitution laws (Kendis, 2019). Even advocates who work to free people from sex trades cannot achieve consensus on who is trafficked and who is a "willing participant" in sex work (United Against Human Trafficking, 2020, p. 1; see also The Advocates for Human Rights, n.d.; see also Kulig & Butler, 2019, for discussion). Some scholars acknowledge that a consensual (but illegal) sex trade exists in the United States involving willing participants who make calculated decisions to violate prostitution laws to earn a living (see Snow et al., 2019, for discussion). Some studies point to experiments with legal sex trades to highlight potential benefits of regulated sex commerce (e.g., in Rhode Island and Nevada) and call for further consideration of legalization and decriminalization of consensual prostitution industries (Gunderson, 2018; Tugee, 2016, but see Cho, 2016).

Other researchers have maintained, for at least the last half-century, that all prostitution is trafficking due to the inherently coercive nature of sex trades (Farrell & Fahy, 2016; Ibrahim, 2016; Kulig & Butler, 2019; Wilson, 2020). Persons who sell sex act under duress created by poverty, addiction, abuse, dependence on their traffickers, psychological manipulation, and trauma-coerced attachment that render victims unable to leave their abusers (Baldwin et al. 2015; Doychak & Raghavan, 2020; Moran & Farley, 2019). The consent/coercion debate has been robust and sustained for decades, if not centuries, and it will remain ripe for discussion for years to come (Doezema, 2020; Jabour, 2013; Jennings, 1976).

Theoretical debate aside, substantial evidence from the medical and social sciences establish that most, if not all, people who are charged with prostitution-related crimes suffer from a constellation of medical, psychological, and physical problems that increase risk for offending and victimization (Blakey et al., 2017; Clawson et al., 2009; HHS, 2009). Concerned communities therefore have begun to emphasize services and interventions that respond to those underlying conditions that correlate with, and may cause, involvement in sex trades. HTCs are one the latest and most interesting community-level developments in that regard (Mueller, 2013).

HTCs, court-based judicially monitored diversionary programs, predominantly focus on sex trafficking as indicated by one or more prostitution-related charges (Kulig & Butler, 2019). They usually do not concern themselves with distinguishing whether someone consented to performing the conduct underlying the charge; they worry about facilitating peoples' movement out of sex trades regardless of level of coercion (Kulig & Butler, 2019). Researchers and practitioners have struggled for decades, if not centuries, with how best to address the intractable problem of criminal sex trade, with everything from zero tolerance arrest policies to social programs nested in rehabilitative models (Shively et al., 2012). All efforts have met with some success, but none have sufficiently addressed the root causes of the sex trade and attendant criminal enterprises (Bales & Lites, 2005). Although scant empirical data exist to analyze HTCs' effectiveness, emerging research suggests HTCs may be as successful as other forms of problem-solving courts at reducing recidivism and providing social services (Beaujolais & Dillard, 2020; Miner-Romanoff, 2017). Much remains to be done in terms of studying these relatively new courts, and the Center for Court Innovation has been particularly assertive in its efforts to establish criteria for best practices and evaluation (see, e.g., Center for Court Innovation [CCI], 2018a; CCI, 2018b).

## TYPES OF HTCS

Communities across the country now support innumerable forms of intervention and service programs for human sex trafficking victims. Some programs compliment court-based programs, but others offer parallel and sometimes redundant efforts. There are faith-based, nonprofit, and community-based service programs for human sex trafficking victims, and several larger cities host pro bono legal clinics for sex trafficking victims (Blakey et al., 2017; Campbell, 2015). Some states employ prosecutor-based programs that attempt to divert persons who run afoul of prostitution laws with pre-arrest and pre-plea programs (Fair and Just Prosecution [FJP], 2017; Office for Victims of Crime, Training and Technical Assistance [OVCTTA], 2020; Mueller, 2013.). Others, like Texas, legislatively mandate programs that connect defendants with prevention and social service providers but do not necessarily operate formal HTCs (Butler, 2011; Wright & Levine, 2020). Finally, a few states have begun to focus on the demand side of sex trafficking. For example, Pennsylvania passed the Buyer Beware Act that elevates sex with a trafficking victim to a felony and increases certain fines and penalties (18 Pa. C.S. § 3013). Pennsylvania's PRIDE court, based in Allegheny County, also runs a "John School" to educate persons who buy sex about the dangers associated with their actions (Mueller, 2013). These programs certainly warrant study, but to be considered a human trafficking *court*, a program must be court-affiliated, and it must have the authority to resolve a criminal charge against a person accused of engaging in a sex act in violation of state laws that criminalize prostitution, pandering, or other terms that connote sex trade (see e.g., 18 Pa. Con. Stat. § 5902).

Working from that baseline, there appear to be at least three general forms of HTCs: (a) stand-alone courts that operate much like drug courts and other problem-solving courts (Campbell, 2015; New York State Unified Court System [NYSUCS], 2020); (b) dedicated dockets within a larger problem solving or community court that dedicates one day, one judge, or one team to human trafficking (Crank, 2014; Mazur& Goodman, 2015); and (c) broad-spectrum courts that handle an array of special cases through a problem-solving court or therapeutic jurisprudence approach (Mueller, 2013). HTCs operate within the criminal justice system, but they resolve criminal charges in a less punitive, more therapeutic way than traditional criminal courts. Some of the older HTCs retain the word "prostitute" in their titles (Blakey et al., 2017). More recent courts have adopted "human trafficking" for philosophical reasons that imply at least partial coercion and victimization (Gruber et al., 2016; Kendis, 2018). Still other courts avoid the prostitute/ victim distinction in their names altogether by using acronyms or neutral language that, they believe, reduces stigma associated with participation (see, e.g., Rosario, 2020, analyzing Ohio CATCH Court).

Not surprisingly, stand-alone courts are more common in more densely populated areas where both needs and resources are greater. Dedicated docket and broad-spectrum courts tend to rely more heavily on community-based programs (McBride, 2020). They collaborate with community members, which "increase[s] awareness among all court and justice actors and communities about trafficking types, dynamics, and reduction strategies," as well as "enhance[ing] regulation of, and vigilance over, trafficking in risky settings and employment sectors such as massage, hair, and manicure parlors, strip clubs, restaurants, bars, pornography production, and the domestic service, construction, agriculture, forestry, and hospitality services" (Martin, 2014, p. 21). Most HTCs contract with external service providers, but a few HTCs hybridize internal and external resources. For example, New York's Midtown Community Court combines "an on-site evidence-based, psychoeducational program known as WISE—Women's Independence, Safety and Empowerment" in conjunction with programming through the local domestic violence shelter (CCI, 2018(c), p. 1).

HTCs might consider borrowing from some aspects of non-judicial programs where the locus of response rests in the prosecuting attorney's office or the police department rather than the judge's office (Johnson et al., 2020; Wright & Levine, 2020). These programs focus on intervention prior to court involvement. They pursue the same diversionary mission as HTCs, but at an earlier point in the process. They also have similar guiding principles to reduce contact with the criminal justice system; rely on clinical staff "to design and run evidence-based and individually-tailored treatment programs; avoid costs to participants as much as possible; be as inclusionary as possible, particularly to moderate and high need individuals; and address underlying causes of behavior" (FJP, 2017, p. 2-3; Beaujolais & Dillard, 2020). They de-emphasize technical violations and avoid imposing absolutes such as "full sobriety" (FJP, 2017, p. 16). They also expressly require internal data tracking and external evaluations (FJP, 2017, p. 16).

## WHO DO HTCS SERVE?

Not all trafficking victims are eligible to participate in HTC programs, as discussed further, but anyone who has been a victim of trafficking hypothetically can be considered for HTC programs. Therefore, the following provides an overview of trafficked populations in general, as well as data on prostitution and sex trafficking. In general, socially vulnerable people with addiction problems, migrant workers, and socially vulnerable women and girls, are most at risk for becoming victims of both forms of trafficking (Bales & Lize, 2005; Hogan & Roe-Sepowitz, 2020; Randle, 2020; Roe-Sepowitz et al., 2011; Russell, 2018). Victims of labor trafficking usually work in agriculture, farming, residential domestic services, construction, and hospitality, while sex trafficking victims most often work in escort services, call-in commercial sex services, illegal massage companies, pornography industries, or "on the streets" (American Bar Association, 2013). Victims of *labor* trafficking generally do not suffer adverse legal consequences for the coerced actions they undertake, whereas victims of *sex* trafficking do, with sentences differing between states. For example, under Pennsylvania state law, someone found engaging in sexual activity for money is subject to conviction for anything from a misdemeanor of the first degree to felony of the third degree (18 Pa. C.S.§ 5902). People who sell sex are prosecuted under prostitution laws that compound their troubles by adding criminal records, fines, and possible jail time to their litany of challenges. Many sex trafficking victims suffer re-victimization at the hands of police and prosecutors who treat them as punitively as offenders, without regard for their victimization (Jorgenson, 2018; Mogulescu, 2011).

Although researchers and advocacy groups concur that human trafficking is endemic and prevalent, there is no reliable data on the number of persons trafficked in the United States. Various sources estimate that, annually, anywhere from 14,500 to 2 million people suffer from trafficking in the United States (Clawson et al., 2009; Crank, 2014, Martin, 2014). These numbers are so inconsistent that they render it impossible to draw any meaningful conclusions.

As noted earlier, HTCs usually focus on adult sex trafficking cases; in other words, cases in which an adult has been charged with a crime related to the sale of sex acts (see e.g., NYSUCS, 2020). Some also serve youth charged with prostitution crimes (Bath et al., 2020). Moreover, HTCs usually focus on the people performing the sex acts, not on the people who broker the acts or buy the acts, commonly known as "pimps" or "johns" (NYSUCS, 2020, but see Mueller, 2013).

Compiling data on this subset of people who violate prostitution laws or are sex trafficked is complicated. "Only a fraction of the estimated . . . trafficking victimization in local communities is captured in either law enforcement or service provider data" (Farrell et al., 2019, p. 2). For example, the Federal Bureau of Investigation's (FBI) Uniform Crime Reports (UCR) began collecting data on human trafficking in 2013, and they distinguish between commercial sex trafficking and forced labor trafficking. In their 2019 report, based on data provided by states, there were 1,607 reported incidents of commercial sex trafficking (FBI, 2019a). However, another data set also managed by the FBI's UCR reported 26,713 arrests for prostitution (FBI,

2019b). There is no explanation for how the states determined who among the prostitution charges were trafficking victims.

"Victims of sex trafficking have the greatest chance of being identified through arrests made by law enforcement pursuant to State prostitution and commercial vice statutes" (Clawson et al., 2009, p. 15). Yet law enforcement protocols for identify trafficking victims are almost "nonexistent," and data collectors' "struggle" with the "challenge of disentangling human trafficking victimization from other offenses" (Farrell et al., 2019, p. 1). Further research should examine how localities define prostitution versus trafficking and consider means of sensitizing law enforcement to underlying issues associated with prostitution and trafficking.

Data from several national organizations provide further insights into the magnitude of the sex trafficking problem. The Polaris Project, the subject of some criticism among advocates and criminal justice reformers, nonetheless produces reports that shed light on trafficking victim demographics. For example, most people who contact their hotline are over the age of eighteen and overwhelmingly female. Among the top five self-reported races and ethnicities, 37 percent identified as Latino, 28 percent as Asian, 17 percent as black, 15 percent as White and 3 percent as multi-ethnic or multi-racial (Polaris Project, 2018). Other evidence also indicates that certain subpopulations are more vulnerable to sex trafficking, including homeless children and adults; children living in foster care; LGBTQ+ individuals; people of color; people who have experienced sexual abuse in their past; people living in poverty; refugees, undocumented immigrants, and migrant workers; people living with addiction; and people struggling with mental illness or intellectual disabilities (Cavett, 2018; Schweig, 2012; Shdaimah & Wiechelt, 2012, 2013). Once people become involved in trafficking, they are likely to be subjected to additional forms of violence at the hands of those to whom they are sold (Macias-Konstantopoulos, 2016). They also suffer from higher rates of sexually transmitted diseases, dental problems, post-traumatic stress, and psychological and emotional problems (Blakey et al., 2017). Even when they break out of illegal sex trades, they experience short- and long-term effects that often lead them into self-destructive behaviors and relationships (Blakey et al., 2017).

Traffickers work to identify and subsequently leverage their victims' vulnerabilities to create dependency and control (Baldwin et al, 2015). Psychological and social science research establishes that traffickers employ a series of power and control tactics over their victims, such as threats, intimidation, economic abuse, emotional abuse, physical abuse, sexual abuse, perpetuation of addiction, and isolation (US Department of State ([US DOS), 2020 b). Traffickers often combine tactics tailored to their victims' vulnerabilities. For example, traffickers promote addiction to create dependency on them as sources of substances, and condition receipt of drugs on sex acts (US DOS, 2020 b). At the same time, trafficking victims may turn to substance abuse to self-medicate trauma, anxiety, and depression (Goodman & Leidholdt, 2013). Although traffickers are not the focus of this chapter, a basic understanding of who they are and how they exert power over victims helps advocates and policymakers develop programming informed by the larger environment in which trafficking occurs. Additionally, those who sell sex must be provided with resources to help them overcome the conditions that made them targets for victimization, and frankly, they must be provided with alternative means of making money. Victims of sex trafficking frequently carry long criminal records for their prostitution offenses. Those criminal records make it almost impossible for those victims to obtain legal employment, access public benefits, or rent an apartment (Shdaimah & Wiechelt, 2012).

A two-pronged approach that partners demand-side reduction with risk reduction programs needs to be employed in place of the traditional catch-and-release approach (Shively et al., 2012). Specialized courts are well-suited to promote this approach. HTCs provide alternatives to traditional court processes for persons who engage in sex acts for profit,[2] focusing on risk reduction, responding to underlying factors that place certain people at greater risk of becoming victims of sex trafficking, and provided essential social, medical, and psychological services to help break the cycle of victimization and offending (Crank, 2014).

HTCs shift the paradigm surrounding commercial sex trades from viewing providers of sex as criminals to understanding that they are victims, as well (Ibrahim, 2016). As noted earlier, past trauma, prior victimization, prior substance abuse, and psychological coercion are common traits among commercial sex workers. Consensus among criminal justice and social service professionals continues to coalesce around the notion that sex trafficking must be redressed with trauma-informed, therapeutic programming that recognizes the complicated duality of the victim as a criminal defendant (Ostad-Hashemi, 2017; Sawicki et al., 2019; Updegrove & Muftic, 2019). HTCs provide judicially monitored intervention programs for individuals facing human trafficking, prostitution, sex trafficking, and other charges related to the sale of sex acts. Traditional criminalization of the sale of sex acts under prostitution and related laws create revolving door offenses that punish sex workers without responding to the underlying issues that led people to become involved in sex trades, leading to an inevitable cycle of arrest, sentencing, release, and reoffending (Hickle & Roe-Sepowitz, 2017; Roe-Sepowitz et al., 2014). HTCs sit at the center of the growing effort to move sex trafficking victims out of jails and into community-based, rehabilitative programming.

## OVERVIEW OF HTC OPERATIONS

The first identifiable HTCs appeared in the mid-2000s, and there are now approximately 40 HTCs in the United States (Kulig & Butler, 2019). HTCs predominantly provide social services and legal alternatives for persons charged with performing sex acts for financial compensation in violation of law, but some HTCs also target persons accused of trafficking, solicitation, and other related crimes (Gruber, Cohen, & Mogulescu, 2016). Very little scholarly research on these courts exists. There have been no identifiable, empirical outcome studies and few process or program evaluations (Kulig & Butler, 2019). Most data on HTCs are anecdotal or collected through nonprofit entities or through convenience samples (see Shdaimah, 2020). While nascent efforts are being made to empirically evaluate these courts, an important conversation is developing about the appropriateness of these courts' punitiveness toward victims and relative inattention to sex buyers (Gruber, Cohen, & Mogulescu, 2016; Kendis, 2019).

### HTC Values, Goals, and Guiding Principles

HTCs' missions evade meaningful typology because there are too many varieties to draw conclusions. But what can be said is that they all appear to subscribe to some guiding principles and goals, summarized as follows:

1.  Facilitation of permanent departure from sex trades through scaffolded social services interventions;
2.  Recidivism reduction with respect to all offending (most often drug or prostitution charges);
3.  Transparency, ensuring that all stakeholders, including victims, offenders, court personnel, regardless of education or language proficiency, understanding court processes, and expectations for participants;
4.  Cost efficiency through coordination with state, local, federal, and nonprofit organizations to reduce overlap of services and achieve efficiencies;
5.  Procedural efficiency through, again, coordination with state, local, federal, and nonprofit organizations to promote timely and effective communication and service delivery;
6.  Procedural justice and equal access to justice;
7.  Comprehensive services through broad spectrum of trauma-informed services tailored to individuals' needs;
8.  Cultural sensitivity and appropriate procedures developed with awareness of global and cultural differences among clients;

9. Mitigation of potential for secondary victimization and unintended consequences of criminal justice involvement; and

10. Reduction of harm to the community and to the clients (synthesized from Beaujolais & Dillard, 2020; Martin, 2014, p. 14, 21–25).

These guiding principles differ somewhat from the ten Key Components espoused by drug and other problem-solving courts, but they are compatible in form and in spirit with their collaborative, treatment-focused concerns (Gallagher et al., 2019; Gallagher & Holmes, 2008). HTCs arguably have a duty, more than other offense-oriented specialized courts, to ground all their work in the scholarship on preventing secondary victimization and ensuring trauma-informed orientation in all their practices. HTC participants arrive in court with a litany of incredibly sensitive, potentially stigmatizing troubles. As noted earlier, they often come from backgrounds of physical abuse and addiction, and the charges they face create fertile soil for secondary victimization by police and court personnel unfamiliar with the victimizing nature of sex trafficking. HTC's guiding principles, as summarized earlier, illustrate these courts' awareness of, and commitment to, mitigating these issues.

## Who Is Eligible to Participate in HTCs?

Generally, participants must establish that they have an open criminal charge for a sex offense (Crank, 2014, p. 38). Critics contend that it is inappropriate to allow persons who do not meet the legal definition of "trafficking victim" to qualify for these diversionary programs. Yet proponents point to the larger mission to break the sex trade cycle, reduce recidivism, and respond to social ills related to sex trafficking. Regardless of whether someone fits the technical definition of victim, they most likely suffer from a multitude of co-occurring conditions, "such as coercive control by abusers, trauma, substance abuse, economic powerlessness, and immigration status, among other challenges, kept these women from leaving a pimp, trafficker, or 'the life' (CCIa, 2018). Importantly, most HTCs recognize that many adult victims entered into prostitution as minors and were still being arrested as adults" (Crank, 2014, p. 38; Gonzalez-Bocinski, 2020).

Outside of the criminal charge requirement, different courts impose different eligibility requirements. Many courts will not accept persons with any history of violent crime, and many only accept misdemeanor cases (Campbell, 2015; Mueller, 2013; NYUCS, 2020). Some systems, such as New York State, accept participants regardless of gender, while others only work with women (Mueller, 2013; NYUCS, 2020). Project DAWN in Philadelphia only serves women with active, nonviolent criminal charges who can pass a psychiatric assessment and are eligible for Medicaid (Mueller, 2013).

Confusion abounds about the legal status of HTC clients because it varies from program to program. Some participants enter shortly after arrest as "pre-plea," meaning that their charges remain pending, and they have not admitted or denied guilt (Leon & Shdaimah, 2012; Schweig et al., 2012; Shdaimah & Wiechelt, 2012; Wiechelt & Shdaimeh, 2011). In these pre-plea courts, judges may suspend charges, reduce charges, or promise to dismiss charges upon successful completion of the program. Other HTCs require clients to plead guilty to at least one charge, and they are "sentenced" to the HTC program (Beaujolais & Dillard, 2020; Campbell, 2015; Kulig & Butler, 2019, Parker & Pizzio, 2017). Most of these post-plea courts reinstate charges and sentences if participants reoffend or otherwise terminate the program early (Beaujolais & Dillard, 2020, citing Leon & Shdaimah, 2012; Miner-Romanoff, 2017, 2014; Roe-Sepowitz et al., 2011).

Participants' legal status invokes at least two concerns about equity. First, most, if not all HTCs insist that clients consent to participate in the program, but there is some discord among scholars about the degree to which consent is truly voluntary (Kinsely, 2016; Luminais & Lovell, 2018). While coerciveness has become an accepted cost of the other specialized courts, HTCs should pay attention to consent with these participants who have a lifetime of adverse experiences with issues related to consent. Second, some HTCs impose significant fines and costs, while others waive all monetary punishments (Campbell, 2015). Many victims of human trafficking return to sex trades after participating in the HTC for financial reasons. These courts that require victims to pay impose significant financial burdens that may be contributing to the problem they claim to want to resolve.

## HTC Operations

Like most problem-solving courts, HTCs use frequent court appearances, periodic check-ins with mentors and therapists, and mandatory treatment to keep tabs on participants (Lee et al., 2013). They require treatment in lieu of jail for minor violations, and they eschew traditional notions of noncompliance. For example, as seen in many other problem-solving courts, substance abuse or "falling off the wagon" is not treated as an act of recidivism; instead, it is viewed as evidence for the need for more treatment (Beaujolais & Dillard, 2020; FJP, 2017). Generally, these programs last anywhere from three months to two years (Beaujolais & Dillard, 2020). The following synopsizes major HTC components.

## The HTC Team or Task Force

HTCs take a trauma-informed team, partnership, or task force approach. The federal Office for Victims of Crime encourages HTC organizers to create "task forces," consistent with the foundational drug court model that recommends a team approach to development and operation of problem-solving court (OVCTTAC, 2020). The CCI recommends HTC teams create working groups, or at least direct their attention to three key concerns: operations, services, and security (CCI, 2018c). Teams include some combination of a judge, a prosecutor, a defense attorney, case managers, service providers, a representative from the probation office, and a data manager (Goodman & Mazur, 2014). Some also include a peer support person or a mentor.

Some teams run themselves on the same principles upon which they run their programming. For example, the Project Dawn Court Diversionary Program in Philadelphia is run exclusively by women, from the presiding judge to the service providers (Mueller, 2013). They meet twice per month and hold each other accountable for promoting trauma-informed care and collaborating with community partners (Office of the District Attorney, n.d.). Similarly, the Tennessee's Cherished HEARTS HTCs impose women-only rules for all court personnel, from police and probation to service providers (Knisely, 2016).

## Screening and Assessment

Many HTCs employ a psychosocial screening tool to assess trauma, victimization, mental health needs, and criminogenic risk factors (Crank, 2014). Clients then are connected with services, treatment, and programming as described further. The CCI advises HTCs to flag cases for consideration and then employ "research-based and gender-responsive screening instruments . . . to identify victims, reveal their needs, and determine program eligibility" (CCI, 2018a, p. 1; CCI, 2018b). Planning is paramount in these courts where participants crave consistency. Their lives have been defined by lack of predictability, and they often regress or recidivate when they feel they cannot depend on processes. Thus, CCI recommends extensive advance planning and inquiries such as: Who will conduct screenings? Where? When in the process? What tools will be used? How will data be recorded and stored? (CCI, 2018c). Experts concur that all plans, including screening and assessment, should be documented, shared, and stored in a transparent fashion (CCI, 2018c).

## Services

In a systematic review of extant literature on HTCs programming, Beaujolais and Dillard (2020) found that many, if not most, HTCs partner with community providers to link participants with life skills training, employment assistance, addiction treatment, and guidance on how to access medical, housing, and social services. HTCs generally require counseling, but they do not necessarily specify type, frequency, or duration of counseling (Beuajolais & Dillard, 2020, citing Collins et al., 2017; Leon, & Shdaimah, 2012; Miner-Romanoff, 2017; Shdaimah, & Wiechelt, 2012). Because of the distinctly decentralized nature of programming within HTCs, it is impossible to draw more concrete conclusions about what they do. Internal descriptions of programming are not enlightening, either. For example, the popular Recovery Oriented System of Care (ROSC) describes itself as "a coordinated network of community-based services and supports that is person-centered and builds on the strengths and resiliencies of individuals, families, and communities to achieve abstinence and improved health, wellness, and quality of life for those with or at risk of alcohol and drug problems" (Campbell et al., 2015, p. 105, quoting Whitter et al., 2010). It is hard to discern from that lengthy description what they actually do. Likewise, Ohio's CATCH program provides wrap around services, including mental health services, housing support, health and lifestyle coaching, interpersonal skill development, and substance abuse treatment (Miner-Romanoff, 2017).

Reflecting trauma-informed, rehabilitative practices, many HTC teams mandate that most participants engage in psycho-educational empowerment programs and skills-building programs. For example, New York HTCs may use the WISE protocol (Women's Independence Safety and Empowerment) or the STEPS program that is offered in partnership with local domestic violence agencies (Crank, 2014, p. 39). Most HTCs also require individual-l and group-level therapy and substance abuse treatment. Many also offer or require financial literacy training, GED classes, legal and employment services, esteem development classes, and housing assistance (Crank, 2014). Many courts offer these programs in English and Spanish, and some have access to language assistance technology (Crank, 2014). For instance, one court in New York offers assistance in Mandarin and Korean (Crank, 2015, p. 40).

HTCs link participants with services, but they have no control over how community-based partners operate. Thus, service delivery can be spotty at times due to scheduling, insurance, and transportation issues, among others (Walters, 2017). Difficulties with access to services, as well as the variety of different individual needs of clients, create barriers to service delivery that demand evaluation.

## Monitoring and Oversight

HTCs impose several monitoring mechanisms among participants to ensure sobriety and program compliance. Probation officers act as enforcers who hold participants accountable. Some programs require 8:00 p.m. to 8:00 a.m. curfews enforced via electronic monitoring, and drug testing is frequent and random (Mueller, 2013). Weekly and biweekly meetings (depending on the HTC) between participants and the judicial team ensure formal periods of monitoring and oversight (Beaujolais & Dillard, 2020). During these meetings, probation officers brief the HTC team on all clients' successes and slip ups. Clients then are given opportunities to report honestly and openly on their successes or transgressions to the presiding judge. The judicial oversight provides the opportunity for continued accountability.

## Enforcement and Sanctions

Violations of the program's terms result in a series of escalating sanctions. These sanctions are gradual and situation dependent. For example, sanctions begin with essay assignments and gradually escalate with punishments such as community service, observing court proceedings for a day in the jury box, and in severe cases spending up to a week in jail (Mueller, 2013). Participants who commit serious violations must restart the phase of the program in which noncompliance occurred.

## Graduation and Termination

On average, it takes participants two years to complete HTC programs, after which their charges are either dropped or dismissed (Mueller, 2013). Some courts offer expungement as an added incentive if participants remain arrest-free for one year following graduation (Mueller, 2013). There are few data points to determine graduation rates or long-term success. But a few programs track and report data. For example, as of 2017, Pennsylvania's Project Dawn reported that more than 70 percent had graduated and remained arrest-free during a one-year follow-up period (Lento, 2020). On the other hand, Pennsylvania's PRIDE court did not enjoy the same levels of success. During the first ten years of its operation, 446 individuals were sentenced or referred to PRIDE Court (Mueller, 2013). Of this base number, only 311 of those individuals chose to receive services. Of these 311 individuals that have participated in the program over the ten years, seventy-nine successful graduates were generated (Mueller, 2013). This translated to a 25 percent graduation rate of those that received services and participated in the treatment court in Allegheny County. While the graduation rate is very low, of the seventy-nine graduates, only five were rearrested for prostitution following their graduation, making the recidivism rate 6 percent, a low number (Mueller, 2013).

## ARE HTCS EFFECTIVE?

HTCs, perhaps more than any other problem-solving courts, suffer from lack of empirical evaluation. In a rigorous 2020 review of research on HTCs, only six studies satisfied the review criteria, and only two of those articulated program goals (Beaujolais & Dillard, 2020). The very limited data on HTC outcomes suggest that they may be effective in at least a few respects. First, they appear to reduce the risk of recidivism and rearrest (Beaujolais & Dillard, 2020; Miner-Romanoff, 2017; Roe-Sepowitz et al., 2011) and the number of nights in jail (Miner-Romanoff, 2017). They increase participants' social scaffolding and access to needed resources, such as employment assistance, social services, and counseling, and otherwise improve their living conditions (Miner-Romanoff, 2017; Roe-Sepowitz et al., 2014). HTCs also might improve participants' perceptions of procedural justice (Martin, 2014).

An evaluation of Ohio's CATCH court found several positive outcomes: graduation rates doubled in a five-year period, and 90 percent of graduates had made positive changes in their lives (Miner-Romanoff, 2017). Participants' mental and physical health improved, and most left feeling that someone cared about them. The majority felt that the program had helped improved their sense of personal safety (85.71 percent), felt it helped with their families (57.14 percent), had more stable housing (71.42 percent), developed healthier life skills (76.20 percent), and were undertaking healthier behaviors (71.42) (Miner-Romanoff, 2017). That same study cited criminal justice cost savings, noting that the CATCH program costs $18,000 per individual annually, far less than the $200,000 necessary to incarcerate someone (Miner-Romanoff, 2017). However, this cost analysis does not account for the expanded court time and personnel required to run these intensive courts. Finally, participants report dramatic improvements in their quality of life after completing HTC programs (Beaujolais & Dillard, 2020; Miner-Romanoff, 2017; Shdaimah & Bailey-Kloch, 2014). These glowing reviews that researchers frequently obtained through interviews should be interpreted with caution considering the tendency of trafficking victims to seek positive interactions, particularly with persons perceived to be in positions of authority.

However, if HTCs' primary goal is to facilitate peoples' exit from sex trades, at least one study finds no significant difference in recidivism rates among those who participated in a diversion program and those who did not (Koegler et al., 2020). Notably, this study involved a program that was not court-based. But it is worthy of mention as one of the few studies that have examined diversion programs' impacts on recidivism. Which leads one to wonder whether a court-based program would enjoy different outcomes: a question ripe for further study.

## CHALLENGES FOR HTCS MOVING FORWARD

As evaluations of HTCs continue to develop, certain issues within these courts that serve participants with complex sequelae of needs should be addressed. The following draws from the extant scholarship to highlight several possible areas of inquiry or analysis.

The "Four P Approach." The NCSL provides a helpful framework for those contemplating what comes next for community-level planning. They encourage (1) *protection* through improved identification procedures that allow police to identify and locate persons at risk for or involved in human trafficking; (2) *prosecution* of traffickers, but not those who are trafficked; (3) *prevention* through public awareness campaigns; and (4) *partnerships* to cut across community silos of services (NCSL, 2018). Operationalization of the Four Ps is a matter for local policy and planning, and academics may find it useful as a frame for building their research agendas.

### Net Widening

Much like many other problem-solving courts, HTCs have been accused of entangling low-level offenders into the criminal justice system under the guise of treatment and rehabilitation (Shdaimah, 2020). Although grounded in benevolent intentions, HTCs may increase the number of people under criminal justice supervision, particularly women of color, through a number of mechanisms (Blakey et al., 2017). Diversionary programs may act as incentives for police officers and prosecutors to pursue minor crimes they previously would not have pursued so as to provide services. This effort may be of noble intent, but one fraught with peril for potential technical violations. Moreover, wealthier people and white people are more likely to have the social and financial capital necessary to extricate themselves from technical violations or other adverse consequences of being under criminal justice control (Kendis, 2019).

On the other hand, New York City, where HTCs operate in four boroughs (Midtown Community Court, Brooklyn Criminal Court, Queens County Criminal Court, and Bronx Community Solutions), offers a positive, partial rebuttal to this criticism. New York City has observed a 20 percent decrease in the number of total arrests for prostitution and loitering between 2014 and 2015 (Cohen, 2016). Optimistically, local law enforcement and court personnel can work together to prevent net widening, possibly by diverting trafficked persons to pre-plea programs that do not file charges unless participants fail out of the program.

## Identification

Given the dearth of data on who are victims of trafficking, there are numerous opportunities to develop helpful information. At the national level, one of the federal agencies that operate trafficking programs could provide training for state- and local-level law enforcement on how to identify trafficking victims (Gallagher & Holmes, 2008). They could contemporaneously provide training on how to track and report trafficking, and how to link victims with community-level services (Gallagher & Holmes, 2008).

## Paternalism

As discussed earlier, sex trafficking victims often have endured years of physical and psychological abuse, anesthetized themselves with drugs and alcohol, and entered sex trade work either involuntarily or under duress (Cavett, 2018; Schweig, 2012; Shdaimah & Wiechelt, 2012, 2013). Their multi-tiered experiences with victimization render theme targets of sympathy for some criminal justice practitioners. Some scholars fear that such sympathy may translate into "white knight syndrome" or inappropriate paternalism (Blakey, et al., 2020; Merry & Ramachandran, 2016). All problem-solving courts could be subject to similar criticism, but the danger of paternalistic overreach in HTCs is particularly acute because of racial and gender aspects of the courts (dominated traditionally by white men) deciding what is "best" for victims of sex trafficking (who are disproportionately women of color and lower socioeconomic status).

## Mitigating Impacts of Bias and Stigma

HTC participants face several sources of potential bias and discrimination as they navigate their way through the requirements of HTC programs. First, they necessarily interact with police because they are arrested. Although police departments continue to improve their employees' sensitivity to issues surrounding victimization and sex trade workers, much work remains to be done. Once they begin HTC programs participants usually are required to undergo mental health evaluations and treatment, which naturally requires them to interact with mental health care providers. There are not yet any established "best practices" for providing mental health services to HTC participants, and any efforts to create such standards should be mindful of potential biases (Judge, 2018). Evidence indicates that mental health workers and social service providers are not immune to these biases, either (Litam, 2019; Weber, 2020).

## Retention and Completion

At least one study found that participants' motivation to stay in the program decreased over time. They were highly incentivized when they discovered that their criminal charges would be resolved and they could get assistance, but the motivation associated with long-term benefits of treatment and a clean record dissipated as the everyday difficulties with complying with program requirements made their near-term realities more difficult (Blakey et al., 2017). Those authors recommended intermittent, prosocial rewards, such as tickets to sporting events or gift cards for restaurants (Blakey et al., 2017). HTCs could borrow from veterans courts and other problem-solving courts and provide tokens or small gifts each time participants pass a milestone, such as ninety days of sobriety or employment.

Blakey and colleagues (2017) also found that the study HTC did not sanction misbehavior other than through jail time. Citing Marlowe (2008), Blakey and colleagues recommend escalating sanctions, reserving jail for the most egregious violations. Creative planners could craft incentive/sanction programs based on resources and opportunities available in their communities.

## Service Provider Partnerships

Perhaps because HTCs are so new, some do not have formalized relationships with their community-based service providers (Blakey et al., 2017). They rely upon "on-call" or ad hoc relationships for providing services to participants. In a similar vein, terms of service provision need to be established before participants begin the program. Trafficking victims crave structure and predictability (Blakey et al. 2017). They prefer to know up front what is expected of them, in small ways and large. For example, participants in the Blakley study were told by the local housing agency with which the HTC partnered that they could only have three smoke breaks per day. Previously, they could take as many smoke breaks as they wanted. The change in the rules disturbed the participants who felt that they were being inexplicably punished and that the rules were unpredictable (Blakey et al., 2017).

## Improved Data Tracking

Generally speaking, HTCs, like most problem-solving courts, do not track much data, and the data they do track are not stored in a manner amenable to analysis. They need to track data in an accessible database—not case management software—so that social scientists can analyze data and provide meaningful, evidence-based evaluation and advice. The Center for Court

Innovation provides baseline guidance in this regard, and consultants can offer insights into what data to track and how best to do it (Mazur et al., 2015). The creation and implementation of a recidivism tracking program is necessary. Data tracking also could help define the scope of the human trafficking problem. As noted earlier, there are no robust, reliable data sets on the number of trafficking victims in the United States (Farrell et al., 2019). HTCs generally protect their participants' identities, but anonymized and aggregated data on participants' experiences would meaningfully expand current understandings of who and how many are victims.

## Culture

Finally, HTCs and their personnel should continue to develop and deploy training programs that promote trust, relationships, reliability, and a trauma-informed approach to all aspects of the court (Blakey et al., 2017). Working from the assumption that these courts have a net positive impact upon the clients they serve, many scholars recommend improved and ongoing education for community stakeholders, such as law enforcement and correctional officers (Leon & Shdaimah, 2012; Miner-Romanoff, 2017; Shdaimah & Wiechelt, 2012). For example, participants in the one of the programs felt that law enforcement officers should be educated about sex trafficking so that officers would understand that the individuals engaging in sex work were themselves victims, and therefore proceed to interface with them in a supportive, helpful manner (Miner-Romanoff, 2017). In another study, participants expressed a desire for the law enforcement officers to "treat [them] like human beings" (Shdaimah & Wiechelt, 2012, p. 159). Another recommendation related to the operational aspects of the programs, such as having consistent protocols and procedures and providing clarity about the responsibilities of the various stakeholder roles (Beaujolais & Dillard, 2020). There was also an expressed need to position services in convenient and accessible locations in the community (Beaujolais & Dillard, 2020; Leon & Shdaimah, 2012).

## CONCLUSION

HTCs are intervention style programs designed to rehabilitate, rather than punish, nonviolent individuals who have charges of prostitution against them. In the past, human trafficking victims have been punished with the same harshness as their perpetrators. This leads to a cycle of revictimization. Due to the coercive nature of sex trafficking and prostitution, the legal system has been forced to adapt its approach when dealing with individuals who, while having technically broken the law, are victims themselves. By combining treatment with judicial supervision, intervention style court programs are designed to provide sex trafficked victims with the means to maintain long-term recovery and stay out of prison. Oftentimes, human trafficking victims have broken the law due to circumstances beyond their control. They are frequently being held against their will physically or lured using a drug addiction. HTC programs are designed to take a victim-centric approach, helping to resolve these issues permanently, rather than punish temporarily without addressing underlying causes and lasting trauma. The victim who has experienced sex trafficking is vital to this process, as they are evidence of a crime committed (Cassidy, 2020). Unfortunately, a lack of standard practices among programs, limited data availability, and poor infrastructure to monitor recidivism after program completion has led to relatively inconclusive results surrounding HTC programs. Concerns also remain about the degree to which HTCs are yet another weapon in the "penal warfare" arsenal against women and people of color (Gruber et al., 2016, p.1332). Nevertheless, however, existing date suggest that HTCs and their more rehabilitative approach help break the cycle of abuse attendant to prosecution of human trafficking victims (Beaujolais & Dillard, 2020).

## NOTES

1. For simplicity and readability, the acronym "HTC" will be used throughout to represent problem-solving courts that provide court-based alternative programs for persons facing charges related to sex trafficking, human trafficking, prostitution, and other interpersonal, adult sexual conduct that is proscribed by law.

2. Demand reduction may be addressed in what are sometimes known as "john courts," and those courts are beyond the scope of this chapter (Bacher et al., 2008). Likewise, there are special programs and courts that focus on challenges unique to child trafficking victims, which also are outside the ambit of this chapter (Micetic, 2018).

## REFERENCES

18 Pa.C.S.A. Crimes and Offenses § 3011.
18 Pa.C.S.A. Crimes and Offenses § 3013.
18 Pa.C.S.A. Crimes and Offenses § 5902.
Advocates for Human Rights. (n.d.). Sex Trafficking. Retrieved from https://www.the advocatesforhumanrights.org/sextrafficking
American Bar Association (2013). Human trafficking. *The Judges' Journal, 52*, 1.
Baldwin, S. B., Fehrenbacher, A. E., & Eisenman, D. P. (2015). Psychological coercion in human trafficking: An application of Biderman's framework. *Qualitative Health Research, 25*(9), 1171–1181.

Bales, K., & Lize, S. (2005). Trafficking in persons in the United States. *Croft Institute for International Studies, University of Mississippi.* Retrieved from https://www.ncjrs.gov/pdffiles1/nij/grants/211980.pdf

Bath, E. P., Godoy, S. M., Morris, T. C., Hammond, I., Mondal, S., Goitom, S., . . . & Barnert, E. S. (2020). A specialty court for US youth impacted by commercial sexual exploitation. *Child Abuse & Neglect, 100,* DOI: 10.1016/j.chiabu.2019.104041.

Barnhart, M. H. (2009). Sex and slavery: An analysis of three models of state human trafficking legislation. *William & Mary Journal of Women and the Law, 16.* 83.

Beaujolais, B., & Dillard, R. L. (2020). Court-affiliated diversion programs for prostitution- related crimes: A comprehensive review of program components and impact. *Violence and Victims, 35*(4), 562–588.

Blakey, J. M., Gunn, A. J., & Canada, K. E. (2020). Supporting the end of prostitution permanently (SEPP) prostitution court: Examining inter-professional collaboration within alternative criminal justice settings. *Journal of Interprofessional Care,* 1–9, DOI: 10.1080/13561820.2020.1751095

Blakey, J. M., & Gunn, A. (2018). The "ickiness factor": Stigma as a barrier to exiting prostitution. *Journal of Offender Rehabilitation, 57*(8), 538–561.

Blakey, J. M., Mueller, D. J., & Richie, M. (2017). Strengths and challenges of a prostitution court model. *Justice System Journal, 38*(4), 364–379.

Beaujolais, B., & Dillard, R. L. (2020). Court-affiliated diversion programs for prostitution-related crimes: A comprehensive review of program components and impact. *Violence and Victims, 35*(4), 562–588.

Begun, A. L., & Hammond, G. C. (2012). CATCH court: A novel approach to "treatment as alternative to incarceration" for women engaged in prostitution and substance abuse. *Journal of Social Work Practice in the Addictions, 12*(3), 328–331.

Brunson et al. (2014). "A guide to human trafficking for state courts." *Human Trafficking and the State Courts Collaborative.* Retrieved from http://www.htcourts.org/wp-content/uploads/00_EntireGuide_140726_v02.pdf. 2020.

Butler, C. N. (2011). Sex slavery in the Lone Star State: Does the Texas human trafficking legislation of 2011 protect minors. *Akron Law Review, 45,* 843.

Campbell, E. (2015). *Michigan's First Human Trafficking Court.* Saint Louis University School of Law. Retrieved from https://scholarship.law.slu.edu/lj/vol60/iss1/6

Cavett, L. J. (2018). *Developing a Residential Treatment Program for Adolescent Females Ages 13–17 Who Have been Rescued from Human Trafficking* (Doctoral dissertation, Mississippi College).

Center for Court Innovation (CCI). (2018) (a). The Center for Court Innovation helps to plan and create off-ramps for justice-involved victims of human trafficking. Retrieved from https://www.courtinnovation.org/areas-of-focus/human-trafficking

Center for Court Innovation (CCI). (2018) (b). Responding to Sex Trafficking in Your Jurisdiction. Retrieved from https://www.courtinnovation.org/sites/default/files/documents/RespondingtoSexTrafficking.pdf_0.pdf

Center for Court Innovation (CCI). (2018) (c). Alternatives to Incarceration. Retrieved from https://www.courtinnovation.org/sites/default/files/media/documen t/2020/MCC_FactShe et_ATI_01142019.pdf

Cho, S. Y. (2016). Liberal coercion? Prostitution, human trafficking and policy. *European Journal of Law and Economics, 41*(2), 321–348.

Clawson, H. J., N. Dutch, A. Solomon, & L. G. Grace. (2009). Human trafficking into and within the United States: A Review of the Literature. *U.S. Department of Health and Human.* Retrieved from *https://aspe.hhs.gov/report/human-trafficking -and-within-united-states-review-literature*

Cohen, A. J. (2016). Trauma and the welfare state: A genealogy of prostitution courts in New York City. *Texas Law Review, 95*, 915.

Crank, K. (2014). Chapter 2: Community courts, specialized dockets, and other approaches to address sex trafficking. *A Guide to Human Trafficking for State Courts.* Human Trafficking and the State Courts Collaborative. Retrieved from http: //www.htcourts.org/wp-content/uploads/00_EntireGuide_140726_v02.pdf. 2020

Department of Health and Human Services (HHS). (2009). Study of HHS programs serving human trafficking victims. Retrieved from tps://aspe.hhs.gov/system/ files/ pdf/75966/index.pdf

Department of Homeland Security (DHS). 2020). DHS launches new center for countering human trafficking. Retrieved from https://www.dhs.gov/news/2020/10 /20/dhs-launches-new-center-countering-human-trafficking

Doezema, J. (2002). Who gets to choose? Coercion, consent, and the UN Trafficking Protocol. *Gender & Development, 10*(1), 20–27.

Doychak, K., & Raghavan, C. (2020). No voice or vote: Trauma-coerced attachment in victims of sex trafficking. *Journal of Human Trafficking, 6*(3), 339–357.

Fair and Just Prosecution. (2017). Promising practices in prosecutor led diversion. Retrieved from https://fairandjustprosecution.org/wpcontent/uploads/2017/09/ FJPBrief.Diversion.9.26.pdf

Farrell, A., Dank, M., Kafafian, M., Lockwood, S., Pfeffer, R., Hughes, A., & Vincent, K. (2019). *Capturing human trafficking victimization through crime reporting.* Washington, DC: US Department of Justice.

Farrell, A., & Fahy, S. (2016). Prostitution and sex trafficking. In C. A. Cuevas & C. M. Rennison (Eds.), *The Wiley Handbook on Psychology of Violence* (pp. 517–532). Wiley.

Federal Bureau of Investigation. (2019) (a). 2019 Crime in the United States: Human trafficking. Retrieved from https://ucr.fbi.gov/crime-in-the-u.s/2019/crime-in-the-u .s.2019/additional-data-collections/human-trafficking

Federal Bureau of Investigation. (2019) (b). 2019 Crime in the United States: Table 29: Retrieved from https://ucr.fbi.gov/crime-in-the-u.s/2019/crime-in-the-u.s.-201 9/tables/table-29

Ferguson, K. M., Soydan, H., Lee, S. Y., Yamanaka, A., Freer, A. S., & Xie, B. (2009). Evaluation of the CSEC Community Intervention Project (CCIP) in five US cities. *Evaluation Review, 33*(6), 568–597.

Gallagher, A., & Holmes, P. (2008). Developing an effective criminal justice response to human trafficking: Lessons from the front line. *International Criminal Justice Review, 18*(3), 318–343.

Foa, E. B., Cashman, L., Jaycox, L., & Perry, K. (2018). *SAFE Court: Results From a 2-year Evaluation of a problem-solving court for prostituted offenders in Harris County, TX.* Report No. 2018-01. Crime Victims' Institute.

Gonzalez Bocinski, S. (n.d.) The economic drivers and consequences of sex trafficking in the United States. *Institute for Women's Policy Research.* Retrieved from iwpr.org/publications/economic-drivers-consequences-sex-trafficking-un ited-states/. 2020.

Goodman, J. L., & Leidholdt, D. A. (2013). *Lawyer's manual on human trafficking.* Supreme Court of the State of New York, Appellate Division, First Department New York State Judicial Committee on Women in the Courts.

Goodman, M., & Mazur, R. (2014). Chapter 5: Identifying and responding to sex trafficking. *A Guide to Addressing Human Trafficking in the State Courts.* pp. 89–100. Human Trafficking and the State Courts Collaborative. Retrieved from http://www.htcourts.org/wp-content/uploads/00_EntireGuide_140726_v02.pdf. 2020

Gruber, A., Cohen, A. J., & Mogulescu, K. (2016). Penal welfare and the new human trafficking intervention courts. *Florida Law Review 68*, 1333.

Gunderson, A. (2018). The Effect of Decriminalizing Prostitution on Public Health and Safety. *Chicago Policy Review (Online).*

Human Trafficking Prosecution Unit (HTPU). (2020). The Department of Justice. https://www.justice.gov/crt/human-trafficking-prosecution-unit-htpu

Hickle, K., & Roe-Sepowitz, D. (2017). "Curiosity and a pimp": Exploring sex trafficking victimization in experiences of entering sex trade industry work among participants in a prostitution diversion program. *Women & Criminal Justice, 27*(2), 122–138.

Hogan, K. A., & Roe-Sepowitz, D. (2020). LGBTQ+ homeless young adults and sex trafficking vulnerability. *Journal of Human Trafficking*, 1–16, DOI: 10.1080/23322705.2020.1841985

Human Trafficking and the State Courts Collaborative. (2020). Retrieved from http://www.htcourts.org/pennsylvania.htm. (2020).

Ibrahim, C. (2016). From prostitutes to victims: The perceptions of human trafficking among law enforcement and victim advocates. (unpublished Master's Thesis). California State University San Marcos.

Jabour, A. (2013). Prostitution politics and feminist activism in modern America: Sophonisba Breckinridge and the morals court in prohibition-era Chicago. *Journal of Women's History, 25*(3), 141–164.

Jennings, M. A. (1976). The victim as criminal: A consideration of California's prostitution law. *California Law Review, 64*, 1235.

Johnson, K. C., Davis, R. C., Labriola, M., Rempel, M., & Reich, W. A. (2020). An overview of prosecutor-led diversion programs: A new incarnation of an old idea. *Justice System Journal, 41*(1), 63–78.

Jorgensen, C. (2018). Badges and brothels: Police officers' attitudes toward prostitution. *Frontiers in Sociology, 3*, 16.

Judge, A. M. (2018). Uncharted waters: Developing mental health services for survivors of domestic human sex trafficking. *Harvard Review of Psychiatry, 26*(5), 287–297.

Justice for Victims of Trafficking Act. (2015). Public Law 114–22.

Kendis, B. (2018). Human trafficking and prostitution courts: Problem solving or problematic. *Case Western Reserve Law Review, 69,* 805.

Kinsely, A. F. (2016) When the defendant is a victim. *Tennessee Bar Association TBA Law Blog.* Retrieved from https://www.phila.gov/districtattorney/diversion/Pages/default.aspx

Koegler, E., Preble, K. M., Cimino, A. N., Stevens, J. E., & Diehl, S. (2020). Examining recidivism in a prostitution diversion program. *International Journal of Offender Therapy and Comparative Criminology, 64*(2–3), 232–248.

Kulig, T. C., & Butler, L. C. (2019). From "whores" to "victims": The rise and status of sex trafficking courts. *Victims & Offenders, 14*(3), 299–321.

Lee, C. G., Cheesman, F., Rottman, D., Swaner, R., Lambson, S., Rempel, M., & Curtis, R. (2013). *A Community court grows in Brooklyn: A comprehensive evaluation of the Red Hook Community Justice Center.* Williamsburg VA: National Center for State Courts.

Lento, J. (2020). What is project dawn court? Retrieved from https://www.josephlento.com/project-dawn-court

Leon, C., & Shdaimah, C. S. (2019). Targeted sympathy in "whore court": Criminal justice actors' perceptions of prostitution diversion programs. Retrieved from https://archive.hshsl.umaryland.edu/bitstream/handle/10713/9496/Leon_Shdaimah_Targeted%20sympathy%2027may19.pdf?sequence=6

Litam, S. D. A. (2019). She's just a prostitute: The effects of labels on counselor attitudes, empathy, and rape myth acceptance. *Professional Counselor, 9*(4), 396–415.

Logan, T. K., Walker, R., & Hunt, G. (2009). Understanding human trafficking in the United States. *Trauma, Violence, & Abuse, 10*(1), 3–30. 2020.

Luminais, M., Lovell, R., & McGuire, M. (2019). A safe harbor is temporary shelter, not a pathway forward: How court-mandated sex trafficking intervention fails to help girls quit the sex trade. *Victims & Offenders, 14*(5), 540–560.

Macias-Konstantopoulos, W. (2016). Human trafficking: The role of medicine in interrupting the cycle of abuse and violence. *Annals of Internal Medicine, 165*(8), 582–588.

Martin, J. A. (2014). *Chapter 9: Addressing the Complexities of Language and Culture in Human Trafficking-Involved Cases.* Guide to Addressing Human Trafficking in the State Courts (pp. 141–166). Human Trafficking and the State Courts Collaborative.

Mazur et al. (2015). Responding to sex trafficking in your jurisdiction: A planning toolkit. *Center for Court Innovation.* Retrieved from https://www.courtinnovation.org/sites/default/files/documents/RespondingtoSexTrafficking.pdf_0.pdf. 2020.

McBride, M. A. (2020). Responding to victims of human trafficking in the United States: A review of treatment providers.

Merry, S., & Ramachandran, V. (2016). The limits of consent: Sex trafficking and the problem of international paternalism. In *Paternalism Beyond Borders* (pp. 224–255). Cambridge University Press.

Micetic, S. F. (2018). Obtaining social justice for victims of domestic minor sex trafficking. *Sociology Compass, 12*(11). DOI: 10.1111/soc4.12635

Miner-Romanoff, K. (2017). CATCH court: Changing actions to change habits—A preliminary evaluation study. *Journal of Human Trafficking, 3*(2), 136–162.

Moran, R., & Farley, M. (2019). Consent, coercion, and culpability: Is prostitution stigmatized work or an exploitive and violent practice rooted in sex, race, and class inequality? *Archives of Sexual Behavior, 48*(7), 1947–1953.

Mogulescu, K. (2011). The public defender as anti-trafficking advocate, an unlikely role: How current New York City arrest and prosecution policies systematically criminalize victims of sex trafficking. *CUNY Law Review, 15*, 471.

Mueller, D. (2013). Treatment courts and court-affiliated diversion projects for prostitution in the united states. *Chicago Coalition for the Homeless*. Retrieved from https://www.issuelab.org/resources/14135/14135.pdf. 2020.

Muftic, L. R., & Updegrove, A. H. (2019). The effectiveness of a problem-solving court for individuals charged with misdemeanor prostitution in Harris County Texas. *Journal of Offender Rehabilitation, 58*(2), 117–132.

National Institute of Justice. (2020). Problem-solving courts. Retrieved from https://nij.ojp.gov/topics/articles/problem-solving-courts. 2020.

National Conference of State Legislatures. (2018). Prosecuting human traffickers: Recent legislative enactments. Retrieved from https://www.ncsl.org/Portals/1/HTML_LargeReports/Prosecuting_Traffickers_091818_32767.pdf

New York State Unified Court System. (2020). Human trafficking intervention courts – Overview. Retrieved from http://ww2.nycourts.gov/courts/problem_solving/htc/index.shtml. 2020.

Office of the District Attorney. (n.d.). Diversion unit: Project Dawn. Retrieved from https://www.phila.gov/districtattorney/diversion/Pages/default.aspx

Office for Victims of Crime Technical and Training Assistance Center. (2020). Office of Justice Programs. Retrieved from https://www.ovcttac.gov/taskforceguide/eguide/6-the-role-of-courts/64-innovative-court-responses/human-trafficking-courts/.2020.

Ostad-Hashemi, L. (2017). Preventing the re-traumatization of individuals who are arrested for prostitution by implementing trauma-informed practices in the criminal justice system. *Columbia Social Work Review, 15*(1), 1–6.

Parker, M., & Pizzio, C. (2017). Effectiveness of a prostitution diversion program: Reset. Retrieved from http://dspace.calstate.edu/bitstream/handle/10211.3/190813/The%20final%20thesis.pdf?sequence=2

Polaris Project. (2018). 2018 U.S. National Human Trafficking Hotline Statistics. Retrieved from https://polarisproject.org/2018-us-national-human-trafficking-hotline-statistics/. 2020.

Randle, L. (2020). Risk factors to the sex trafficking victimization of female refugees. *MUNDI, 1*(1), 6–7.

Rosario, E. (2020). *CATCH Court: An innovative method to combating human trafficking in women* (Doctoral dissertation, The Ohio State University).

Roe-Sepowitz, D. E., Gallagher, J., Hickle, K. E., Pérez Loubert, M., & Tutelman, J. (2014). Project ROSE: An arrest alternative for victims of sex trafficking and prostitution. *Journal of Offender Rehabilitation, 53*(1), 57–74.

Russell, A. (2018). Human trafficking: A research synthesis on human-trafficking literature in academic journals from 2000–2014. *Journal of Human Trafficking*, *4*(2), 114–136.

Sawicki, D. A., Meffert, B. N., Read, K., & Heinz, A. J. (2019). Culturally competent health care for sex workers: An examination of myths that stigmatize sex work and hinder access to care. *Sexual and Relationship Therapy*, *34*(3), 355–371.

Schultz, T., Canning, S. S., Estabrook, H., & Wong, P. (2020). Mental health needs and coping resources of participants in a prostitution pre-sentencing court program. *Journal of Offender Rehabilitation*, *59*(8), 456–477.

Schweig, S., Malangone, D., & Goodman, M. (2012). *Prostitution diversion programs*. Center for Court Innovation, New York, NY. Retrieved from www .courtinnovation.org. 2020.

Shdaimah, C., & Bailey-Kloch, M. (2014). "Can you help with that instead of putting me in jail?": Participant insights on Baltimore City's specialized prostitution diversion program. *Justice System Journal*, *35*(3), 287–300.

Shdaimah, C. S., & Wiechelt, S. A. (2012). Converging on empathy: Perspectives on Baltimore city's specialized prostitution diversion program. *Women & Criminal Justice*, *22*(2), 156–173.

Shdaimah, C. S., & Wiechelt, S. A. (2013). Crime and compassion: Women in prostitution at the intersection of criminality and victimization. *International Review of Victimology*, *19*(1), 23–35.

Shdaimah, C. (2020). Problem-solving courts, street level bureaucrats, and clients as policy agents in a prostitution diversion program. *Qualitative Data repository*. DOI: 10.5064/F6C8VUHP

Shively, M., Kliorys, K., Wheeler, K., & Hunt, D. (2012). A national overview of prostitution and sex trafficking demand reduction efforts, final report. Washington, DC: National Institute of Justice.

Shively, M., Jalbert, S., Kling, R., Rhodes, W., Finn, P., Flygare, C., & Wheeler, K. (2008). *Final report on the evaluation of the first offender prostitution program: Report summary*. Washington, DC: National Institute of Justice, US Department of Justice.

Smith, K., & Block, W. E. (2019). Legalization of prostitution: A cost-benefit analysis. *Journal of Accounting, Ethics & Public Policy*, *20*(3), 351-368.

Snow, N. M., Smith, M., & Radatz, D. L. (2019). Human trafficking and prostitution. *The Encyclopedia of Women and Crime*, 1–3.

Trafficking Victims Protection Act (TVPA). (2000). 22 U.S.C. § 7102 et seq.

Tugee, J. (2016). Reassessing the justifiability of the criminalization of prostitution in the United States of America. DOI: 10.2139/ssrn.2808849

United Against Human Trafficking. (2020). Prostitution and human trafficking: What's the difference? Retrieved from https://uaht.org/prostitution-and-human-tr afficking/

US Department of State. (2020) (a). U.S. Advisory Council on Human Trafficking: Office to Monitor and Combat Trafficking in Persons. Retrieved from https://www .state.gov/u-s-advisory-council-on-human-trafficking/.

US Department of State (2020) (b) Trafficking in Persons Report: 20th Edition. https://www.state.gov/wp-content/uploads/2020/06/2020-TIP-Report-Complete-062420-FINAL.pdf

Updegrove, A. H., & Muftic, L. R. (2019). Childhood polyvictimization, adult violent victimization, and trauma symptomatology: An exploratory study of prostitution diversion program participants. *Journal of Family Violence, 34*(8), 733–743.

Valente, B. M. (2018). Treatment with a side of stigma: The influence of sex work stigma on the Chicago Prostitution and Trafficking Intervention Court. *DePaul Law Review, 68*, 777.

Walters, J. H., Krieger, K., Kluckman, M., Feinberg, R., Orme, S., Asefnia, N., Gremminger, M., & Gibbs, D. (2017). *Evaluation of Domestic Victims of Human Trafficking Demonstration Projects: Final report from the first cohort of projects. Report # 2017-57*, Washington, DC: Office of Planning, Research and Evaluation, Administration for Children and Families, U.S. Department of Health and Human Services. Retrieved from https://www.acf.hhs.gov/sites/default/files/opre/sc1_final_report_508_compliant.pdf

Weber, A. (2020). *Choice, circumstance, or coercion: Prostitution stigma's effects on mental health professionals' perceptions of sex workers and sex work* (Doctoral dissertation, Boston College).

Wilson, L. N. (2020). Pimps, prostitutes, and providers: How educating healthcare providers impacts beliefs, knowledge, and perceptions on sex trafficking. Retrieved from https://repository.asu.edu/items/56818

Wiechelt, S. A., & Shdaimah, C. S. (2011). Trauma and substance abuse among women in prostitution: Implications for a specialized diversion program. *Journal of Forensic Social Work, 1*(2), 159–184.

Wright, R. F., & Levine, K. L. (2020). Models of Prosecutor-Led Diversion Programs in the United States and Beyond. *Annual Review of Criminology, 4*. DOI: 10/1146/annurey-criminol-061020-022236.

## Chapter 12

# Sex Offense Courts

## *A Historical and International Overview*

### Ashley Kilmer and Amanda Emmert

### INTRODUCTION AND OVERVIEW OF EXISTING
### SEX OFFENSE POLICIES AND PRACTICES

The emergence of Sex Offense Courts (SOCs) in Canada, South Africa, and the United States during the past three decades can be viewed as extensions of existing frameworks of statutes, policies, and practices aimed at monitoring and controlling people convicted of sex offenses. Most of these efforts seek to reduce the risk of sex offense recidivism through the use of intensive surveillance, mandated programming, and social exclusion in the realms of housing, employment, and social interaction. The use of the judicial system as part of this surveillance and control strategy adds additional legal oversight and application of formal sanctions to an existing network of formal and informal policies and practices limiting people convicted of sex offenses from full social and civic participation.

  This chapter begins with an overview of the emergence of sex offense courts within a historical framework of past and current sex offense policies utilized in Canada, South Africa, and the United States. Next, the chapter reviews existing SOCs in these same countries, which include discussion of the goals and operations of SOCs in each country and available research findings of the courts' impacts on case outcomes, sex offense behavior, and victim experiences. The chapter then transitions to an evaluation and discussion of current SOC practices. Particular attention is given to the paucity of evaluations of SOCs; little evidence exists that SOCs improve public safety through increased monitoring, limiting offending opportunities, or encouraging rehabilitation. Additionally, the chapter considers questions about the added benefits of SOCs in comparison to existing laws and practices focusing on surveillance and control of people convicted of sex offenses. This is especially important in light of the unintended consequences existing policies already produce (with relatively little to no public safety benefits) for individuals convicted of sex offenses and their families. The chapter concludes by identifying additional questions and areas for future inquiry that could provide needed insight into determining whether SOCs can provide benefits beyond existing sex offense policies or if alternative strategies could be more effective at reducing new victimizations while minimizing unintended consequences.

## Historical Sex Offense Policies

Official state responses to sex offending behavior have taken various forms throughout the past several hundred years. There is documentation of an early form of specialized court in the eighteenth century dedicated to formally sanctioning behaviors deemed sexually deviant such as incest, bestiality, homosexuality, and inter-generational relationships (Wright, 2014). The current practices and court models in use today reflect a history of specialized responses to sex offenses that often are not applied similarly to other offense types.

Historically, treatment and rehabilitation approaches have been coupled with formal sanctions. The medicalization and pathologization of sexual offending appear in the late nineteenth and early twentieth centuries through the use of physical and chemical castration as a means to incapacitate or suppress the sexual arousal of those convicted of sex offenses or those found to have deviant sexual desires (Wright, 2014). It was not uncommon during this time for those convicted of sex offenses to be sterilized as they were deemed "unfit" to reproduce and risk passing on their sexual deviance to their offspring (Wright, 2014). Modern-day regard of sexual offending behaviors as psychologically abnormal has resulted in indeterminant Civil Commitment laws, mandated psychological and cognitive-behavioral treatment, and the use of chemical castration. All still are accepted, even required, in some countries, including parts of the United States (Cohen & Jelic, 2007; Daley, 2008; Lee & Cho, 2013; Aagaard, 2014; Sudewo & Abdurrachman, 2020).

In addition to the use of mandated treatment, individuals convicted of sex offenses often are subjected to a wide variety of supervision and management policies and practices. For example, Canada, South Africa, the United States, and twenty-seven other countries have registries of individuals who have committed sexual offenses (SMART Summary, 2016). Modern-day sex offender[1] registry and notification (SORN) policies initially were implemented to facilitate law enforcement agencies in the ongoing tracking and monitoring of people convicted of sex offenses. Proponents hoped law enforcement-managed registries would reduce future victimizations by collecting and maintaining updated information about the individuals, including details of their offense, locations of residency and employer, and other personal identification information, along with whether they were compliant with registration requirements. In the United States, the push to make at least some registry information available to the public (via Megan's Law in 1996) was intended to make it easier for members of the community to ascertain whether someone convicted of a sex offense resided in their neighborhood. The often-stated intention of providing public-facing information is to "protect children" from becoming potential victims by coming into contact with an individual on the registry. However, registries often do more to perpetuate the "stranger danger" myth of sexual offending and increase stigmatization of those on the registry versus meaningfully reduce sex offense recidivism (Sample & Bray, 2006; Cohen & Jeglic, 2007; Leon & Kilmer, 2013).

The United States is not the only nation that makes its registry data available to the public (SMART Summary, 2016). However, despite the availability of registries in the United States, registries are under-utilized by the public, with studies finding only 17–45 percent of surveyed individuals ever accessed their state's registry (Boyle et al., 2014; Harris & Cudmore, 2018; Kernsmith et al., 2009).

Further, we provide a brief overview of the existing frameworks of sex offense laws and registries in Canada, South Africa, and the United States, as these nations have implemented SOCs. Later in the chapter, we discuss how the motivations, goals, and effects of existing sex offense policies and practices overlap with the purpose and operations of SOCs and whether these specialized courts produce unique benefits to individuals and communities impacted by sex offending behavior or function more as an expansion of the existing SO framework.

## Canada

Canada's legislative history regarding sexual offenses began in 1948 with the Criminal Sexual Psychopath Act, enacting "special criminal legislation for dangerous sexual offenders without certifiable mental disorder" (Petrunik, Murphy, & Fedoroff, 2008, p. 116). In the decades following, Canada enacted habitual offender and dangerous sexual offender statutes, which were later abolished and replaced by a dangerous offender (DO) statute. The DO statute applies to individuals convicted of serious violent offenses who demonstrate patterns of aggressive behaviors or "an inability to control their sexual impulses," and results in a lifetime probation sentence (Petrunik, Murphy, & Fedoroff, 2008, p. 116).

Local and provincial community notification policies have evolved to forewarn the public when people convicted of sex offenses are released from jails and prisons. These policies began informally, as some individual police forces and provincial governments developed community notification policies, in part to avoid liability suits if released individuals commit crimes in the community (Petrunik, Murphy, & Fedoroff, 2008). In 1995, Manitoba established Canada's first legally mandated public notification system, with British Columbia, Alberta, Newfoundland, Saskatchewan, and Ontario going on to create their own formal notification systems (Petrunik, Murphy, & Fedoroff, 2008).

Bill C-126, enacted in 1994, allows judges to issue life-long probation orders prohibiting visiting playgrounds and areas children might be present (Petrunik, Murphy, & Fedoroff, 2008). While §810 of the Criminal Code enables courts to issue orders restricting movement, personal interaction, residence, and access to firearms or alcohol (Petrunik, Murphy, & Fedoroff, 2008). And an amendment to Code (§810.1) places restrictions on individuals determined to be at high risk of committing sex offenses, but who have not been convicted been convicted of doing so (Petrunik, Murphy, & Fedoroff, 2008).

In 2001, Christopher's Law (Sex Offender Registry) created a private (not accessible to the public) registry of individuals convicted or found not criminally responsible by reason of mental disorder of sex offenses in Ontario, Canada (Ontario Sex Offender Registry, 2019). Thereafter, Canada launched a national registry in 2004 under the control of the Royal Canadian Mounted Police (RCMP) (Petrunik, Murphy, & Fedoroff, 2008; SMART Summary, 2016). An individual is included on the registry only after legal proceedings, during which the Crown presents evidence that registration is necessary for public safety, and individuals convicted of sex offenses have opportunity to present evidence of why registration is not warranted (Petrunik, Murphy, & Fedoroff, 2008). The national registry is intended to facilitate police investigations, as access to the registry is only granted to law enforcement officials by the RCMP after specific sex crimes have been reported (Petrunik, Murphy, & Fedoroff, 2008). However, in 2015, legislation creating a national public registry website, available to the public, was passed (SMART Summary, 2016).

## South Africa

Much of South Africa's sex offense legislation post-dates establishment of SOCs in South Africa in 1993. Public outrage over high-profile rape cases in the early 1990s, and public perceptions that sentencing outcomes were too lenient for sex offenses, led the South African Parliament to enact what were intended to be temporary emergency measures against crime (Baehr, 2008). The "temporary" act was made permanent in 2007. The Criminal Law Amendment Act 105 of 1997 established mandatory minimum sentencing for multiple crimes, including rape (Baehr, 2008). The act divides rape into two categories, with the mandated minimum sentence for Part I offenses being life in prison, and for Part II offenses being ten years imprisonment for first offense, fifteen years for second offense, and twenty years for third offenses (Baehr, 2008). These minimum sentence requirements far exceed the median sentences given before enactment (Baehr, 2008).

In 2007, South Africa created the National Register for Sex Offenders (NRSO) via Chapter 6 of Criminal Law (Sexual Offences and Related Matters) Amendment Act, 2007 (Act 32 of 2007). The NRSO is managed by the Minister of the Department of Justice and Constitutional Development, and includes the names, professions/trades, addresses, offense, and other details of individuals convicted of sexual offenses against children and people with mental disabilities (FAQ, n.d.).

While the NRSO is not publicly accessible, public and private sector employers like schools and hospitals can check the registry for people being hired (FAQ, n.d.). Individuals convicted of sex offenses against children or people with intellectual disabilities are not allowed to work with children or people with intellectual disabilities, apply for foster care, or adopt (FAQ, n.d.).

## The United States

The United States was the first country to institute a national-level registry of individuals convicted of sex offenses. These federally mandated registration requirements were a result of a series of laws passed in the 1990s and early 2000s in response to public outcry over high-profile cases involving children (many of whom the laws were named after). First, the Jacob Wetterling Crimes against Children and Sexually Violent Offender Registration Act of 1994 required states to implement and manage their own registries. Megan's law expanded the Jacob Wetterling Act to include community notification and make a subset of information in the registry publicly available. In 1996, the Pam Lynchner Sex Offender Tracking and Identification Act created a federal database managed by the FBI and available to law enforcement to track the location and personal information of anyone convicted of a sex offense in the United States.

Over the next ten years, legislation passed that allocated additional resources to manage state-run registries, improve identification and tracking of offenses related to human trafficking and child pornography, and develop the child abduction emergency alert (Amber Alert) system (Protection of Children from Sexual Predators Act 1998; PROTECT Act 2003). Finally, in 2006, the Adam Walsh Child Protection and Safety Act provided states with a set of national standards related to registration requirements, community notification (signs, flyers, or mailed letters notifying residents of someone convicted of certain sex offenses has moved into the neighborhood), civil commitment (hospitalization), and prevention of child pornography and internet-based offenses. States must comply with these established national standards or risk losing 10 percent of their federal funding they receive as part of the Omnibus Crime Control Act. In addition to national- and state-level legislation related to registration and tracking databases, individuals convicted of sex offenses are often placed under intensive community supervision that may include electronic monitoring and curfews (Button, DeMichele, & Payne, 2009; Center for Sex Offender Management, 2008; Payne & Gainey, 2004).

Many local jurisdictions also enact ordinances to further control those convicted of sex offenses within the community. One of the most popular and widely used are residency restrictions. These ordinances prevent a person convicted of a sex offense from living within a specified distance (typically 1,000 to 2,500 feet) of a building or physical space where children are likely to congregate. Depending on the specific ordinance, these locations often include schools, parks, daycare centers, public pools, libraries, and bus stops (Duwe, Donnay, & Tewksbury, 2008). Additionally, individuals convicted of sex offenses often face numerous formal and informal collateral consequences in the areas of employment, housing, and socialization that further control and limit their participation in society (Kilmer & Leon 2017; Leon & Kilmer, 2013; Levenson, 2008; Levenson & Tewksbury, 2009). Despite the well-meant intentions of such extensive tracking, supervision, and control of an offending population in order to reduce future sex offending and victimization, there is little empirical support that current sex offense policies meaningfully reduce sex offense recidivism (Duwe & Donnay, 2008; Duwe, Donnay, & Tewksbury, 2008; Letourneau et al., 2010; Levenson & Cotter, 2005; Sample & Bray, 2006; Sandler, Freeman, & Socia 2008; Tewksbury & Zgoba, 2010; Veysey, Zgoba, & Dalessandro, 2009).

## THE EMERGENCE OF SEX OFFENSE COURTS

The overview of policies related to sex offending behaviors in the previous section provides a useful context for understanding the development and implementation of SOCs within these same nations. In most cases, the aims and operations of SOCs can be viewed as a natural expansion of existing sex offense policies and practices rather than a novel strategy to attempt to reduce sexual victimization. Therefore, the network of existing policies and practices targeting those convicted of sex offenses discussed in the previous section allows for the identification of similarities and differences in the scope, aims, and practices of the SOCs that have emerged in the past thirty years.

## SOCs in South Africa

South Africa established it first SOC in 1993 with the goal of reducing secondary harm to victims as witnesses in sex offense cases (Walker & Louw, 2003). The Sexual Offences Court sought to recruit prosecutors who had experience working with children or the ability to relate to the victims in sex offense cases. They try to increase the speed and efficiency with which cases were tried. A second aim of the court is to reduce secondary trauma to victims and witnesses by making efforts to familiarize them with the courtroom layout and process before the trial takes place (Parkinson, 2016). A 1997 evaluation of the court found it partially successful in "eliminating victim trauma, establishing collaboration between various agencies dealing with sexual offences and in improving reporting, prosecution and conviction rates in the Cape Town area" (South African Human Rights Commission, 2002, p. 26). Findings from subsequent evaluation studies suggest the reduction in secondary trauma to victims was driven by the availability and use of CCTV, separate waiting rooms for victims, and physical examinations and counseling carried out by sensitive medical staff (Reyneke & Kruger, 2006; Sadan, Dikweni, & Cassiem 2001).

SOCs in South Africa had two other perceived benefits, higher conviction rates and greater court efficiency. Studies found that conviction rates for sexual offenses in specialist courts were routinely higher (in some cases as high as 95 percent) than in generalist courts (Kruger & Reyneke, 2008; Reyneke & Kruger, 2006; Sadan, Dikweni, & Cassiem, 2001). And sex offense case proceedings concluded in less than six-months (Walker & Louw, 2005). While these changes were, in part, attributed to better training of court personnel, the reduction in case time combined with high conviction rates may indicate SOCs provide less nuanced case management, not more.

Despite being one of the earliest to implement an SOC and positive outcomes for conviction rates and victim satisfaction with court proceedings, many of South Africa's SOCs closed in 2008 or reverted to being generalist courts. As a result, conviction rates began to decline to pre-SOC implementation levels. After several years, they judicial system re-established the specialized courts (Parkinson, 2016).

## SOCs in Canada

While not exclusively focused on sex offenses, the Family Violence Court (FVC) of Winnipeg, Manitoba deals with intimate partner sexual assault cases and child sexual abuse cases as part of its purview (Family Violence in Canada, 2000; Parkinson, 2016). Sexual assault cases comprise 2 percent of the courts' adult victim cases, and child sexual abuse cases account for 45 percent of child abuse cases presided over by the court (Family Violence in Canada, 2000).

Similar to the SOCs in South Africa, the Canadian FVC's goals include expedient case processing, reduced case attrition through improved victim cooperation, and victim protection via appropriate sentencing (Final Report, 2003; Ursel, 1995). FVC pursues its aims through a pro-arrest/zero tolerance policy, a witness/victim advocacy program, a specialized prosecution unit, designated courts for case processing, and "a special unit in the probation office to deliver court mandated treatment programs" (Family Violence in Canada, 2000, p. 45). Court policy outlines that successful case management involves balancing rigorous prosecution with victims' well-being (Family Violence in Canada, 2000).

Ultimately, the FVC demonstrated higher incarceration rates incarceration for individuals convicted of child sexual abuse (63 percent compared to 54 percent nationwide) and longer sentence lengths (37 percent of individuals convicted in the FVC are sentenced to two or more years, compared to 6 percent at the national level; Ursel & Gorkoff, 2001). Based on these statistics, it appears sex offense cases managed by the FVC result in a more punitive response to those convicted of sex offenses, with increased rates of imprisonment and longer periods of incarceration. While this may serve a retributive function of those seeking "just deserts" for people convicted of sex offenses, the limited rehabilitative and public safety benefits associated with more severe and lengthier punishment should be considered and is discussed later in this chapter.

## SOCs in the United States

The first SOC in the United States began in 2005, far after implementation of the specialized courts in South Africa and Canada. The first court in the United States closely followed a blueprint developed by LaFond and Winick (2003) and was initially a response to and departure from the "one-size-fits-all" approach of existing sex offense policy. The court used actuarial risk assessment instruments to inform initial sentencing and supervision decisions, and to make periodic adjustments in supervision levels through continued risk assessment during an individual's probation, incarceration, or post-release supervision (La Fond & Winick, 2003). Risk-assessment instruments allow correctional agencies to focus their surveillance and control resources on those perceived to be most likely to present a safety risk to the public. Assessment-informed decision-making aims to reduce the cost and resources required for the incarceration and intensive monitoring of people convicted of sex offenses by only using those limited resources on individuals who score as "high-risk."

LaFond and Winick (2003) also suggested these specialized courts promote rehabilitation goals, such as stable housing and employment, social support, and counseling or other programming needs. This approach recognizes that reentry is a dynamic process, not an outcome or status following incarceration; therefore, risk assessment must be ongoing, so new stressors related to the pursuit of reentry and rehabilitation goals, interpersonal challenges, and offending opportunities can be identified and addressed. This court model uses a specially trained, multi-disciplinary case management team, including probation, treatment providers, and a polygraph examiner with the aim of reducing access to potential victims and opportunities re-offend (English, 2003; La Fond & Winick, 2003). Supervision intensity, restrictions, and sanctions are applied and adjusted regularly based on information reported by the supervised individual, verification from the polygraph, and assessment by the case management team.

La Fond and Winick (2003) also proposed that this court model include an active judiciary component beginning at criminal prosecution, continuing through the sentencing and supervision process, and ending when the individual receives a final discharge from the program. They believed the ongoing interaction between the judge and court participant throughout the duration of the individual's time under community supervision would increase the supervised individual's "buy-in" to programming and accept sanctions for non-compliance with their conditions of supervision. Finally, LaFond and Winick (2003) also sought to incorporate therapeutic jurisprudence, a philosophy that involves mindful application of the law and use of the legal system to minimize the "antitherapeutic" effects of the law. This approach relies upon legal and social science scholars to study how involvement in the legal system and the application of laws and sanctions create consequences for the well-being of those directly impacted. A discussion of whether such therapeutic aims are (or can be) realized with the practices of sex offense courts occurs later in this chapter. However, LaFond and Winick's proposed court model appears to recognize the collateral consequences of existing sex offense policies and offers a more individually tailored, support-focused approach to the management of those convicted of sex offenses. Similarly, the Center for Court Innovation promoted a court model that involves ongoing collaboration between judges, treatment providers, and victim services (Grant, 2007; Thomforde-Hauser & Grant, 2010). The center identified seven elements of a successful sex offense court: "(1) criteria for diversion; (2) risk assessments; (3) monitoring; (4) victim outreach; (5) judicial-offender relationships; (6) community of stakeholders; and (7) specialized training, assistance, and evaluation" (Herman, 2007; Richmond & Richmond, 2015). The overlap in vision for the development of specialized sex offense courts makes it clear that dynamic, wrap-around style of case management and programming was valued over more traditional forms of supervision and control.

Using the blueprint developed by LaFond and Winick and the elements identified by the Center for Court Innovation, the first SOC in the United States began in Oswego County, New York, in 2005. Oswego County's SOC set out to establish judicial monitoring of individuals on probation, protect the public, increase interagency collaboration, and support victims (Thomforde-Hauser & Grant, 2010). New York SOCs preside over all cases with felony sex offense charges from beginning to end (processing to adjudication).

Premised on the necessity for "offender accountability" and community safety (Herman, 2007), key features of New York SOCs include early intervention, post-disposition monitoring, consistency, and accountability (Thomforde-Hauser & Grant, 2010). Additionally, literature on New York SOCs highlights the intention to train judges and court personnel to handle sex offense cases and keep up to date on research and best practices for issues relating to sexual offending behaviors (Parkinson, 2016). This has primarily manifested itself in the form of incorporation of evidence-based risk-assessment instruments in determining supervision and treatment needs of individuals managed by the court (Hauser, 2017; Richmond & Richmond, 2015).

Evaluations and statistics on New York SOCs are extremely limited (Parkinson, 2016). Research from one study notes that in Oswego SOC's first year, the court oversaw sixty-eight individuals on probation and sixty-five individuals in prison (Grant, 2007). None of whom were arrested on new charges (Grant, 2007). While Cossins (2010) notes that New York SOCs have the technology and facilities to enable witnesses to appear in court via CCTV; however, the technology is not used often. And Parkinson (2016) notes that public articles on New York SOCs focus on "offender management" as opposed to the courts' role in supporting victims.

Allegheny County, Pennsylvania, initiated a SOC in 2011 similar to New York's in Pittsburgh, citing their primary aims as "procedural justice, offender accountability, and victim safety" (Hauser, 2017, p. 1). The court was specifically designed to address "inefficiencies" related to processing and adjudication of people charged with sex offenses, the lack of a specialized court docket for sex offense cases, and the ability to impose charge-specific conditions (Hauser, 2017). Allegheny's SOC oversees all cases where individuals are charged with and convicted of Megan's Law violations (Administrative Office of Pennsylvania Courts, 2011). Cases are managed by the court from arrest, sentencing, and community supervision and ongoing monitoring (Hauser, 2017). Since its inception, the court has seen a 37 percent reduction in the time to disposition of sex offense cases in the county, thus achieving the greater efficiency in processing cases that was originally sought. In addition, a 2017 report found that recidivism rates of those managed by the SOC were low, but acknowledged that recidivism rate for this population (people convicted of sex offenses) is already typically low and may not be a result of the specific supervision and management practices implemented by the court (Hauser, 2017). As mentioned earlier with the New York court, evaluation data on the Allegheny SOC focus primarily on case processing and management of people convicted of sex offenses. There is only a brief statement about "increasing collaboration with victim advocates" and no discussion on what this entails beyond the opportunity to submit a victim impact statement and be connected to victim support services, which typically already exist in existing court models (Hauser, 2017).

The task of coordinating services across multiple agencies in order to provide effective supervision, management, and support for people convicted of sex offenses is not always successful. While the SOCs in New York and Pennsylvania were able to implement and maintain their court model over the past decade or more, other efforts to develop such a court model have failed (Budd, Burbrink, & Connor, 2016). In an evaluation of a proposed SOC that failed to launch, researchers found that breakdowns in collaboration between stakeholders within the criminal justice system and community, a lack of coordination with service and treatment providers, and resistance to a more therapeutic approach to management of sex offense cases were all contributing factors (Budd, Burbrink, & Connor, 2016).

## Summary

While the SOCs in each of these nations emerged out of different historical and legal frameworks of sex offense policies and practices, they do share some similarities. First, all of the courts described earlier had overarching aims of (1) increasing efficiency in the prosecution of sex offense cases; (2) producing greater accountability in the form of formal social control and legal sanctions; and (3) recruiting and using specially trained legal actors and other court personnel. The courts in South African and Canada are primarily an expansion of existing supervision and control practices, providing greater efficiency in case processing and disposition, as well as more punitive sentencing outcomes. The courts in the United States differ from these other models in that their intentions appear to be the development of a more therapeutic response to sex offense cases, integrating greater treatment and support services with dynamic and intensive supervision practices. Finally, the SOCs all include statements regarding a commitment to the needs of victims by providing trauma-informed support resources and specialized advocates to victims. The next section discusses the advantages and limitations of SOCs in achieving their intended aims and functions.

## EVALUATION OF CURRENT SOC PRACTICES

SOCs differ significantly from other specialized courts. Most specialized courts provide offenders with resources and support services not available through traditional courts. In contrast, SOCs do not provide additional resources to individuals accused and convicted of sex offenses (despite LaFond and Winick's model for U.S. courts that includes an inter-disciplinary specialized management team). In some cases, SOCs provide additional support and resources to victims (such as in South Africa) or court/parole personnel (purportedly in Canada, South Africa, and the United States in the form of training). In reality, SOCs do not serve the interests of individuals charged or convicted with sex offenses, and the support they provide to victims appears minimal. As mentioned previously, the response to victims has largely been limited to opportunities to prepare impact statements or referrals to victims' services. While Richmond and Richmond (2015) claimed that specialized sex offense courts could result in increased reporting of sex crimes, there is no data to support this assertion. Furthermore, there is lack of evidence that SOCs lead to increases in utilization of victim services or whether victims feel more included or supported (Hauser, 2017). Additionally, existing evaluation studies do not provide data on whether individuals managed by SOCs are receiving greater access to housing and employment resources, treatment programming, or having their supervision levels and conditions adjusted based on ongoing risk and need assessments. Instead, available evaluation data suggests that the dynamic and therapeutic court model elements originally promoted by La Fond and Winick and the Center for Court Innovation have been de-emphasized and focus has primarily been on increasing efficiency in court operations and maintaining existing supervision and control practices (Hauser, 2017).

SOCs do have some benefits. They reduce the number of judges deciding similar cases, which can increase uniformity of decision making (Baum, 2009). Hypothetically, as judges, prosecutors, and court personnel focus on specific types of cases, they can be trained on the content matter, develop expertise enabling knowledge-informed decision making, and increase case processing efficiency (Altbecker, 2003; Baum, 2009). However, these philosophical advantages may not hold true for SOCs. For example, the extent and type of training received by SOC judges, prosecutors, and court personnel is unclear. The center spearheading the United States SOCs reported the Oswego County SOC judge, court staff, and partner organizations received initial training in "sex offender management" (Grant, 2007). However, it is unclear whether this holds true for other U.S. SOCs, or if training continued as originally intended. Similarly, a study by Muller and Van der Merwe (2004) found limited or no training was provided to prosecutors in South African SOCs.

Moreover, studies suggest specialized court judges are as—and potentially more—prone to bias, as generalist judges (Baum, 2010; Leibovitch, 2017; Rachlinski, Guthrie, & Wistrich, 2006). Case management techniques enable increased efficiency, even without specialized courts (Jacoby, 1994). Thus, many of the perceived advantages of SOCs cannot be, or have not been, verified.

Disadvantages of SOCs include the potential for rote or automated case treatment, the diminished role of adversarial defense lawyers, increased demands on individuals convicted, and the potential for increased oversight and demands that can lead to more technical violations. For example, South Africa's SOCs fast case processing and higher conviction rates (than generalist courts) have been noted as signs that the courts are successful. However, speedy processing and high conviction rates may demonstrate that cases are receiving less attention, as opposed to more, as it is easy to process cases quickly if you convict everyone (or most) without attention to case details.

Additionally, SOCs invoke "net-widening" concerns due to their long-term, intensive supervision practices. When individuals are subjected to lengthy periods of intense community supervision and social restrictions, it can be counterproductive to the original aims of these court-mandated practices. Research on community supervision outcomes indicates more individuals ultimately cycle back into the prison system, not less (Phelps, 2013). It is well-documented that formerly incarcerated individuals encounter significant barriers when attempting to reintegrate into communities (Mercado, Alvarez, & Levenson, 2008; Petersilia, 2003; Travis & Visher, 2005). These challenges are often worse when an individual is convicted of a sex offense, due to the increased stigma associated with this offense type (Cubellis, Evans, & Fera, 2019; Tewksbury, 2005). Specifically, securing full-time, stable employment can be a significant obstacle to long-term reentry success. Ongoing court appointments, mandated counseling appointments, and regular check-ins with supervision officers can make it even more difficult to find an employer willing to accommodate such a schedule. In addition, supervision requirements and restrictions can create obstacles to accessing stable housing, maintaining supportive relationships, and even parenting (Kilmer & Leon, 2017; Naser & Visher, 2006; Tewksbury, 2005). These challenges to community reintegration can result in strain (Ackerman & Sacks, 2012), frustration, hopelessness, and social withdrawal (Jeglic, Mercado, & Levenson, 2009; Levenson, D'Amora, & Hern 2007; Mercado, Alvarez, & Levenson, 2008; Winnick & Bodkin, 2008), all of which can result in higher risk of relapse into criminal behavior and recidivism (Ackerman & Sacks, 2012; Center for Sex Offender Management, 2008; Cortoni, 2009).

It is critical to note, the vast majority of people convicted of sex offenses who are re-incarcerated are *not* re-incarcerated for committing new sex offenses. Over 50 percent of probation revocations for people convicted of sex offenses arise from technical violations of the conditions of their supervision, not new criminal offenses. Less than 10 percent are rearrested or re-incarcerated as a result of a new sex offense (Bench & Allen, 2013; Hepburn & Griffen, 2004; Johnson, 2006; Sample & Bray, 2006). Technical violations can include failure to make a court appointment or check-in appointment with their supervision officer, being outside of an approved geographic area, not following curfew rules, or failure to maintain employment (Johnson, 2006). Additionally, research indicates that the longer people are on community supervision, the greater the likelihood of committing a technical violation, being re-incarcerated, or having the supervision window extended, thereby further increasing the chance of "failure."

Therefore, long-term, intensive supervision practices, such as those utilized by SOCs, might offer minimal success at reducing re-offending behavior (Georgiou, 2014; Hyatt & Barnes, 2014), and may actually contribute to an *increase* in recidivism (Petersilia & Turner, 1993; Phelps, 2013; Lerman & Weaver, 2014; Wright, 2014), which is in direct opposition to their original intent. With very little research conducted on SOCs or SOCs' outcomes, it is difficult to evaluate the exact impact of SOCs. However, the substantial literature on the ineffectiveness of SORN and other policies targeting people convicted of sex offenses suggests SOCs have the potential to increase technical violations and re-incarceration. Research consistently finds intensive supervision and social restrictions do little to deter engagement in first-time sex offending behavior, nor are they effective at reducing sex offense recidivism (Freeman, 2012; Sandler, Freeman, & Socia, 2008). Based on this body of existing data and research, it is reasonable to view SOCs with significant skepticism. Existing SOCs have incorporated many of the same surveillance, monitoring, and social restriction practices already implemented by law enforcement and community supervision agencies, while offering little unique resources or attention to supporting victims or increasing rehabilitation and community re-integration opportunities for those convicted of sex offenses.

## CONCLUSION

SOCs developed in Canada, South Africa, and the United States under similar social and political environments. They extend existing networks of agencies, policies, and practices that monitor, control, and apply legal sanctions to people convicted of sex offenses. However, extensive empirical evaluation of these policies, particularly those implemented in the United States, have found that they are largely ineffective at reducing sex offending behaviors or providing meaningful public safety benefits. In some cases, these overly restrictive policies can actually lead to increased risks of recidivism due to the extreme stigmatization and social rejection they produce.

Based on a review of existing SOC models and limited evaluation data, it can be argued that SOCs are largely an extension of these existing frameworks, prioritizing accountability and oversight of people who commit sex offenses, and to a lesser extent, reducing trauma for victims/survivors or providing support for rehabilitation and community reintegration for individuals who are funneled into these court programs. Courts in each of the three nations reviewed have documented increased efficiency in processing sex offense cases and some success in reducing secondary victimization during court proceedings. However, the lack of evaluation research on SOCs and their outcomes, intended and unintended, is a primary area of concern. These courts largely operate as "black boxes," with little to no transparency about training of key court actors, the processes used to hear cases and making sentencing or supervision recommendations, or whether intended outcomes—such as reducing sex-offending behaviors, increasing utilization of victim services, and increasing accountability—are being achieved. In addition, more research is needed to determine whether there have been any unintended consequences as a result of the implementation of these courts. For example, courts in South Africa tout higher conviction rates as an indicator of the courts' success. The courts have attributed this as a result of more expedient processing of DNA evidence and close partnerships between prosecutors and investigators (Parkinson, 2016). However, investigative bodies responsible for analyzing evidence for the prosecution it is directly aligned with could raise some ethical concerns about whether the increase in conviction rates is truly a judicial success or an indication of prioritizing speedy case processing at the expense of potentially higher risk of wrongful convictions. In Canada, the Family Violence Court funnels people convicted of sex offenses into incarceration settings for longer periods of time than other courts (Ursel & Gorkoff, 2001). While Canada's correctional facilities may not be as punitive as those in the United States, they still have criminogenic elements that can lead to increased risk of future offending behavior than if an individual was supervised within the community with greater access to rehabilitative resources and reintegration support, which can reduce risk of recidivism. In the United States, these courts largely have been used to facilitate and expand an already-extensive framework of surveillance and control policies. This is of particular concern given that the SOCs in the United States were developed off of a model emphasizing the importance of therapeutic jurisprudence and reducing the "painful" effects and unintended consequences of legal system involvement and one-size-fits-all approaches to supervision.

Due to the limited evaluation of SOCs and their consequences, additional research on the operations and outcomes of the courts is critically needed to develop an informed conclusion about their effectiveness at their primary aims of increasing public safety and reducing secondary traumatization of victims. However, a larger question remains of whether the use of SOCs is an ideal approach for working with individuals convicted of sex offenses or reducing future victimizations. Most individuals convicted of sex offenses are "first time offenders," and while recidivism rates do vary, people convicted of sex offenses have generally low rates of sex-offense recidivism. In addition, most existing sex offense policies focus on preventing offenses where victims are strangers to perpetrators, but research indicates that the majority of all sex offense victims know their perpetrator (Craun & Theriot, 2009). Despite this body of research, many existing policies do not target the more common sex offense behaviors, such as those committed by first time offenders against victims known to the perpetrator. This can help explain why current sex offense policies are largely ineffective and reducing sex offending behavior.

In order to address the needs of both victims and offenders more successfully, SOCs may need to consider alternative approaches that are less oriented toward maintaining or expanding existing sex offense policy. One example could be the incorporation of restorative justice principles. Recently, SOC and sex offense management models in Australia (for youth convicted of sex offenses), New Zealand, and Canada have incorporated restorative justice conferencing both before and after prosecution (Center for Innovative Justice, 2014). The primary aim in restorative justice conferencing is to repair harm through attending to victims' needs, holding those convicted of sex offenses accountable, and support reintegration into the community (Marshall, 1999; Zehr, 2015). While this may sound similar to the aims of the therapeutic SOC model, restorative justice centers victims in the process rather than supervision and control. As a result, restorative justice prioritizes the needs and preferences of victims while generally offering more options for accountability and rehabilitation (Marshall, 1999; Stubbs, 2012). Early evaluation studies on these restorative justice-oriented models find greater victim satisfaction with the justice process as well as lower rates of re-offending behavior (Center for Innovative Justice, 2014; Joudo-Larsen, 2014). The use of restorative justice techniques is worth further study and consideration as one alternative approach that could yield greater success regarding public safety outcomes than current SOC operations may be capable of achieving.

# NOTE

1. While supervision, registration, and notification policies targeting those convicted of sex offenses are often referred to as "sex offender" policies, the authors seek to avoid dehumanizing "offender"-based terminology when discussing individuals impacted by these policies and will instead use person-centered terminology such as "person or individual convicted of a sex offense."

# REFERENCES

Aagaard, L. (2014). Chemical castration of Danish sex offenders. *Journal of Bioethical Inquiry, 11*(2), 117–118.

Ackerman, A. R., & Sacks, M. (2012). Can general strain theory be used to explain recidivism among registered sex offenders? *Journal of Criminal Justice, 40*(3), 187–193.

Administrative Office of Pennsylvania Courts (AOPC). (2011). Commonwealth's first sex offender court opens in Pittsburgh. Pittsburgh, Pennsylvania. Retrieved from http://www.pacourts.us/assets/files/newsrelease-1/file-1239.pdf?cb=5934e9

Altbecker, A. (2003). Justice through specialisation? The case of the specialised commercial crime court. Monograph 76. Pretoria, South Africa: Institute for Security Studies. Retrieved from https://issafrica.org/research/monographs/monograph-76-justice-through-specialisation-the-case-of-the-specialised-commercial-crime-court-antony-altbeker.

Baehr, K. S. (2008). Mandatory minimums making minimal difference: Ten years of sentencing sex offenders in South Africa. *Yale Journal of Law and Feminism, 20*, 213–246.

Baum, L. (2009). Probing the effects of judicial specialization. *Duke Law Journal, 58*, 1667–1684.

Baum, L. (2010). Fortieth annual Administrative Law Symposium: Judicial specialization and the adjudication of immigration cases. *Duke Law Journal, 59*(8), 1501–1561.

Belanger, K., & Stone, W. (2008). The social service divide: Service availability and accessibility in rural versus urban counties and impact on child welfare outcomes. *Child Welfare, 87*(4), 101–124.

Bench, L. L., & Allen, T. D. (2013). Assessing sex offender recidivism using multiple measures: A longitudinal analysis. *The Prison Journal, 93*(4), 411–428.

Boyle, D.J., Ragusa-Salerno, L.M., Marcus, A.F., Passannante, M.R., & Furrer, S. (2014). Public knowledge and use of sexual offender internet registries: Results from a random digit dialing telephone survey." *Journal of Interpersonal Violence, 29*(10), 1914–1932.

Budd, K. M., Burbrink, M. J., & Connor, T. A. (2016). Team member's perceptions on a sex offender reentry court's failure to launch: a pilot study. *Journal of Sexual Aggression, 22*(3), 394–409.

Button, D. M., DeMichele, M., & Payne, B. K. (2009). Using electronic monitoring to supervise sex offenders: Legislative patterns and implications for community corrections officers. *Criminal Justice Policy Review, 20*(4), 414–436.

Center for Sex Offender Management. (2008*). Legislative trends in sex offender management.* Washington D.C.: U.S. Department of Justice, Office of Justice Programs.

Cohen, M., & Jeglic. E. (2007). Sex offender legislation in the United States: What do we know? *International Journal of Offender Therapy and Comparative Criminology, 51*(4), 369–383.

Cortoni, F. (2009). Factors associated with sexual recidivism. In A. R. Beech, L. A. Craig, & K. D. Browne (Eds.), *Assessment and treatment of sex offenders: A handbook* (pp. 39–52). Wiley.

Cossins, A. (2010). Alternative models for prosecuting child sex offences in Australia. Report of the National Child Sexual Assault Reform Committee. University of New South Wales.

Craun, S. W., & Theriot, M. T. (2009). Misperceptions of sex offender perpetration: Considering the impact of sex offender registration. *Journal of Interpersonal Violence, 24*(12), 2057–2072.

Cubellis, M. A., Evans. D. N., & Fera, A. G. (2019). Sex offender stigma: An exploration of vigilantism against sex offenders. *Deviant Behavior, 40*(2), 225–239.

Daley, M. V. (2008). A flawed solution to the sex offenders situation in the United States: The legality of chemical castration for sex offenders. *Indiana Health Law Review, 5,* 87.

Duwe, G., & Donnay, W. (2008). The impact of Megan's Law on sex offender recidivism: The Minnesota experience. *Criminology, 46,* 411–446.

Duwe, J., Donnay, W., & Tewksbury, R. (2008). Does residential proximity matter? A geographic analysis of sex offense recidivism. *Criminal Justice and Behavior, 35*(4), 484–504.

English, K. (2003). The containment approach to managing sex offenders. *Seton Hall Law Review, 34,* 1255–1272.

Family Violence in Canada: A Statistical Profile. (2000). Catalogue no. 85-224-XIE. Statistics Canada. Ottawa: Canadian Centre for Justice Statistics. Retrieved from https://www150.statcan.gc.ca/n1/en/pub/85-224-x/85-224-x2000000-eng.pdf?st=MiuTtXUb.

FAQ: National Register for Sex Offenders (NRSO). n.d. Government. Republic of South Africa: The Department of Justice and Constitutional Development. Retrieved from https://www.justice.gov.za/vg/nrso.html.

Final Report of the Ad Hoc Federal-Provincial-Territorial Working Group Reviewing Spousal Abuse Policies and Legislation. 2003. Ottawa, Canada: Department of Justice. Retrieved from https://www.justice.gc.ca/eng/rp-pr/cj-jp/fv-vf/pol/spo_e-con_a.pdf.

Freeman, N. J. (2012). The public safety impact of community notification laws: Rearrest of convicted sex offenders. *Crime & Delinquency, 58*(4), 539–564.

Georgiou, G. (2014). Does increased post-release supervision of criminal offenders reduce recidivism? Evidence from a statewide quasi-experiment. *International Review of Law and Economics, 37,* 221–243.

Grant, J. (2007). Establishing a model court: A case study of the Oswego Sex Offense Court. New York, NY: Center for Court Innovation. Retrieved from https://www.courtinnovation.org/

Harris, A. J., & Cudmore, R. (2018). Community experience with public sex offender registries in the United States: A national survey. *Criminal Justice Policy Review, 29*(3), 258–279.

Hauser, R. T. (2017). *The Allegheny County Sex Offense Court: Using evidence-based practices to increase accountability and safety.* New York, NY: Center for Court Innovation. Retrieved from https://www.courtinnovation.org/

Hepburn, J. R., & Griffin, M. L. (2002). *An analysis of risk factors contributing to the recidivism of sex offenders on probation.* National Institute of Justice, Washington D.C. Retrieved from https://citeseerx.ist.psu.edu/viewdoc/download?doi=10.1.1.1 40.8357&rep=rep1&type=pdf

Herman, K. (2007). Sex offense courts: The next step in community management. New York, NY: Center for Court Innovation. Retrieved from http://www.courtinno vation.org/research/sex-offense-courts-next-step-community-management

Hyatt, J. M., & Barnes, G. C. (2014). An experimental evaluation of the impact of intensive supervision on the recidivism of high-risk probationers. *Crime & Delinquency, 63*(1), 3–38.

Jacoby, J. (1994). Expedited drug case management programs: Some lessons in case management reform. *The Justice System Journal, 17*, 19–40.

Jeglic, E. L., Mercado, C. C., & Levenson, J. S. (2012). The prevalence and correlates of depression and hopelessness among sex offenders subject to community notification and residence restriction legislation. *American Journal of Criminal Justice, 37*(1), 46–59.

Johnson, J. L. (2006). Sex offenders on federal community supervision: Factors that influence revocation. *Federal Probation, 70*, 18.

Joudo-Larsen, J. (2014). Restorative justice in the Australian criminal justice system." *AIC reports. Research and Public Policy series.*

Kernsmith, P.D., Comartin, E., Craun, S.W., & Kernsmith, R. M. (2009). The relationship between sex offender registry utilization and awareness. *Sexual Abuse, 21*(2), 181–193.

Kilmer, A., & Leon, C. S. (2017). 'Nobody worries about our children': Unseen impacts of sex offender registration on families with school-age children and implications for desistance. *Criminal Justice Studies, 30*(2), 181–201.

Kruger, H. B., & Reyneke, J. M. (2008). Sexual offences courts in South Africa: Quo Vadis? *Journal for Juridical Science, 33*, 32–75.

La Fond, J. Q., & Winick, B. J. (2003). Sex offender reentry courts: A proposal for managing the risk of returning sex offenders to the community. *Seton Hall Law Review, 34*, 1173–1212.

Lee, J. Y., & Cho, K. S. (2013). Chemical castration for sexual offenders: Physicians' views." *Journal of Korean Medical Science, 28*(2), 171–172.

Leibovitch, A. (2017). Punishing on a curve. *Northwestern University Law Review, 111*(5), 1205–1280.

Leon, C., & Kilmer, A. (2013). Controlling the sex offender. In S. L. Mallicoat & C. L. Gardiner (Eds.), *Criminal Justice Policy.* Thousand Oaks, CA: SAGE Publications, Inc.

Lerman, A. E., & Weaver, V. M. (2014). *Arresting citizenship: The democratic consequences of American crime control.* Chicago, IL: University of Chicago Press.

Letourneau, E. J., Levenson, J. S., Bandyopadhyay, D., Sinha, D., & Armstrong, K. S. (2010). Evaluating the effectiveness of sex offender registration and notification policies for reducing sexual violence against women: Final Report for National Institute of Justice. MUSC, Medical University of South Carolina.

Levenson, J. S. (2008). Collateral consequences of sex offender residence restrictions. *Criminal Justice Studies, 21*, 153–166.

Levenson, J. S., & Cotter, L. P. (2005). The impact of sex offender residence restrictions: 1,000 feet from danger, or one step from absurd? *International Journal of Offender Therapy and Comparative Criminology, 49*(1), 168–178.

Levenson, J. S., D'Amora, D. A., & Hern, A. L. (2007). Megan's law and its impact on community re-entry for sex offenders. *Behavioral Sciences & the Law, 25*(4), 587–602.

Levenson, J. S., & Tewksbury, R. (2009). Collateral damage: Family members of registered sex offenders. *American Journal of Criminal Justice, 34*, 54–68.

Marshall, T. F. (1999). *Restorative justice: An overview*. Home Office.

Mercado, C. C., Alvarez, S., & Levenson, J. (2008). The impact of specialized sex offender legislation on community reentry." *Sexual Abuse: A Journal of Research and Treatment, 20*(2), 188–205.

Ministerial Advisory Task Team on the Adjudication of Sexual Offence Matters. (2013). *Report on the re-establishment of sexual offences courts*. South Africa: Department of Justice and Constitutional Development.

Muller, K., & van de Merwe, I. A. (2004). The sexual offences prosecutor: A new specialisation? *Journal for Juridical Sciences, 29*, 135–151.

Naser, R. L., & Visher, C. A. (2006). Family members' experiences with incarceration and reentry. *Western Criminology Review, 7*(2), 20–31.

Ontario Sex Offender Registry. (2019). Government website. Ontario, Canada: Ontario Ministry of the Solicitor General. Retrieved from https://www.mcscs.jus.gov.on.ca/english/police_serv/sor/sor.html.

Payne, B. K., & Gainey, R. R. (2004). The electronic monitoring of offenders released from jail or prison: Safety, control, and comparisons to the incarceration experience. *The Prison Journal, 84*(4), 413–435.

Parkinson, P. (2016). Specialist prosecution units and courts: A review of the literature. *Sydney Law School Research Paper* 16/26. Commonwealth of Australia, Australia: Sydney Law School. Retrieved from https://ssrn.com/abstract=2756305.

Petersilia, J. (2003). *When prisoners come home: Parole and prisoner reentry*. New York, NY: Oxford University Press.

Petersilia, J., & Turner, S. (1993). Intensive probation and parole. *Crime and Justice, 17*, 281–335.

Petrunik, M., Murphy, L., & Fedoroff, J. P. (2008). American and Canadian approaches to sex offenders: A study of the politics of dangerousness. *Federal Sentencing Reporter, 21*(2), 111–123.

Phelps, M. S. (2013). The paradox of probation: Community supervision in the age of mass incarceration. *Law & Policy, 35*(1–2), 51–80.

Rachlinski, J. J., Guthrie, C., & Wistrich, A. J. (2006). Inside the bankruptcy judge's mind. *Boston University Law Review, 86*(5), 1227–1265.

Reyneke, J. M., & Kruger, H. B. (2006). Sexual offences courts: Better justice for children? *Journal for Juridical Science, 31*, 73–107.

Richmond, C., & Richmond, M. (2015). The future of sex offense courts: How expanding specialized sex offense courts can help reduce recidivism and improve victim reporting. *Cardozo Journal of Law & Gender, 21*, 443.

Sadan, M., Dikweni, L., & Cassiem, S. (2001). Pilot assessment: The sexual offences court in Wynberg & Cape Town and related services. *IDASA*. Retrieved from http://www.endvawnow.org/uploads/browser/files/assessment_sexual_offences_courts_sa.pdf.

Sample, L. L., & Bray, T. M. (2006). Are sex offenders different? An examination of rearrest patterns. *Criminal Justice Policy Review, 17*(1): 83–102.

Sandler, J. C., Freeman, N. J., & Socia, K. M. (2008). Does a watched pot boil? A time-series analysis of New York State's sex offender registration and notification law. *Psychology, Public Policy, and Law, 14*(4), 284–302.

SMART Summary: Global Survey of Sex Offender Registration and Notification Systems. (2016). Washington, DC: Office of Sex Offender Sentencing, Monitoring, Apprehending, Registering, and Tracking. Retrieved from https://smart.ojp.gov/sites/g/files/xyckuh231/files/media/document/global-survey-2016-final.pdf.

South African Human Rights Commission. (2002). *Does the criminal justice system protect children?* Johannesburg: South African Human Rights Commission. Retrieved from https://www.gov.za/sites/default/files/gcis_document/201409/childsexoff0.pdf.

Stubbs, J. (2012). Justice for gendered violence: What does restorative justice offer? In J. Bolitho, J. Bruce, & G. Mason (Eds.), *Restorative Justice: Adults and Emerging Practice*. Alexandria, Austrailia: Federation Press.

Sudewo, F. A., & Abdurrachman, H. (2020). The use of castration punishment toward perpetrators of sexual violence in Indonesia." In *International Conference on Agriculture, Social Sciences, Education, Technology and Health (ICASSETH 2019)* (pp. 165–170). Atlantis Press.

Tewksbury, R. (2005). Collateral consequences of sex offender registration. *Journal of Contemporary Criminal Justice, 21*(1), 67–81.

Tewksbury, R., & Zgoba, K. M. (2010). Perceptions and coping with punishment: How registered sex offenders respond to stress, internet restrictions, and the collateral consequences of registration. *International Journal of Offender Therapy and Comparative Criminology, 54*(4), 537–551.

Thomforde-Hauser, R., & Grant, J. A. (2010). *Sex offense courts: Supporting victim and community safety through collaboration*. Center for Court Innovation. Retrieved from https://www.courtinnovation.org/sites/default/files/Sex_Offense_Courts.pdf.

Travis, J., & Visher, C. (Eds.). (2005). *Prisoner reentry and crime in America*. New York, NY: Cambridge University Press.

Ursel, E. J. (1994). Winnipeg Family Violence Court. *Juristat, 14*(12), 1–15.

Ursel, J., & Gorkoff, K. (2001). Court processing of child sexual abuse cases: The Winnipeg Family Violence Court experience. In D. Hiebert-Murphy & L. Burnside (Eds.), *Pieces of a Puzzle: Perspectives on Child Sexual Abuse* (pp. 79–94). Nova Scotia, Canada: Fernwood Publishing.

Ursel, J. (1995). The Winnipeg Family Violence Court. In M. Valverde, L. MacLeod, & K. Johnson (Eds.). *Wife Assault and the Canadian Criminal Justice System: Issues and Policies*. Toronto, Canada: University of Toronto Press.

Veysey, B., Zgoba, K., & Dalessandro, M. (2009). A preliminary step towards evaluating the impact of Megan's Law: A trend analysis of sexual offenses in New Jersey from 1985 to 2005. *Justice Research and Policy, 10*(2), 1–18.

Walker, S. P., & Louw, D. (2003). The South African Court for sexual offences. *International Journal of Law & Psychiatry, 26*, 73–85.

Walker, S. P., & Louw, D. (2005). The court for sexual offences: Perceptions of the victims of sexual offences. *International Journal of Law & Psychiatry, 28*, 231–245.

Ward, K. C., & Merlo, A. V. (2015). Rural jail reentry and mental health identifying challenges for offenders and professionals. *The Prison Journal, 96*(1), 27–52.

Winnick, T. A., & Bodkin, M. (2008). Anticipated stigma and stigma management among those to be labeled "ex-con." *Deviant Behavior, 29*(4), 295–333.

Wright, R. G. (Ed.). (2014). *Sex offender laws: Failed policies, new directions.* New York, NY: Springer Publishing Company, LLC.

Zehr, H. (2015). *The little book of restorative justice: Revised and updated.* New York, NY: Good Books.

*Chapter 13*

# Opioid Intervention Courts

## Lisa Shannon, Monica Himes, Shondrah Nash, and Jennifer Newell

### INTRODUCTION

What was introduced as a class of drugs to reduce pain and discomfort ultimately has caused individual misuse, addiction, and a national public health crisis. Over the past twenty years, the United States has experienced an increase in opioid use, misuse, and abuse (Dart et al., 2015). National Survey on Drug Use and Health (NSDUH) 2018 findings suggest approximately 10.3 million individuals aged twelve and older misused opioids in the past year; approximately 2 million individuals aged twelve or older had an opioid use disorder (OUD; Substance Use and Mental Health Service Administration [SAMHSA], 2019)).

This chapter provides an overview of opioid dependence and the opioid crisis, along with evidence-based rehabilitative responses, including problem-solving courts and the recent inception of Opioid Intervention Courts (OICs). The chapter also compares and contrasts OICs with other problem-solving courts, includes a qualitative account of court operations and proceedings of the nation's first OIC, and closes with a discussion of other developing OICs and future directions.

### Opioid Dependence

Drug dependence is a complex and debilitating illness characterized by uncontrollable cravings and compulsive drug-seeking, despite devastating consequences (National Institute on Drug Abuse, 2018b). Specifically, opioid dependence is "a problematic pattern of opioid use leading to clinically significant impairment or distress" often manifested by increased tolerance, inability to stop or control use, and the presence of physical withdrawal symptoms when use decreases or stops (American Psychiatric Association, 2013, p. 541).

Initially, individuals may use prescribed opioids to control pain or to experience feelings of euphoria, but tolerance builds quickly and the euphoric feelings diminish soon thereafter (Wang, 2019). Opioid receptors are G-protein coupled receptors located throughout the brain, spinal cord, skin, and gastrointestinal system (Stein, 2016; Waldoer et al., 2004; Wang, 2019). When opioid use is chronic, these receptors are continuously activated, and tolerance builds. Then, when use ceases, a person can experience severe withdrawal symptoms similar to severe influenza. According to the Clinical Opiate Withdrawal Scale (COWS), the most distressing withdrawal symptoms are increased pulse, sweating, restlessness, bone or joint aches, diarrhea, and tremors (Wesson & Ling, 2003). Additionally, many experience gooseflesh, as well as increased yawning, runny nose, anxiety, and irritability (Wesson & Ling, 2003). Scientists found chronic use of opioids creates a "cascade of cellular and synaptic changes" and "together, these events underpin the manifestation of opioid tolerance, dependence, and addiction" (Waldoer et al., 2004, p. 982).

## The Opioid Crisis

Drug overdose deaths have reached an unprecedented rate in the United States, and the majority are associated with opioid use (Scholl et al., 2019). Over 446,000 Americans died from opioid overdose between 1999 and 2018 (Wilson et al., 2020). Of the 67,367 drug overdose deaths in the United States in 2018, 69.5 percent (46,802) were opioid-related (Centers for Disease Control [CDC], 2020a). Increases in opioid-related overdoses have been reported across rural/urban districts, racial/ethnic groups, and multiple states (Scholl et al., 2019). States with the highest death rates related to drug overdose in 2018, of which synthetic opioids were the main culprit, included (in descending order) West Virginia, Delaware, Maryland, Pennsylvania, Ohio, and New Hampshire (CDC, 2020a).

The rise in opioid use and related deaths in the United States occurred in three distinct waves. The first wave began with increased opioid prescriptions (natural/semi-synthetic opioids and methadone) in the 1990s. This wave was fueled by aggressive advertising from pharmaceutical companies, particularly Purdue Pharma, touting opioids as non-addictive, based on one obscure study by Porter and Jick. Misleading advertising promised minimal addiction risk of prescription opioids and encouraged widespread and generous prescribing as an act of compassion to patients in pain (Van Zee, 2009). From the 1990s through 2010, there was a dramatic increase in "pill mills," a term used to describe a doctor's office/clinic that prescribed controlled drugs inappropriately. People who became addicted to prescription opioids could access a virtually unlimited supply by traveling to visit multiple pill mills (Rigg et al., 2010). The second wave began around 2010, as access to natural/semi-synthetic opioids and methadone decreased, and heroin overdose-related deaths rapidly increased. During this time, prescription monitoring programs implemented in nearly every state allowed the government to oversee and control prescription opioids. Additionally, pill mills were closed, and many doctors were charged for a variety of crimes, including distribution of narcotics and conspiracy; however, there has been sentencing disparities between "white collar" doctors, compared to street dealing counterparts (Gershowitz, 2019). The flow of prescription opioids drying up combined with a perfectly timed influx of heroin into the United States from Mexico led to increased heroin use. "Some researchers suggest that the very policies and practices that have been designed to address inappropriate prescribing are now fueling the increases in rates of heroin use and death" (Compton et al., 2016, p. 155). A 2014 study found that 75 percent of heroin users were introduced to opioids through prescription drugs (Cicero et al., 2014). Finally, in 2013, there was a third wave with a significant spike in overdose deaths involving synthetic opioids, particularly fentanyl (CDC, 2020b). Fentanyl is a synthetic opioid fifty times more potent than heroin (CDC, 2019). Overdose deaths involving non-methadone synthetic opioids, including fentanyl, increased on average by 8 percent per year from 1999 to 2013 and by 71 percent per year from 2013 to 2017 (Hedegaard et al., 2020, 2018).

For every opioid-overdose fatality, there are non-fatal opioid overdoses, which can result in serious complications. Individuals who experience a single opioid overdose are more likely to undergo subsequent overdoses. Recurring opioid overdoses are linked to increased symptoms of depression and suicidal ideation, decreasing cognitive performance, and a greater risk for long-term physical consequences resulting in opioid-induced respiratory depression compared with those experiencing a single overdose (Zibbell et al., 2019).

While opioid use and overdose rates have created a public health crisis, there has been a corresponding influx impacting the criminal justice system and public safety. Specifically, opioid use may often lead to criminal justice system involvement (McGreevey & Forkey, 2019); approximately 25 percent of the incarcerated population are opioid addicted (Rich & Satel, 2018). The demand for innovation in treating opioid use, relapse, and overdose has not gone unnoticed by American jurisprudence. Recently, specialized court programs have been developed to meet the needs of opioid-dependent individuals. These OICs emphasize individuals' long-term recovery over punishment via a judicially-supervised program where non-violent, opioid-dependent individuals with justice system involvement receive behavioral health services and medication-assisted treatment (MAT) within hours after arrest. These emergent OICs build on the problem-solving court model, which is briefly reviewed further.

## Problem-Solving Courts Overview

Problem-solving courts are community-based programs that provide rehabilitation opportunities to individuals with various risks, needs, and characteristics involved in the criminal justice system. The most commonly known is drug court. Developed in the late 1980s to address the national influx of substance abuse-related crimes, drug courts coordinate efforts of judges, prosecuting and defense attorneys, law enforcement, probation/parole as well as mental health, social service, and treatment providers to break the cycle of substance abuse, addiction, and crime (National Association of Drug Court Professionals [NADCP], 1997). The NADCP's *Key Components* offers general operational guiding principles (NADCP, 1997). Two more recent publications, *Best Practice Standards (Volumes I* and *II)*, offer specific guidelines based on extant adult drug court research (NADCP 2013, 2015). Most programs accept participants via various referral pathways and use a thorough screening and assessment process for acceptance. Participants advance through phases via individualized program plans, consisting of various components such as substance abuse treatment, case management, supervision and monitoring, drug testing, and status hearings before a judge. Additional services, including job skills training, trauma and family therapy, and mental health treatment, are also provided (Segal et al., 2013).

Research supports the effectiveness of problem-solving courts; retention rates are higher for drug court participants compared with the general treatment-seeking population (Cissner & Rempel, 2005). Reduced recidivism is an often-cited benefit of drug court participation (Brown, 2011; Huddleston & Marlowe, 2011; Shaffer, 2011). A meta-analytic review of 154 studies on drug court showed overall recidivism reduced from 50 percent to 38 percent, and drug-related recidivism reduced from 50 percent to 37 percent (Mitchell et al., 2012). The success of the problem-solving court model via drug courts has encouraged the development of other specialized court dockets (e.g., Veterans Treatment Courts [VTCs] and Mental Health Courts [MHCs]), which target unique and individualized needs.

## Problem-Solving Courts and Gaps Related to Opioid Use

Based on extant research, drug court success may depend on a variety of individual characteristics, including past substance use history and drug of choice. Termination, or non-completion, from traditional problem-solving courts may result from cocaine and opioid use (Dutra et al., 2008) and a history of intravenous drug use (Roll et al., 2005). Gallagher and colleagues (2018) showed participants who reported opioids as drug of choice were 80 percent less likely to complete drug court compared with participants with a non-opioid drug of choice. Emerging research has suggested that participants reporting opioids as drug of choice have different factors associated with drug court completion compared with participants who report other drugs of choice. Specifically, research examining participants identifying opioids as drug of choice has suggested that individual characteristics (e.g., age, living with partner/children) are important factors for program completion (Shannon et al., 2020a). Furthermore, in regard to completion of drug court for individuals reporting opioids as drug of choice, program-related factors emerged as especially critical (e.g., number of days in program, number of positive drug tests, and sanctions/therapeutic responses), which suggests the critical importance of program-related services and occurrences for individuals using opioids (Shannon et al., 2020b).

For individuals who may be eligible for problem-solving courts and are using opioids, time is a crucial consideration related to overdose risk. *Key Component* #3 states, "Eligible participants are identified early and promptly placed in the drug court program" (NADCP, 1997, pg. 5). Interaction with the justice system, particularly an arrest, is a critical window of opportunity for engaging individuals in treatment services (Center for Substance Abuse Treatment [CSAT], 2005; NADCP, 1997). However, prior to beginning most traditional problem-solving courts, there are necessary activities to complete. These activities can include legal proceedings (e.g., arraignment and court appearance) as well as legal screenings (e.g., to determine if a non-violent offender) and clinical assessment (e.g., to determine treatment needs; CSAT, 2005; Picard-Fritsche, 2010); each activity takes time. While there is a dearth of published data, some studies purport only a small window of time passes between entry into the criminal justice system and problem-solving court participation. For example, one study examining an effort to broaden access to court-mandated treatment in Brooklyn (Screening and Treatment Enhancement Project; STEP) showed the median time between arrest and drug court intake was two and a half days; however, median wait time from intake to participation was nine days (Picard-Fritsche, 2010). For individuals using opioids, an eleven-day wait period may be too long, given the increased risk of overdose and related need for medication-assisted and other treatment opportunities.

While much of American society and governmental agencies acknowledge addiction as a legitimate, treatable disorder (SAMHSA, 2019), prompt and early access to treatment remains a barrier for many opioid users. Although problem-solving court options, such as drug court, have been shown as a viable option for criminal justice-involved opioid users, death can occur before they get through the entrance activities/wait period (Picard-Fritsche, 2010). Therefore, OICs developed to fill gaps in services within the problem-solving court framework and to expedite access to treatment, including the immediate use of life-saving MAT.

## Problem-Solving Courts and Medication-Assisted Treatment

In 2011, the NADCP Board of Directors approved a resolution on MAT availability (NADCP, 2011), which applied to all problem-solving courts. The resolution encouraged professionals to become educated on MAT, make reasonable efforts toward collaborating with MAT experts for increased availability, and not impose generalized restrictions on participants' MAT use (NADCP, 2011). Examining application of this resolution, a 2013 study suggested a little over half (56 percent) of drug courts reported MAT was available under specific conditions, a little over one-third (34 percent) reported agonist therapy was permitted, and 40 percent reported continued maintenance was allowed (Matusow et al., 2013). A recent study showed successful integration of MAT in problem-solving courts has positive long-term outcomes (i.e., reduced recidivism; Jun & Fairbairn, 2018). Research has suggested MAT use among problem-solving court participants is feasible and resulted in enhanced performance (e.g., fewer missed sessions and fewer positive drug tests; Finigan, et al., 2011). One study showed MAT also significantly lowers re-arrest rates (compared with those who did not receive naltrexone) and produced considerable cost-benefits (Finigan et al., 2014). Recent publications offer strategies to enhance successful incorporation of MAT in criminal justice settings (Matejkowski et al., 2015) and specifically in problem-solving courts (Friedman & Wagner-Goldstein, 2015).

## Medication-Assisted Treatment Options

Studies have shown that individuals who complete detoxification and enter an entirely abstinence-based program are more likely to return to drug use (Bart, 2012). As a result, the medical community has sought additional forms of treatment to bridge the gap between detoxification and long-term recovery. The Food and Drug Administration (FDA) has approved several medications for OUD treatment, the most common of which are methadone, buprenorphine, and naltrexone. Findings on their use in OUD treatment, safety and effectiveness, dosing, and other important factors are discussed further (American Society of Addiction Medicine [ASAM], 2015).

## Methadone

Methadone is a long-acting opioid agonist used to manage opioid withdrawal symptoms and treat OUD (ASAM, 2015). Opioid agonist medications bind to opioid receptors in the brain, and pharmacologically occupy them, thereby reducing acute withdrawal symptoms and cravings (Wang, 2019). Methadone use for treating opioid dependence began in the 1950s, after an increase in heroin use following World War II (World Health Organization, 2009). Dr. Vincent Dole developed the methadone maintenance daily dosing protocol in the 1960s that is still used today (Dole, 1971, 1994). Currently, methadone is only dispensed from certified Opioid Treatment Programs (OTPs), and clients visit clinics daily to receive their dose for the first ninety days. Clients are then given incrementally increasing amounts of take-home doses, as their length of sobriety increases, with a maximum one-month supply take-home dose (Federal Opioid Treatment Standards, 2019). Listed on the World Health Organization's List of Essential Medicines, methadone is a vital medicinal tool in the treatment of OUD (World Health Organization, 2019).

## Buprenorphine

The partial opioid agonist, buprenorphine, was approved by the FDA to treat OUD in 2002. Partial agonist drugs bind to the same opioid receptors as do full agonist drugs; however, they do not activate receptors as powerfully. The result is that cravings and withdrawal symptoms are reduced, but without euphoric effects associated with use of opioid agonists (National Institute on Drug Abuse, 2018a). Although there are multiple pharmaceutical combinations of buprenorphine, the most commonly used and recommended is a combined version of buprenorphine and naloxone (e.g., Suboxone, Zubsolv, Bunavail; ASAM, 2015). The addition of naloxone (an opioid antagonist) dissuades intravenous misuse of buprenorphine, because if the buprenorphine/naloxone combination is injected, it precipitates withdrawal symptoms, whereas those symptoms are averted when the buprenorphine/naloxone is taken orally as prescribed (ASAM, 2015). Buprenorphine can be prescribed in office-based treatment settings by certified physicians, which is markedly different from methadone. There are currently 86,646 medical practitioners in the U.S. who are certified to prescribe buprenorphine (SAMHSA, 2020). Buprenorphine is taken sublingually and is available in two, four, and eight-milligram doses, with the maximum recommended daily dose being 24 mg. Most opioid users will start with a 12–16 mg daily dose, in addition to recommended psychosocial treatments, including (as clinically indicated): mutual help programs, couples counseling, cognitive behavioral therapy, and motivational enhancement (ASAM, 2015).

## Naltrexone

Naltrexone is a long-acting opioid antagonist used to prevent opioid relapse. Antagonist medications occupy the opioid receptors in the brain but do not activate them, thereby, blocking the euphoric effects of opioids subsequently taken (ASAM, 2015). Naltrexone was approved by the FDA in 1984 for use in OUD treatment and is now available in a daily oral form (e.g., ReVia, Depade), as well as an extended-release injectable (e.g., Vivitrol) taken monthly (ASAM, 2015). Precaution must be taken with patients using naltrexone, as their tolerance to opioids will diminish over time while taking the medication, and relapse to opioid use at their pre-treatment levels places them at-risk of overdose (ASAM, 2015; SAMHSA, 2014).

## Development and Essential Elements of Opioid Intervention Courts (OICs)

OICs have emerged as a recent adaptation of the problem-solving court model, developed in response to a myriad of needs. While problem-solving courts, such as drug courts, have been in existence for over thirty years with well-documented success (Mitchell et al., 2012), opioid users have been at high-risk for fatal overdose before being processed into a traditional problem-solving court. In response, the nation's first OIC began in Buffalo, New York, in 2017 (hereafter Buffalo-OIC).

Utilizing the *Key Components* as a guide, OICs have worked to develop their own list of *Essential Elements* specific to the needs of opioid users. *The Ten Essential Elements of OICs* are summarized here.

1. Broad legal eligibility. OIC eligibility is based on clinical need rather than criminogenic risk, attempting to include the broadest array of non-violent offenders who are clinically appropriate (i.e., at-risk for overdose).
2. Immediate screening for overdose risk. Court staff visit the local jail daily to screen individuals in the holding unit for OUD and overdose risk.
3. Informed consent after consultation with defense counsel. Individuals meet with defense counsel and complete informed consent.
4. Suspension of prosecution or expedited plea. Offenders are diverted at arraignment, and charges are held in abeyance while medical stabilization and treatment begins.
5. Rapid clinical assessment and treatment engagement. Assessment and treatment linkage occur within twenty-four hours; MAT services are vital.
6. Recovery Support Services. Use of community-based recovery services, including MAT, peer support, recovery support, and connections to primary care are integral.

7. Frequent judicial supervision and compliance monitoring. Daily court appearance for ninety days, nightly "check-in," close coordination between court and treatment providers.
8. Intensive case management. Treatment services are coordinated by an OIC case manager.
9. Program completion and continuing care. There is an established minimum of ninety days of treatment and supervision to complete the program.
10. Performance evaluation and continuous improvement. An independent research team evaluates the court process (Center for Court Innovation, 2019).

## Case Study: Buffalo-OIC

Given the recent inception of OICs and dearth of published information on the model, the authors (hereafter identified as the research team) conducted an in-depth case study of the Buffalo-OIC. The examination included data collection from key stakeholders involved in program implementation and ethnographic observations from a Buffalo-OIC court session.

Started in 2017, the Buffalo-OIC's goal is to save lives of high-risk opioid users engaged in the court system by way of linkages to specialized treatment (medication-assisted and behavioral therapies) within hours of arrest and providing participants with tools toward initiating and sustaining recovery. From the Buffalo-OIC perspective, it did not matter if other effective problem-solving courts existed if people were dying before they could access available services. The Buffalo-OIC utilizes *The Ten Essential Elements of OICs* and evidence-based principles of traditional problem-solving courts in its operational framework. Consequently, a participant's engagement with the justice system may transition into an opportunity to undergo monitored, recovery-based services.

### Key Stakeholder Data

Three research team members visited the Buffalo-OIC and discussed facets of court development and implementation with key stakeholders on December 9 and 10, 2019. The research team developed a list of questions/topics that covered program implementation (e.g., cost, funding) and operations (e.g., phases, treatment). Discussions with Buffalo-OIC administrators and staff occurred over the course of the two-day visit at various times via both formal and informal dialogue. The information presented in this chapter provides presents a summary of the Buffalo-OIC's implementation, operations, and other developments based on key stakeholder data.

*OIC Implementation and Operations*

The Buffalo-OIC is state-funded, as are other problem-solving courts in New York. Its operating team consists of a judge and various court system personnel.

To identify eligible participants for the Buffalo-OIC, relevant court staff are notified of individuals who are arrested and in holding. Each morning, two individuals from the Court Outreach Unit: Referral and Treatment Services (COURTS) conduct assessments with individuals who are detained/in holding. The eligibility assessment is brief and focuses on the following topics: (1) history of use; (2) history of overdose; (3) desire for help, treatment, and MAT; and (4) linkages to treatment. Similar to other problem-solving courts, clinical need determines program eligibility; individuals with dual diagnoses are eligible.

Involvement with the Buffalo-OIC is pre-adjudication; individuals who consent to participate have not pled/been found guilty of a crime, but have a pending charge. At the time of data collection, there was no Buffalo-OIC capacity mentioned.

The Buffalo-OIC follows the medical model for treatment and service provision. One analogy used by key personnel when explaining treatment and services was that, "OIC is an emergency room for specialty courts for dealing with the time of crises." Translated, the Buffalo-OIC focuses on only immediate, pressing needs, which ultimately aligns with the mission to save lives. Accordingly, if an individual needs longer-term services, he or she could be referred to another appropriate problem-solving court.

Unlike many other problem-solving courts, there are no set phases to demarcate progression in the Buffalo-OIC. Given the program was intended as relatively short term (90 days), court staff described its structure as "static," meaning requirements for all participants are the same. Participants must see the judge daily for at least the first thirty days; after this time, the court has the discretion to reduce court appearances. Additional monitoring of participants occurs via a nightly curfew call with court staff. Aside from terms associated with court appearances and monitoring, there are few other rules and no formal participant handbook, a contrast to other problem-solving courts. The goal is not necessarily to achieve abstinence, but to save lives by reducing high-risk substance use and rapidly connecting participants to appropriate forms of treatment. The program, therefore, strives to keep participants engaged and not overwhelmed with rules and punitive measures.

The Buffalo-OIC links participants with treatment, including various MAT options. MAT is readily accessible with mobile units close to the courthouse to provide nearly immediate participant access. Other treatment services and referrals are conveniently located on the fourth floor of the courthouse (at COURTS). In terms of participant cost, participants' insurance covers treatment sessions; however, no one is turned away for not having insurance. Program termination would only occur if the individual no longer desired help. In contrast to other problem-solving courts, there are no sanctions for failing to follow through with programmatic or treatment requirements. Some Buffalo-OIC participants are discharged and then participate in drug court or VTC. However, the option exists to participate in the Buffalo-OIC, later face criminal charges, and not continue in another problem-solving court.

## OIC Development, Partnerships, and Successes

In order to implement such a unique programmatic opportunity, community partnerships were necessary. To develop these, one key stakeholder discussed how all needed partners were "invited to the table" to discuss the new program. As a result, based on discussions with key stakeholders, the overall feeling was that everyone had been supportive of the Buffalo-OIC. Initially, there were some discussions about due process, since court staff at times were visiting/screening individuals prior to an attorney visit. However, when the stakeholders realized that participants need to begin treatment immediately, and within hours if possible, these concerns dismissed.

The Buffalo-OIC stakeholders could easily discuss countless accomplishments. Some accomplishments were the quick intervention, treatment within twenty-four hours (unless the individual is admitted over the weekend) and working toward the mission of saving lives. Buffalo-OIC participants stayed in the program longer than anticipated. While the court was planned for 90 days, at the time of the research team's visit, the average length of participation was 116 days. The Buffalo-OIC had even been able to secure a federal SAMHSA grant. Further, despite the novelty of the court, the Buffalo-OIC had data to support and highlight accomplishments. At the time of the research team's visit, the Buffalo-OIC reported serving 506 individuals with 124 active clients. The court had a 96 percent retention rate, with only six deaths. After participation in the Buffalo-OIC, 70 percent of the individuals had their charges dismissed.

Fortunately, according to key stakeholders, there were no sustained barriers to Buffalo-OIC implementation, which is not always the case when starting a new program. There was some discussion about select individuals' perceptions the program was "soft" on crime or those who did not immediately see the value of the first-and-fast treatment approach. However, these perceptions were relatively short-lived and were overcome by having strong leaders and advocates implementing the program.

## Court Observation

Extant research on other problem-solving courts suggests judicial interactions are a best practice and integral to participant success (Carey et al., 2012). Research emphasizes the importance of the frequency of judicial appearances and the time spent in front of the judge during court appearances (Carey et al., 2012). As part of this team's exploration of the Buffalo-OIC, the same three research team members observed and recorded proceedings from a court session.

Researchers recorded data using a modified protocol originally developed by Satel (1998) during a national study of fifteen adult drug court programs. The presumption when selecting this method to organize court observations was the Buffalo-OIC would operate similarly to other problem-solving courts. This modified protocol provided guidance and structure to allow for systematic descriptions of the interactional (e.g., exchanges between judge, court staff, and participants) and environmental (e.g., physical characteristics/ setting) variables of the court session across the various observers. This modified protocol involved recording occurrences during the session for specific characteristics of potential importance, including the interaction between the judge and participants (e.g., eye contact, physical proximity, conversation, and time spent with participant), and courtroom setting (e.g., seating arrangements and noise level). During the court session, each research team member independently recorded observations. It is important to note this was an ethnographic observation of court proceedings; there was no direct interactions or feedback solicited from program participants. Transcriptions of compiled notes from each research team member provided a summary of the court session from multiple perspectives.

The court observation was coordinated with Buffalo-OIC staff and conducted on December 10, 2019. At that time, the presiding judge had been with the Buffalo-OIC for approximately ten months. Individuals entered the courtroom at approximately 9:30 a.m. The court session was called to order at approximately 9:40 a.m. Before the judge called the session to order, individuals in the courtroom interacted with various court personnel, including lawyers and the bailiff. There did not appear to be arranged seating in the courtroom. After the session was called to order, in terms of noise level or potential distractions, the court's gallery was quiet.

Buffalo-OIC proceedings were integrated within a regularly scheduled court session, resulting in individuals within the courtroom who were not program participants. Compared with some other problem-solving court dockets, which are only for program participants, this is a different feature of the Buffalo-OIC. Once the court was in session, the judge called docket members, including Buffalo-OIC participants, to the bench. There was no apparent order for appearing before the judge; however, incarcerated individuals and those represented by an attorney seemed to have prioritized appearances before the judge. Individuals were permitted to walk in and out throughout the court session. Buffalo-OIC participants arrived at various times throughout the court session due to work, appointments, drug testing, and other morning commitments. Individuals did not remain throughout the entire session; each participant left the courtroom after completing his/her one-on-one discussion with the judge.

## Observations of Judge-Participant Interaction

The overall atmosphere created by the judge and court staff was positive. During participants' one-on-one time with the judge, there was no physical contact. Instead, participants approached the bench when called and stood directly on the other side of the bench. Having the ability to walk directly to the bench was a distinguishing characteristic of the Buffalo-OIC. Individuals in the courtroom for other matters often stood with a lawyer behind a podium. In one instance, a potential participant was brought in from jail for his or her first appearance to see if he or she wanted to join the program. The individual arrived in a jumpsuit, handcuffed, and stood by the podium instead of directly in front of the bench. The judge discussed program participation in understandable terms; upon leaving, the potential participant thanked the judge for the opportunity.

Overall, the research team observed positive social interaction between Buffalo-OIC participants, the presiding judge, and court staff. The judge smiled while sustaining direct, consistent eye contact with all individuals who approached the bench. The judge conveyed a general interest in the status of participants' lives, well-being, safety, and, in some cases, that of their families. In fact, from all appearances, the judge's sociable, conversant temperament was constructive toward earning participants' trust. Further, the judge complimented defendants on their "attitude" to succeed, told participants they were "doing good," she was "proud" of their commitment to improve, and to "keep it up" or not be discouraged by "one little hiccup." The Buffalo-OIC coordinator, who was seated or stood close to the bench, additionally offered encouragement.

The judge delicately fielded questions that encouraged discussions on how Buffalo-OIC participants were functioning. Alongside talks regarding treatment, conversations extended to individuals' housing situation, transportation, and insurance coverage. There were no microphones used in the courtroom to enhance others' ability to hear conversations. All conversations were relatively private between the individual and the judge; there were no general announcements or information shared with the gallery by either the judge or participants. Unrestricted by a podium, participants' short proximity to the judge, along with persistent court appearances and monitoring, may have fostered what appeared to be a highly structured, yet individualized court experience.

For each appearance, the judge seamlessly and personably followed up on aspects regarding individuals' systems of support, personal welfare, and other life challenges that might affect recovery. During these discussions, participants spent at least three to five minutes in front of the judge, sometimes more. One participant, who had been late and did not answer when initially called to the bench, expressed worry over a sick school-aged child. Throughout, the judge listened attentively, agreeably inserted the benefits of therapy, and later asked the individual about his or her grandmother's well-being. When addressing another participant, who had missed the previous night's curfew call, the judge inquired about a spouse's welfare. In the case of another participant, who had discussed chronic issues with employment, the judge offered that the individual "make (her/his) mom happy" and added that "earning your own money builds self-esteem."

As with most problem-solving courts, the Buffalo-OIC participants appear frequently before the judge. For most, based on conversations with the judge, and from listening to the discussion of the next court appearance, court appearances are daily. There were a handful of participants where court appearances varied a bit (e.g., three days/week and every other day). For these individuals, with more varied court appearances, there appeared to be a longer duration of Buffalo-OIC participation based on conversations with the judge about past events. Additional monitoring of Buffalo-OIC participants is conducted via a nightly curfew call-in taken by court staff, another stipulation of the program.

## Observations of Court Structure and Judicial Responses

Although efficient, the court session and the processes were neither tactless nor without empathy. The judge and program coordinator were provided with documentation on each Buffalo-OIC participant, allowing both to have up-to-date knowledge about the individual and potentially important life events. Related, when participants appeared before the judge, most brought yellow slips that documented drug-testing results. Within the Buffalo-OIC's program structure, drug testing is not utilized to "catch" the individual in the act of continued substance use for punishment. The function of drug testing is to show compliance with MAT, to look for dangerous drug use patterns (e.g., continued opioid use) and, if needed, to introduce therapeutic adjustments. Varying from other problem-solving courts, many Buffalo-OIC participants continued to use other legal, illegal, or illicit substances. This use, if detected via screening, was a topic discussed with the judge. For example, one participant discussed alcohol use, which had been detected during drug screening.

Another contrast to other problem-solving courts was the absence of sanctions. For example, a participant informed the court of an unapproved decision to discontinue approved MAT (Suboxone). The judge mildly admonished the person, stating there should not be revisions to a treatment plan without first being cleared by a doctor. The judge offered a similar response when addressing Buffalo-OIC participants who appeared to still be using illicit substances or not following program requirements (e.g., not adhering to the nightly call-in requirement). Several individuals, for example, violated the program's nightly "check-in"/call with court staff. These instances were invariably met with a gentle prompting to resume nightly contact. At least one participant tested positive for fentanyl, to which the judge offered a moderate warning about the dangers of the drug. One participant, who apologized for missing several court appearances, was reminded, "This is to keep you on the straight and narrow (path)."

### Observations of Program Support

The research team saw support for Buffalo-OIC participants via efforts to affirm their programmatic progress. One participant, for example, received a bus pass for transportation to counseling if he or she agreed to enroll in a treatment group. As a reward, another Buffalo-OIC participant was excused from one court date weekly related to personal progress and allowed to select the absence date. At one point during the session, a peer support personnel entered the courtroom and shared feedback from participants regarding their rapport and positive interactions with the judge and court staff. While not all participants had legal representation, those escorted into the court detained and handcuffed were accompanied by a lawyer, one of whom acted as a translator, if needed. No family members were present with program participants.

Some decisions regarding participants' health and recovery were weighed by both the court and the individual. A participant, who had been recently released from jail, tested positive for substance use and shared ongoing struggles with alcohol dependency. Consequently, the court spent significant time unpacking the individual's recovery aspirations and needs, specifically those linked to inpatient services. The judge scheduled an alcohol assessment and additional treatment services, which were to commence that month. Appearing in shackles and in a jail jumpsuit, a participant entered court apologizing profusely after an apparent disturbance during a previous court date. The judge permitted the individual's entry into a MAT program and informed of his or her court appearance the next day.

Based on data collected from key stakeholders and court observations, the Buffalo-OIC is making an impact on participants' lives. As the opioid epidemic continues, it is fair to say that more and continued efforts to help serve these individuals will follow.

## Other Developed and Emerging Opioid Intervention Courts

Inarguably, the Buffalo-OIC is a groundbreaking endeavor that builds upon the traditional problem-solving court framework and advances it exponentially for individuals with OUD. However, it is important to recognize that, while the Buffalo-OIC model was the nation's first and selected for this analysis, it is not the only OIC in operation. When the *Ten Essential Elements of Opioid Intervention Courts* was published in 2019, there were at least four additional states with operational OICs: Pennsylvania, Arizona, Tennessee, and Wisconsin. In fact, key stakeholders from these established OICs participated in work groups that developed the *Essential Elements guidelines.*

Interestingly, even among this small number of operational OICs, there were already unique differences in implementation and operations (e.g., target population, judicial process). For example, the Brown County (Wisconsin) Opiate Treatment Court employs a parallel track to the drug court for those individuals with OUD (Lucas & Arnold, 2019). The Recovery Oriented Compliance Strategy (ROCS; Tennessee) program includes both pre-/post-plea individuals and gives special attention to pregnant women with OUD (Lucas & Arnold, 2019). Seemingly, much like the *Key Components* for drug courts, the *Essential Elements* serve as a guiding framework offering both structure and flexibility to fit unique contextual needs.

Buffalo-OIC stakeholders acknowledged a steady number of visitors and that court teams from multiple states were interested in developing this type of problem-solving court. Stakeholders also posited that OICs will be more successful in jurisdictions where there are established drug courts and existing community supports in place. Therefore, by the time of publication, it is likely that the number of states with operational OICs will be much higher.

## FUTURE DIRECTIONS AND
## CONCLUDING COMMENTS

OICs are emerging, promising problem-solving courts working to save the lives of a vulnerable and at-risk group of individuals. At the time of preparing this publication, the *Essential Elements* and preliminary findings on the Buffalo-OIC had been published for approximately one year (The State University of New York, 2019). While there is support and much interest in the OIC model, future directions should include more research on these emerging specialty courts, given the diversity in implementation even among the small number of existing OICs. Further, there should be focused research on the *Essential Elements* to understand the impact of adherence to and modifications of on programmatic effectiveness and participant outcomes.

For many individuals, problem-solving courts and community-based rehabilitation efforts offer a second chance. Since the first problem-solving court in Miami, Florida, in 1989, the model has focused on providing individualized treatment for those involved in the criminal justice system who struggle with substance use disorder. Given the well-documented success via positive outcomes, the model has evolved over time to serve individuals with specialized/unique needs (e.g., VTCs and MHCs). OICs are the most recent example of this evolution, as program participants engage in intense judicial supervision and treatment resources *during the early stages of recovery*. The goal of saving lives via early intervention and treatment is a valuable piece of the OIC model and has shown early success. As these specialized courts continue to evolve and expand, it will be important to systematically examine outcomes, along with what is most suitable in terms of best practices, to build a robust peer-reviewed literature base focusing on OICs.

## REFERENCES

American Psychiatric Association. (2013). *Diagnostic and statistical manual of mental disorders* (5th ed.). Author.

American Society of Addiction Medicine. (2015). *The ASAM national practice guideline for the use of medications in the treatment of addiction involving opioid use.* Retrieved from: https://www.asam.org/docs/default-source/practice-support/guidelines-and-consensus-docs/asam-national-practice-guideline-supplement.pdf

Bart, G. (2012). Maintenance medication for opiate addiction: The foundation of recovery. *Journal of Addictive Diseases, 21*(3), 207–225.

Brown, R. (2011). Drug court effectiveness: A matched cohort study in the Dane County drug treatment court. *Journal of Offender Rehabilitation, 50*(4), 191–201.

Carey, S. M., Mackin, J. R., & Finigan, M. W. (2012). What works? The ten key components of drug court: Research-based best practices. *Drug Court Review, VIII*(1), 6–42.

Center for Court Innovation. (2019). *The 10 essential elements of opioid intervention courts.* Retrieved from: https://www.courtinnovation.org/sites/default/files/media/documents/2019-07/report_the10essentialelements_07092019.pdf

Center for Substance Abuse Treatment (2005). *Substance abuse treatment for adults in the criminal justice system.* Treatment Improvement Protocol (TIP) Series 44, DHHS Publication No. (SMA) 05-4056. Substance Abuse and Mental Health Services Administration.

Centers for Disease Control and Prevention. (2019). *Opioid overdose: Synthetic opioid overdose data.* Retrieved from: https://www.cdc.gov/drugoverdose/data/fentanyl.html#overdose-deaths-synthetic

Centers for Disease Control and Prevention. (2020a). *Drug overdose deaths.* Retrieved May 27, 2020 from: https://www.cdc.gov/drugoverdose/data/statedeaths.html

Centers for Disease Control and Prevention. (2020b). *Understanding the epidemic.* Retrieved May 29, 2020 from: https://www.cdc.gov/drugoverdose/epidemic/index.html

Cicero, T., Ellis, M., & Surratt, H. (2014). The changing face of heroin use in the Unites States: A retrospective analysis of the past 50 years. *JAMA Psychiatry, 71*(1), 821–826.

Cissner, A. B., & Rempel, M. (2005). *The state of drug court research: Moving beyond 'do they work?'* Retrieved from: http://www.courtinnovation.org/.

Compton, W., Jones, C., & Baldwin, G. (2016). Relationship between nonmedical prescription-opioid use and heroin use. *New England Journal of Medicine, 374*, 154–163.

Dart, R. C., Surratt, H. L., Cicero, T. J., Parrino, M. W., Severtson, G., Bucher-Bartelson, B., & Green, J. L. (2015). Trends in opioid analgesic abuse and mortality in the United States. *The New England Journal of Medicine, 372*(3), 241–248.

Dole, V. P. (1971). Methadone maintenance treatment for 25,000 addicts. *Journal of the American Medical Association, 215*, 1131–1134.

Dole, V. P. (1994). What we have learned from three decades of methadone maintenance treatment. *Drug and Alcohol Review, 13*, 3–4.

Dutra, L., Stathopoulou, G., Basden, S., Leyro, T., Powers, M., & Otto, M. (2008). A meta-analytic review of psychosocial interventions for substance use disorders. *American Journal of Psychiatry, 165*, 179–187.

Federal Opioid Treatment Standards, 42 Code of Federal Regulations, §8.12 (2019).

Finigan, M. W., Perkins, T., Sullivan, J. E., & Kandrevas, J. A. (2014). Is there a role for extended-release naltrexone in drug courts? Results of a pilot study. *Drug Court Review, IX(1),* 23–42.

Finigan, M. W., Perkins, T., Zold-Kilbourn, P., Parks, J., & Stringer, M. (2011). Preliminary evaluation of extended-release naltrexone in Michigan and Missouri drug courts. *Journal of Substance Abuse Treatment, 41*(3), 288–293.

Friedman, S., & Wagner-Goldstein, K. (2015). *Medication-assisted treatment in drug courts. Recommended strategies.* New York State: Legal Action Center, Center for Court Innovation.

Gallagher, J. R., Wahler, E. A., Lefebvre, E., Paiano, E., Carlton, J., et al. (2018). Improving graduation rates in drug court through employment and schooling opportunities and Medication-Assisted Treatment (MAT), *Journal of Social Service Research, 44*(3), 343–349.

Gershowitz, A. (2019). *Punishing pill mill doctors: Sentencing disparities in the opioid epidemic* [Unpublished Research Paper], William & Mary Law School. Retrieved from: https://dx.doi.org/10.2139/ssrn.3503662

Hedegaard, H., Miniño, A. M., & Warner, M. (2018) *Drug overdose deaths in the United States, 1999–2017. NCHS Data Brief, no 329.* National Center for Health Statistics.

Hedegaard, H., Miniño, A. M., & Warner, M. (2020). *Drug overdose deaths in the United States, 1999–2018. NCHS Data Brief, no 356.* National Center for Health Statistics.

Huddleston, W., & Marlowe, D. B. (2011). *Painting the current picture: A national report on drug courts and other problem-solving court programs in the United States.* National Drug Court Institute.

Jun, J. H., & Fairbairn, N. (2018). Integrating injectable opioid agonist treatment into a drug treatment court program: A case study. *Substance Abuse, 39*(4), 493–496.

Lucas, D., & Arnold, A. (2019). *Court responses to the opioid epidemic: Happening now.* Center for Court Innovation. Retrieved: https://www.courtinnovation.or g/sites/default/files/media/document/2019/Handout_HappeningNowOpioid_0717 2019.pdf

Matejkowski, J., Dugosh, K. L., Clements, N. T., & Festinger, D. S. (2015). Pilot testing of an online training for criminal justice professionals on medication-assisted treatment. *Journal of Addictions & Offender Counseling, 36*(1), 13–27.

Matusow, H., Dickman, S., Rick, J. D., Fong, C., Dumont, D. M., Hardin, C., et al. (2013). Medication assisted treatment in U.S. drug courts: Results from a nation-wide survey of availability, barriers, and attitudes. *Journal of Substance Abuse Treatment, 44,* 473–480.

McGreevey, J., & Forkey, K. (2019). The legacy of addition and incarceration on reentry. *Journal for Advancing Justice,* II, 21–37.

Mitchell, O., Wilson, D. B., Eggers, A., & MacKenzie, D. (2012). Assessing the effectiveness of drug courts on recidivism: A meta-analytic review of traditional and non-traditional drug courts. *Journal of Criminal Justice, 40*(1), 60–71.

National Association of Drug Court Professionals. (1997). *Defining drug courts: The ten key components.* United States Department of Justice, Office of Justice Programs, Drug Court Program Office.

National Association of Drug Court Professionals. (2011). *Resolution on the availability of medically assisted treatment (MAT) for addiction in drug courts.* Author.

National Association of Drug Court Professionals. (2013). *Adult drug court best practice standards* (vol. I). Author.

National Association of Drug Court Professionals. (2015). *Adult drug court best practice standards* (vol. II). Author.

National Institute on Drug Abuse. (2018a). *Medications to treat opioid use disorder.* https://www.drugabuse.gov/publications/research-reports/medications-to-treat-opi oid-addiction/overview

National Institute on Drug Abuse. (2018b). *Principles of drug addiction treatment: A research-based guide,* 3rd ed. Retrieved from: https://www.drugabuse.gov/node /pdf/675/principles-of-drug-addiction-treatment-a-research-based-guide-third-edition

Picard-Fritsche, S. (2010). *Expanding access to drug court: An evaluation of Brooklyn's centralized drug screening and referral initiative.* Retrieved from: https ://www.courtinnovation.org/sites/default/files/Expanding_Access.pdf

Rich, J., & Satel, S. (2018). Access to maintenance medications for opioid addiction is expanding. Prisons need to get on board. *Slate.* Retrieved on July 25, 2019 from: https://slate.com/technology/2018/05/opioid-crisis-prisons-need-to-expand-access -to-maintenance-medication.html

Rigg, K., March, S., & Inciardi, J. (2010). Prescription drug abuse and diversion: Role of the pain clinic. *Journal of Drug Issues, 40*(3), 681–702.

Roll, J. M., Prendergast, M., Richardson, K., Burdon, W., & Ramirez, A. (2005). Identifying predictors of treatment outcome in a drug court program. *The American Journal of Drug and Alcohol Abuse, 31*, 642–656.

Satel, S. (1998). Observational study of courtroom dynamics in selected drug courts. *National Drug Court Institute Review, 1*, 43–72.

Scholl, L., Seth, P., Kariisa, M., Wilson, N., & Baldwin, G. (2019). Drug and opioid-involved overdose deaths—United States, 2013–2017. *Morbidity and Mortality Weekly Report*, 67(5152), 1419.

Segal, E. A., Gerdes, K. E., & Steiner, S. (2013). *Empowerment series: An introduction to the profession of social work: Becoming a change agent.* (4th ed.). Brooks/Cole.

Shaffer, D. K. (2011). Looking inside the black box of drug courts: A meta-analytic review. *Justice Quarterly, 28*(3), 493–521.

Shannon, L. M., Jones, A. J., Newell, J., Nash, S., & Nichols, E. (2020a). Examining contextual differences in participant characteristics and during-program occurrences with drug court program completion. *Journal of Drug Issues, 50*(2), 191–208.

Shannon, L. M., Jones, A. J., Newell, J., & Nichols, E. (2020b). Examining predisposing factors and program performance indicators associated with program completion: A comparison of opioid and non-opioid-preferring participants in drug court. *International Journal of Offender Therapy and Comparative Criminology, 64*(12), 1236–1257.

Stein, C. (2016). Opioid receptors. *Annual Review of Medicine, 67*, 433–451.

Substance Abuse and Mental Health Services Administration. (2014). *Clinical use of extended-release injectable naltrexone in the treatment of opioid use disorder: A brief guide.* Retrieved from: https://store.samhsa.gov/product/Clinical-Use-of-E xtended-Release-Injectable-Naltrexone-in-the-Treatment-of-Opioid-Use-Disorder -A-Brief-Guide/SMA14-4892R

Substance Abuse and Mental Health Services Administration (2019). *Key substance use and mental health indicators in the United States: Results from the 2018 National Survey on Drug Use and Health (HHS Publication No. PEP 19-5068, NSDUH Series, H-54).* Center for Behavioral Health Statistics and Quality, Substance Abuse and Mental Health Services Administration. Retrieved January 27, 2020 from: https://www.samhsa.gov/data/

Substance Abuse and Mental Health Services Administration. (2019). *Understanding addiction.* Retrieved from: https://findtreatment.gov/content/understanding-addicti on/addiction-can-affect-anyone

Substance Abuse and Mental Health Services Administration. (2020). *National waiver totals.* Retrieved May 27, 2020 from: https://www.samhsa.gov/medication -assisted-treatment/practitioner-program-data/certified-practitioners

The State University of New York at Buffalo Primary care research Institute. (2019). *Report on the Buffalo opioid intervention court.* Retrieved from http://medicine .buffalo.edu/about/community_outreach/opioid-intervention-court.html

Van Zee, A. (2009). The promotion and marketing of Oxycontin: Commercial triumph, public health tragedy. *American Journal of Public Health, 99*(2), 221–227.

Waldoer, M., Bartlett, S., & Whistler, J. (2004). Opioid receptors. *Annual Review of Biochemistry, 73*, 953–990.

Wang, S. (2019). Historical review: Opiate addiction and opioid receptors. *Cell Transplant, 28*(3), 233–238.

Wesson, D. R., & Ling, W. (2003). The Clinical Opioid Withdrawal Scale (COWS). *Journal of Psychoactive Drugs, 35*(2), 253–259.

Wilson, N., Kariisa, M., Set, P., Smith, H., & Davis, N. (2020). Drug and opioid-involved overdose deaths—United States 2017-2018. *Morbidity and Mortality Weekly Report, 69*(11), 290–297.

World Health Organization. (2009). *Clinical guidelines for withdrawal management and treatment of drug dependence in closed settings.* Retrieved from: https://iris.wpro.who.int/bitstream/handle/10665.1/5480/9789290614302_eng.pdf

World Health Organization. (2019). *WHO Model List of Essential Medicines, 21st Ed.* Retrieved from: https://apps.who.int/iris/bitstream/handle/10665/325771/WHO-MVP-EMP-IAU-2019.06-eng.pdf?ua=1

Zibbell, J., Howard, J., Clarke, S. D., Ferrell, A., & Karon, S. L. (2019). *Non-fatal opioid overdose and associated health outcomes: Final summary report.* U.S. Department of Health & Human Services.

# Conclusion

Twenty-four scholars' analysis of thirteen different types of problem-solving courts has brought you to this point and the need to contemplate some fundamental questions. First, to what extent are problem-solving courts scalable? Problem-solving courts began as an alternative to incarceration for justice-involved persons with readily identifiable criminogenic needs. Drug courts were intended to address substance abuse problems among program participants. Could and should, this model be adapted to other issues facing individuals in the criminal justice system, and to what extend can the model appropriately be applied? Relatedly, is there a place in legal and therapeutic communities for standardized models of these courts? Is there a one-size-fits-all, or most likely, or are they inherently reflective of local-level needs and wishes? If the justice system as a whole should be individualized and each person allowed to have the law individually applied to their condition, research on problem-solving courts reveals that there is more than one way to successfully implement this model. The question remains. Are there enough commonalities among these courts to create a meaningful typology that can be adopted, adapted, and implemented in a comprehensive, meaningful response to certain populations' criminogenic needs, and their individual or offense characteristics, or are they destined to remain ad hoc efforts? We contend that answering this question requires a three-part process.

First, we must understand the current situation with respect to problem-solving courts—a state-of-the-courts scoping. This book surveys the landscape of problem-solving courts and creates common ground for consideration of next-level questions. Each chapter establishes that problem-solving courts share certain features; they all: (1) work with persons facing criminal charges; (2) rely upon the power of the judicial system to motivate participants to comply with program requirements; (3) provide access to an array of mental health, social, medical, and psychological services; (4) require that participants engage in one or more of the aforementioned services, with threat of legal sanctions if they do not; (5) use lack of recidivism as at least one measure of success; and (6) appear to be operated by groups of highly engaged believers who want to help their participants.

The nuts and bolts of what constitutes a problem-solving court are sufficiently developed and have been tested over time. But do these courts share a common foundation? Based on the analysis in this book, we offer that they do, in part. All courts examined in this book operate from the premise that the traditional criminal justice system falls short in some respect regarding a specific individual characteristic or type of offense. All these courts also share a therapeutic perspective that the offenses, or the individuals themselves, have identifiable needs that cannot be met through normal prosecutorial procedures. They require specialized attention from people trained in social and medical sciences to assist the court in achieving desirable outcomes.

At this point, however, consistency begins to fall apart. There is not much consensus on the mechanisms by which these courts achieve alleged successes and what type of success is preferential. Should success in a court setting hinge on recidivism, or are other indicators of success just as valid? Success might look like ability to support oneself through gainful employment after receiving job training; improved access to mental health treatment; stronger ties to the community; or safe family environment for children of parents who have neglected or abused their sons or daughters. Perhaps such consistency is impossible, given the topic-specific focus of each court; for example, it is hard to wrap one's mind around what commonalities exist between a court that works with sex offenders and a court that helps people escape homelessness. There are, nevertheless, some indications that these courts share operational features that could be tested through theoretically informed evaluation.

Certain features appear to be valued across all models of problem-solving courts, and those who work in these court settings contend that they contribute to participants' success. They are dictated by the ten Key Components adapted for the varying courts. But only a small body of scholarship inquires how these features contribute (or do not contribute) to positive outcomes for participants. Taking the components, developing hypotheses about the way they work, and operationalizing those concepts into evaluations is critical to continued development of this now permanent fixture and popular model of justice. There are, undoubtedly, many questions to pose and investigate. We offer three final thoughts on what some of those components are and what future researchers could query to further our collective understanding of problem-solving courts and this ever-adapting model of justice.

First, all of these courts employ a dedicated courtroom work group. That work group always includes a judge, but that judge sits not as a traditional neutral arbiter of facts, but as a referee, a coach, a mentor, and an adjudicator. If the criminal justice system continues down the problem-solving court path and expands the criminogenic, individual, and offense characteristics that they should apply to, more attention should be given to how, whether, and which roles within the courtroom work group influence participants' behaviors. Is program compliance a result of judges' positional authority, or is there something more nuanced about the participant-judge relationship that increase participants' likelihood of success? What about the courtroom work group contributes to success, and how can we leverage it to increase successful completion of these programs? These answers to these questions remain surprisingly out of reach with current data given that problem-solving courts are more than thirty years old.

Second, is it still appropriate to look at recidivism as an outcome measure for these courts' success? Most of the research shared in this book indicate that reducing recidivism is a goal, but definitions of recidivism are as varied as the courts that apply them. Moreover, is it appropriate to assess addiction recovery with traditional recidivism analysis? Arguably, drug courts originated after recognizing that old-school definitions of recidivism were irrelevant to breaking the substance abuse addiction cycle. In fact, addiction recovery almost always entails at least one recidivistic event. Which other problem-solving courts are constrained by a focus on recidivism and the criminal events that brought participants to seek an alternative to jail or prison? Many outcome evaluations address more than recidivism, though through a criminal justice lens, a strong aim of these programs seeks to eliminate criminality. In this volume, we sought to include the perspective of scholars from various fields—including social work, criminal justice, and public policy—and embrace the practitioner perspective by securing contributions by scholars who work closely with courts to evaluate them. At the granular level, we see that a focus on crime is limiting; these courts offer so much more, and their scope appears unlimited.

Third is the issue of coercion. To the extent that these courts are successful at reducing criminal activity and achieving other outcomes among their target populations and target offenses, do those successes derive from transactional understandings of coercion, or do they offer something more? Is the threat of future prosecution and incarceration essential to their work? Has the possibility of having criminal charges been dismissed or expunged the primary motivator for participants? Or is something more going on to motivate participation and drive success? Perhaps these courts provide communities of care that participants had not experienced before. Or perhaps the "second chance" nature appeals to some participants. These courts all seem to believe in their therapeutic value and credit their treatment-focused approach with their participants' successes. The research community needs to parse those relationships.

Once we have better understandings of how and why these courts work (and the extent to which they do based on rigorous evaluation), we can more fully explore the appropriateness of scalability. The chapters in this volume demonstrate that scalability is in full swing, but all problem-solving courts deserve deeper analysis of how they work and if taking problem-solving courts to scale has indeed been effective in achieving desired outcomes. The evidence often suggests that problem-solving courts "work"—however defined—but the black box remains unopened or its contents ambiguous because we still, thirty years later, do not quite understand why or how they work. Instead of retrofitting theoretical models on problem-solving courts, we must generate informed hypotheses, then test them, to fill gaps in knowledge. We offer this book as a foundation upon which to build those hypotheses and understand these complex courts that currently operate in a muddy arena of treatment, punishment, and subculture.

# Index

# About the Contributors

**Eileen M. Ahlin**, PhD, is an associate professor of criminal justice at Penn State Harrisburg. Prior to her current faculty appointment, she was senior study director at Westat where over a period of fifteen years she managed national, state, and local process and outcome evaluations on different problem-solving courts, including drug courts, community courts, and family treatment courts. Her recent research appears in *Journal of Interpersonal Violence*, *Aggression and Violent Behavior*, *Race and Justice*, and *The Prison Journal*. She is author and coauthor of several books and edited volumes, including *The Veterans Treatment Court Movement: Striving to Serve Those Who Served* (2019, Routledge) and the forthcoming title *Youth Violence in Context* (Routledge). Ahlin was the 2020 recipient of Penn State Harrisburg's Excellence in Research and Scholarly Activity Award.

**Maria João Lobo Antunes**, PhD, is an assistant professor in the Department of Sociology, Anthropology and Criminal Justice at Towson University. She is currently on the editorial board for the *Journal of Mass Violence Research* and was recently elected to a three-year term as executive counselor of the Division of Victimology of the American Society of Criminology. As a National Institute of Justice W.E.B. Du Bois Fellow, her research interests focus on youth violence: perpetration and exposure, in addition to immigrant and minority youth deviant and prosocial outcomes. Antunes's forthcoming book, with Eileen M. Ahlin, is dedicated to contextualizing youth violence. Her work appears in *Aggression and Violent Behavior*, *Feminist Criminology*, *Youth Violence and Juvenile Justice*, and *Journal of Youth and Adolescence*.

**Elyshia D. Aseltine**, PhD, is an associate professor in the Department of Sociology, Anthropology, and Criminal Justice at Towson University in

Maryland. Her current teaching and research interests focus on racial/ethnic inequality, prison-based education, and prison reentry.

**Cassandra Atkin-Plunk**, PhD, is an associate professor and associate director in the School of Criminology and Criminal Justice at Florida Atlantic University (FAU). Her research interests span both institutional and community corrections with an emphasis on contemporary issues in corrections, including the reentry and reintegration of offenders and problem-solving courts. Atkin-Plunk examines evidence-based practices and conducts program and policy evaluations in an effort to identify what works in corrections. She is the recipient of over $500,000 in external funding. Her research is largely community-based, and for this work, she was awarded the 2018 FAU Presidential Award for Outstanding Community-Engaged Research. Her research has been published in *Justice Quarterly*, *Criminal Justice and Behavior*, *Journal of Criminal Justice*, *Journal of Interpersonal Violence*, *Criminal Justice Policy Review*, and *Journal of Offender Rehabilitation*.

**Kealy A. Cassidy**, BA, earned two degrees from Gettysburg College in political science and public policy with a minor in peace and justice studies. Kealy would start law school in August 2022 and pursue a career in human rights law.

**Amanda B. Cissner** is the director of research writing at the Center for Court Innovation in New York, New York, editing and overseeing the written work produced by the center's research departments. She is currently working on several projects assessing efforts to safely reduce the use of jail in jurisdictions across the country, including one study focusing specifically on cases involving intimate partner violence. Her past research includes studies on violence prevention; intimate partner and dating violence; specialized court models, including domestic violence, drug, mental health, and reentry courts; and restorative justice practices. She received her MA in sociology from New York University.

**Tyrell Connor**, PhD, is an assistant professor in the Department of Sociology at State University of New York, New Paltz. He received his BA in psychology from Hampton University and his PhD in sociology (2015) from Purdue University.

**Anne S. Douds**, JD, PhD, is a retired trial attorney and an assistant professor of public policy at Gettysburg college. She earned her BA in political science from Duke University, her JD from Emory University School of Law, and her PhD from George Mason University. Her trial practice focused mainly on civil rights, and her recent research and consulting work include court evaluations, victim advocacy program evaluations, and criminal justice systems analysis. Her recent publications have appeared in *Victims & Offenders* and *Criminal Justice Policy Review*. Douds has published two books: *Rethinking American Correctional Policies: Commonsense Choices from Uncommon Voices* (2017) and *The Veterans Treatment Court Movement: Striving to Serve Those Who Served* (2019). Her next book, *Feminism, Leadership, and the 1950s: Bold Women of the Eisenhower Era*, will go to press in 2021.

**Amanda Emmert**, PhD, earned her doctorate in criminal justice from the University at Albany-SUNY. Her primary research interests include incarceration, employment, offender reintegration, weapon carrying, and policy.

**Irina Fanarraga**, MA, is a criminal justice doctoral student at John Jay College of Criminal Justice / The Graduate Center, CUNY. She has secured research fellowships at the Center for Court Innovation and the Kings County District Attorney's Office. Her research interests include alternatives to incarceration, risk assessment, and corrections.

**Lama Hassoun Ayoub** is a senior fellow at the Center for Court Innovation. She leads research studies on a wide range of topics, including community supervision and reentry, tribal justice systems, and schools and youth. She has been principal investigator on numerous federally funded studies, including a randomized controlled trial evaluating a reentry court in Harlem and worked with partners to complete a national multi-site evaluation of reentry courts across the country. She continues to do research on community supervision and reentry, as well as risk-need assessment in tribal jurisdictions, schools and youth, and the impact of incarceration on families. She received her MSc in public health from Harvard University and is currently pursuing a doctorate in developmental psychology from Wayne State University.

**Rebecca Thomforde Hauser** is the associate director of Gender and Family Justice Programs at the Center for Court Innovation in New York, New York. Working from a perspective of social justice and grounded in collaboration, Rebecca assists jurisdictions nationally to enhance their court and community response to domestic and sexual violence. Rebecca engages communities to identify internal strengths and challenges in their efforts to address such violence and provides ongoing support in those efforts, including training to judges and court stakeholders, incorporating evidence-based best practices, risk needs assessment, abusive partner intervention programming, and victim safety. She has previously served as the Domestic Violence Accountability Coordinator for the state of Vermont. She graduated from

Earlham College—where she received a Fulbright Scholarship—and Boston University School of Theology.

**Monica Himes**, PhD, LCSW, is an assistant professor of social work in the Department of Sociology, Social Work and Criminology at Morehead State University. Himes's doctoral dissertation focused on the implementation and evaluation of veterans' treatment courts in Kentucky. Her current funded projects include five Bureau of Justice Assistance grants for the evaluation of veterans' treatment courts and drug courts in Kentucky. Her research interests are substance use and mental health disorders, veterans' issues, bias, discrimination, and racism within social work education. She is the current president of the Kentucky Association of Social Work Educators.

**Mitra Z. Honardoost**, MA, is a supervisor in the Family Preservation Unit with York County (PA) Children Youth and Families. She received her MA in criminal justice from Penn State Harrisburg.

**Ashley Kilmer**, PhD, earned her doctorate in Criminology from the University of Delaware. Prior to joining the faculty at Towson University in the fall of 2018, Kilmer was an assistant professor of criminal justice at Bridgewater State University in Massachusetts. She is also a trained Inside-Out Prison Exchange Program facilitator. She studies the impact of criminal justice-related policies and practices on justice-involved individuals and their families.

**Deborah Koetzle**, PhD, is an associate professor and the executive officer of the Criminal Justice PhD Program at John Jay College of Criminal Justice/CUNY. She is a research fellow with the University of Cincinnati Corrections Institute. Her research interests center around effective correctional interventions with a focus on problem-solving courts, risk/need assessment, probation practices, and cross-cultural comparisons of correctional practices and policies.

**Jared A. Michaels** is a senior at Gettysburg College pursuing degrees in political science and public policy. He is a member of the Phi Sigma Alpha honor society and plans to pursue a career in state or local government after graduation.

**Shondrah Nash**, PhD, is a professor of sociology in the Department of Sociology, Social Work and Criminology at Morehead State University. Nash has conducted research on marginalized groups for close to twenty years, including rurality and women's experiences substance abuse and the intersection of race, gender, religion, and spousal violence.

**Jennifer Newell**, BA, completed her BA in social work from the University of Kentucky. She has over twelve years of experience on multiple evaluation studies. Newell is currently working for the Department of Sociology, Social Work, and Criminology at Morehead State University as a project leader on several grants with Volunteers of America of Los Angeles, Skid Row Development Corporation, and Kentucky Specialty Courts.

**Carrie Petrucci**, MSW, PhD, has twenty years of experience in evaluation research. She specializes in evaluation of criminal justice and social welfare programs for underserved populations. Her areas of expertise include partici- patory and collaborative techniques using mixed methods, including concept mapping. She has been involved in multiple evaluations on problem-solving courts, including domestic violence courts, DUI courts, and drug courts. She has also been co-principal investigator for a statewide evaluation of Family Justice Centers, and Principal Investigator for two statewide evalu- ations in California on child abuse treatment and law enforcement special- ized units. Her publications include qualitative and quantitative analyses in peer-reviewed journals, including the *Community College Journal of Research and Practice*, *Oñati Socio-Legal Series*, *Transportation Research Circular*, *Victims and Offenders*, *Journal of Social Service Research*, *The Journal of Law, Medicine, and Ethics*, *Washington University Journal of Law and Policy*, *Behavioral Sciences and the Law*, *Criminal Law Bulletin*, and *Brief Treatment and Crisis Intervention*. She has also published several chapters on therapeutic jurisprudence and social work, domestic violence, and juvenile justice. She was formerly a child protective services worker in Los Angeles and a community corrections program director in San Francisco. In addition to conducting evaluation research, she is also Adjunct Faculty at Alliant International University in their Psychology Doctorate Counseling and Family Therapy Program.

**Michael Rempel** is director of jail reform at the Center for Court Innovation, overseeing strategic planning and research related to reducing incarceration in New York City. His current projects include studying and reducing the harmful effects of money bail, pretrial detention, case processing delays, racial and ethnic disparities, and jail incarceration amid the COVID-19 pandemic. Most recently, he consulted extensively with the Mayor's Office of Criminal Justice in New York on expanding the city's supervised release program to all charges and risk levels; and he recently published articles on jail trends in the COVID-19 era, bail reform, pretrial supervision, racial bias in risk assessment, and prosecutor-led diversion. He also previously served as staff to the Independent Commission on New York City Criminal Justice and Incarceration Reform (a.k.a. the Lippman Commission). Prior to 2018, he served for sixteen years as the center's research director, supervising a twenty-person department that studied a wide range of reform topics. His past work includes leading national studies of prosecutor-led diversion, adult drug courts, reentry courts, and court responses to domestic violence. He served, for example, as co-PI on NIJ's Multi-Site Adult Drug Court Evaluation and co-PI on NIJ's Evaluation of Second Chance Act Adult Reentry Courts. He also led an analysis of decision-making at each stage of criminal case processing in New York City (NYC) and served as PI on a study of the main drivers of felony case delay in the city. He has long been interested in bridging the gap between the worlds of research and policy and, while research director, frequently consulted on evidence-based technical assistance initiatives in New York, nationally, and internationally (the latter in partnership with the Organization of American States).

**Lisa Shannon**, PhD, MSW, is an associate professor of social work in the Department of Sociology, Social Work, and Criminology at Morehead State University. Her current funded projects focus primarily on evaluations of community-based substance abuse treatment programs. She is currently the evaluator for multiple Center for Substance Abuse Treatment (CSAT) Substance Abuse and Mental Health Services Administration (SAMHSA) projects examining outcomes associated with community-based services (i.e., drug courts, other specialty courts, and Volunteers of America). She recently completed a Bureau of Justice Assistance (BJA) statewide evaluation of Kentucky Drug Courts as well as multiple BJA-funded evaluations of specific specialty court sites using evidence-based or best practices. Her research interests are substance use/abuse, victimization, and treatment-seeking behaviors as well as community-based treatment alternatives for those involved in the criminal justice system. Additionally, she is a nominated/elected board member for the National Association of Drug Court Professionals, an editorial board member for the *Advancing Justice* and *Drug Court Review* journals as well as a reviewer for the National Institutes of Health.

**Kyle C. Troeger** is a senior at Gettysburg College. He is pursuing his undergraduate degree with a double major in public policy and political science. His research interests include constitutional law, regulatory policy, and political theory. After graduation, he hopes to work for a policy think tank.

**Ella R. Warburton** is a junior at Gettysburg College studying public policy and Spanish, and she studies with the Eisenhower Institute. She works with a nonprofit in Lancaster County, Pennsylvania, that serves orphaned children. After college, she hopes to attend graduate school and then continue to work in the nonprofit sector.

www.ingramcontent.com/pod-product-compliance
Lightning Source LLC
Chambersburg PA
CBHW022301280326
41932CB00010B/933